CHILD ABUSE
AND DOMESTIC VIOLENCE

ISSN 1935-1216

CHILD ABUSE AND DOMESTIC VIOLENCE

Melissa J. Doak

INFORMATION PLUS® REFERENCE SERIES
Formerly Published by Information Plus, Wylie, Texas

THOMSON
GALE

Detroit • New York • San Francisco • New Haven, Conn. • Waterville, Maine • London

THOMSON

GALE

Child Abuse and Domestic Violence
Melissa J. Doak
Paula Kepos, Series Editor

Project Editor
John McCoy

Permissions
Lisa Kincade, Jackie Jones, Lista Person

Composition and Electronic Prepress
Evi Seoud

Manufacturing
Cynde Bishop

ISBN-13: 978-0-7876-5103-9 (set)
ISBN-10: 0-7876-5103-6 (set)
ISBN-13: 978-1-4144-0745-6
ISBN-10: 1-4144-0745-9
ISSN: 1935-1216

This title is also available as an e-book.
ISBN-13: 978-1-4144-2868-0 (set), ISBN-10: 1-4144-2868-5 (set)
Contact your Thomson Gale sales representative for ordering information.

Printed in the United States of America
10 9 8 7 6 5 4 3 2 1

TABLE OF CONTENTS

PREFACE

Child Abuse and Domestic Violence is part of the *Information Plus Reference Series*. It updates and replaces two earlier titles in the series: *Child Abuse: Betraying a Trust* and *Violent Relationships: Battering and Abuse among Adults*. The purpose of each volume of the series is to present the latest facts on a topic of pressing concern in modern American life. These topics include today's most controversial and most studied social issues: abortion, capital punishment, care for the elderly, child abuse, crime, health care, the environment, immigration, minorities, social welfare, women, youth, and many more. Although written especially for the high school and undergraduate student, this series is an excellent resource for anyone in need of factual information on current affairs.

By presenting the facts, it is Thomson Gale's intention to provide its readers with everything they need to reach an informed opinion on current issues. To that end, there is a particular emphasis in this series on the presentation of scientific studies, surveys, and statistics. These data are generally presented in the form of tables, charts, and other graphics placed within the text of each book. Every graphic is directly referred to and carefully explained in the text. The source of each graphic is presented within the graphic itself. The data used in these graphics are drawn from the most reputable and reliable sources, in particular from the various branches of the U.S. government and from major independent polling organizations. Every effort was made to secure the most recent information available. The reader should bear in mind that many major studies take years to conduct and that additional years often pass before the data from these studies are made available to the public. Therefore, in many cases the most recent information available in 2007 dated from 2004 or 2005. Older statistics are sometimes presented as well, if they are of particular interest and no more-recent information exists.

Although statistics are a major focus of the *Information Plus Reference Series*, they are by no means its only content. Each book also presents the widely held positions and important ideas that shape how the book's subject is discussed in the United States. These positions are explained in detail and, where possible, in the words of those who support them. Some of the other material to be found in these books includes: historical background; descriptions of major events related to the subject; relevant laws and court cases; and examples of how these issues play out in American life. Some books also feature primary documents, or have pro and con debate sections giving the words and opinions of prominent Americans on both sides of a controversial topic. All material is presented in an even-handed and unbiased manner; the reader will never be encouraged to accept one view of an issue over another.

HOW TO USE THIS BOOK

Tragically, every year millions of American adults are subjected to physical, sexual, verbal, or emotional abuse by their intimate partners. Perhaps even more disturbingly, millions of children suffer from such abuse at the hands of the people who are supposed to care for them. Many more have their basic needs neglected. This volume provides the best information available on the prevalence, causes, and devastating consequences of this intimate violence. The challenges that domestic violence and child abuse pose to the legal system are also covered in detail.

Child Abuse and Domestic Violence consists of nine chapters and three appendixes. Each chapter covers an aspect of the problems of child abuse and domestic violence in the United States. For a summary of the information covered in each chapter, please see the synopses provided in the Table of Contents at the front of the book. Chapters generally begin with an overview of the basic facts and background information on the chapter's topic, then proceed to examine subtopics of particular interest. For example, Chapter 1: Defining Child Abuse and

Domestic Violence begins by explaining how the modern definition of domestic violence has evolved. This is backed up by a history of how intimate abuse has been dealt with by society. Care is given to explaining how the problem goes beyond purely physical attacks to include mental and emotional abuse. The existence of intimate abuse in same-sex relationships and the special risks faced by immigrant women are highlighted. Next the chapter moves on to the issue of child abuse. Legal definitions of child abuse are provided. Characteristic signs of child abuse are explored next. This is followed by several sections on laws, regulations, and government services designed to protect children. The chapter concludes with a section highlighting the high-profile controversy of child abuse in religious settings. Readers can find their way through a chapter by looking for the section and subsection headings, which are clearly set off from the text. Or, they can refer to the book's extensive Index, if they already know what they are looking for.

Statistical Information

The tables and figures featured throughout *Child Abuse and Domestic Violence* will be of particular use to the reader in learning about these issues. These tables and figures represent an extensive collection of the most recent and important statistics on child abuse and domestic violence. For example, graphics include statistics on the prevalence of child maltreatment and on the relationship between childhood victimization and later criminality. They also cover the link between alcohol usage and domestic violence and the effectiveness of mandatory arrest policies in preventing additional domestic violence. Thomson Gale believes that making this information available to the reader is the most important way in which we fulfill the goal of this book: to help readers understand the issues and controversies surrounding child abuse in the United States and reach their own conclusions about them.

Each table or figure has a unique identifier appearing above it for ease of identification and reference. Titles for the tables and figures explain their purpose. At the end of each table or figure, the original source of the data is provided.

In order to help readers understand these often complicated statistics, all tables and figures are explained in the text. References in the text direct the reader to the relevant statistics. Furthermore, the contents of all tables and figures are fully indexed. Please see the opening section of the Index at the back of this volume for a description of how to find tables and figures within it.

Appendixes

In addition to the main body text and images, *Child Abuse and Domestic Violence* has three appendixes. The first is the Important Names and Addresses directory. Here the reader will find contact information for a number of organizations that study child abuse and domestic violence, fight these crimes, or advocate influential positions on these issues. The second appendix is the Resources section, which is provided to assist the reader in conducting his or her own research. In this section the author and editors of *Child Abuse and Domestic Violence* describe some of the sources that were most useful during the compilation of this book. The final appendix is this book's Index.

ADVISORY BOARD CONTRIBUTIONS

The staff of Information Plus would like to extend its heartfelt appreciation to the Information Plus Advisory Board. This dedicated group of media professionals provides feedback on the series on an ongoing basis. Their comments allow the editorial staff who work on the project to make the series better and more user-friendly. Our top priorities are to produce the highest-quality and most useful books possible, and the Advisory Board's contributions to this process are invaluable.

The members of the Information Plus Advisory Board are:

- Kathleen R. Bonn, Librarian, Newbury Park High School, Newbury Park, California
- Madelyn Garner, Librarian, San Jacinto College—North Campus, Houston, Texas
- Anne Oxenrider, Media Specialist, Dundee High School, Dundee, Michigan
- Charles R. Rodgers, Director of Libraries, Pasco-Hernando Community College, Dade City, Florida
- James N. Zitzelsberger, Library Media Department Chairman, Oshkosh West High School, Oshkosh, Wisconsin

COMMENTS AND SUGGESTIONS

The editors of the *Information Plus Reference Series* welcome your feedback on *Child Abuse and Domestic Violence*. Please direct all correspondence to:

Editors
Information Plus Reference Series
27500 Drake Rd.
Farmington Hills, MI, 48331-3535

CHAPTER 1

DEFINING CHILD ABUSE AND DOMESTIC VIOLENCE

DOMESTIC VIOLENCE

"Violence against women" means any act of gender-based violence that results in, or is likely to result in, physical, sexual or psychological harm or suffering to women, including threats of such acts, coercion or arbitrary deprivation of liberty, whether occurring in public or in private life.

—UN Declaration on the Elimination of Violence against Women (December 1993, http://www.unhchr.ch/huridocda/huridoca.nsf/ (Symbol)/A.RES.48.104.En?Opendocument)

The UN Populations Fund, in its report *State of the World Population 2005: The Promise of Equality: Gender Equity, Reproductive Health and the Millennium Development Goals* (2005, http://www.unfpa.org/swp/2005/pdf/ en_swp05.pdf), states that "violence against women has long been shrouded in a culture of silence." Sometimes, women as well as men accept gender violence as a normal aspect of relationships between men and women. For these reasons, reliable statistics about violence against women of all kinds, including domestic violence, are hard to come by. However, the report states that worldwide an estimated one out of three women will be beaten, coerced into sex, or otherwise abused in their lifetime, usually by a member of their own family or an acquaintance. Clearly, many women suffer as a result of ongoing domestic violence.

So what is domestic abuse? Early definitions focused exclusively on physical assault and bodily injury. For example, the Colorado Advisory Committee to the U.S. Commission on Civil Rights offered this definition of a battered wife in *The Silent Victims: Denver's Battered Women* (1977): "A woman who has received deliberate, severe and repeated physical injury from her husband, the minimal injury being severe bruising." This definition excluded acts such as pushing, slapping, pinching, or other violent acts perpetrated by husbands on their wives that produced no or minimal bruising, as well as threats of violence.

In their groundbreaking work based on their 1975 National Family Violence Survey and 1985 National Family Violence Resurvey, Murray A. Straus and Richard J. Gelles define spousal violence in specific actions, known as the Conflict Tactics Scale. That scale is now the measure most widely used to estimate the extent of spousal abuse. According to the scale, a spouse can be considered abusive if he or she:

- Throws something at a partner
- Pushes, grabs, or shoves
- Slaps
- Kicks, bites, or hits the partner with a fist
- Hits or tries to hit the partner with an object
- Beats up the partner
- Threatens the partner with a knife or a gun
- Uses a knife or fires a gun at the partner

Today, a broader interpretation is accepted, and abuse is understood to include sexual and psychological actions and harm, such as marital rape and forced isolation. Richard J. Gelles notes in "Estimating the Incidence and Prevalence of Violence against Women: National Data Systems and Sources" (*Violence against Women*, July 2000) that feminist scholars and advocates have expanded the definition to encompass issues of intent, control, and power, and conceptualize the problem of violence against women as "coercive control." The National Coalition against Domestic Violence (2006, http://www.ncadv.org/) defines battering as a pattern of behavior through which a person establishes power and control over another person by means of fear and intimidation. The incorrect belief that abusers are entitled to control their partners is a primary cause of aggression and abuse, according to the coalition.

The National Coalition against Domestic Violence also describes battering as emotional, economic, and sexual abuse, as well as using threats, male privilege, isolation, and various other strategies, including the involvement of the children of those being battered, to maintain power through fear and intimidation. The organization argues it is important to view all these behaviors as battering to understand how verbal threats, a single slap, or an insult can escalate to a life-threatening situation.

An international examination of violence by Etienne G. Krug et al., in a World Health Organization publication titled *World Report on Violence and Health* (2002, http://www.who.int/violence_injury_prevention/violence/world_report/en/full_en.pdf), also defines domestic abuse in terms broad enough to include the wide variety of abuses that occur throughout the world. Krug et al. note that "the overwhelming burden of partner violence is borne by women at the hands of men," although women can also be violent toward men and violence is also sometimes found in same-sex relationships. They define intimate partner violence as any behavior that causes physical, psychological, or sexual harm, including physically aggressive acts, such as slapping, hitting, kicking, or beating; psychological abuse, such as intimidation and belittling; forced sexual activity or intercourse; and various controlling behaviors, including isolating a partner from friends and family and restricting the partner's access to outside information or assistance from others. Table 1.1 shows definitions of violence against women developed by different organizations around the world.

In *Violence against Women: The Hidden Health Burden* (1994, http://www.iwhc.org/resources/vawhiddenburden.cfm), Lori L. Heise, Adrienne Germain, and Jacqueline Pitanguy caution against using the overly broad definitions of abuse proposed by some organizations, which encompass gender inequalities such as unequal pay or lack of access to contraception or other health care services. They term such inequalities *discrimination*, rather than *abuse*. Abuse against women, according to their study, is verbal or physical force, coercion, or deprivation directed against a woman or girl that causes physical or psychological harm, humiliation, loss of liberty, or other female subordination.

Historical Recognition of the Problem

Societal recognition of domestic violence as a problem is a recent historical development. Domestic violence has existed in almost all societies throughout history. Vivian C. Fox notes in "Historical Perspectives on Violence against Women" (*Journal of International Women's Studies*, November 2002) that its origin can be traced back centuries to the development of patriarchal and hierarchical systems of authority in which males controlled all property. In such systems women and children were often considered to be the property of men. The growth of male-oriented societies promoted

TABLE 1.1

Definitions of the term "violence against women" from around the world

Behavior by the man, adopted to control his victim, which results in physical, sexual and/or psychological damage, forced isolation, or economic deprivation or behavior which leaves a woman living in fear. (Australia, 1991)

Any act involving use of force or coercion with an intent of perpetuating/promoting hierarchical gender relations. (Asia Pacific Forum on Women, Law and Development, 1990)

Any act of gender-based violence that results in, or is likely to result in, physical, sexual or psychological harm or suffering to women, including threats of such acts, coercion or arbitrary deprivations of liberty, whether occurring in public or private life. Violence against women shall be understood to encompass but not be limited to:

Physical, sexual and psychological violence occurring in the family and in the community, including battering, sexual abuse of female children, dowry-related violence, marital rape, female genital mutilation and other traditional practices harmful to women, non-spousal violence, violence related to exploitation, sexual harassment and intimidation at work, in educational institutions and elsewhere, trafficking in women, forced prostitution, and violence perpetrated or condoned by the State. (UN Declaration against Violence against Women)

Any act, omission or conduct by means of which physical, sexual or mental suffering is inflicted, directly or indirectly, through deceit, seduction, threat, coercion or any other means, on any woman with the purpose or effect of intimidating, punishing or humiliating her or of maintaining her in sex-stereotyped roles or of denying her human dignity, sexual self-determination, physical, mental and moral integrity or of undermining the security of her person, her self-respect or her personality, or of diminishing her physical or mental capacities. (Draft Pan American Treaty against Violence against Women)

Any act or omission which prejudices the life, the physical or psychological integrity or the liberty of a person or which seriously harms the development of his or her personality. (Council of Europe, 1986)

SOURCE: Lori L. Heise, Adrienne Germain, and Jacqueline Pitanguy, "Appendix Box B1. Definitions of Violence against Women," in *Violence against Women: The Hidden Health Burden,* World Bank, 1994, http://www.iwhc.org/resources/vawhiddenburden.cfm (accessed August 25, 2006)

the widely accepted belief in male superiority that in turn formed the basis for women's subordination. This belief in men's domination over women, which was often supported by economic, social, cultural, and religious institutions, made it acceptable for men to use violence as a way to control women. As the UN Declaration on the Elimination of Violence against Women states:

> Violence against women is a manifestation of historically unequal power relations between men and women, which have led to domination over and discrimination against women by men and to the prevention of the full advancement of women. . . . Violence against women is one of the crucial social mechanisms by which women are forced into a subordinate position compared with men.

In fact, U.S. law supported a man's right to control his wife by force until the end of the late nineteenth century. In a landmark Alabama case in 1871, a court found that a husband did not have the right to physically abuse his wife, even "moderately" or with "restraint." In the case, *Fulgham v. State*, the court ruled that a married woman deserved protection under the law. The ruling stated:

> A rod which may be drawn through the wedding ring is not now deemed necessary to teach the wife her duty

and subjection to the husband. The husband is therefore not justified or allowed by law to use such a weapon, or any other, for her moderate correction. The wife is not to be considered as the husband's slave. And the privilege, ancient though it be, to beat her with a stick, to pull her hair, choke her, spit in her face or kick her about the floor, or to inflict upon her like indignities, is not now acknowledged by our law.

Also in 1871, the Massachusetts Supreme Court rejected a husband's manslaughter defense that he had a right to chastise his wife for drunkenness. He had hit his inebriated wife several times on the cheek and temple; she had fallen as a result, hit her head, and died. In this case, *Commonwealth v. McAfee*, the Massachusetts Supreme Court announced that "beating or striking a wife violently with the open hand is not one of the rights conferred on a husband by the marriage, even if the wife be drunk or insolent."

Although the Alabama and Massachusetts cases declared husbands did not have the right to physically chastise their wives, no criminal penalties were yet attached to physical abuse. In fact, in a case three years earlier, *State v. Rhodes*, the North Carolina Supreme Court declared that although a husband's whipping of his wife "would without question have constituted a battery if the subject of it had not been the defendant's wife," it refused to convict him of assault and battery, ruling that if domestic assaults were prosecuted, "the evil of publicity would be greater than the evil involved in the trifles complained of."

Although Maryland enacted a law in 1882 that punished wife beaters with forty lashes with a whip or a year in jail, even in the early twentieth century courts still refused to convict wife batterers. In 1910 the U.S. Supreme Court ruled in *Thompson v. Thompson* that a wife had no cause for action on an assault and battery charge against her husband because it "would . . . open the doors of the courts to accusations of all sorts of one spouse against the other, and bring into public notice complaints for assault, slander, and libel."

Thus, although court decisions affirmed that a husband could no longer legally beat his wife, in almost all cases a battered wife in the early twentieth century still had no legal recourse against her husband. Any criminal proceedings against a wife batterer had to be initiated by the state; women could not sue their husbands. Instead, the criminal justice system set up a separate court system—the family court—to deal with domestic complaints. According to Reva B. Siegel in "'The Rule of Love': Wife Beating as Prerogative and Privacy" (*Yale Law Journal*, June 1996), this act decriminalized physical abuse of women. Rather than punishing wife beaters, judges and social workers urged couples to reconcile and provided counseling designed to prevent divorce.

Assault in this context was viewed as an inappropriate expression of emotions; wives and husbands needed to learn how to express emotions in different ways.

The ruling of a 1962 landmark case changed the legal consequences of physical abuse of a spouse. In *Self v. Self* the California Supreme Court agreed with earlier rulings, stating that a spouse's right to sue would "destroy the peace and harmony of the house." Despite that finding, the court observed that this outdated assumption was based "on the bald theory that after a husband has beaten his wife there is a state of peace and harmony left to be disturbed." Therefore, "one spouse may maintain an action against the other" for physical abuse.

Despite the ruling enabling victims to seek legal recourse, by 1965 there had been little change. Jurisdictions throughout the United States ignored the complaints of battered women. For example, in Washington, D.C., according to police records, seventy-four hundred women filed official complaints that year but just two hundred arrest warrants were issued.

Social and Legal Recognition of Domestic Violence

Public perception and handling of domestic violence began to change significantly in the 1970s. The consciousness-raising groups that emerged during the rise of U.S. feminism in the 1960s and 1970s provided small groups of women a place to discuss their problems. Their analysis of personal problems—including domestic violence—allowed them to understand women's collective oppression. This became the basis for feminist collective action.

Efforts to aid battered women arose out of this feminist consciousness. The first battered women's shelter was founded in 1971 by Erin Pizzey in London. Pizzey, the recognized founder of the modern women's shelter movement, wrote the first book to be published on domestic violence, *Scream Quietly, or the Neighbors Will Hear*, in 1974. Authors in the United States followed suit. In 1975 Susan Brownmiller's *Against Our Will: Men, Women, and Rape*, a book about the politics and sociology of rape, was published, and in 1976 Del Martin's book *Battered Wives* appeared, focusing specifically on violence within marriage functioning as part of male dominance of women.

In 1973 the first battered women's shelter in the United States opened in St. Paul, Minnesota. By 1976 there were four hundred programs for battered women operating in the United States. EMERGE, the first treatment program for male offenders, opened in Boston, Massachusetts, in 1977, and the following year many states enacted laws to protect victims of domestic violence. More than a decade later, in 1988, the U.S. surgeon general declared domestic abuse the leading health hazard to women in the United States. According to "Women/Children Fleeing Abuse" (2002, http://www.npr.org/news/specials/housingfirst/whoneeds/abuse.html), a special report by National Public Radio, by 2002 more than two thousand shelters and service programs for battered women existed across the nation.

In the late twentieth century domestic violence was the subject of countless books, movies, and stage plays. Of these, one of the most memorable was *The Burning Bed*, which was based on the true story of Francine Hughes, an East Lansing, Michigan, woman. After having suffered seventeen years of abuse, she burned her abusive husband to death in 1977 as he slept. Hughes was acquitted of murder based on a defense of temporary insanity caused by years of physical and psychological abuse. Her case gave rise to the battered woman's defense, which subsequently was widely used to defend abused women who killed their partners. A made-for-television movie based on Hughes's case aired in 1984 to an audience of seventy-five million, giving momentum to the battered women's movement and significantly influencing legislative reform.

In 1978 the U.S. Commission on Civil Rights held the forum "Consultation on Battered Women" in Washington, D.C., and considered violence against women as a civil rights issue. The testimony from that forum was published as *Battered Women—Issues of Public Policy*. The following year, the first congressional hearings were held on the issue of domestic violence.

The subject dominated the media in 1995 with the highly publicized murder trial of O. J. Simpson, who was accused of the brutal slaying of his former wife, Nicole Brown, and her friend, Ronald Goldman. Simpson, a former football star and popular sports commentator, was acquitted of murder, but not until millions of Americans had heard a recording of Brown begging police for help in a prior domestic violence incident involving Simpson, and had seen a photo of her face, bruised and bloody from a beating prior to the murder, which was among the evidence presented at Simpson's trial.

LEGISLATION AGAINST VIOLENCE. In 1994 the Violence against Women Act granted female victims of violence, including battered women, federal civil rights protection. The civil rights section of the act was tested in 1999, when Christy Brzonkala filed a civil suit after being raped by two football players from Virginia Polytechnic Institute. In a five-to-four decision in *U.S. v. Morrison*, the U.S. Supreme Court ruled that Congress could not enact a federal civil remedy "for victims of gender-motivated violence." Individuals who committed crimes motivated by a gender bias, the Court ruled, could not be held accountable at the federal level.

Congress passed a revised act in October 2000—Victims of Trafficking and Violence Protection Act—which included the sections Strengthening Law Enforcement to Reduce Violence against Women, Strengthening Services to Victims of Violence, Limiting the Effects of Violence on Children, and Strengthening Education and Training to Combat Violence against Women. The new legislation made no mention of women's civil rights. Although spouse abuse is illegal in the United States and women may now sue their abusers for damages at the state level, battering continues. Many women still feel helpless and trapped in abusive relationships, unable to tell others about their problems and unsure of where to seek and obtain help.

EMOTIONAL AND PSYCHOLOGICAL ABUSE

Most definitions of abuse focus on situations where physical violence was either threatened or used. Official definitions used by the courts and police do not include emotional or psychological abuse, although domestic violence activists believe that such abuse can cause as much long-term damage as acts of physical violence.

Emotional and psychological abuse is usually harder to define than physical abuse, where bruises and scars are clearly evident. Almost all couples scream and shout at one another at some point. However, abuse is distinguished from the heated arguments that may follow in the course of otherwise healthy relationships because the abuser uses words to project power over a mate in a demeaning way. This can produce serious and often debilitating emotional or psychological consequences.

Some domestic violence researchers and counselors equate emotional abuse with the Amnesty International definition of psychological torture, which includes verbal degradation, denial of power, isolation, monopolizing perceptions, and threats to kill. Health and social service workers who counsel victims cite emotional violence as one of several factors that may paralyze women, preventing them from fleeing dangerous and abusive relationships. Furthermore, they believe that early identification of and effective intervention to end emotional abuse may prevent this emotional violence from escalating to physical abuse.

Verbal Aggression

Murray A. Straus, along with Stephen Sweet, examined verbal aggression as it was measured in the 1985 National Family Violence Resurvey data in their study "Verbal/Symbolic Aggression in Couples: Incidence Rates and Relationships to Personal Characteristics" (*Journal of Marriage and the Family*, 1992). Straus and Sweet find no significant differences between man-to-woman and woman-to-man verbal aggression. They also find that when one partner engages in verbal aggression, the other responds in similar fashion. Women report more abuse regardless of who initiated the aggression, but Straus and Sweet are unable to determine whether men minimize the incidence of verbal abuse or women exaggerate it.

Straus and Sweet's study finds no correlation between race or socioeconomic status and verbal aggression, although other studies report increased frequency of verbal aggression among African-American couples. They do find, however, a link between age and levels of abuse, indicating that verbal aggression declines with age regardless of how much conflict there is in a relationship. Straus and Sweet's analysis also reveals a direct connection between alcohol consumption and verbal aggression—the more often men drink excessively, the more likely they are to be verbally abusive. Similarly, the more women use drugs, the greater the probability of verbal abuse. For men, however, drug use does not significantly affect the use of verbal abuse. Straus and Sweet caution that their research reveals a correlation between these two variables, but not causation—in other words, it demonstrates a relationship between alcohol consumption and abuse, but it does not show whether men and women drink to provide themselves with excuses for abusive behavior or whether drinking causes their aggression.

Several studies find that verbal aggression is a precursor to physical violence. Margareta Hyden finds in "Verbal Aggression as a Prehistory of Woman Battering" (*Journal of Family Violence*, March 1995) that in most cases a "verbal fight," with the aim of making one's partner feel worthless, precedes battering. One study finds that verbal aggression is correlated with physical violence during pregnancy. Lynda M. Sagrestano et al., in "Demographic, Psychological, and Relationship Factors in Domestic Violence during Pregnancy in a Sample of Low-Income Women of Color" (*Psychology of Women Quarterly*, December 2004), find that pregnant women who report verbal aggression in their relationships are more likely to report physical abuse than their nonpregnant peers. In addition, those who report verbal aggression experience more frequent physical abuse than women who do not experience verbal aggression.

ABUSE OF IMMIGRANT WOMEN

Luke J. Larsen reports in *The Foreign-Born Population in the United States: 2003* (August 2004, http://www.census.gov/prod/2004pubs/p20-551.pdf) that in March 2003 the total foreign-born population was 33.5 million people, or 11.7% of the U.S. population. Abuse of immigrant women remains a problem in the United States. Immigrant women may be at increased risk for various reasons, including a cultural background that teaches them to defer to their husbands. Many foreign-born women cannot speak English and do not know their rights in the United States. Others fear they will be deported or have no resources or support systems to turn to for help.

In March 2003 Asian immigrants accounted for 25% of all immigrants in the United States and in 2005 were

FIGURE 1.1

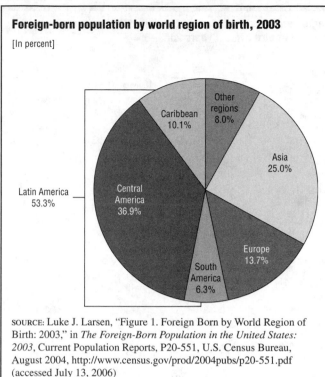

Foreign-born population by world region of birth, 2003

[In percent]

SOURCE: Luke J. Larsen, "Figure 1. Foreign Born by World Region of Birth: 2003," in *The Foreign-Born Population in the United States: 2003*, Current Population Reports, P20-551, U.S. Census Bureau, August 2004, http://www.census.gov/prod/2004pubs/p20-551.pdf (accessed July 13, 2006)

35.7% of legal permanent residents, or green-card holders. (See Figure 1.1 and Table 1.2.) Along with other immigrant groups, the Asian immigrant community has become increasingly aware of domestic abuse. Some Asian women have been sent to the United States as the result of arranged marriages to live with men they barely know. In some cases the husband takes his immigrant bride's money, jewelry, and passport, leaving her completely dependent on him. The abusive husband often tells his immigrant wife that if she leaves him, she will be deported. For some abused immigrant women, it would be worse to return home and bring shame on their family than to stay with the abusive partner. In some cultures divorced women are outcasts with no place in society.

U.S. immigration laws have unintentionally contributed to the problem of abuse among immigrant women. The Immigration Marriage Fraud Amendment was passed in 1986 in an attempt to prevent immigrants from illegally obtaining resident status through a sham marriage to a U.S. citizen. The amendment requires that spouses, usually husbands, petition for conditional resident status for an undocumented mate. Conditional status lasts a minimum of two years during which time the couple must remain married. If the marriage dissolves, the immigrant loses conditional status and may be deported. As a result, some wives become prisoners of abusive husbands for as long as the husbands control their conditional resident status.

TABLE 1.2

Legal permanent residents in the United States by region and country of birth, fiscal years 2003–05

Region/country of birth	2005 Number	2005 Percent	2004 Number	2004 Percent	2003 Number	2003 Percent
Total	1,122,373	100.0	957,883	100.0	705,827	100.0
Region:						
Africa	85,102	7.6	66,462	6.9	48,738	6.9
Asia	400,135	35.7	334,551	34.9	244,759	34.7
Europe	176,569	15.7	133,181	13.9	100,769	14.3
North America	345,575	30.8	342,399	35.7	250,667	35.5
Carribbean	108,598	9.7	89,075	9.3	68,756	9.7
Central America	53,470	4.8	62,287	6.5	54,565	7.7
Other North America	183,507	16.3	191,037	19.9	127,346	18.0
Oceania	6,546	0.6	5,985	0.6	4,377	0.6
South America	103,143	9.2	72,060	7.5	55,247	7.8
Unknown	5,303	0.5	3,245	0.3	1,270	0.2
Country:						
Mexico	161,445	14.4	175,411	18.3	115,864	16.4
India	84,681	7.5	70,151	7.3	50,372	7.1
China	69,967	6.2	55,494	5.8	40,659	5.8
Philippines	60,748	5.4	57,846	6.0	45,397	6.4
Cuba	36,261	3.2	20,488	2.1	9,304	1.3
Vietnam	32,784	2.9	31,524	3.3	22,133	3.1
Dominican Republic	27,504	2.5	30,504	3.2	26,205	3.7
Korea	26,562	2.4	19,678	2.1	12,512	1.8
Colombia	25,571	2.3	18,846	2.0	14,777	2.1
Ukraine	22,761	2.0	14,156	1.5	11,666	1.7
Canada	21,878	1.9	15,569	1.6	11,446	1.6
El Salvador	21,359	1.9	29,807	3.1	28,296	4.0
United Kingdom	19,800	1.8	14,915	1.6	11,666	1.7
Jamaica	18,346	1.6	14,430	1.5	13,384	1.9
Russia	18,083	1.6	17,410	1.8	13,951	2.0
Guatemala	16,825	1.5	18,920	2.0	14,415	2.0
Brazil	16,664	1.5	10,556	1.1	6,357	0.9
Peru	15,676	1.4	11,794	1.2	9,444	1.3
Poland	15,352	1.4	14,326	1.5	10,526	1.5
Pakistan	14,926	1.3	12,086	1.3	9,444	1.3
All other countries	395,180	35.2	316,058	33.0	237,453	33.6

SOURCE: Kelly Jefferys and Nancy Rytina, "Table 3. Legal Permanent Resident Flow by Region and Country of Birth: Fiscal Years 2003 to 2005," in *U.S. Legal Permanent Residents: 2005*, Annual Flow Report, Office of Immigration Statistics, April 2006, http://www.uscis.gov/graphics/shared/statistics/publications/USLegalPermEst_5.pdf (accessed August 24, 2006)

The law was amended under the Immigration Act of 1990 to permit a waiver of conditional status if the immigrant could prove battery or extreme cruelty. While the new law attempts to provide relief for battered brides, the initial filing for conditional status is still in the hands of the husband; if the abuse begins before he chooses to file the petition, the woman has no legal recourse.

In addition, the Medicare Modernization Act of 2003, an aid package meant to defray the costs of providing health care to immigrants, potentially harms battered immigrant women, according to the Family Violence Prevention Fund in "Hospital Regulation Would Threaten Battered Immigrant Women, Experts Warn" (September 2004, http://www.endabuse.org/newsflash/index.php3?Search=Article&NewsFlashID=552). Under the proposal, hospitals wanting aid are required to ask uninsured patients intimidating questions about their immigration status.

These regulations may keep battered women from seeking medical care.

Many immigrants come from cultures that are radically different from the predominant American society. Among the Asian-American community, including Chinese, Vietnamese, Indians, Koreans, Thai, and Cambodians, there is widespread acceptance of male dominance and a belief that the community and the family take priority over the individual. Asian women are generally raised to accept their husbands' dominance and are more reluctant to complain or to leave than their native-born counterparts. Complicating the problem of domestic abuse in this community are strong family ties, economic dependency, the stigma of divorce, and fear of bringing shame to the family. In "Immigrant Women and Domestic Violence: Common Experiences in Different Countries" (*Gender and Society*, December 2002), Cecilia Menjívar and Olivia Salcido state that "the experiences of immigrant women in domestic violence situations are often exacerbated by their specific position as immigrants, including limited host-language skills, lack of access to dignified jobs, uncertain legal statuses, and experiences in their home countries; thus, their alternatives to living with their abusers are very limited."

Still, researchers find that rates of domestic abuse in immigrant communities are no higher than among the native population. There is, however, documented evidence of abuse in practically every immigrant community in the United States. For example, research conducted during the 1990s by the Immigrant Woman's Task Force of the Northern California Coalition for Immigrant Rights found that 34% of Latinas and 25% of Filipinas surveyed had experienced domestic violence. Findings were reported by Deena L. Jang, Leni Marin, and Gail Pendleton in *Domestic Violence in Immigrant and Refugee Communities: Asserting the Rights of Battered Women* (1997).

Jang, Marin, and Pendleton also note that language barriers compound immigrant women's problems, often making it difficult for women to seek and obtain help. Women who do not speak English generally do not know how to find help, have difficulties in availing themselves of the help that does exist, and do not know their rights in the United States. Social workers report that interpreters, often male, do not always translate correctly, preferring to maintain community values rather than support the battered wife. In addition, many Asian women do not know the law and are misinformed by their husbands that they will be deported or lose their children if they report the abuse.

Some of the distinctive ways that battered immigrant women are abused include threatening to report a woman to the Immigration and Naturalization Service, to have her deported, or to withdraw her petition to legalize her immigration status are among the actions an abusive husband may take to control his immigrant wife.

In September 1994 President Bill Clinton signed the Violence against Women Act as part of the Violent Crime Control and Law Enforcement Act of 1994. The Violence against Women Act permitted undocumented battered women to obtain lawful permanent resident status by petitioning for that status or through the suspension of deportation. To take advantage of this law, however, immigrant women must hire a lawyer and enter a system many of them misunderstand and mistrust.

New policies and programs for recent immigrant victims have emerged across the country, especially in cities with large immigrant populations. To improve the communication between immigrants and the criminal justice system, authorities have made special efforts to reach immigrant victims by hiring multicultural criminal justice staffs and providing informational materials in a variety of languages. Police representatives also attend meetings of immigrant groups, and members of the immigrant community are encouraged to serve as representatives on citizen police committees.

The most effective programs to assist immigrant women acknowledge the multiple pressures these women face during their efforts to become oriented and to assimilate themselves into American culture and society. Along with cultural shock and language barriers, many immigrant women confront racism, class prejudice, and sexism. Fear of authority and the absence of social networks and support services compound the problem. Finally, recognizing that many women are brought to the United States in circumstances that increase the likelihood of victimization—as mail-order brides, child care workers, or prostitutes—is an important step in stemming the crisis and addressing the crime of domestic violence. According to Marianne Sullivan et al. in "Participatory Action Research in Practice: A Case Study in Addressing Domestic Violence in Nine Cultural Communities" (*Journal of Interpersonal Violence*, August 2005), promising experimental programs include battered immigrant women themselves in the development of programs to address battering in their communities.

DOMESTIC ABUSE AMONG SAME-SEX COUPLES

One aspect of domestic abuse that often has been overlooked is violence between men or women in same-sex relationships. There are few published studies about this subject, but Vernon R. Wiehe in *Understanding Family Violence* (1998) finds that comparable forms of physical, emotional, and sexual abuse occur between partners in same-sex relationships as heterosexual partners, with one difference: emotional abuse may also include threats to disclose a partner's homosexuality.

Researchers have difficulty comparing the prevalence of partner abuse in same-sex relationships with abuse rates in heterosexual relationships because they must rely on nonrandom, self-selected samples. These studies consider people who identify themselves as homosexuals and agree to participate in a research study as opposed to randomly selected people representative of the population to be studied. As with other forms of abuse, same-sex partners may underreport violence in their relationships. Most of the published studies examining same-sex domestic violence indicate that abuse rates for same-sex couples are about the same as for heterosexual couples, including one study by Michelle Aulivola, "Outing Domestic Violence: Affording Appropriate Protections to Gay and Lesbian Victims" (*Family Court Review*, January 2004). Stephen Owen and Tod Burke, in "An Exploration of the Prevalence of Domestic Violence in Same Sex Relationships" (*Psychological Reports*, August 2004), also find that gays and lesbians who responded had experienced violence at the same rate as heterosexuals. While violence rates against heterosexual and homosexual women are comparable, violence against homosexual men is higher than against heterosexual men.

How Abusive Are Women in Same-Sex Relationships?

Some survey data about women in same-sex relationships indicate that lesbians endure considerable levels of physical and sexual violence. In "Physical and Sexual Violence Experienced by Lesbian and Heterosexual Women" (*Violence against Women*, January 2000), Linda A. Bernhard observes that while lesbians, like other women, are at risk of abuse from past and present male partners, they also risk being victimized by their female partners. In addition, because lesbians are also at greater risk for hate crimes than their heterosexual counterparts, they may experience more violence than heterosexual women.

Based on the limited research done on lesbian violence, it appears the risk factors for abuse are similar to those of heterosexual women. Dependency and jealousy, both of which may precipitate abuse in heterosexual relationships, have been identified as the main contributors of lesbian battering. The literature about this subject also contains clinical case studies and anecdotal reports indicating that lesbian batterers may also abuse alcohol or drugs, feel powerless, and suffer from low self-esteem. Kimberly F. Balsam and Dawn M. Szymanski state in "Relationship Quality and Domestic Violence in Women's Same-Sex Relationships: The Role of Minority Stress" (*Psychology of Women Quarterly*, September 2005) that the stress specific to living as a lesbian correlates with both domestic violence perpetration and victimization.

Battered lesbians are among the most underserved population of battered women, often facing denial from other lesbians and homophobia from health and social service providers. Many states have narrow definitions of family that deny gay and lesbian victims of domestic violence the possibility of seeking family court orders of protection or other civil redress. Complicating the issue are the myths that same-sex violence is mutual and the abuse is not as dangerous or destructive as heterosexual abuse. In fact, according to health care providers, the abuse is rarely mutual and can be just as harmful as abuse in heterosexual relationships.

WHAT IS CHILD ABUSE?

Child abuse is often a secret. Since the 1960s, however, Americans have become increasingly aware of the problems of child abuse and neglect (together referred to as child maltreatment). According to the report *Juvenile Court Statistics* (1966), the Children's Bureau of the U.S. Department of Health, Education, and Welfare (and later of the U.S. Department of Health and Human Services) reports that in 1963 some 150,000 young victims of maltreatment were reported to authorities. The U.S Department of Health and Human Services notes in *Child Maltreatment 2004* (2006, http://www.acf.hhs.gov/programs/cb/pubs/cm04/cm04.pdf) that in 2004 state child protective services (CPS) agencies received about three million reports of child maltreatment involving about 5.5 million children.

There is still no agreement on what constitutes child abuse. In August 2002 a mother in Brilliant, Ohio, was charged with three counts of felony child endangerment for allegedly allowing her three children to become seriously sunburned. A sheriff's deputy had arrested the woman after noticing that her three young children had sunburned faces while at the county fair in 95°F weather. The woman spent eight days in jail. Authorities later released the mother after determining that the children were not that badly burned. She was charged with a single count of misdemeanor child endangerment, which the prosecutor dismissed two months later.

In September 2002 a surveillance camera in a store in Mishawaka, Indiana, recorded a mother apparently beating and punching her four-year-old daughter inside her car. The videotape, which aired nationally, caused public outrage. The mother was charged with battery to a child, a felony that could bring her a maximum of three years in jail. The child was put in foster care while the case was under investigation. While extreme cases such as the Indiana one are easy to label, less severe cases, such as the sunburned children, are viewed differently by different people.

Researchers disagree on the definition of child abuse as well. The National Research Council identifies inadequate and conflicting definitions of abuse and neglect as a problem in conducting research in the area of child maltreatment. Debate about definitions continues,

as evidenced by numerous articles and reports, including three that appeared in the May 2005 edition of the journal *Child Abuse and Neglect*: Desmond K. Runyan et al., "Describing Maltreatment: Do Child Protective Service Reports and Research Definitions Agree?"; Jody Todd Manly, "Advances in Research Definitions of Child Maltreatment"; and Howard Dubowitz et al., "Defining Child Neglect Based on Child Protective Services Data."

OFFICIAL DEFINITIONS OF CHILD ABUSE

Official definitions of child abuse and neglect differ among institutions, government bodies, and experts. The Child Abuse Prevention and Treatment Act (CAPTA) Amendments of 1996, which amended the 1974 CAPTA and was reauthorized by the Keeping Children and Families Safe Act of 2003, defines child maltreatment in this way:

> The term "child abuse and neglect" means, at a minimum, any recent act or failure to act, on the part of a parent or caretaker [including any employee of a residential facility or any staff person providing out-of-home care who is responsible for the child's welfare], which results in death, serious physical or emotional harm, sexual abuse or exploitation, or an act or failure to act which presents an imminent risk of serious harm. [A child is a person under the age of eighteen, unless the child protection law of the state in which the child resides specifies a younger age for cases not involving sexual abuse.]

It should be noted that this definition of child abuse and neglect specifies that only parents and caregivers can be considered perpetrators of child maltreatment. Abusive or negligent behavior by other people—strangers or people known to the child—is considered child assault.

Based on a concern that severely disabled newborns may be denied medical care, CAPTA also considers as child abuse and neglect the "withholding of medically indicated treatment," including appropriate nutrition, hydration, and medication, which in the treating physician's medical judgment would most likely help, improve, or correct an infant's life-threatening conditions. This definition, however, does not refer to situations where treatment of an infant, in the physician's medical judgment, would prolong dying, be ineffective in improving or correcting all the infant's life-threatening conditions, or would be futile in helping the infant to survive. In addition, this definition does not include circumstances where the infant is chronically or irreversibly comatose.

CAPTA Defines Four Main Types of Child Maltreatment

PHYSICAL ABUSE. Physical abuse is the infliction of physical injury through punching, beating, kicking, biting, burning, shaking, or otherwise harming a child. Physical abuse is generally a willful act. There are cases, however, in which the parent or caretaker may not have intended to hurt the child. In such cases, the injury may have resulted from overdiscipline or corporal (physical) punishment. Nonetheless, if the child is injured, the act is considered abusive.

SEXUAL ABUSE. Sexual abuse includes fondling a child's genitals, intercourse, incest, rape, sodomy, exhibitionism, and commercial exploitation through prostitution or the production of pornographic materials.

PSYCHOLOGICAL ABUSE. Psychological abuse includes acts or omissions by the parents or by other caregivers that have caused, or could cause, serious behavioral, cognitive, emotional, or mental disorders. In some cases of emotional abuse, the abuser's action alone, without any harm evident in the child's behavior or condition, is enough cause for intervention by CPS agencies. For example, the parent or caregiver may use extreme or bizarre forms of punishment, such as locking a child in a dark room or closet.

Other forms of psychological abuse may involve more subtle acts, such as habitual scapegoating (erroneously blaming the child for things that go wrong), belittling, or rejection of the child. For CPS to intervene, demonstrable harm to the child is often required. Although any of the types of child maltreatment may be found separately, different types of abuse often occur in combination with one another. Emotional abuse is almost always present when other types are identified.

CHILD NEGLECT. Child neglect is an act of omission characterized by failure to provide for the child's basic needs. Neglect can be physical, educational, or emotional. Physical neglect includes failure to provide food, clothing, and shelter; refusal of or delay in seeking health care (medical neglect); abandonment; inadequate supervision; and expulsion from the home or refusal to allow a runaway to return home. Educational neglect includes permitting chronic truancy, failure to enroll a child of mandatory school age in school, and failure to take care of a child's special educational needs. Emotional neglect includes substantial inattention to the child's need for affection, failure to provide needed psychological care, spousal abuse in the child's presence, and allowing drug or alcohol use by the child. It is important to distinguish between willful neglect and a parent's or a caretaker's failure to provide the necessities of life because of poverty or cultural factors.

State Definitions

CAPTA provides a foundation for states by identifying a minimum set of acts or behaviors that characterize child abuse and neglect. Each state, based on CAPTA guidelines, has formulated its own definitions of the different types of child maltreatment. State definitions, however, such as of neglect, may be unclear. For example, states typically define neglect as the failure to provide adequate food, clothing, shelter, or medical care. About one-fifth of states do not have a separate definition for neglect. Moreover, most CPS agencies consider recent incidence of neglect instead of patterns of behavior that may constitute chronic, or continuing, neglect.

States define child abuse and neglect in three areas in state statutes: reporting laws for child maltreatment, criminal codes, and juvenile court laws. Most state laws also include exceptions, such as religious exemptions, corporal punishment, cultural practices, and poverty.

A DESCRIPTION OF MALTREATED CHILDREN

Perhaps better than a definition of child abuse is a description of the characteristics likely to be exhibited by abused and/or neglected children. The fact sheet "Recognizing Child Abuse and Neglect: Signs and Symptoms" (2006, http://www.childwelfare.gov/pubs/factsheets/signs.cfm), which is maintained by the Child Welfare Information Gateway, indicates that, in general, abused or neglected children are likely to have at least several of the following characteristics:

- Their behavior or school performance suddenly changes.
- They do not get medical attention for problems brought to their parents' attention.
- They seem always watchful for something bad to happen.
- They are passive and withdrawn.
- They do not want to go home.

Physically abused children may:

- Have unexplained burns, bruises, or broken bones
- Have fading bruises still visible after a school absence
- Seem frightened of parents
- Shrink away from adults
- Report injury at the hands of a parent or other caregiver

Sexually abused children may:

- Exhibit difficulty walking or sitting
- Suddenly refuse to change for gym
- Begin having nightmares or wetting the bed
- Show sudden appetite changes
- Demonstrate bizarre or precocious sexual knowledge or behavior
- Contract a venereal disease, especially before age fourteen
- Run away from home
- Report sexual abuse at the hands of a parent or other caregiver

Victims of Physical Abuse

Victims of physical abuse often display bruises, welts, contusions, cuts, burns, fractures, lacerations, strap marks, swellings, and/or lost teeth. While internal injuries are seldom detectable without a hospital examination, anyone in close contact with children should be alert to multiple injuries, a history of repeated injuries, new injuries added to old ones, and untreated injuries, especially in young children. Older children may attribute an injury to an improbable cause, lying for fear of parental retaliation. Younger children, however, may be unaware that a severe beating is unacceptable and may admit to having been abused.

Physically abused children frequently have behavior problems. Especially among adolescents, chronic and unexplainable misbehavior should be investigated as possible evidence of abuse. Some children come to expect abusive behavior as the only kind of attention they can receive and so act in a way that invites abuse. Others break the law deliberately to come under the jurisdiction of the courts to obtain protection from their parents. Children who have been abused may display a wide array of behavioral problems including being aggressive or disruptive; displaying intense anger or rage; being self-abusive or self-destructive; feeling suicidal or depressed; using drugs or alcohol; fearing certain adults; and avoiding being at home.

Parents who inflict physical abuse generally provide necessities, such as adequate food and clean clothes. Nevertheless, they get angry quickly, have unrealistic expectations of their children, and are overly critical and rejecting of their children. According to the Child Welfare Information Gateway, parents who physically abuse their children may offer unconvincing explanations for injuries to their children, describe their children in negative ways (for example, as "evil"), or use harsh physical discipline with their children. Abusive parents may avoid other parents in the neighborhood and school activities. While many abusive parents have been mistreated as children themselves and are following a learned behavior, an increasing number who physically abuse their own children do so under the influence of alcohol and drugs.

Victims of Physical Neglect

Physically neglected children are often hungry. They may go without breakfast and have neither food nor money for lunch. Some take the lunch money or food of other children and hoard whatever they obtain. They show signs of malnutrition, such as paleness, low weight relative to height, lack of body tone, fatigue, inability to participate in physical activities, and lack of normal strength and endurance.

These children are usually irritable. They show evidence of inadequate home management and are unclean and unkempt. Their clothes are often torn and dirty. They may lack proper clothing for different weather conditions, and their school attendance may be irregular. In addition, these children may frequently be ill and may exhibit a generally repressed personality, inattentiveness, and withdrawal. They are in obvious need of medical attention for correctable conditions such as poor eyesight, poor dental care, and lack of immunizations.

A child who suffers physical neglect also generally lacks parental supervision at home. For example, the child may frequently return from school to an empty house. While the need for adult supervision is, of course, relative to both the situation and the maturity of the child, it is generally held that a child younger than age twelve should always be supervised by an adult or at least have immediate access to a concerned adult when necessary.

Parents of neglected children are either unable or unwilling to provide appropriate care. Some neglectful parents are mentally deficient. Most lack knowledge of parenting skills and tend to be discouraged, depressed, and frustrated with their role as parents. Alcohol or drug abuse may also be involved.

Medical neglect refers to the parents' failure to provide medical treatment for their children, including immunizations, prescribed medications, recommended surgery, and other intervention in cases of serious disease or injury. Some situations involve a parent's inability to care for a child or lack of access to health care. Other situations involve a parent's refusal to seek professional medical care, particularly because of a belief in spiritual healing.

Victims of Emotional Abuse and Neglect

Emotional abuse and neglect are as serious as physical abuse and neglect, although this condition is far more difficult to describe or identify. Emotional maltreatment often involves a parent's lack of love or failure to give direction and encouragement. The parent may either demand far too much from the child in the area of academic, social, or athletic activity or withhold physical or verbal contact, indicating no concern for the child's successes and failures and giving no guidance or praise.

Parents who commit emotional abuse and neglect are often unable to accept their children as fallible human beings. The effects of such abuse can often be far more serious and lasting than those of physical abuse and neglect. Emotionally abused children are often extremely aggressive, disruptive, and demanding in an attempt to gain attention and love. They are rarely able to achieve the success in school that tests indicate they can achieve.

Emotional maltreatment can be hard to determine. Is the child's abnormal behavior the result of maltreatment on the part of the parents, or is it a result of inborn or internal factors? Stuart N. Hart et al., in "Psychological

Maltreatment" (John E. B. Myers et al., eds., *The APSAC Handbook on Child Maltreatment*, 2002), list problems associated with emotional abuse and neglect, including poor appetite, lying, stealing, enuresis (bed-wetting), encopresis (passing of feces in unacceptable places after bowel control has been achieved), low self-esteem, low emotional responsiveness, failure to thrive, inability to be independent, withdrawal, suicide, and homicide.

GOVERNMENT SERVICES FOR CHILDREN

The federal government first provided child welfare services with the passage of the Social Security Act of 1935. Under Title IV-B (Child Welfare Services Program) of the act, the Children's Bureau received funding for grants to states for "the protection and care of homeless, dependent, and neglected children and children in danger of becoming delinquent." Before 1961 Title IV-B was the only source of federal funding for child welfare services.

The 1962 Social Security Amendments required each state to make child welfare services available to all children. The law further required states to provide coordination between child welfare services (under Title IV-B) and social services (under Title IV-A, or the Social Services program), which served families on welfare. The law also revised the definition of child welfare services to include the prevention and remedy of child abuse. In 1980 Congress created a separate Foster Care program under Title IV-E.

Title IV-A became Title XX (Social Services Block Grant) in 1981, giving states more options regarding the types of social services to fund. Today, child abuse prevention and treatment services have remained an eligible category of service.

State Programs That Help Children at Risk

Under Title IV-B Child Welfare Services (Subpart 1) and Promoting Safe and Stable Families (Subpart 2) programs, families in crisis receive preventive intervention so that children will not have to be removed from their homes. If this cannot be achieved, children are placed in foster care until they can be reunited with their families. If reunification is not possible, parents' rights are terminated and the children are made available for adoption.

States use the Foster Care (Title IV-E) program funds for the care of foster children and for the training of foster parents, program personnel, and private-agency staff. Title XX funds provide services such as child day care, CPS, information and referral, counseling, and employment.

The Child Abuse Reporting Network

In 1961 C. Henry Kempe, a pediatric radiologist, and his associates proposed the term *battered child syndrome* at a symposium on the problem of child abuse held under the auspices of the American Academy of Pediatrics. The term refers to the collection of injuries sustained by a child as a result of repeated mistreatment or beatings. The following year, Kempe et al. published the landmark article "The Battered Child Syndrome" (*Journal of the American Medical Association*, July 7, 1962). The term *battered child syndrome* developed into the word *maltreatment*, encompassing not only physical assault but also other forms of abuse, such as malnourishment, failure to thrive, medical neglect, and sexual and emotional abuse.

Kempe proposed that physicians be required to report child abuse. According to the National Association of Counsel for Children, by 1967, after Kempe's findings had gained general acceptance among health and welfare workers and the public, forty-four states had passed legislation that required the reporting of child abuse to official agencies, and the remaining six states had voluntary reporting laws. This was one of the most rapidly accepted pieces of legislation in U.S. history. Initially, only doctors were required to report and then only in cases of "serious physical injury" or "nonaccidental injury." Today, all the states have laws that require not only doctors but most professionals who serve children to report all forms of suspected abuse and either require or permit any citizen to report child abuse.

One of the reasons for the lack of prosecution of early child abuse cases was the difficulty in determining whether a physical injury was a case of deliberate assault or an accident. In the latter part of the twentieth century, however, doctors of pediatric radiology were able to determine the incidence of repeated child abuse through sophisticated developments in x-ray technology. These advances allowed radiologists to see more clearly such things as subdural hematomas (blood clots around the brain resulting from blows to the head) and abnormal fractures. As a result, these advances brought about more recognition in the medical community of the widespread incidence of child abuse, along with growing public condemnation of abuse.

FEDERAL CHILD ABUSE LEGISLATION

The passage of CAPTA in 1974 created the National Center on Child Abuse and Neglect (NCCAN), which developed standards for handling reports of child maltreatment. NCCAN also established a nationwide network of CPS and served as a clearinghouse for information and research on child abuse and neglect.

Since 1974 CAPTA has been amended a number of times. (See Figure 1.2.) In 1978 the Child Abuse Prevention and Treatment and Adoption Reform Act promoted the passage of state laws providing comprehensive adoption assistance. The act provided grants to encourage the adoption of children with special needs and broadened the definition of abuse, adding a specific reference to sexual abuse and exploitation to the basic definition. That

FIGURE 1.2

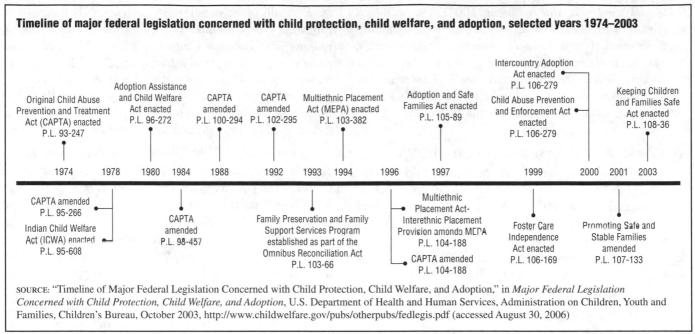

Timeline of major federal legislation concerned with child protection, child welfare, and adoption, selected years 1974–2003

SOURCE: "Timeline of Major Federal Legislation Concerned with Child Protection, Child Welfare, and Adoption," in *Major Federal Legislation Concerned with Child Protection, Child Welfare, and Adoption*, U.S. Department of Health and Human Services, Administration on Children, Youth and Families, Children's Bureau, October 2003, http://www.childwelfare.gov/pubs/otherpubs/fedlegis.pdf (accessed August 30, 2006)

same year the Indian Child Welfare Act was also enacted to reestablish tribal jurisdiction over the adoption of Native American children.

In response to the public outcry about the placement of an increasing number of children in foster care, Congress passed the Adoption Assistance and Child Welfare Act of 1980, with the goal of promoting family reunification. In 1988 the Child Abuse Prevention, Adoption, and Family Services Act replaced the original 1974 CAPTA, mandating, among other things, the establishment of a system to collect national data on child maltreatment.

In 1994 Congress passed the Multiethnic Placement Act, directing states to actively recruit adoptive and foster families, especially for minority children waiting a long time for placement in a home. Pursuant to the Child Abuse Prevention and Treatment Act Amendments of 1996, NCCAN was abolished. Its functions have subsequently been consolidated within the Children's Bureau of the Department of Health and Human Services.

By 1997 the federal government had realized that reuniting abused children with their families did not always work in the best interests of the children. Congress revisited the "reasonable efforts" for family reunification originally mandated by the 1980 Adoption Assistance and Child Welfare Act. Under the 1997 Adoption and Safe Families Act, "reasonable efforts" was clarified to mean the safety of the child comes first. States were directed to indicate circumstances under which an abused child should not be returned to the parents or caretakers. According to the Government Accountability Office

report *Foster Care: Recent Legislation Helps States Focus on Finding Permanent Homes for Children, but Long-Standing Barriers Remain* (June 2002, http://www.gao.gov/new.items/d02585.pdf), despite the legislation's intention to increase adoptions of children from foster care, many barriers to obtaining permanent families for foster children remain.

The Promoting Safe and Stable Families Amendments of 2001 was enacted partly to address the rising number of children with incarcerated parents. The law provided a grant program for creating mentoring services for these children. The law also created a new program to assist youth aging out of foster care, helping them pursue an education or vocational training.

In 2003 CAPTA received reauthorization through 2008 under the Keeping Children and Families Safe Act. The law, among other things, directs more comprehensive training of CPS personnel, including a mandate that they inform alleged abusers, during the first contact, of the nature of complaints against them. The law calls for child welfare agencies to coordinate services with other agencies, including public health, mental health, and developmental disabilities agencies. The law also directs the collection of data for the Fourth National Incidence Study of Child Abuse and Neglect, which will be completed in February 2008.

Federal Legislation Dealing with the Prosecution of Child Abusers

The Children's Justice and Assistance Act of 1986 offers grants to states to improve the investigation and prosecution of cases of child abuse and neglect, especially sexual abuse and exploitation. The act aims to reduce additional trauma to the child by training people who are involved in child maltreatment cases, such as law enforcement, mental health personnel, prosecutors, and judges. The act also supports legislation that would allow indirect testimony from children, shorten the time children spend in court, and make children's courtroom experiences less intimidating.

Until 1995 none of the federal child abuse legislation dealt specifically with punishing sex offenders. In December of that year, with growing acknowledgment of and concern about sex crimes against minors, Congress passed the Sex Crimes against Children Prevention Act of 1995. The act increased penalties for those who sexually exploit children by engaging in illegal conduct, or for exploitation conducted via the Internet, as well as for those who transport children with the intent to engage in criminal sexual activity.

Three years later Congress enacted the Protection of Children from Sexual Predators Act of 1998 that, among other things, established the Morgan P. Hardiman Child Abduction and Serial Murder Investigative Resources Center (CASMIRC). The purpose of CASMIRC, as stated in the text of the act, is "to provide investigative support through the coordination and provision of federal law enforcement resources, training, and application of other multidisciplinary expertise, to assist federal, state, and local authorities in matters involving child abductions, mysterious disappearance of children, child homicide, and serial murder across the country."

Congress passed the Prosecutorial Remedies and Other Tools to End the Exploitation of Children Today Act on April 30, 2003. Among other things, the act establishes a national Amber Alert Program for recovering abducted children and provides that there will be no statute of limitations for sex crimes and abduction of children. (Under previous laws, the statute of limitations expired when the child turned twenty-five years old.) The law also provides for severe penalties for sex tourism (defined as travel with intent to engage in illicit sexual conduct) and the denial of pretrial release for suspects in federal child rape or kidnap cases. The Amber Alert Program is named after Amber Hagerman of Texas, who was abducted and murdered in 1996. She was nine years old. A witness notified police, giving a description of the vehicle and the direction it had gone, but police had no way of alerting the public. Amber Alert allows for a voluntary partnership between law enforcement, broadcasters, and transportation agencies, whereby an urgent bulletin is broadcast to the public via the Emergency Alert System giving a description of the abducted child and the alleged abductor.

ABUSE OF CHILDREN IN RELIGIOUS SETTINGS

Allegations of child abuse have surfaced among several religious denominations. For example, according to the report *The Nature and Scope of the Problem of Sexual Abuse of Minors by Catholic Priests and Deacons in the United States* (June 2002, http://www.usccb.org/nrb/johnjaystudy), a survey of Roman Catholic dioceses in the United States commissioned by the U.S. Conference of Catholic Bishops, 10,667 incidents of alleged sexual abuse occurred between 1950 and 2002 involving 4,392 priests and deacons. During most of this period, church leaders who knew of the abuse worked to keep it secret by paying millions of dollars to victims' families and moving the abusive priests from parish to parish. Allegations of sexual abuse by priests have also surfaced in Mexico, Ireland, Canada, Colombia, Venezuela, Italy, Spain, England, Australia, and Hong Kong.

Other religious denominations have also been involved in sexual abuse allegations. Some members of the Jehovah's Witnesses spoke out against their church's policy of handling reports of child sexual abuse. The church follows biblical standards to resolve problems. A group of church elders meet in secret to decide each case of sexual abuse allegation. The elders require two credible witnesses, including the accuser, to determine whether or not the allegations are true. William Bowen, a former elder and founder of silentlambs (http://www.silentlambs.org), a group that monitors sexual abuse in the Jehovah's Witnesses, claims that it is usually impossible for a child victim to have a witness to the incident. Without the witnesses to attest to the abuse, the alleged perpetrator is considered innocent and the charges are kept confidential. According to church officials, they do report suspected abuse if the state law requires it.

In June 2000 former Hare Krishna children sued the International Society for Krishna Consciousness (ISKCON), a sect of Hinduism that became popular in the United States during the 1960s. The parents left the children in boarding schools while they went out to recruit new members and to solicit donations. The plaintiffs alleged physical, emotional, and sexual abuse, including being deprived of food and sleep, being severely beaten, being locked up in roach-infested rooms, and being offered in marriage to older men who were patrons of ISKCON. ISKCON officials, while substantiating that the abuse had occurred, denied that hundreds of children were involved.

The lawsuit attempted to use a federal law, Racketeer-Influenced and Corrupt Organizations (RICO) chapter of the Organized Crime Control Act of 1970, which was originally intended to curb organized crime. The lawsuit sought $400 million in damages from ISKCON congregations and individuals. In September 2001 the U.S. District Court of Dallas, Texas, permanently dismissed the case.

CHAPTER 2

DETECTING, MEASURING, AND PREVENTING CHILD ABUSE

INCIDENCE AND PREVALENCE OF CHILD MALTREATMENT

Statistics on child abuse are difficult to interpret and compare because there is little consistency in how information is collected. The definitions of abuse vary from study to study, as do the methods of counting incidents of abuse. Some methods count only reported cases of abuse. Some statistics are based on estimates projected from a small study, whereas others are based on interviews.

Researchers use two terms—*incidence* and *prevalence*—to describe the estimates of the number of victims of child abuse and neglect. Andrea J. Sedlak and Diane D. Broadhurst, in the Third National Incidence Study of Child Abuse and Neglect (1993; NIS-3), define incidence as the number of new cases occurring in the population during a given period. The incidence of child maltreatment is measured in terms of incidence rate: the number of children per one thousand children in the U.S. population who are maltreated annually. Surveys based on official reports by child protective services (CPS) agencies and community professionals are a major source of incidence data. (The term "child protective services" refers to the services provided by an agency authorized to act on behalf of a child when his or her parents are unable or unwilling to do so. This term is also often used to refer to the agency itself.)

Prevalence, as defined by NIS-3, refers to the total number of child maltreatment cases in the population at a given time. Some researchers use lifetime prevalence to denote the number of people who have had at least one experience of child maltreatment in their lives. To measure the prevalence of child maltreatment, researchers use self-reported surveys of parents and child victims. Examples of self-reported surveys are the landmark 1975 National Family Violence Survey and the 1985 National Family Violence Resurvey conducted by Murray A. Straus and Richard J. Gelles.

Studies based on official reports depend on a number of things happening before an incident of abuse can be recorded. The victim must be seen by people outside the home, and these people must recognize that the child has been abused. Once they have recognized this fact, they must then decide to report the abuse and find out where to report it. Once CPS receives and screens the report for appropriateness, it can then take action.

In some cases the initial call to CPS is prompted by a problem that must be handled by a different agency. It may be a case of neglect because of poverty rather than abuse, although the initial report is still recorded as abuse.

For the data to become publicly available, CPS must keep records of its cases and then pass them on to a national group that collects those statistics. Consequently, final reported statistics are understated estimates—they are valuable as indicators but not definitive findings. Because of the hidden nature of child abuse, it is unlikely that accurate statistics on it will ever be available.

COLLECTING CHILD MALTREATMENT DATA

The 1974 Child Abuse Prevention and Treatment Act (CAPTA) created the National Center on Child Abuse and Neglect (NCCAN) to coordinate nationwide efforts to protect children from maltreatment. As part of the former U.S. Department of Health, Education, and Welfare, NCCAN commissioned the American Humane Association to collect data from the states.

In 1985 the federal government stopped funding data collection on child maltreatment. In 1986 the National Committee to Prevent Child Abuse (NCPCA; now called Prevent Child Abuse America) picked up where the government left off. The NCPCA started collecting detailed information from the states on the number of children abused, the characteristics of child abuse, the number of child abuse deaths, and the changes in the funding and extent of child welfare services.

In 1988 the Child Abuse Prevention, Adoption, and Family Services Act replaced the 1974 CAPTA. The new law mandated that NCCAN, as part of the U.S. Department of Health and Human Services (HHS), establish a national data collection program on child maltreatment. In 1990 the National Child Abuse and Neglect Data System (NCANDS), designed to fulfill this mandate, began collecting and analyzing child maltreatment data from CPS agencies in the fifty states and the District of Columbia. The first three surveys were known as *Working Paper 1*, *Working Paper 2*, and *Child Maltreatment 1992*. NCANDS has since conducted the Child Maltreatment survey annually. The most current survey as of this writing was *Child Maltreatment 2004* (2006, http://www.acf.hhs.gov/programs/cb/pubs/cm04/cm04.pdf).

The data collected from states cannot be completely relied on because each state has its own method of gathering and classifying the information. Most states collect data on an incident basis; that is, they count each time a child is reported for abuse or neglect. If the same child is reported several times in one year, each incident is counted. Consequently, the reported number of incidents of child maltreatment may be greater than the reported number of maltreated children.

As part of the 1974 CAPTA, Congress also mandated NCCAN to conduct a periodic National Incidence Study of Child Abuse and Neglect (NIS). Data on maltreated children are collected not only from CPS agencies but also from professionals in community agencies, such as law enforcement, public health, juvenile probation, mental health, and voluntary social services, as well as from hospitals, schools, and day care centers. The NIS is the single most comprehensive source of information about the incidence of child maltreatment in the United States, because it analyzes the characteristics of child abuse and neglect that are known to community-based professionals, including those characteristics not reported to CPS. The most recent study is the above-mentioned NIS-3 (1993). This report is based on a nationally representative sample of more than 5,600 professionals in 842 agencies serving forty-two counties. NIS-3 includes not only child victims investigated by CPS agencies but also children seen by community institutions (such as day care centers, schools, and hospitals) and other investigating agencies (such as public health departments, police, and courts). In addition, victim counts were unduplicated, which means that each child was counted only once.

In 2003 the Keeping Children and Families Safe Act directed the collection of data for the Fourth National Incidence Study of Child Abuse and Neglect. Data from this study will be available by February 2008.

Definition Standards

NIS-3 used two standardized definitions of abuse and neglect:

- Harm Standard—required that an act or omission must have resulted in demonstrable harm to be considered as abuse or neglect

- Endangerment Standard—allowed children who had not yet been harmed by maltreatment to be counted in the estimates of maltreated children if a non-CPS professional considered them to be at risk of harm or if their maltreatment was substantiated or indicated in a CPS investigation

VICTIMS OF MALTREATMENT

Rates of Victimization

CPS DATA. According to *Child Maltreatment 2004*, in 2004 CPS agencies received an estimated three million referrals, or reports, alleging the maltreatment of about 5.5 million children, which may include some children who were reported and counted more than once. States may differ in the rates of child maltreatment reported. States differ not only in definitions of maltreatment but also in the methods of counting reports of abuse. Some states count reports based on the number of incidents or the number of families involved, rather than on the number of children allegedly abused. Other states count all reports to CPS, whereas others count only investigated reports.

In 2004 forty-five states and the District of Columbia submitted child-level data for each report of alleged maltreatment. Child-level data include, among other things, the demographics about the children and the perpetrators, types of maltreatment, and dispositions (findings after investigation or assessment of the case). The remaining five states submitted only summary statistics, such as the number of child victims of maltreatment. CPS agencies screened in (accepted for further assessment or investigation) nearly 1.3 million (62.7%) referrals. Overall, the rate of maltreatment referrals ranged from 22.8 per one thousand children (Hawaii) to 102.2 per one thousand children (Colorado) under age eighteen. (See Table 2.1.)

In 2004 an estimated 872,000 children were victims of maltreatment in the United States. A total of 11.9 children for every one thousand children in the population were victims of abuse or neglect. (See Table 2.2.) According to *Child Maltreatment 2002* (2004, http://www.acf.hhs.gov/programs/cb/pubs/cm02/cm02.pdf), this was the lowest victim rate since 1999, when the rate was 11.8 children per one thousand children in the population. The rate of maltreatment peaked at 15.3 per one thousand children in 1993.

Table 2.3 shows the types of maltreatment children suffered in 2004. In that year 544,050 of the 872,088 children reported maltreated to CPS agencies had suffered neglect. Another 17,968 suffered medical neglect.

TABLE 2.1

Screened-in and screened-out referrals by state, 2004

State	Child population	Screened-in referrals Number	Screened-in referrals %	Screened-out referrals Number	Screened-out referrals %	Total referrals Number	Total referrals Rate
Alabama	1,094,533	19,081	59.8	12,812	40.2	31,893	29.1
Alaska							
Arizona	1,547,260	35,623	99.0	370	1.0	35,993	23.3
Arkansas	676,550	20,076	62.5	12,046	37.5	32,122	47.5
California	9,596,463	234,718	66.1	120,521	33.9	355,239	37.0
Colorado	1,178,889	29,540	24.5	90,978	75.5	120,518	102.2
Connecticut							
Delaware	193,506	5,276	76.5	1,625	23.5	6,901	35.7
District of Columbia	109,547	4,977	94.0	320	6.0	5,297	48.4
Florida	4,003,290	145,393	72.2	55,956	27.8	201,349	50.3
Georgia	2,332,567	85,817	84.1	16,169	15.9	101,986	43.7
Hawaii	298,693	3,608	53.0	3,200	47.0	6,808	22.8
Idaho	372,411	6,502	44.6	8,083	55.4	14,585	39.2
Illinois							
Indiana	1,600,295	35,817	61.1	22,769	38.9	58,586	36.6
Iowa	680,437	24,366	64.1	13,674	35.9	38,040	55.9
Kansas	683,491	15,729	52.6	14,193	47.4	29,922	43.8
Kentucky	980,187	46,951	90.1	5,141	9.9	52,092	53.1
Louisiana							
Maine	282,129	5,358	31.2	11,809	68.8	17,167	60.8
Maryland							
Massachusetts	1,464,189	38,940	61.1	24,806	38.9	63,746	43.5
Michigan							
Minnesota	1,240,280	17,471	37.8	28,801	62.2	46,272	37.3
Mississippi	749,569	15,801	72.4	6,013	27.6	21,814	29.1
Missouri	1,384,542	54,216	50.5	53,038	49.5	107,254	77.5
Montana	208,093	7,450	55.5	5,981	44.5	13,431	64.5
Nebraska	434,566	10,962	64.3	6,098	35.7	17,060	39.3
Nevada	603,596	13,062	65.4	6,898	34.6	19,960	33.1
New Hampshire	304,994	6,400	38.1	10,378	61.9	16,778	55.0
New Jersey							
New Mexico	492,287	16,005	58.0	11,606	42.0	27,611	56.1
New York							
North Carolina							
North Dakota							
Ohio							
Oklahoma	859,870	36,070	60.2	23,818	39.8	59,888	69.6
Oregon	852,357	23,529	50.6	22,995	49.4	46,524	54.6
Pennsylvania							
Rhode Island	243,813	6,707	54.5	5,608	45.5	12,315	50.5
South Carolina	1,024,700	17,186	65.9	8,893	34.1	26,079	25.5
South Dakota	190,874	4,620	29.8	10,899	70.2	15,519	81.3
Tennessee	1,391,289	48,622	63.9	27,415	36.1	76,037	54.7
Texas	6,266,779	140,038	85.6	23,616	14.4	163,654	26.1
Utah	740,114	21,132	67.6	10,114	32.4	31,246	42.2
Vermont	134,894	2,690	21.8	9,664	78.2	12,354	91.6
Virginia	1,804,900	28,105	53.3	24,631	46.7	52,736	29.2
Washington	1,486,020	32,314	43.9	41,218	56.1	73,532	49.5
West Virginia	384,641	18,508	70.7	7,688	29.3	26,196	68.1
Wisconsin							
Wyoming	116,932	2,018	40.2	3,001	59.8	5,019	42.9
Total	**48,009,547**	**1,280,678**		**762,845**		**2,043,523**	
Percent			62.7		37.3		
Weighted rate							42.6
Number reporting	38	38	38	38	38	38	38

Note: Screened-in referrals are those that are accepted for investigation or assessment by Child Protective Services (CPS); screened-out referrals are those that are not accepted or pursued by CPS.

SOURCE: "Table 2.1. Screened-in and Screened-out Referrals, 2004," in *Child Maltreatment 2004*, U.S. Department of Health and Human Services, Administration on Children, Youth, and Families, 2006, http://www.acf.hhs.gov/programs/cb/pubs/cm04/cm04.pdf (accessed June 12, 2006)

In other words, 64.5% of all children found to be maltreated by CPS agencies in 2004 were victims of neglect or medical neglect. Another 152,250 children (17.5%) were victims of physical abuse and 84,398 children (9.7%) were victims of sexual abuse. *Child Maltreatment 2004* reports that 61,272 children (7%) were victims of emotional, or psychological, maltreatment, and another 126,856 children (14.5%) experienced other types of maltreatment, including abandonment, congenital drug addiction, and threats to harm them. Some children were victims of more than one type of maltreatment.

TABLE 2.2

Rates of children who were subjects of an investigation and victimization, 2000–04

Reporting year	Child population	Investigation rate	States reporting	Total children subjects of an investigation	Victim rate	States reporting	Total victims
2000	72,342,618	42.0	49	3,038,000	12.2	50	883,000
2001	72,603,552	43.2	48	3,136,000	12.5	51	905,000
2002	72,846,774	43.9	50	3,198,000	12.3	51	897,000
2003	73,043,506	46.3	50	3,382,000	12.2	51	893,000
2004	73,277,998	47.8	49	3,503,000	11.9	50	872,000

SOURCE: Adapted from "Table 3.3. Rates of Children Who Were Subjects of an Investigation and Victimization, 1990–2004," in *Child Maltreatment 2004*, U.S. Department of Health and Human Services, Administration on Children, Youth, and Families, 2006, http://www.acf.hhs.gov/programs/cb/pubs/cm04/cm04.pdf (accessed June 12, 2006)

Figure 2.1 shows that while rates of different types of abuse fluctuate somewhat from year to year, they remained fairly steady between 2000 and 2004. According to CPS statistics, in 2004, 2.1 out of every one thousand children were physically abused; 7.4 out of every one thousand children were neglected; 1.2 out of every one thousand children were sexually abused; 0.9 out of every one thousand children were emotionally abused; and 3.2 out of every one thousand children suffered from some other form of abuse.

NIS DATA. The NIS, while providing older data, gives a clearer picture of the incidence of child maltreatment because it collects data not just from child protective service agencies but also from other community professionals as well. In 1993, under the Harm Standard, nearly 1.6 million children were victims of maltreatment, a 66.9% increase from the Second National Incidence Study of Child Abuse and Neglect (1986; NIS-2) estimate (931,000 children) and a 148.5% increase from the First National Incidence Study of Child Abuse and Neglect (1980) estimate (625,100 children). Significant increases occurred for all types of abuse and neglect, as compared with the two earlier NIS surveys. The 1.6 million child victims of maltreatment in 1993 reflected a yearly incidence rate of 23.1 per one thousand children under age eighteen. (See Table 2.4.)

In 1993, under the Endangerment Standard, more than 2.8 million children experienced some type of maltreatment. This figure doubled the NIS-2 estimate of 1.4 million. As with the Harm Standard, marked increases occurred for all types of abuse and neglect. The incidence rate was 41.9 per one thousand children under age eighteen. (See Table 2.5.)

Gender of Victims

CPS DATA. In 2004 CPS agencies found a higher rate of child maltreatment among girls (12.6 cases per one thousand children) than among boys (11.2 cases per one thousand children). About 48.3% of maltreated children were boys and 51.7% were girls. (See Table 2.6.)

NIS DATA. NIS data allow comparisons of types of maltreatment suffered by boys and girls. Under both the Harm and Endangerment Standards of NIS-3, more females were subjected to maltreatment than males. Females were sexually abused about three times more often than males. Males, however, were more likely to experience physical and emotional neglect under the Endangerment Standard. Under both standards, males suffered more physical and emotional neglect, whereas females suffered more educational neglect. Males were at a somewhat greater risk of serious injury and death than females. (See Table 2.7 and Table 2.8.)

Age of Victims

CPS DATA. Younger children represented most of the maltreated victims among CPS agencies in 2004. Older children are less likely to be victimized than younger children. The victimization rate for infants and toddlers up through age three was 16.1 per one thousand children of the same age group, compared with 13.4 per one thousand for children ages four to seven. The rate of victimization for children ages eight to eleven was 10.9 per one thousand; for ages twelve to fifteen, 9.3 per one thousand; and for ages sixteen and seventeen, 6.1 per one thousand. (See Figure 2.2.)

Children of different ages suffered different types of maltreatment in 2004. Nearly three-quarters (72.9%) of the youngest children under age three suffered from neglect, whereas only a little more than half (52.4%) of those age sixteen and older did. By contrast, only 12.8% of the youngest group suffered physical abuse and only 2.2% of this group suffered sexual abuse. However, 24.9% of maltreated children age sixteen and older suffered physical abuse, and 16.3% of these children suffered sexual abuse. (See Table 2.9.)

NIS DATA. NIS-3 finds a low incidence of maltreatment in younger children, particularly among those ages zero to five. This may be because, before reaching school age, children are less observable to community professionals, especially educators—the group most likely to report suspected maltreatment. NIS-3 notes a disproportionate increase in the incidence of maltreatment among children as they reach ages six through fourteen. (See Figure 2.3 and Figure 2.4.) Sedlak and Broadhurst note the incidence of maltreatment among children older than age fourteen decreases.

TABLE 2.3

Types of maltreatment sustained by victims, by state, 2004

State	Victims	Physical abuse		Neglect		Medical neglect		Sexual abuse	
		Number	%	Number	%	Number	%	Number	%
Alabama	9,414	3,811	40.5	4,108	43.6			2,263	24.0
Alaska									
Arizona	7,344	1,502	20.5	5,628	76.6			426	5.8
Arkansas	7,276	1,340	18.4	4,132	56.8	223	3.1	2,021	27.8
California	98,201	13,693	13.9	66,580	67.8			7,932	8.1
Colorado	9,578	1,821	19.0	5,157	53.8	133	1.4	1,024	10.7
Connecticut	13,285	1,379	10.4	9,354	70.4	430	3.2	631	4.7
Delaware	1,581	415	26.2	465	29.4	51	3.2	208	13.2
District of Columbia	2,378	364	15.3	2,041	85.8			109	4.6
Florida	129,914	17,092	13.2	38,753	29.8	2,071	1.6	5,384	4.1
Georgia	52,851	5,701	10.8	36,461	69.0	2,591	4.9	2,447	4.6
Hawaii	3,629	400	11.0	547	15.1	56	1.5	196	5.4
Idaho	1,856	350	18.9	1,293	69.7	28	1.5	117	6.3
Illinois	29,150	8,238	28.3	18,496	63.5	912	3.1	5,912	20.3
Indiana	18,869	2,763	14.6	13,271	70.3	561	3.0	3,922	20.8
Iowa	13,804	1,963	14.2	10,404	75.4	188	1.4	849	6.2
Kansas	4,895	1,238	25.3	1,260	25.7	117	2.4	813	16.6
Kentucky	19,186	2,865	14.9	15,878	82.8			927	4.8
Louisiana	10,862	3,219	29.6	8,144	75.0			776	7.1
Maine	4,235	1,138	26.9	2,993	70.7			521	12.3
Maryland	15,180	4,617	30.4	8,981	59.2			1,885	12.4
Massachusetts	36,201	5,441	15.0	32,762	90.5			1,067	2.9
Michigan	28,035	5,487	19.6	20,170	71.9	617	2.2	1,451	5.2
Minnesota	8,183	1,465	17.9	6,171	75.4	101	1.2	847	10.4
Mississippi	5,674	1,282	22.6	2,980	52.5	190	3.3	905	15.9
Missouri	9,616	2,768	28.8	4,857	50.5	291	3.0	2,619	27.2
Montana	1,753	221	12.6	1,217	69.4	28	1.6	152	8.7
Nebraska	4,785	869	18.2	3,789	79.2	3	0.1	384	8.0
Nevada	4,377	787	18.0	3,600	82.2	83	1.9	169	3.9
New Hampshire	948	202	21.3	605	63.8	18	1.9	176	18.6
New Jersey	8,159	2,167	26.6	4,264	52.3	958	11.7	662	8.1
New Mexico	6,150	1,838	29.9	4,270	69.4	120	2.0	340	5.5
New York	74,483	9,031	12.1	67,619	90.8	2,925	3.9	2,867	3.8
North Carolina	29,085	1,157	4.0	25,606	88.0	758	2.6	1,178	4.1
North Dakota	1,668	293	17.6	1,464	87.8			156	9.4
Ohio	43,093	9,178	21.3	24,141	56.0	5	0.0	7,541	17.5
Oklahoma	12,483	2,372	19.0	10,990	88.0	353	2.8	867	6.9
Oregon	11,759	1,145	9.7	3,156	26.8	534	4.5	1,150	9.8
Pennsylvania	4,647	1,596	34.3	121	2.6	102	2.2	2,822	60.7
Rhode Island	3,068	594	19.4	2,302	77.0	56	1.8	163	5.3
South Carolina	9,950	3,216	32.3	6,715	67.5	366	3.7	849	8.5
South Dakota	1,917	279	14.6	1,514	79.0			76	4.0
Tennessee	14,840	4,696	31.6	7,698	51.9	327	2.2	3,579	24.1
Texas	50,891	13,308	26.2	33,757	66.3	2,319	4.6	6,822	13.4
Utah	13,559	1,708	12.6	2,842	21.0	57	0.4	2,552	18.8
Vermont	1,138	562	49.4	65	5.7	30	2.6	520	45.7
Virginia	6,959	1,709	24.6	4,299	61.8	170	2.4	1,100	15.8
Washington	6,730	1,275	18.9	5,393	80.1			464	6.9
West Virginia	8,446	2,335	27.6	4,622	54.7	127	1.5	451	5.3
Wisconsin	9,325	1,304	14.0	2,629	28.2	52	0.6	4,034	43.3
Wyoming	678	56	8.3	426	62.8	17	2.5	72	10.6
Total	**872,088**	**152,250**		**544,050**		**17,968**		**84,398**	
Percent			17.5		62.4		2.1		9.7
Number reporting	50	50	50	50	50	38	38	50	50

Note: Child maltreatment is defined by the U.S. Department of Health and Human Services as abuse or neglect of children.

SOURCE: "Table 3.5. Maltreatment Types of Victims, 2004," in *Child Maltreatment 2004*, U.S. Department of Health and Human Services, Administration on Children, Youth, and Families, 2006, http://www.acf.hhs.gov/programs/cb/pubs/cm04/cm04.pdf (accessed June 12, 2006)

Older children are more likely to escape if the abuse becomes more prevalent or severe. They are also more able to defend themselves and/or fight back.

Under the Harm Standard only ten per one thousand children in the zero-to-two age group experienced overall maltreatment. The numbers were significantly higher for children ages six to seventeen. Under the Endangerment Standard twenty-six per one thousand children ages zero to two were subjected to overall maltreatment. A slightly higher number of children (thirty-three per one thousand children) in the oldest age group (fifteen to seventeen years old) suffered maltreatment of some type. As with the Harm Standard, children between the ages of six and fourteen had a higher incidence of maltreatment.

FIGURE 2.1

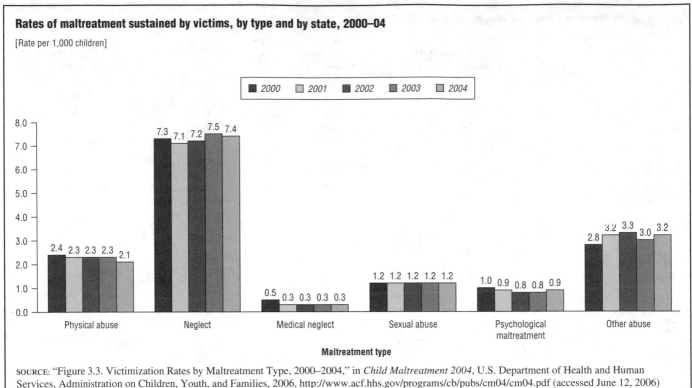

Rates of maltreatment sustained by victims, by type and by state, 2000–04

[Rate per 1,000 children]

Legend: 2000 | 2001 | 2002 | 2003 | 2004

Maltreatment type	2000	2001	2002	2003	2004
Physical abuse	2.4	2.3	2.3	2.3	2.1
Neglect	7.3	7.1	7.2	7.5	7.4
Medical neglect	0.5	0.3	0.3	0.3	0.3
Sexual abuse	1.2	1.2	1.2	1.2	1.2
Psychological maltreatment	1.0	0.9	0.8	0.8	0.9
Other abuse	2.8	3.2	3.3	3.0	3.2

SOURCE: "Figure 3.3. Victimization Rates by Maltreatment Type, 2000–2004," in *Child Maltreatment 2004*, U.S. Department of Health and Human Services, Administration on Children, Youth, and Families, 2006, http://www.acf.hhs.gov/programs/cb/pubs/cm04/cm04.pdf (accessed June 12, 2006)

TABLE 2.4

Comparison of actual maltreatment incidence rates to estimates of maltreatment incidence rates, by Harm Standard guidelines, selected years 1980–93

Harm Standard maltreatment category	NIS-3 estimates 1993		Comparisons with earlier studies			
			NIS-2: 1986		NIS-1: 1980	
	Total number of children	Rate per 1,000 children	Total number of children	Rate per 1,000 children	Total number of children	Rate per 1,000 children
All maltreatment	1,553,800	23.1	931,000	14.8	625,100	9.8
Abuse:						
All abuse	743,200	11.1	507,700	8.1	336,600	5.3
Physical abuse	381,700	5.7	269,700	4.3	199,100	3.1
Sexual abuse	217,700	3.2	119,200	1.9	42,900	0.7
Emotional abuse	204,500	3.0	155,200	2.5	132,700	2.1
Neglect:						
All neglect	879,000	13.1	474,800	7.5	315,400	4.9
Physical neglect	338,900	5.0	167,800	2.7	103,600	1.6
Emotional neglect	212,800	3.2	49,200	0.8	56,900	0.9
Educational neglect	397,300	5.9	284,800	4.5	174,000	2.7

Note: Estimated totals are rounded to the nearest 100.

SOURCE: Andrea J. Sedlak and Diane E. Broadhurst, "National Incidence of Maltreatment under the Harm Standard in the NIS-3 (1993) and Comparison with the NIS-2 (1986) and the NIS-1 (1980) Harm Standard Estimates," in *The Third National Incidence Study of Child Abuse and Neglect*, U.S. Department of Health and Human Services, National Center on Child Abuse and Neglect, 1996

Race and Ethnicity of Victims

CPS DATA. In 2004 rates of child maltreatment as recorded by CPS agencies were highest among African-American children (19.9 per one thousand children) and lowest among Asian-American children (2.9 per one thousand children). Pacific Islanders had a rate of 17.6 per one thousand children; Native American and Alaskan Native children had a rate of 15.5 per one thousand children; whites had a rate of 10.7 per one thousand children; and Hispanics had a rate of 10.4 per one thousand children. (See Figure 2.5.)

TABLE 2.5

Comparison of actual maltreatment incidence rates to estimates of maltreatment incidence rates, by Endangerment Standard guidelines, 1986 and 1993

Endangerment Standard maltreatment category	NIS-3 estimates 1993		Comparison with NIS-2 1986	
	Total no. of children	Rate per 1,000 children	Total no. of children	Rate per 1,000 children
All maltreatment	2,815,600	41.9	1,424,400	22.6
Abuse:				
All abuse	1,221,800	18.2	590,800	9.4
Physical abuse	614,100	9.1	311,500	4.9
Sexual abuse	300,200	4.5	133,600	2.1
Emotional abuse	532,200	7.9	188,100	3.0
Neglect:				
All neglect	1,961,300	29.2	917,200	14.6
Physical neglect	1,335,100	19.9	507,700	8.1
Emotional neglect	584,100	8.7	203,000	3.2
Educational neglect	397,300	5.9	284,800	4.5

Note: Estimated totals are rounded to the nearest 100.

SOURCE: Andrea J. Sedlak and Diane E. Broadhurst, "National Incidence of Maltreatment under the Endangerment Standard in the NIS–3 (1993) and Comparison with the NIS–2 (1986) Endangerment Standard Estimates," in *The Third National Incidence Study of Child Abuse and Neglect*, U.S. Department of Health and Human Services, National Center on Child Abuse and Neglect, 1996

WHY ARE MINORITY CHILDREN OVERREPRESENTED IN CPS DATA? In *Children of Color in the Child Welfare System: Perspectives from the Child Welfare Community* (2003, http://www.childwelfare.gov/pubs/otherpubs/children/index.cfm), Susan Chibnall et al. of the HHS's Children's Bureau explore the attitudes and perceptions of CPS personnel regarding the overrepresentation of minority children, particularly African-American children, in the child welfare system. According to Chibnall et al., while African-American children make up 15% of all children in the United States, they represent 25% of substantiated maltreatment victims. In addition, these children account for 45% of all children in foster care.

Chibnall et al. conducted the study in nine child welfare agencies across the country. They interviewed agency administrators, supervisors, and caseworkers. The child welfare personnel gave a variety of reasons minority children are overrepresented in the child welfare system, including:

- Poverty and poverty-related issues—Child welfare personnel thought that African-American families are more likely to be poorer than are other ethnic/racial groups. This makes them more vulnerable to social problems such as child maltreatment, domestic violence, and substance abuse. Moreover, these families typically live in areas lacking resources where they can go for assistance.

- Visibility—Poor families are more likely to use public services, such as public health care, making them more visible to mandated reporters when they are

TABLE 2.6

Sex of victims by state, 2004

State	Boys			
	Population	Number	Rate	Percent
Alabama	560,579	3,984	7.1	42.4
Alaska				
Arizona	791,665	3,632	4.6	49.6
Arkansas	346,241	3,138	9.1	43.1
California	4,914,300	46,986	9.6	47.9
Colorado	604,120	4,638	7.7	48.4
Connecticut	428,940	6,482	15.1	48.9
Delaware	99,224	748	7.5	47.3
District of Columbia	55,356	1,125	20.3	47.4
Florida	2,049,418	64,418	31.4	49.6
Georgia	1,192,387	26,164	21.9	49.5
Hawaii	153,362	1,760	11.5	48.7
Idaho	190,932	898	4.7	48.4
Illinois	1,655,171	14,094	8.5	48.8
Indiana	819,933	8,542	10.4	45.4
Iowa	348,882	6,795	19.5	49.2
Kansas	352,041	2,295	6.5	46.9
Kentucky	502,874	9,420	18.7	49.5
Louisiana	595,159	5,253	8.8	48.4
Maine	144,796	2,092	14.4	49.7
Maryland	712,620	7,234	10.2	48.0
Massachusetts	749,875	17,707	23.6	50.0
Michigan	1,298,124	13,689	10.5	48.8
Minnesota	636,209	3,932	6.2	48.1
Mississippi	382,712	2,591	6.8	45.7
Missouri	708,711	4,162	5.9	43.3
Montana	107,103	835	7.8	48.8
Nebraska	222,433	2,322	10.4	49.0
Nevada	309,918	2,187	7.1	50.1
New Hampshire	156,400	435	2.8	45.9
New Jersey	1,102,192	3,963	3.6	48.8
New Mexico	250,157	2,934	11.7	48.5
New York	2,338,744	36,800	15.7	49.7
North Carolina	1,082,630	14,421	13.3	49.6
North Dakota	71,470	803	11.2	48.3
Ohio	1,420,015	20,347	14.3	47.3
Oklahoma	440,952	6,133	13.9	49.1
Oregon	436,545	5,617	12.9	47.8
Pennsylvania	1,452,429	1,616	1.1	34.8
Rhode Island	124,670	1,524	12.2	49.8
South Carolina	524,065	4,794	9.1	48.7
South Dakota	97,817	918	9.4	48.4
Tennessee	713,724	6,674	9.4	45.0
Texas	3,202,108	24,249	7.6	47.8
Utah	380,741	6,198	16.3	45.9
Vermont	69,463	456	6.6	40.1
Virginia	921,865	3,259	3.5	46.8
Washington	761,970	3,367	4.4	50.0
West Virginia	196,733	4,132	21.0	49.1
Wisconsin	670,296	3,647	5.4	39.3
Wyoming	60,292	333	5.5	49.1
Total	37,408,363	419,743		
Weighted rate			11.2	
Weighted percent				48.3
Number reporting	50	50	50	50

experiencing problems, including child abuse and neglect.

- Overreporting—Many study participants proposed that, because poor families are more visible to mandated reporters such as doctors and nurses, they are more likely to be reported to CPS.

- Worker bias—When investigating particular families, some caseworkers may not understand the cultural norms and practices of minorities; this may influence

TABLE 2.6

Sex of victims by state, 2004 [CONTINUED]

State	Population	Number	Rate	Percent
		Girls		
Alabama	533,954	5,402	10.1	57.6
Alaska				
Arizona	755,595	3,694	4.9	50.4
Arkansas	330,309	4,136	12.5	56.9
California	4,682,163	51,143	10.9	52.1
Colorado	574,769	4,940	8.6	51.6
Connecticut	409,848	6,763	16.5	51.1
Delaware	94,282	832	8.8	52.7
District of Columbia	54,191	1,250	23.1	52.6
Florida	1,953,872	65,363	33.5	50.4
Georgia	1,140,180	26,687	23.4	50.5
Hawaii	145,331	1,854	12.8	51.3
Idaho	181,479	958	5.3	51.6
Illinois	1,582,979	14,796	9.3	51.2
Indiana	780,362	10,260	13.1	54.6
Iowa	331,555	7,009	21.1	50.8
Kansas	331,450	2,600	7.8	53.1
Kentucky	477,313	9,604	20.1	50.5
Louisiana	569,802	5,609	9.8	51.6
Maine	137,333	2,121	15.4	50.3
Maryland	682,188	7,824	11.5	52.0
Massachusetts	714,314	17,697	24.8	50.0
Michigan	1,235,315	14,345	11.6	51.2
Minnesota	604,071	4,251	7.0	51.9
Mississippi	366,857	3,081	8.4	54.3
Missouri	675,831	5,447	8.1	56.7
Montana	100,990	877	8.7	51.2
Nebraska	212,133	2,418	11.4	51.0
Nevada	293,678	2,179	7.4	49.9
New Hampshire	148,594	513	3.5	54.1
New Jersey	1,053,867	4,157	3.9	51.2
New Mexico	242,130	3,121	12.9	51.5
New York	2,233,619	37,239	16.7	50.3
North Carolina	1,035,862	14,664	14.2	50.4
North Dakota	67,485	861	12.8	51.7
Ohio	1,359,197	22,626	16.6	52.7
Oklahoma	418,918	6,349	15.2	50.9
Oregon	415,812	6,142	14.8	52.2
Pennsylvania	1,384,580	3,031	2.2	65.2
Rhode Island	119,143	1,538	12.9	50.2
South Carolina	500,635	5,045	10.1	51.3
South Dakota	93,057	980	10.5	51.6
Tennessee	677,565	8,158	12.0	55.0
Texas	3,064,671	26,518	8.7	52.2
Utah	359,373	7,317	20.4	54.1
Vermont	65,431	682	10.4	59.9
Virginia	883,035	3,700	4.2	53.2
Washington	724,050	3,362	4.6	50.0
West Virginia	187,908	4,290	22.8	50.9
Wisconsin	637,690	5,638	8.8	60.7
Wyoming	56,640	345	6.1	50.9
Total	**35,681,406**	**449,416**		
Weighted rate			**12.6**	
Weighted percent				**51.7**
Number reporting	**50**	**50**	**50**	**50**

SOURCE: "Table 3.8. Sex of Victims, 2004," *Child Maltreatment 2004*, U.S. Department of Health and Human Services, Administration on Children, Youth, and Families, 2006, http://www.acf.hhs.gov/programs/cb/pubs/cm04/cm04.pdf (accessed June 12, 2006)

their decisions at different stages of child welfare services, including child maltreatment reporting, investigation, substantiation, and the child's removal from home and placement in foster care. A caseworker's bias may also make it more likely, for example, that he or she would remove an African-American child than a white child from comparable home environments.

TABLE 2.7

Maltreatment rates under the Harm Standard by gender, 1993

[Per 1,000 children]

Harm Standard maltreatment category	Males	Females
All maltreatment	21.7	24.5
Abuse:		
All abuse	9.5	12.6
Physical abuse	5.8	5.6
Sexual abuse	1.6	4.9
Emotional abuse	2.9	3.1
Neglect:		
All neglect	13.3	12.9
Physical neglect	5.5	4.5
Emotional neglect	3.5	2.8
Educational neglect	5.5	6.4
Severity of injury:		
Fatal	0.04	0.01
Serious	9.3	7.5
Moderate	11.3	13.3
Inferred	1.1	3.8

SOURCE: Adapted from Andrea J. Sedlak and Diane D. Broadhurst, "Sex Differences in Incidence Rates per 1,000 Children for Maltreatment under the Harm Standard in the NIS-3 (1993)," in *The Third National Incidence Study of Child Abuse and Neglect*, U.S. Department of Health and Human Services, National Center on Child Abuse and Neglect, 1996

Some child welfare personnel who were interviewed for the study believed that the Multi-ethnic Placement Act of 1994, which allows the placement of African-American children in nonminority homes, does not serve children's best interests. They were concerned that transracial placements might be harmful to minority children's self-esteem and ethnic/racial identity.

NIS DATA. NIS-3 finds no significant differences in race in the incidence of maltreatment. Sedlak and Broadhurst note that this finding may be somewhat surprising, considering the overrepresentation of African-American children in the child welfare population and in those served by public agencies. They attribute this lack of race-related difference in maltreatment incidence to the broader range of children identified by NIS-3, compared with the smaller number investigated by public agencies and the even smaller number receiving child protective and other welfare services. NIS-2 also had not found any disproportionate differences in race in relation to maltreatment incidence.

Children with Disabilities Particularly at Risk

Children with disabilities are potentially at risk for maltreatment because society generally treats them as different and less valuable, thus possibly tolerating violence against them. Some parents may feel disappointment at not having a "normal" child. Others may expect too much and feel frustrated if the child does not live up to their expectations. These children require special care and attention, and parents may not have the social

TABLE 2.8

Maltreatment rates under the Endangerment Standard by gender, 1993

Endangerment Standard maltreatment category	Males	Females
All maltreatment	40.0	42.3
Abuse:		
All abuse	16.1	20.2
Physical abuse	9.3	9.0
Sexual abuse	2.3	6.8
Emotional abuse	8.0	7.7
Neglect:		
All neglect	29.2	27.6
Physical neglect	19.7	18.6
Emotional neglect	9.2	7.8
Educational neglect	5.5	6.4
Severity of injury:		
Fatal	0.04	0.01
Serious	9.4	7.6
Moderate	14.1	15.3
Inferred	2.1	4.6
Endangered	14.5	14.8

SOURCE: Adapted from Andrea J. Sedlak and Diane D. Broadhurst, "Sex Differences in Incidence Rates per 1,000 Children for Maltreatment under the Endangerment Standard in the NIS-3 (1993)," in *The Third National Incidence Study of Child Abuse and Neglect*, U.S. Department of Health and Human Services, National Center on Child Abuse and Neglect, 1996

FIGURE 2.2

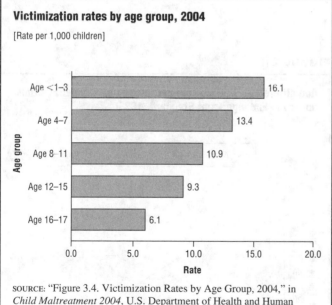

Victimization rates by age group, 2004

[Rate per 1,000 children]

SOURCE: "Figure 3.4. Victimization Rates by Age Group, 2004," in *Child Maltreatment 2004*, U.S. Department of Health and Human Services, Administration on Children, Youth, and Families, 2006, http://www.acf.hhs.gov/programs/cb/pubs/cm04/cm04.pdf (accessed June 12, 2006)

support to help ease stressful situations. Caring for children with disabilities can also be expensive, creating even more stress and with it risk of maltreatment.

In "Assessment of Maltreatment of Children with Disabilities" (*Pediatrics*, August 2001), the Committee on Child Abuse and Neglect and the Committee on Children with Disabilities—two committees of the American Academy of Pediatrics—note that children with disabilities may also be vulnerable to sexual abuse. Dependent on caregivers for their physical needs, these children may not be able to distinguish between appropriate and inappropriate touching of their bodies. The opportunities for sexual abuse may also be increased if the child depends on several caregivers for his or her needs.

Patricia M. Sullivan, in "Violence against Children with Disabilities: Prevention, Public Policy, and Research Implications" (Dorothy K. Marge, ed., *A Call to Action: Ending Crimes of Violence against Children and Adults with Disabilities—A Report to the Nation*, 2003), calls attention to the fact that the federal government does not collect specific data on children with disabilities in its crime statistics systems nor in national incidence studies mandated by law. Although CAPTA required that national incidence studies of child maltreatment include data on children with disabilities, the latest survey, the NIS-3, does not satisfy this mandate. Moreover, NCANDS, which releases annual state data on maltreated children, does not gather information relating to children's disability status.

Sullivan undertook two epidemiological studies on maltreated children with disabilities. (Epidemiological studies consider individuals' sex, age, race, social class, and other demographics.) The incidence of maltreatment (the number of new cases during a given period, such as per week, per month, or per year) and its prevalence (the total number of maltreated children with disabilities at a given time) were measured. The hospital-based study of six thousand children found a 64% prevalence rate of maltreatment among disabled children, twice the prevalence rate (32%) among nondisabled children. The school-based study included 4,954 children; 31% of disabled children had been maltreated, 3.4 times that of the nondisabled comparison group.

Family Characteristics of Victims

The only reliable information on family characteristics of victims come from NIS data, as the living arrangements data on children reported to CPS were incomplete. For example, in 2004 nearly half (44.2%) had living arrangement data that were missing or incomplete. The following discussion comes from NIS-3.

FAMILY STRUCTURE. According to NIS-3, under the Harm Standard, among children living with single parents, an estimated 27.3 per one thousand under age eighteen suffered some type of maltreatment—almost twice the incidence rate for children living with both parents (15.5 per one thousand). The same rate held true for all types of abuse and neglect. Children living with single parents also had a greater risk of suffering serious

TABLE 2.9

Victims by age group and by type of maltreatment, 2004

[Based on data from 45 states]

Age group	Total victims	Physical abuse		Neglect		Medical neglect		Sexual abuse	
		Number	%	Number	%	Number	%	Number	%
Age <1–3	232,409	29,733	12.8	169,311	72.9	5,981	2.6	5,145	2.2
Age 4–7	187,275	31,389	16.8	119,794	64.0	2,870	1.5	17,018	9.1
Age 8–11	160,940	30,793	19.1	96,205	59.8	2,584	1.6	18,294	11.4
Age 12–15	158,104	36,089	22.8	85,362	54.0	2,617	1.7	26,133	16.5
Age 16 and older	45,946	11,460	24.9	24,098	52.4	713	1.6	7,480	16.3
Unknown or missing	2,397	532	22.2	1,462	61.0	26	1.1	278	11.6
Total	**787,071**	**139,996**		**496,232**		**14,791**		**74,348**	
Percent			17.8		63.0		1.9		9.4

Age group	Psychological abuse		Other abuse		Unknown		Total	
	Number	%	Number	%	Number	%	Number	%
Age <1–3	11,067	4.8	37,673	16.2	653	0.3	259,563	111.8
Age 4–7	11,954	6.4	27,377	14.6	497	0.3	210,899	112.7
Age 8–11	11,881	7.4	23,617	14.7	365	0.2	183,739	114.2
Age 12–15	10,716	6.8	22,222	14.1	424	0.3	183,563	116.2
Age 16 and older	2,871	6.2	6,689	14.6	136	0.3	53,447	116.3
Unknown or missing	207	8.6	76	3.2	5	0.2	2,586	107.9
Total	**48,696**		**117,654**		**2,080**		**893,797**	
Percent		6.2		14.9		0.3		113.5

SOURCE: "Table 3.11. Victims by Age Group and Maltreatment Type, 2004," in *Child Maltreatment 2004*, U.S. Department of Health and Human Services, Administration on Children, Youth, and Families, 2006, http://www.acf.hhs.gov/programs/cb/pubs/cm04/cm04.pdf (accessed June 12, 2006)

FIGURE 2.3

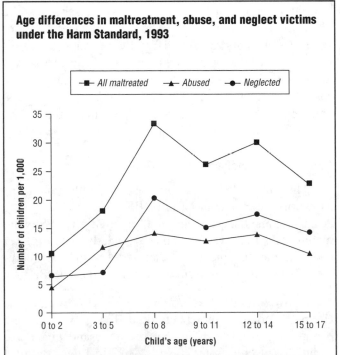

Age differences in maltreatment, abuse, and neglect victims under the Harm Standard, 1993

SOURCE: Andrea J. Sedlak and Diane D. Broadhurst, "Age Difference in All Maltreatment, Abuse, and Neglect under the Harm Standard," in *The Third National Incidence Study of Child Abuse and Neglect*, U.S. Department of Health and Human Services, National Center on Child Abuse and Neglect, 1996

FIGURE 2.4

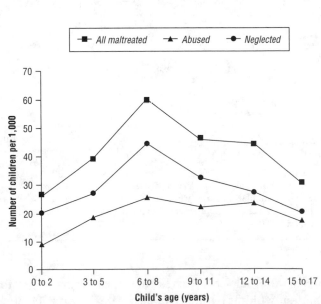

Age differences in maltreatment, abuse, and neglect victims under the Endangerment Standard, 1993

SOURCE: Andrea J. Sedlak and Diane D. Broadhurst, "Age Difference in All Maltreatment, Abuse, and Neglect under the Endangerment Standard," in *The Third National Incidence Study of Child Abuse and Neglect*, U.S. Department of Health and Human Services, National Center on Child Abuse and Neglect, 1996

24   Detecting, Measuring, and Preventing Child Abuse   Child Abuse and Domestic Violence

FIGURE 2.5

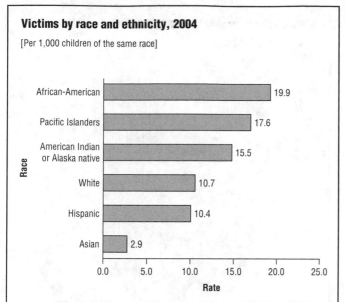

Victims by race and ethnicity, 2004

[Per 1,000 children of the same race]

Race	Rate
African-American	19.9
Pacific Islanders	17.6
American Indian or Alaska native	15.5
White	10.7
Hispanic	10.4
Asian	2.9

SOURCE: "Figure 3.5. Race and Ethnicity of Victims, 2004," in *Child Maltreatment 2004*, U.S. Department of Health and Human Services, Administration on Children, Youth, and Families, 2006, http://www.acf.hhs.gov/programs/cb/pubs/cm04/cm04.pdf (accessed June 12, 2006)

TABLE 2.10

Maltreatment incidence rates under the Harm Standard by family structure, 1993

[Per 1,000 children]

Harm Standard maltreatment category	Both parents	Single parent — Either mother or father	Mother only	Father only	Neither parent
All maltreatment:	15.5	27.3	26.1	36.6	22.9
Abuse:					
All abuse	8.4	11.4	10.5	17.7	13.7
Physical abuse	3.9	6.9	6.4	10.5	7.0
Sexual abuse	2.6	2.5	2.5	2.6	6.3
Emotional abuse	2.6	2.5	2.1	5.7	5.4
Neglect:					
All neglect	7.9	17.3	16.7	21.9	10.3
Physical neglect	3.1	5.8	5.9	4.7	4.3
Emotional neglect	2.3	4.0	3.4	8.8	3.1
Educational neglect	3.0	9.6	9.5	10.8	3.1
Severity of injury:					
Fatal	0.019	0.015	0.017	0.005	0.016
Serious	5.8	10.5	10.0	14.0	8.0
Moderate	8.1	15.4	14.7	20.5	10.1
Inferred	1.6	1.4	1.3	2.1	4.8

SOURCE: Adapted from Andrea J. Sedlak and Diane D. Broadhurst, "Incidence Rates per 1,000 children for Maltreatment under the Harm Standard in the NIS-3 (1993) for Different Family Structures," in *The Third National Incidence Study of Child Abuse and Neglect*, U.S. Department of Health and Human Services, National Center on Child Abuse and Neglect, 1996

injury (10.5 per one thousand) than did those living with both parents (5.8 per one thousand). (See Table 2.10.)

Under the Endangerment Standard an estimated 52 per one thousand children living with single parents

TABLE 2.11

Maltreatment incidence rates under the Endangerment Standard by family structure, 1993

[Per 1,000 children]

Endangerment Standard maltreatment category	Both parents	Single parent — Either mother or father	Mother only	Father only	Neither parent
All maltreatment	26.9	52.0	50.1	65.6	39.3
Abuse:					
All abuse	13.5	19.6	18.1	31.0	17.3
Physical abuse	6.5	10.6	9.8	16.5	9.2
Sexual abuse	3.2	4.2	4.3	3.1	6.6
Emotional abuse	6.2	8.6	7.7	14.6	7.1
Neglect:					
All neglect	17.6	38.9	37.6	47.9	24.1
Physical neglect	10.8	28.6	27.5	36.4	17.1
Emotional neglect	6.4	10.5	9.7	16.2	8.3
Educational neglect	3.0	9.6	9.5	10.8	3.1
Severity of injury:					
Fatal	0.020	0.015	0.017	0.005	0.016
Serious	5.9	10.5	10.0	14.0	8.0
Moderate	9.6	18.5	17.7	24.8	11.5
Inferred	2.1	2.5	2.0	6.0	4.7
Endangered	9.3	20.5	20.4	20.7	15.1

SOURCE: Adapted from Andrea J. Sedlak and Diane D. Broadhurst, "Incidence Rates per 1,000 children for Maltreatment under the Endangerment Standard in the NIS-3 (1993) for Different Family Structures," in *The Third National Incidence Study of Child Abuse and Neglect*, U.S. Department of Health and Human Services, National Center on Child Abuse and Neglect, 1996

suffered some type of maltreatment, compared with 26.9 per one thousand living with both parents. Children in single-parent households were abused at a 45% higher rate than those in two-parent households (19.6 versus 13.5 per one thousand) and suffered more than twice as much neglect (38.9 versus 17.6 per one thousand). Children living with single parents (10.5 per one thousand) were also more likely to suffer serious injuries than those living with both parents (5.9 per one thousand). (See Table 2.11.)

FAMILY INCOME. Family income was significantly related to the incidence rates of child maltreatment. Under the Harm Standard children in families with annual incomes less than $15,000 had the highest rate of maltreatment (47 per one thousand). The figure is almost twice as high (95.9 per one thousand) using the Endangerment Standard. Children in families earning less than $15,000 annually also sustained more serious injuries than did children living in families earning more than that amount. (See Table 2.12 and Table 2.13.)

PERPETRATORS OF CHILD MALTREATMENT
CPS Data

The law considers perpetrators of child abuse to be those people who abuse or neglect children under their care. They may be parents, foster parents, other relatives,

TABLE 2.12

Maltreatment incidence rates under the Harm Standard by family income, 1993

[Per 1,000 children]

Harm Standard maltreatment category	<$I5K/year	$15–29K/year	$30K+/year
All maltreatment	47.0	20.0	2.1
Abuse:			
All abuse	22.2	9.7	1.6
Physical abuse	11.0	5.0	0.7
Sexual abuse	7.0	2.8	0.4
Emotional abuse	6.5	2.5	0.5
Neglect:			
All neglect	27.2	11.3	0.6
Physical neglect	12.0	2.9	0.3
Emotional neglect	5.9	4.3	0.2
Educational neglect	11.1	4.8	0.2
Severity of injury:			
Fatal	0.060	0.002	0.001
Serious	17.9	7.8	0.8
Moderate	23.3	10.5	1.3
Inferred	5.7	1.6	0.1

SOURCE: Adapted from Andrea J. Sedlak and Diane D. Broadhurst, "Incidence Rates per 1,000 children for Maltreatment under the Harm Standard in the NIS-3 (1993) for Different Levels of Family Income," in *The Third National Incidence Study of Child Abuse and Neglect*, U.S. Department of Health and Human Services, National Center on Child Abuse and Neglect, 1996

TABLE 2.13

Maltreatment incidence rates under the Endangerment Standard by family income, 1993

[Per 1,000 children]

Endangerment Standard maltreatment category	<$15K/year	$15–29K/year	$30K=/year
All maltreatment	95.9	33.1	3.8
Abuse:			
All abuse	37.4	17.5	2.5
Physical abuse	17.6	8.5	1.5
Sexual abuse	9.2	4.2	0.5
Emotional abuse	18.3	8.1	1.0
Neglect:			
All neglect	72.3	21.6	1.6
Physical neglect	54.3	12.5	1.1
Emotional neglect	19.0	8.2	0.7
Educational neglect	11.1	4.8	0.2
Severity of injury:			
Fatal	0.060	0.002	0.003
Serious	17.9	7.9	0.8
Moderate	29.6	12.1	1.5
Inferred	7.8	2.7	0.2
Endangered	40.5	10.3	1.3

SOURCE: Adapted from Andrea J. Sedlak and Diane D. Broadhurst, "Incidence Rates per 1,000 Children for Maltreatment under the Endangerment Standard in the NIS-3 (1993) for Different Levels of Family Income," in *The Third National Incidence Study of Child Abuse and Neglect*, U.S. Department of Health and Human Services, National Center on Child Abuse and Neglect, 1996

or other caretakers. People who victimize children that are not under their care are not considered to have committed child abuse, but rather assault, battery, rape, or other crimes. According to CPS data, perpetrators are

FIGURE 2.6

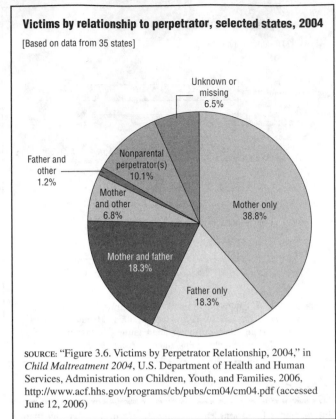

Victims by relationship to perpetrator, selected states, 2004

[Based on data from 35 states]

SOURCE: "Figure 3.6. Victims by Perpetrator Relationship, 2004," in *Child Maltreatment 2004*, U.S. Department of Health and Human Services, Administration on Children, Youth, and Families, 2006, http://www.acf.hhs.gov/programs/cb/pubs/cm04/cm04.pdf (accessed June 12, 2006)

more likely to be women (57.8%) than men (42.2%). In 2004, 38.8% of victims were maltreated by their mothers acting alone; 18.3% experienced maltreatment from their fathers acting alone. Another 18.3% were maltreated by both parents. About 6.8% of the victims were maltreated by their mothers and another person whose relationship with the mother was not known, and 1.2% were maltreated by their fathers and another person. One in ten victims (10.1%) were maltreated by nonparental perpetrators, and another 6.5% were maltreated by unknown individuals. (See Figure 2.6.)

CPS data indicate that most perpetrators of child maltreatment are in their twenties and thirties. In 2004 the median age of female perpetrators was thirty-one years; the median age of male perpetrators was thirty-four years. Almost half (44.4%) of the female perpetrators were younger than thirty, whereas only about one-third (34.1%) of male perpetrators were. (See Figure 2.7.)

CPS data show that overall, more than half of perpetrators of maltreatment (57.9%) neglected one or more children, 10.3% physically abused children, and 6.9% sexually abused children. Variations existed in this pattern, however, depending on the perpetrator's relationship to the child or children. Parents who maltreated their children were most likely to neglect them (62.9%). Ten percent of parental perpetrators physically abused their children, and 2.6% sexually abused their children.

FIGURE 2.7

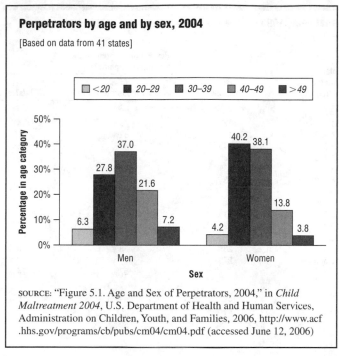

Perpetrators by age and by sex, 2004

[Based on data from 41 states]

Legend: ☐ <20 ■ 20–29 ■ 30–39 ■ 40–49 ■ >49

Men:
- <20: 6.3
- 20–29: 27.8
- 30–39: 37.0
- 40–49: 21.6
- >49: 7.2

Women:
- <20: 4.2
- 20–29: 40.2
- 30–39: 38.1
- 40–49: 13.8
- >49: 3.8

Y-axis: Percentage in age category (0%–50%)
X-axis: Sex

SOURCE: "Figure 5.1. Age and Sex of Perpetrators, 2004," in *Child Maltreatment 2004*, U.S. Department of Health and Human Services, Administration on Children, Youth, and Families, 2006, http://www.acf.hhs.gov/programs/cb/pubs/cm04/cm04.pdf (accessed June 12, 2006)

Among friends and neighbors who maltreated children, 73.8% sexually abused them, 9.9% neglected them, and 4.1% physically abused them. Residential facility staff members (as well as other professionals) were relatively more likely to physically abuse children; 19.8% of residential facility perpetrators physically abused children, 46.7% neglected children, and 12.1% sexually abused children. (See Figure 2.8.)

NIS Data

Like CPS data, NIS-3 finds that most child victims (78%) were maltreated by their birth parents. Parents accounted for 72% of physical abuse and 81% of emotional abuse. Almost half (46%) of sexually abused children, however, were violated by someone other than a parent or parent substitute. More than a quarter (29%) were sexually abused by a birth parent, and 25% were sexually abused by a parent substitute, such as a stepparent or a mother's boyfriend. In addition, sexually abused children were more likely to sustain fatal or serious injuries or impairments when birth parents were the perpetrators. (See Table 2.14.)

Overall, children were somewhat more likely to be maltreated by female perpetrators (65%) than by males (54%). Among children maltreated by their natural parents, most (75%) were maltreated by their mothers, and almost half (46%) were maltreated by their fathers. (Children who were maltreated by both parents were included in both "male" and "female" perpetrator counts.) Children who were maltreated by someone other than parents and parent substitutes were more likely to have been maltreated by a

FIGURE 2.8

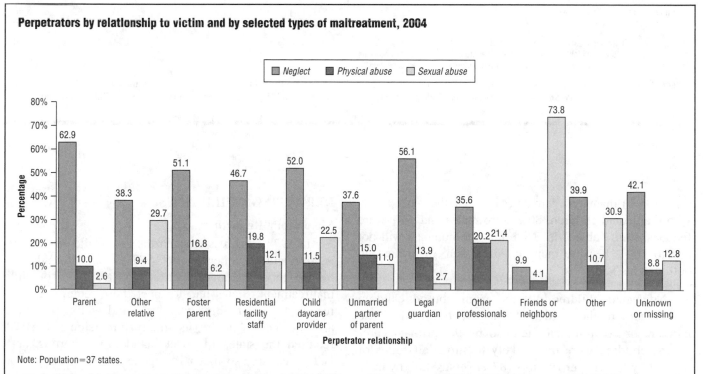

Perpetrators by relationship to victim and by selected types of maltreatment, 2004

Legend: ☐ Neglect ■ Physical abuse ☐ Sexual abuse

- Parent: Neglect 62.9, Physical abuse 10.0, Sexual abuse 2.6
- Other relative: Neglect 38.3, Physical abuse 9.4, Sexual abuse 29.7
- Foster parent: Neglect 51.1, Physical abuse 16.8, Sexual abuse 6.2
- Residential facility staff: Neglect 46.7, Physical abuse 19.8, Sexual abuse 12.1
- Child daycare provider: Neglect 52.0, Physical abuse 11.5, Sexual abuse 22.5
- Unmarried partner of parent: Neglect 37.6, Physical abuse 15.0, Sexual abuse 11.0
- Legal guardian: Neglect 56.1, Physical abuse 13.9, Sexual abuse 2.7
- Other professionals: Neglect 35.6, Physical abuse 20.2, Sexual abuse 21.4
- Friends or neighbors: Neglect 9.9, Physical abuse 4.1, Sexual abuse 73.8
- Other: Neglect 39.9, Physical abuse 10.7, Sexual abuse 30.9
- Unknown or missing: Neglect 42.1, Physical abuse 8.8, Sexual abuse 12.8

Y-axis: Percentage (0%–80%)
X-axis: Perpetrator relationship

Note: Population=37 states.

SOURCE: "Figure 5.3. Perpetrators by Relationship to Victims and Selected Types of Maltreatment, 2004," in *Child Maltreatment 2004*, U.S. Department of Health and Human Services, Administration on Children, Youth, and Families, 2006, http://www.acf.hhs.gov/programs/cb/pubs/cm04/cm04.pdf (accessed June 12, 2006)

TABLE 2.14

Perpetrator's relationship to child and severity of harm, by type of maltreatment, 1993

Category	Percent children in maltreatment category	Total maltreated children	Percent of children in row with injury/impairment . . .		
			Fatal or serious	Moderate	Inferred
Abuse:	100%	743,200	21%	63%	16%
Natural parents	62%	461,800	22%	73%	4%
Other parents and parent/substitutes	19%	144,900	12%	62%	27%
Others	18%	136,600	24%	30%	46%
Physical abuse	100%	381,700	13%	87%	a
Natural parents	72%	273,200	13%	87%	a
Other parents and parent/substitutes	21%	78,700	13%	87%	a
Others	8%	29,700	b	82%	a
Sexual abuse	100%	217,700	34%	12%	53%
Natural parents	29%	63,300	61%	10%	28%
Other parents and parent/substitutes	25%	53,800	19%	18%	63%
Others	40%	100,500	26%	11%	63%
Emotional abuse	100%	204,500	26%	68%	6%
Natural parents	81%	166,500	27%	70%	2%
Other parents and parent/substitutes	13%	27,400	b	57%	24%
Others	5%	10,600	b	b	b
Neglect:	100%	879,000	50%	44%	6%
Natural parents	91%	800,600	51%	43%	6%
Other parents and parent/substitutes	9%	78,400	35%	59%	b
Others	c	c	c	c	c
Physical neglect	100%	338,900	64%	15%	21%
Natural parents	95%	320,400	64%	16%	20%
Other parents and parent/substitutes	5%	18,400	b	b	b
Others	c	c	c	c	c
Emotional neglect	100%	212,800	97%	3%	a
Natural parents	91%	194,600	99%	b	a
Other parents and parent/substitutes	9%	b	b	b	a
Others	c	c	c	c	a
Educational neglect	100%	397,300	7%	93%	a
Natural parents	89%	354,300	8%	92%	a
Other parents and parent/substitutes	11%	43,000	b	99%	a
Others	c	c	c	c	a
All maltreatment	100%	1,553,800	36%	53%	11%
Natural parents	78%	1,208,100	41%	54%	5%
Other parents and parent/substitutes	14%	211,200	20%	61%	19%
Others	9%	134,500	24%	30%	46%

aThis severity level not applicable for this form of maltreatment.
bFewer than 20 cases with which to calculate estimate; estimate too unreliable to be given.
cThese perpetrators were not allowed by countability requirements for cases of neglect.

SOURCE: Andrea J. Sedlak and Diane D. Broadhurst, "Distribution of Perpetrator's Relationship to Child and Severity of Harm by the Type of Maltreatment," in *The Third National Incidence Study of Child Abuse and Neglect*, U.S. Department of Health and Human Services, National Center on Child Abuse and Neglect, 1996

male (85%) than by a female (41%). Of the other adults who maltreated children, 80% were males and 14% were females. (See Table 2.15. Note that the numbers will not add to 100% because many children were maltreated by both parents.)

Neglected children differed from abused children with regard to the gender of the perpetrators. Because mothers or other females tend to be the primary caretakers, children were more likely to suffer all forms of neglect by female perpetrators (87%, versus 43% by male perpetrators). In contrast, children were more often abused by males (67%) than by females (40%). (See Table 2.15.)

REPORTING CHILD ABUSE

Mandatory Reporting

In 1974 Congress enacted the first Child Abuse Prevention and Treatment Act (CAPTA) that set guidelines for the reporting, investigation, and treatment of child maltreatment. States had to meet these requirements to receive federal funding to assist child victims of abuse and neglect. Among its many provisions, CAPTA required the states to enact mandatory reporting laws and procedures so that CPS agencies could take action to protect children from further abuse.

The earliest mandatory reporting laws were directed at medical professionals, particularly physicians, who

TABLE 2.15

Perpetrator's gender, by type of maltreatment and by relationship to child, 1993

Category	Percent children in maltreatment category	Total maltreated children	Percent of children in row with perpetrator whose gender was . . .		
			Male	Female	Unknown
Abuse:	100%	743,200	67%	40%	a
Natural parents	62%	461,800	56%	55%	a
Other parents and parent/substitutes	19%	144,900	90%	15%	a
Others	18%	136,600	80%	14%	a
Physical abuse	100%	381,700	58%	50%	a
Natural parents	72%	273,200	48%	60%	a
Other parents and parent/substitutes	21%	78,700	90%	19%	a
Others	8%	29,700	57%	39%	a
Sexual abuse	100%	217,700	89%	12%	a
Natural parents	29%	63,300	87%	28%	a
Other parents and parent/substitutes	25%	53,800	97%	a	a
Others	46%	100,500	86%	8%	a
Emotional abuse	100%	204,500	63%	50%	a
Natural parents	81%	166,500	60%	55%	a
Other parents and parent/substitutes	13%	27,400	74%	a	a
Others	5%	10,600	a	a	a
All neglect:	100%	879,000	43%	87%	a
Natural parents	91%	800,600	40%	87%	a
Other parents and parent/substitutes	9%	78,400	76%	88%	a
Others	b	b	b	b	b
Physical neglect	100%	338,900	35%	93%	a
Natural parents	95%	320,400	34%	93%	a
Other parents and parent/substitutes	5%	18,400	a	90%	a
Others	b	b	b	b	b
Emotional neglect	100%	212,800	47%	77%	a
Natural parents	91%	194,600	44%	78%	a
Other parents and parent/substitutes	9%	18,200	a	a	a
Others	b	b	b	b	b
Educational neglect	100%	397,300	47%	88%	a
Natural parents	89%	354,300	43%	86%	a
Other parents and parent/substitutes	11%	43,000	82%	100%	a
Others	b	b	b	b	b
All maltreatment	100%	1,553,800	54%	65%	1%
Natural parents	78%	1,208,100	46%	75%	a
Other parents and parent/substitutes	14%	211,200	85%	41%	a
Others	9%	134,500	80%	14%	7%

[a]Fewer than 20 cases with which to calculate, estimate too unreliable to be given.
[b]These perpetrators were not allowed by countability requirements for cases of neglect.

SOURCE: Andrea J. Sedlak and Diane D. Broadhurst, "Distribution of Perpetrator's Gender by Type of Maltreatment and Perpetrator's Relationship to Child," in *The Third National Incidence Study of Child Abuse and Neglect*, U.S. Department of Health and Human Services, National Center on Child Abuse and Neglect, 1996

were considered the most likely to see abused children. As of 2006 each state designated mandatory reporters, including health care workers, mental health professionals, social workers, school personnel, child care providers, and law enforcement officers. Any individual, however, whether or not he or she was a mandatory reporter, could report incidents of abuse or neglect.

Some states also require maltreatment reporting from other individuals, such as firefighters, Christian Science practitioners, battered women's counselors, animal control officers, veterinarians, commercial/private film or photograph processors, and even lawyers. As of June 2003, nineteen states and Puerto Rico required all citizens to report suspected child maltreatment. (See Table 2.16.)

Some state statutes include provisions pertaining to the right of confidentiality of communications between professionals and their clients. In "Clergy as Mandatory Reporters of Child Abuse and Neglect" (March 2005, http://childwelfare.gov/systemwide/laws_policies/statutes/clergymandated.cfm), the Child Welfare Information Gateway reports that as of March 2005 clergy were mandated reporters in twenty-five states. In eighteen other states any person who suspected child abuse or neglect was required to report—including clergy. In twenty-one states, "pastoral communications" between clergy and penitent (a person repenting sin) were privileged (pastoral communications are confessions or conversations in which the member of the clergy is acting in the capacity of spiritual adviser), but in two states that privilege was denied in cases of child abuse and neglect. Few states recognized the physician-patient and mental health professional-client privileges as exempt from mandatory reporting laws. Ohio and Wyoming recognized

TABLE 2.16

Mandatory reporting of child abuse and neglect, 2003

State	Professions that must report					Others who must report		Standard for reporting	Privileged communications
	Health care	Mental health	Social work	Education/ child care	Law enforcement	All persons	Other		
Alabama § 26-14-3(a) § 26-14-10	✔	✔	✔	✔	✔		Any other person called upon to give aid or assistance to any child	Known or suspected	Attorney/client
Alaska § 47.17.020(a) § 47.17.023 § 47.17.060	✔	✔	✔	✔	✔		Paid employees of domestic violence and sexual assault programs and drug and alcohol treatment facilities Members of a child fatality review team or multidisciplinary child protection team Commercial or private film or photograph processors	Have reasonable cause to suspect	
American Samoa § 45.2002	✔	✔	✔	✔			Medical examiner or coroner Christian Science practitioner	Have reasonable cause to know or suspect Have observed conditions which would reasonably result	
Arizona § 13-3620(A) § 8-805(B)-(C)	✔	✔	✔	✔	✔		Parents Anyone responsible for care or treatment of children Clergy/Christian Science practitioners Domestic violence victim advocates	Have reasonable grounds to believe	Clergy/penitent Attorney/client
Arkansas § 12-12-507(b)-(c) § 12-12-518(b)(1)	✔	✔	✔	✔	✔		Prosecutors Judges Department of Human Services employees Domestic violence shelter employees and volunteers Foster parents Court Appointed Special Advocates Clergy/Christian Science practitioners	Have reasonable cause to suspect Have observed conditions which would reasonably result	Clergy/penitent Attorney/client
California Penal Code § 11166(a), (c) § 11165.7(a)	✔	✔	✔	✔	✔		Firefighters Animal control officers Commercial film and photographic print processors Clergy Court Appointed Special Advocates	Have knowledge of or observe Know or reasonably suspect	Clergy/penitent
Colorado § 19-3-304(1), (2) (2.5) § 19-3-311	✔	✔	✔	✔	✔		Christian Science practitioners Veterinarians Firefighters Victim advocates Commercial film and photographic print processors Clergy	Have reasonable cause to know or suspect Have observed conditions which would reasonably result	Clergy/penitent
Connecticut § 17a-101(b) § 17a-103(a)	✔	✔	✔	✔	✔		Substance abuse counselors Sexual assault counselors Battered women's Clergy Child advocates	Have reasonable cause to suspect or believe	
Delaware tit. 16, § 903 § 909	✔	✔	✔	✔		✔		Know or in good faith suspect	Attorney/client Clergy/penitent

TABLE 2.16

Mandatory reporters of child abuse and neglect, 2003 [CONTINUED]

State	Professions that must report					Others who must report		Standard for reporting	Privileged communications
	Health care	Mental health	Social work	Education/ child care	Law enforcement	All persons	Other		
District of Columbia § 4-1321.02(a), (b), (d) § 4-1321.05	✔	✔	✔	✔	✔			Know or have reasonable cause to suspect	
Florida § 39.201(1) § 39.204	✔	✔	✔	✔	✔	✔	Judges Religious healers	Know or have reasonable cause to suspect	Attorney/client
Georgia § 19-7-5(c)(1), (g) § 16-12-100(c)	✔	✔	✔	✔	✔		Persons who produce visual or printed matter	Have reasonable cause to believe	
Guam Tit. 19 § 13201	✔	✔	✔	✔	✔		Christian Science practitioners Commercial film and photographic print processors	Have reason to suspect Have knowledge or observe	
Hawaii § 350-1.1(a) § 350-5	✔	✔	✔	✔	✔		Employees of recreational or sports activities	Have reason to believe	
Idaho § 16-1619(a), (c) § 16-1620	✔	✔	✔	✔	✔	✔		Have reason to believe Have observed conditions which would reasonably result	Clergy/penitent Attorney/client
Illinois 325 ILCS § 5/4	✔	✔	✔	✔	✔		Homemakers, substance abuse treatment personnel Christian Science practitioners Funeral home directors Commercial film and photographic print processors Clergy	Have reasonable cause to believe	Clergy/penitent
Indiana § 31-33-5-1 § 31-33-5-2 § 31-32-11-1	✔	✔	✔	✔	✔	✔	Staff member of any public or private institution, school, facility, or agency	Have reason to believe	
Iowa § 232.69(1)(a)-(b) § 728.14(1) § 232.74	✔	✔	✔	✔	✔		Commercial film and photographic print processors Employees of substance abuse programs Coaches	Reasonably believe	
Kansas § 38-1522(a), (b)	✔	✔	✔	✔	✔		Firefighters Juvenile intake and assessment workers	Have reason to suspect	
Kentucky § 620.030(1), (2) § 620.050(2)	✔	✔	✔	✔	✔	✔		Know or have reasonable cause to believe	Attorney/client Clergy/penitent
Louisiana Ch. Code art. § 603(13) § 609(A)(1) § 610(F)	✔	✔	✔	✔	✔		Commercial film or photographic print processors Mediators	Have cause to believe	Clergy, Christian Science practitioner/ penitent
Maine tit. 22, §4011(1) tit. 22, § 4015	✔	✔	✔	✔	✔		Guardians *ad litem* and Court Appointed Special Advocates Fire inspectors Commercial film processors Homemakers Humane agents Clergy	Know or have reasonable cause to suspect	Clergy/penitent

State	Professions that must report					Others who must report		Standard for reporting	Privileged communications
	Health care	Mental health	Social work	Education/ child care	Law enforcement	All persons	Other		
Maryland Family Law § 5-704(a) § 5-705(a)(1)	✔	✔	✔	✔	✔	✔		Have reason to believe	Attorney/client Clergy/penitent
Massachusetts ch. 119, § 51A ch. 119, § 51B	✔	✔	✔	✔	✔		Drug and alcoholism counselors Probation and parole officers Clerks/magistrates of district courts Firefighters Clergy/Christian Science practitioners	Have reasonable cause to believe	Clergy/penitent
Michigan § 722.623(1), (8) § 722.631	✔	✔	✔	✔	✔		Clergy	Have reasonable cause to suspect	Attorney/client Clergy/penitent
Minnesota § 626.556 Subd. 3(a), 8	✔	✔	✔	✔	✔			Know or have reason to believe	Clergy/penitent
Mississippi § 43-21-353(1)	✔	✔	✔	✔	✔	✔	Attorneys Ministers	Have reasonable cause to suspect	
Missouri § 210.115(1) § 568.110 § 210.140	✔	✔	✔	✔	✔		Persons with responsibility for care of children Christian Science practitioners Probation/parole officers Commercial film processors Internet service providers Clergy	Have reasonable cause to suspect Have observed conditions which would reasonably result	Attorney/client Clergy/penitent
Montana § 41-3-201 (1)-(2), (4)	✔	✔	✔	✔	✔		Guardians *ad litem* Clergy Religious healers Christian Science practitioners	Know or have reasonable cause to suspect	Clergy/penitent
Nebraska § 28-711(1) § 28-714	✔		✔	✔		✔		Have reasonable cause to believe Have observed conditions which would reasonably result	
Nevada § 432B.220(3), (5) § 432B.250	✔		✔	✔		✔	Religious healers Alcohol/drug abuse counselors Clergy/Christian Science practitioners Probation officers Attorneys Youth shelter workers	Know or have reason to believe	Clergy/penitent Attorney/client
New Hampshire § 169-C:29 § 169-C:32	✔	✔	✔	✔	✔	✔	Christian Science practitioners Clergy	Have reason to suspect	Attorney/client *Clergy/penitent privilege denied*
New Jersey § 9:6-8.10						✔		Have reasonable cause to believe	
New Mexico § 32A-4-3(A) § 32A-4-5(A)	✔	✔	✔	✔	✔	✔	Judges Clergy	Know or have reasonable suspicion	Clergy/penitent
New York Soc. Serv. Law § 413(1)	✔	✔	✔	✔	✔		Alcoholism/substance abuse counselors District attorneys Christian Science practitioners	Have reasonable cause to suspect	
North Carolina § 7B-301 § 7B-310						✔	Any institution	Have cause to suspect	Attorney/client *Clergy/penitent privilege denied*

TABLE 2.16

Mandatory reporters of child abuse and neglect, 2003 [CONTINUED]

State	Professions that must report					Others who must report		Standard for reporting	Privileged communications
	Health care	Mental health	Social work	Education/ child care	Law enforcement	All persons	Other		
North Dakota § 50-25.1-03 § 50-25.1-10	✔	✔	✔	✔	✔		Clergy Religious healers Addiction counselors	Have knowledge of or reasonable cause to suspect	Clergy/penitent Attorney/client
Northern Mariana Islands Tit. 6, § 5313(a); § 5316	✔			✔	✔		Medical examiners/ coroners Religious healers	Know or have reasonable cause to suspect	Attorney/client
Ohio § 2151.421 (A)(1), (A)(2), (G)(1)(b)	✔	✔	✔	✔			Attorneys Religious healers Agents of humane societies	Know or suspect	Attorney/client Physician/ patient
Oklahoma tit. 10, § 7103(A)(1) tit. 10, § 7104 tit. 10, § 7113	✔			✔		✔	Commercial film and photographic print processors	Have reason to believe	
Oregon § 419B.005(3) § 419B.010(1)	✔	✔	✔	✔	✔		Attorneys Clergy Firefighters Court Appointed Special Advocates	Have reasonable cause to believe	Mental health/ patient Clergy/penitent Attorney/client
Pennsylvania 23 Pa. § 6311(a),(b)	✔	✔	✔	✔	✔		Funeral directors Christian Science practitioners Clergy	Have reasonable cause to suspect	Clergy/penitent
Puerto Rico Tit. 8, § 441a; § 411b	✔	✔	✔	✔	✔	✔	Professionals or public officials Processors of film or photographs	Should know or have knowledge of Suspects Observes	
Rhode Island § 40-11-3(a) § 40-11-6(a) § 40-11-11	✔					✔		Have reasonable cause to know or suspect	Attorney/client *Clergy/penitent privilege denied*
South Carolina § 20-7-510(A) § 20-7-550	✔	✔	✔	✔	✔		Judges Funeral home directors and employees Christian Science practitioners Film processors Religious healers Substance abuse treatment staff Computer technicians	Have reason to believe	Attorney/client Clergy/penitent
South Dakota § 26-8A-3 § 26-8A-15	✔	✔	✔	✔	✔		Chemical dependency counselors Religious healers Parole or court services officers Employees of domestic abuse shelters	Have reasonable cause to suspect	
Tennessee § 37-1-403(a) § 37-1-605(a) § 37-1-411	✔	✔	✔	✔	✔	✔	Judges Neighbors Relatives Friends Religious healers	Knowledge of/ reasonably know Have reasonable cause to suspect	
Texas Family Code § 261.101(a)-(c) § 261.102	✔			✔		✔	Juvenile probation or detention officers Employees or clinics that provide reproductive services	Have cause to believe	*Clergy/penitent privilege denied*
Utah § 62A-4a-403(1)-(3) § 62A-4a-412(5)	✔					✔		Have reason to believe Have observed conditions which would reasonably result	Clergy/penitent

TABLE 2.16

Mandatory reporters of child abuse and neglect, 2003 [CONTINUED]

State	Professions that must report					Others who must report		Standard for reporting	Privileged communications
	Health care	Mental health	Social work	Education/ child care	Law enforcement	All persons	Other		
Vermont tit. 33, §4913(a), (f)-(h)	✔	✔	✔	✔	✔		Camp administrators and counselors Probation officers Clergy	Have reasonable cause to believe	Clergy/penitent
Virgin Islands Tit. 5, § 2533(a) § 2538	✔	✔	✔	✔	✔			Have reasonable cause to suspect Observe conditions which would reasonably result	Attorney/client
Virginia § 63.2-1509(A) § 63.2-1519	✔	✔	✔	✔	✔		Mediators Christian Science practitioners Probation officers Court Appointed Special Advocates	Have reason to suspect	
Washington § 26.44.030 (1), (2) § 26.44.060(3)	✔	✔	✔	✔	✔		Any adult with whom a child resides Responsible living skills program staff	Have reasonable cause to believe	
West Virginia § 49-6A-2 § 49-6A-7	✔	✔	✔	✔	✔		Clergy Religious healers Judges, family law masters or magistrates Christian Science practitioners	Reasonable caused suspect When believe Have observed	Attorney/client *Clergy/penitent privilege denied*
Wisconsin § 48.981(2), (2m)(c)-(e)	✔	✔	✔	✔	✔		Alcohol or drug abuse counselors Mediators Financial and employment planners Court Appointed Special Advocates	Have reasonable cause to suspect Have reason to believe	
Wyoming § 14-3-205(a) § 14-3-210					✔			Know or have reasonable caused believe or suspect Have observed conditions which would reasonably result	Attorney/client Physician/ patient Clergy/penitent

SOURCE: *State Statute Series: Mandatory Reporters of Child Abuse and Neglect, Summary of State Laws*, U.S. Department of Health and Human Services, Children's Bureau, Child Welfare Information Gateway, March 2005, http://www.childwelfare.gov/systemwide/laws_policies/statutes/mandaall.pdf (accessed August 21, 2006)

privileged communications between physicians and patients, while Oregon exempted from mandatory reporting privileged communications between mental heath professionals and patients.

Who Reports Child Abuse?

In 2004 more than half (55.7%) of all reports of alleged child maltreatment came from professional sources—educators (16.5%); legal, law enforcement, and criminal justice personnel (15.6%); social services personnel (10.5%); medical personnel (7.9%); mental health personnel (3.8%); child day care providers (0.9%); and foster care providers (0.5%). Friends and neighbors, parents, and other relatives comprised nearly one-fifth (19.6%) of the reporters, whereas alleged victims and self-identified perpetrators reported abuse in 0.7% of the cases. Another 17.8% of reports came from anonymous and other sources. (See Figure 2.9.)

All states offer immunity to individuals who report incidents of child maltreatment "in good faith" or with sincerity. Besides physical injury and neglect, most states include mental injury, sexual abuse, and the sexual exploitation of minors as cases to be reported.

Failure to Report Child Maltreatment

Many states impose penalties, either a fine and/or imprisonment, for failure to report child maltreatment. A mandated reporter, such as a physician, may also be sued for negligence for failing to protect a child from harm. Although all states have enacted legislation requiring, among other things, the mandatory reporting of child maltreatment by certain professionals, states vary in the standard for reporting. The standard to report child maltreatment varies from having "reasonable cause to suspect," to having "reason to believe," to having "observed conditions which would reasonably result," to "know or suspect."

FIGURE 2.9

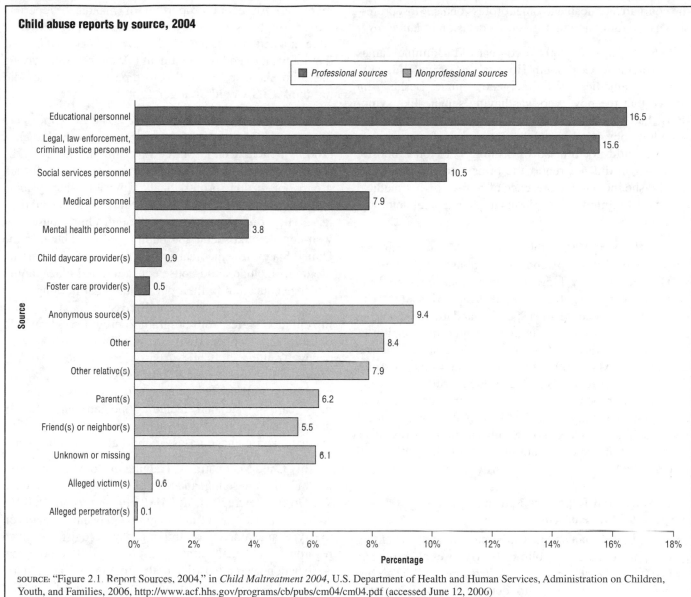

Child abuse reports by source, 2004

■ *Professional sources* ▨ *Nonprofessional sources*

Source	Percentage
Educational personnel	16.5
Legal, law enforcement, criminal justice personnel	15.6
Social services personnel	10.5
Medical personnel	7.9
Mental health personnel	3.8
Child daycare provider(s)	0.9
Foster care provider(s)	0.5
Anonymous source(s)	9.4
Other	8.4
Other relative(s)	7.9
Parent(s)	6.2
Friend(s) or neighbor(s)	5.5
Unknown or missing	6.1
Alleged victim(s)	0.6
Alleged perpetrator(s)	0.1

SOURCE: "Figure 2.1 Report Sources, 2004," in *Child Maltreatment 2004*, U.S. Department of Health and Human Services, Administration on Children, Youth, and Families, 2006, http://www.acf.hhs.gov/programs/cb/pubs/cm04/cm04.pdf (accessed June 12, 2006)

The 1976 landmark California case *Landeros v. Flood et al.* illustrates a case involving a physician's failure to report child maltreatment. Eleven-month-old Gita Landeros was brought by her mother to the San Jose Hospital in California for treatment of injuries. Besides a fractured lower leg, the girl had bruises on her back and abrasions on other parts of her body. She also appeared scared when anyone approached her. At the time Gita was also suffering from a fractured skull, but this was never diagnosed by the attending physician, Dr. A. J. Flood.

Gita returned home with her mother and subsequently suffered further serious abuse at the hands of her mother and the mother's boyfriend. Three months later Gita was brought to another hospital for medical treatment, where the doctor identified and reported the abuse to the proper authorities. After surgery for her injuries the child was placed with foster parents. The mother and boyfriend were eventually convicted of the crime of child abuse. The guardian *ad litem* (a court-appointed special advocate) for Gita filed a malpractice suit against Dr. Flood and the San Jose Hospital, citing painful permanent physical injury to the plaintiff as a result of the defendants' negligence.

The trial court of Santa Clara County dismissed the Landeros complaint, and the case was appealed to the California Supreme Court. The California Supreme Court agreed that Dr. Flood should have identified Gita's abuse. The court ruled that the doctor's failure to do so contributed to the child's continued suffering, and Dr. Flood and the hospital were found liable. While this case applied specifically to a medical doctor, the principles reached by the court are applicable to other professionals. Most professionals are familiar with the court's decision in *Landeros*.

On August 10, 2002, two-year-old Dominic James was brought to Cox South Hospital in Springfield, Missouri. Paramedics told emergency nurse Leslie Ann Brown that the boy, who was having seizure-like symptoms, had bruises on his back and to report this to the attending physician. Told by Dominic's foster parents that the child got bruised by leaning back on a booster seat, Brown did not report the bruises to the physician, nor did she include the presence of bruises on her medical reports. Dominic was hospitalized again a week later and died soon after.

In February 2003 the state of Missouri charged Brown with failure to report child abuse. In September 2003 Green County Judge Calvin Holden dismissed the criminal charges, stating that the Missouri statute with the "reasonable cause to suspect" standard for reporting child abuse was unconstitutionally vague in violation of the U.S. and Missouri Constitutions. The state appealed the case in May 2004. In August 2004 the Missouri Supreme Court reversed Judge Holden's ruling, allowing the case to proceed to trial. However, later that year charges were dismissed against Brown after an agreement was reached requiring Cox South Hospital to revise its training for mandated reporters and implement annual refresher courses.

Why Mandated Reporters Fail to Report Suspected Maltreatment

Gail L. Zellman and C. Christine Fair, in "Preventing and Reporting Abuse" (John E. B. Myers et al., eds., *The APSAC Handbook on Child Maltreatment*, 2002), conducted a national survey to determine why mandated reporters may not report suspected maltreatment. The researchers surveyed 1,196 general and family practitioners, pediatricians, child psychiatrists, clinical psychologists, social workers, public school principals, and heads of child care centers. Nearly eight out of ten (77%) survey participants had made a child maltreatment report at some time in his or her professional career. More than nine out of ten (92%) elementary school principals reported child maltreatment at some time, followed closely by child psychiatrists (90%) and pediatricians (89%). A lesser proportion of secondary school principals (84%), social workers (70%), and clinical psychologists (63%) reported child maltreatment at some time in their careers.

Nearly 40% of the mandated reporters, however, indicated that at some time in their careers they had failed to report even though they had suspected child maltreatment. Almost 60% failed to report child maltreatment because they did not have enough evidence that the child had been maltreated. One-third of the mandated reporters

thought the abuse was not serious enough to warrant reporting. An equal proportion of mandated reporters did not report suspected abuse because they felt they were in a better position to help the child (19.3%) or they did not want to end the treatment (19%) they were giving the child. Almost 16% failed to report because they did not think CPS would do a good job.

In *Confronting Chronic Neglect: The Education and Training of Health Professionals on Family Violence* (2002), Felicia Cohn, Marla E. Salmon, and John D. Stobo examined the curricula on family violence for six groups of health professionals: physicians, physician assistants, nurses, psychologists, social workers, and dentists. They find that, in fact, although child abuse is a well-documented social and public health problem in the United States, few medical schools and residency training programs include child abuse education and other family violence education in their curricula. What training there is consists of lectures and case discussions, and the training duration varies from program to program. Suzanne P. Starling and Stephen Boos, in "Core Content for Residency Training in Child Abuse and Neglect" (*Child Maltreatment*, November 2003), suggest offering a core curriculum in residency programs that would enable primary care physicians (including pediatricians, family doctors, and emergency-medicine doctors) to recognize, evaluate, and manage cases of child abuse and neglect.

In "Child Maltreatment Training in Doctoral Programs in Clinical, Counseling, and School Psychology: Where Do We Go from Here?" (*Child Maltreatment*, August 2003), Kelly M. Champion et al. sought to gain information on the type and amount of training psychologists received regarding child maltreatment in American Psychological Association-accredited doctoral programs. Their study examined surveys sent to training directors of doctoral programs in 1992 and 2001. Champion et al. find that doctoral programs had generally remained unchanged within those years. Few doctoral programs offered specific courses on child maltreatment in 1992 and 2001, just 13% and 11%, respectively. Although 65% of programs in 1992 and 59% in 2001 covered child maltreatment in three or more courses, these courses were rarely required to complete a doctoral program. Twenty percent of programs in 1992 and 22% in 2001 offered training in child maltreatment in clinical settings; most programs, however, reported that students completed just 1% to 10% of such training. Finally, research activities in child maltreatment decreased from 60% in 1992 to 47% in 2001.

What Happens after a Child Maltreatment Report?

CPS. On receipt of a report of suspected child maltreatment, CPS screens the case to determine its proper jurisdiction. For example, if it is determined that the alleged perpetrator of sexual abuse is the victim's parent or caretaker, CPS screens in the report and conducts further investigation. If the alleged perpetrator is a stranger or someone who is not the parent or caregiver of the victim, the case is screened out, or referred elsewhere, in this case, to the police because it does not fall within CPS jurisdiction as outlined under federal law.

A state's child welfare system, under which CPS functions, consists of other components designed to ensure a child's well-being and safety. These include foster care, juvenile and family courts, and other child welfare services. Other child welfare services include family reunification, granting custody to a relative, termination of parental rights, and emancipation (releasing a subject from the system because he or she is now recognized by the court as an adult). Cases of reported child abuse or neglect typically undergo a series of steps through the child welfare system. (See Figure 2.10.)

DISPOSITIONS OF INVESTIGATED REPORTS. After a CPS agency screens in a report of child maltreatment, it initiates an investigation. Some states follow one time frame for responding to all reports, whereas others follow a priority system, investigating high-priority cases within one to twenty-four hours. According to *Child Maltreatment 2004*, the twenty-six states that reported response time in 2004 showed an average response time of ninety-seven hours, or approximately four days.

Following investigation of the report of child maltreatment, the CPS agency assigns a disposition, or finding, to the report. Before 2000, reports of alleged child maltreatment received one of three dispositions—indicated, substantiated, or unsubstantiated. In 2000 several states announced plans to establish an alternative response program to reports of alleged child maltreatment. If the child is at a serious and immediate risk of maltreatment, CPS responds with the traditional formal investigation, which may involve removing the child from the home. If it is determined, however, that the parent will not endanger the child, CPS workers use the alternative response to help the family. This involves a more informal approach. Instead of removing the child from the home environment, CPS steps in to assist the whole family by, for example, helping reduce stress that may lead to child abuse through provision of child care, adequate housing, and education in parenting skills. In 2004 ten states implemented the alternative response program.

Other dispositions, used by all states, included:

- A disposition of "substantiated," which means that sufficient evidence existed to support the allegation of maltreatment or risk of maltreatment

- A disposition of "indicated or reason to suspect," which means that the abuse and/or neglect could not be confirmed, but there was reason to suspect that the child was maltreated or was at risk of maltreatment

FIGURE 2.10

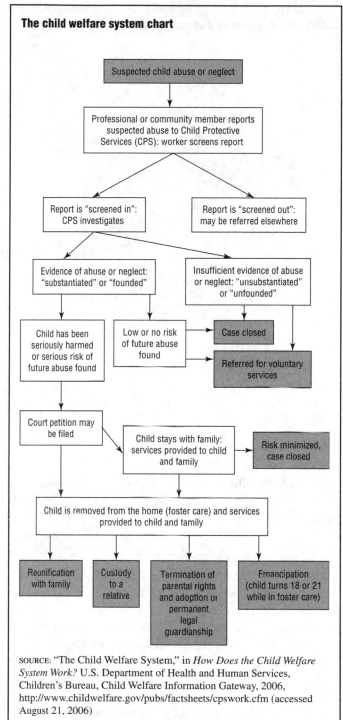

The child welfare system chart

SOURCE: "The Child Welfare System," in *How Does the Child Welfare System Work?* U.S. Department of Health and Human Services, Children's Bureau, Child Welfare Information Gateway, 2006, http://www.childwelfare.gov/pubs/factsheets/cpswork.cfm (accessed August 21, 2006)

- A disposition of "unsubstantiated," which means that no maltreatment occurred or sufficient evidence did not exist to conclude that the child was maltreated or was at risk of being maltreated

Of the 1.9 million investigated reports in 2004, 60.7% were unsubstantiated. More than one-fourth (25.7%) were substantiated, and another 3% were indicated. Dispositions that were identified "closed with no finding" referred to

FIGURE 2.11

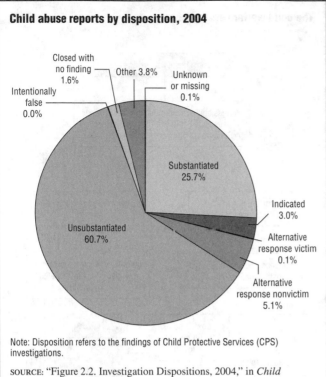

Child abuse reports by disposition, 2004

Closed with no finding 1.6%

Other 3.8%

Unknown or missing 0.1%

Intentionally false 0.0%

Substantiated 25.7%

Indicated 3.0%

Unsubstantiated 60.7%

Alternative response victim 0.1%

Alternative response nonvictim 5.1%

Note: Disposition refers to the findings of Child Protective Services (CPS) investigations.

SOURCE: "Figure 2.2. Investigation Dispositions, 2004," in *Child Maltreatment 2004*, U.S. Department of Health and Human Services, Administration on Children, Youth, and Families, 2006, http://www.acf .hhs.gov/programs/cb/pubs/cm04/cm04.pdf (accessed June 12, 2006)

cases in which the investigation could not be completed because the family moved out of the jurisdiction, the family could not be found, or the needed reports were not filed within the required time limit. Such dispositions accounted for 1.6% of investigated cases. (See Figure 2.11.)

COURT INVOLVEMENT. The juvenile or family court hears allegations of maltreatment and decides if a child has been abused and/or neglected. The court then determines what should be done to protect the child. The child may be left in the parents' home under the supervision of the CPS agency, or the child may be placed in foster care. If the child is removed from the home and it is later determined that the child should never be returned to the parents, the court can begin proceedings to terminate parental rights so that the child can be put up for adoption. The state may also prosecute the abusive parent or caretaker when a crime has allegedly been committed.

THE DEBATE ABOUT FAMILY PRESERVATION. The Adoption Assistance and Child Welfare Act of 1980 mandated: "In each case, reasonable efforts will be made (A) prior to the placement of a child in foster care, to prevent or eliminate the need for removal of the child from his home, and (B) to make it possible for the child to return to his home." Because the law, however, did not define the term *reasonable efforts*, states and courts interpreted the term in different ways. In many cases

child welfare personnel took the "reasonable efforts" of providing family counseling, respite care, and substance abuse treatment, thus preventing the child from being removed from abusive parents.

The law was a reaction to what was seen as zealousness in the 1960s and 1970s, when children, especially African-American children, were taken from their homes because their parents were poor. At the beginning of the twentieth-first century, however, some feel that problems of drug or substance abuse can mean that returning the child to the home is likely a guarantee of further abuse. Others note that some situations exist where a parent's live-in partner, who has no emotional attachment to the child, may also present risks to the child.

Richard J. Gelles, a prominent family violence expert and once a vocal advocate of family preservation, had a change of heart after studying the case of fifteen-month-old David Edwards, who was suffocated by his mother after the child welfare system failed to come to his rescue. Although David's parents had lost custody of their first child because of abuse, and despite reports of David's abuse, CPS made "reasonable efforts" to let the parents keep the child. In *The Book of David: How Preserving Families Can Cost Children's Lives* (1996), Gelles points out that CPS needed to abandon its blanket solution to child abuse in its attempt to use reasonable efforts to reunite the victims and their perpetrators. He contends that those parents who seriously abuse their children are incapable of changing their behaviors.

By contrast, in "Foster Care vs. Family Preservation: The Track Record on Safety" (August 2005, http:// www.nccpr.org/newissues/1.html), the National Coalition for Child Protection Reform (NCCPR), a nonprofit organization of experts on child abuse and foster care who are committed to the reform of the child welfare system, contends that many allegedly maltreated children are unnecessarily removed from their homes—and in fact that children are in more danger when placed in foster care than when given services to help preserve the family. The NCCPR recognizes that, while there are cases in which the only way to save a child is to remove him or her from an abusive home, in many cases providing support services to the family in crisis, while letting the child remain at home, helps ensure child safety.

The NCCPR states in "What Is 'Family Preservation'?" (December 2003, http://www.nccpr.org/newissues/ 10.html) that, with the proper assistance, a family in crisis can change its behavior. This assistance can range from basic, concrete monetary help (e.g., a place in a day care center) to intensive intervention procedures involving twenty-four-hour, on-call counseling and emergency services. Above all, the organization insists that the current system of CPS must be reformed.

CONTROVERSIES SURROUNDING THE CHILD PROTECTIVE SERVICES SYSTEM

Child Welfare Workforce

Child welfare caseworkers perform multiple tasks in the course of their jobs. Among other things, they investigate reports of child maltreatment, coordinate various services (mental health, substance abuse, etc.) to help keep families together, find foster care placements for children if needed, make regular visits to children and families, arrange placement of children in permanent homes when they cannot be safely returned to their parents or caretakers, and document all details pertaining to their cases. Caseworker supervisors monitor and support their caseworkers, sometimes taking on some of the cases when there is a staff shortage or heavy caseload. In the report *Child Welfare: HHS Could Play a Greater Role in Helping Child Welfare Agencies Recruit and Retain Staff* (March 2003, http://www.gao.gov/new.items/d03357.pdf), the Government Accountability Office (GAO), the investigative arm of Congress, examines the child welfare workforce and how challenges in recruiting and retaining caseworkers affect the children under their care and reported its findings. Among other things, GAO examines exit interview documents of caseworkers who had left their jobs from seventeen states, forty counties, and nineteen private child welfare agencies. The GAO also interviewed child welfare officials and experts and conducted on-site visits to agencies in four states: California, Illinois, Kentucky, and Texas.

The GAO finds that CPS agencies continued to have difficulty attracting and retaining experienced caseworkers. The low pay not only made it difficult to attract qualified workers but also contributed to CPS employees leaving for better-paying jobs. Because the federal government has not set any national hiring policies, employees have college degrees that may not necessarily be related to social work. Workers whom the GAO interviewed in different states also mentioned risk to personal safety, increased paperwork, lack of supervisory support, and insufficient time to attend training as things that affected their job performance and influenced their decision to leave.

Heavy Caseloads

In the four states GAO visited, caseworkers spent from 50% to 80% of their time doing paperwork. Staff shortage because of workers quitting their jobs resulted in excessive caseloads. Figure 2.12 shows the GAO's findings for worker caseloads as compared with recommended standards. The Child Welfare League of America, a private child welfare organization, recommends a caseload of twelve to fifteen cases per caseworker, while the Council on Accreditation for Children and Family Services, which evaluates organizations against best-practice standards, recommends no more than eighteen cases per worker. The GAO finds that, in reality, individual case-

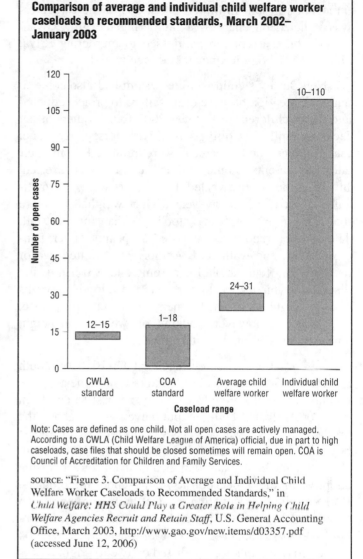

FIGURE 2.12

Comparison of average and individual child welfare worker caseloads to recommended standards, March 2002–January 2003

Note: Cases are defined as one child. Not all open cases are actively managed. According to a CWLA (Child Welfare League of America) official, due in part to high caseloads, case files that should be closed sometimes will remain open. COA is Council of Accreditation for Children and Family Services.

SOURCE: "Figure 3. Comparison of Average and Individual Child Welfare Worker Caseloads to Recommended Standards," in *Child Welfare: HHS Could Play a Greater Role in Helping Child Welfare Agencies Recruit and Retain Staff*, U.S. General Accounting Office, March 2003, http://www.gao.gov/new.items/d03357.pdf (accessed June 12, 2006).

workers handled anywhere from ten to 110 cases, with the average being twenty-four to thirty-one cases.

SLIPPING THROUGH THE CRACKS. Some CPS workers at times fail to monitor the children they are supposed to protect. In Florida the Department of Children and Families could not account for the disappearance of a five-year-old foster child, Rilya Wilson, who had been missing for more than a year before the agency noticed her absence in April 2002. At around that time the agency had reportedly lost track of more than 530 children. Rilya's disappearance was only discovered after her caseworker was fired and the new caseworker could not locate the child. The former caseworker had reported that Rilya was fine, even though that caseworker had not visited the child at her foster home for months. Authorities discovered that her foster mother continued to receive welfare payments for the girl in her absence. Witnesses had also testified that the foster mother and her roommate abused the child before her disappearance. The women faced charges of aggravated child abuse, and her foster mother was convicted of fraud and sentenced to three years in jail. In March 2005, one of the caregivers was indicted on charges of murdering the girl. Rilya's foster mother eventually confessed to murdering Rilya, although her body has never been recovered.

New Jersey's child welfare system had also come to national attention because of its failure to protect adopted and foster children. In October 2003 four brothers of the Jackson family in Collingswood, New Jersey, ages nine, ten, fourteen, and nineteen, were removed from their adoptive parents' home and the couple was arrested. Investigations later revealed the brothers were systematically starved over many years. They weighed no more than forty five pounds and stood less than four feet tall. The children reportedly subsisted on peanut butter, pancake batter, and wallboard. Authorities admitted two of the boys had fetal alcohol syndrome and two had eating disorders, which were the reasons the adoptive parents gave to neighbors for the brothers' emaciated appearance. The brothers, however, had put on weight and height since living with other foster families.

Investigations also revealed that Division of Youth and Family Services (DYFS) workers visited the adoptive parents' home thirty-eight times in the past to check on three other foster children but never asked about the brothers. In 1995, when DYFS was notified by the oldest boy's school that he seemed malnourished, DYFS did not require a medical examination and even agreed to the adoptive mother's decision to home school the brothers. DYFS policies regulating foster homes required an annual medical evaluation and interview of each household member, but these never took place. In May 2004 the adoptive parents were indicted on twenty-eight counts of aggravated assault and child endangerment.

These cases and others like them serve to focus public and media attention on the failure of CPS. While many departments are conscientiously and effectively doing their jobs, there are sometimes failures that result in great harm and even death to the children under their care.

Holding States Accountable

The HHS released *Child Welfare Outcomes 2002: Annual Report—Safety, Permanency, Well-Being* (http://www.acf.hhs.gov/programs/cb/pubs/cwo02/cwo02.pdf), the fifth in a series of annual reports on states' performances in meeting the needs of at-risk children who have entered the child welfare system. The report finds that states were succeeding in some areas and failing in others. For instance, in 2002 many states were unable to prevent many recurrences of child maltreatment; several states with a high percentage of reunifications between foster children and birth families also had a high percentage of those children reentering foster care;

TABLE 2.17

What were the outcomes for the children exiting foster care for the fiscal year 2003?

Reunification with parent(s) or primary caretaker(s)	55%	155,499
Living with other relative(s)	11%	31,572
Adoption	18%	50,355
Emancipation	8%	22,432
Guardianship	4%	10,959
Transfer to another agency	2%	6,439
Runaway	1%	4,158
Death of child	0%	586

Note: Deaths are attributable to a variety of causes including medical conditions, accidents and homicide.

SOURCE: "What Were the Outcomes for the Children Exiting Foster Care during FY 2003?" in *The AFCARS Report*, U.S. Department of Health and Human Services, Administration for Children and Families, 2006, http://www.acf.hhs.gov/programs/cb/stats_research/afcars/tar/report10.pdf (accessed August 21, 2006). Data from Adoption and Foster Care Analysis and Reporting System (AFCARS), National Data Archive on Child Abuse and Neglect, Cornell University, Ithaca, New York.

and few states met national standards for getting children adopted into permanent homes within twenty-four months of their entry into foster care. By contrast, most states kept children in foster care safer in 2002 than they had in 1999 by using a variety of measures such as tougher licensing requirements for foster homes; most states were successful in achieving permanency for foster children leaving care; and most states had improved their adoption rates in the past few years.

According to *The AFGARS Report: Interim FY 2003 Estimates as of June 2006* (June 2006, http://www.acf.hhs.gov/programs/cb/stats_research/afcars/tar/report10.pdf), an estimated 282,000 children entered and 281,000 exited foster care in 2003. Of those children who exited foster care, 55% were reunited with their parents or primary caretakers, 11% went to live with relatives, 18% were adopted, and 8% were emancipated (they became legal adults). Two percent were transferred to another CPS agency, and another 4% were put under guardianship. One percent of foster children had run away. Another 586 children had died. (See Table 2.17.) As of September 30, 2003, an estimated 523,000 children remained in foster care.

States Should Use the Adoption and Safe Families Act

Richard Wexler notes in "Take the Child and Run: Tales from the Age of ASFA" (*New England Law Review*, Fall 2001) that "in passing ASFA [Adoption and Safe Families Act], Congress failed to learn the lessons some states have begun to learn after experiencing foster care panics—huge, sudden increases in placements that follow intensive media coverage of the death of a child who was known to the [child welfare] system." Wexler describes how, in the aftermath of foster care panics, child abuse deaths tend to increase. Caseworkers, fearing the scrutiny of politicians and the media and overwhelmed with more cases, may remove children from homes that could have been made safe with the right services, while leaving others in dangerous homes.

Wexler observes that while the ASFA encourages states to terminate parental rights within a restricted time period and provides monetary incentives for adoptions, nothing in the law prevents states from providing parents with housing or child care. States do not have to use the "take the child and run" approach. Instead, states can provide rent subsidies so that parents will not lose their children because of lack of decent housing. Moreover, states can provide day care so that single working parents who might otherwise leave children unsupervised to earn a living will not lose those children because they have been found neglectful.

Lives Saved

Although CPS agencies have had many problems and are often unable to perform as effectively as they should, many thousands of maltreated children have been identified, many lives have been saved, and many more have been taken out of dangerous environments. It is impossible to tally the number of child abuse cases that might have ended in death; these children have been saved by changes in the laws, by awareness and reporting, and by the efforts of the professionals who intervened on their behalf.

CHAPTER 3
CAUSES AND EFFECTS OF CHILD ABUSE

CAUSES OF CHILD ABUSE

Child abuse is primarily a problem within families. While abuse by nonfamily members does occur, most victims are abused by one or more of their parents. For this reason, much of the research into the causes of child abuse has focused on families and the characteristics and circumstances that can contribute to violence within them.

The 1975 National Family Violence Survey and the 1985 National Family Violence Resurvey, conducted by Murray A. Straus and Richard J. Gelles, are the most complete studies of spousal and parent-child abuse yet prepared in the United States. Unlike most studies of child abuse, the data from these surveys came from detailed interviews with the general population, not from cases that came to the attention of official agencies and professionals. Straus and Gelles therefore had a more intimate knowledge of the families and an awareness of incidences of child abuse that were not reported to authorities or community professionals.

Straus and Gelles believe that cultural standards permit violence in the family. The family, which is the center of love and security in most children's lives, is also the place where the child is punished, sometimes physically. They incorporated research from the two surveys and additional chapters into the book *Physical Violence in American Families: Risk Factors and Adaptations to Violence in 8,145 Families* (1990).

Understanding Factors that Contribute to Child Abuse

The factors contributing to child maltreatment are complex. In the Third National Incidence Study of Child Abuse and Neglect (1993; NIS-3), the most comprehensive federal source of information about the incidence of child maltreatment in the United States, Andrea J. Sedlak and Diane D. Broadhurst find that family structure and size, poverty, alcohol and substance abuse, domestic violence, and community violence are contributing factors to child abuse and neglect.

While these and other factors impact the likelihood of child maltreatment, they do not necessarily lead to abuse. It is important to understand that the causes of child abuse and the characteristics of families in which child abuse occurs are only indicators. Most parents, even in the most stressful and demanding situations, and even with a personal history that might predispose them to be more violent than parents without such a history, do not abuse their children.

Murray A. Straus and Christine Smith note in "Family Patterns and Child Abuse" (Straus and Gelles, *Physical Violence in American Families: Risk Factors and Adaptations to Violence in 8,145 Families*, 1989) that one cannot simply single out an individual factor as the cause of abuse. Straus and Smith find that a combination of several factors is more likely to result in child abuse than is a single factor alone. Also, the sum of the effects of individual factors taken together does not necessarily add up to what Straus and Smith call the "explosive combinations" of several factors interacting with one another. Nonetheless, even "explosive combinations" do not necessarily lead to child abuse.

FAMILIES AT RISK FOR CHILD MALTREATMENT

While it is impossible to determine whether child maltreatment will occur, generally a family may be at risk if the parent is young, has little education, has had several children born within a few years, and is highly dependent on social welfare. According to Judith S. Rycus and Ronald C. Hughes in the *Field Guide to Child Welfare* (1998), a family at high to moderate risk includes parents who do not understand basic child development and who may discipline inappropriately for the child's age; those who lack the necessary skills for caring for and managing a child; those who use physical punishment harshly and excessively; and those who do not appropriately supervise their children.

Furthermore, families under stress are more likely to produce abusive parents and abused or neglected children, such as during divorce or other problems with adult relationships, death, illness, disability, incarceration, or loss of a job, according to Rycus and Hughes. Small stresses can have a cumulative effect and become explosive with a relatively minor event. For potentially abusive parents, high levels of ongoing stress, coupled with inadequate coping strategies and limited resources, produce an extremely high-risk situation for children involved.

According to "Child Maltreatment: Fact Sheet" (April 2006, http://www.cdc.gov/ncipc/factsheets/cmfacts.htm), which is maintained by the Centers for Disease Control and Prevention, a family may also be at risk if:

- A child in the family has a disability or mental retardation.

- It is socially isolated.

- Parents do not understand child development.

- Domestic violence exists in the home.

- The family is economically disadvantaged.

- Family members are substance abusers.

- The parents are young or single.

- The parents are depressed or have other mental health conditions.

- The surrounding community is particularly violent.

Psychological Abuse

Psychological abuse can cause great harm to children but tends to be less well recognized than physical or sexual abuse or neglect. In "Family Dynamics Associated with the Use of Psychologically Violent Parental Practices" (*Journal of Family Violence*, April 2004), Marie-Hélène Gagné and Camil Bouchard identify four family characteristics that are likely to result in parental psychological violence. The first involves a scapegoat child, who may be different from other family members by his or her unattractiveness, disability, having been adopted, or being the child of a former spouse. This child is typically neglected by the parents, treated harshly, and excluded from family intimacy. The second type of family has a domineering father, who intimidates the children and may even turn physically violent. The mother herself may be a victim of spousal violence. The children may be psychologically abused by both parents. The authoritarian mother typifies the third family characteristic leading to parental psychological abuse. She controls the household, and the children are expected to do as she bids. The fourth family characteristic involves the "broken parent,"

FIGURE 3.1

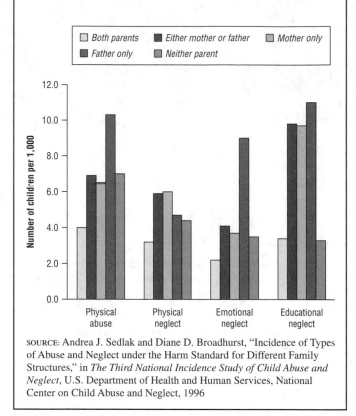

Incidence of types of abuse and neglect under the Harm Standard, by family structure, 1993

SOURCE: Andrea J. Sedlak and Diane D. Broadhurst, "Incidence of Types of Abuse and Neglect under the Harm Standard for Different Family Structures," in *The Third National Incidence Study of Child Abuse and Neglect*, U.S. Department of Health and Human Services, National Center on Child Abuse and Neglect, 1996

who has not attained maturity and a feeling of self-worth because of a difficult past. This type of parent takes care of the children when things are going smoothly, but falls apart when difficulties arise.

Family Structure

Single parents families appear to be at greater risk of child maltreatment. NIS-3 found that under the Harm Standard (see Chapter 2 for a definition of the Harm Standard and Endangerment Standard), children in single-parent households were at a higher risk of physical abuse and all types of neglect than were children in other family structures. Children living with only their fathers suffered the highest incidence rates of physical abuse and emotional and educational neglect. (See Figure 3.1.) Under the Endangerment Standard higher incidence rates of physical and emotional neglect occurred among children living with only their fathers than among those living in other family structures. (See Figure 3.2.)

The Problem of Substance Abuse

Child protective services (CPS) workers are faced with the growing problem of substance abuse among families involved with the child welfare system. According to the National Household Survey on Drug Abuse's

FIGURE 3.2

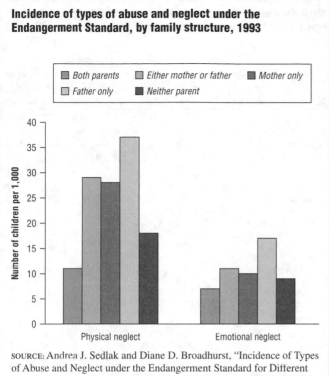

Incidence of types of abuse and neglect under the Endangerment Standard, by family structure, 1993

SOURCE: Andrea J. Sedlak and Diane D. Broadhurst, "Incidence of Types of Abuse and Neglect under the Endangerment Standard for Different Family Structures," in *The Third National Incidence Study of Child Abuse and Neglect*, U.S. Department of Health and Human Services, National Center on Child Abuse and Neglect, 1996

TABLE 3.1

Children age 17 or younger living with one or more parents with past-year substance abuse or dependence, by number and percentage, 2001

Ages of children (years)	Estimated numbers (in thousands)	Percentage
Younger than 3	1,078	9.8
3 to 5	1,115	9.8
6 to 11	1,816	7.5
12 to 17	2,100	9.2

Notes: Children include biological, step, adoptive, or foster. Children aged 17 or younger who were not living with one or more parents for most of the quarter of the NHSDA interview are excluded from the present analysis. According to the 2000 Current Population Survey, this amounts to approximately 3 million or 4 percent of children aged 17 or younger.

SOURCE: "Table 2. Estimated Numbers (in Thousands) and Percentages of Children Aged 17 or Younger Living with One or More Parents with Past Year Substance Abuse or Dependence: 2001," in *Children Living with Substance-Abusing or Substance-Dependent Parents*, U.S. Department of Health and Human Services, Substance Abuse and Mental Health Services Administration, Office of Applied Studies, June 2, 2003, www.oas.samhsa .gov/2k3/children/children.pdf (accessed June 19, 2006)

NHSDA Report (June 2003, http://www.oas.samhsa.gov/ 2k3/children/children.pdf), in 2001 nearly seventy million children under age eighteen lived with at least one parent; about 6.1 million of these children (comprising 8.7% percent of all children in the nation) lived with one or more parents with past-year substance abuse or dependence. About one-fifth (19.6%) were five years

FIGURE 3.3

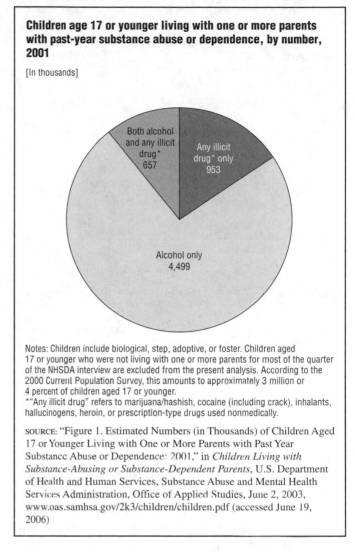

Children age 17 or younger living with one or more parents with past-year substance abuse or dependence, by number, 2001

[In thousands]

Notes: Children include biological, step, adoptive, or foster. Children aged 17 or younger who were not living with one or more parents for most of the quarter of the NHSDA interview are excluded from the present analysis. According to the 2000 Current Population Survey, this amounts to approximately 3 million or 4 percent of children aged 17 or younger.
*"Any illicit drug" refers to marijuana/hashish, cocaine (including crack), inhalants, hallucinogens, heroin, or prescription-type drugs used nonmedically.

SOURCE: "Figure 1. Estimated Numbers (in Thousands) of Children Aged 17 or Younger Living with One or More Parents with Past Year Substance Abuse or Dependence: 2001," in *Children Living with Substance-Abusing or Substance-Dependent Parents*, U.S. Department of Health and Human Services, Substance Abuse and Mental Health Services Administration, Office of Applied Studies, June 2, 2003, www.oas.samhsa.gov/2k3/children/children.pdf (accessed June 19, 2006)

old or younger. (See Table 3.1.) Among these children, about 4.5 million lived with an alcoholic parent, an estimated 953,000 lived with a parent with an illicit drug problem, and approximately 657,000 lived with parents who abused both alcohol and illicit drugs. (See Figure 3.3.) Fathers (7.8%) were more likely than mothers (4%) to report having had a past-year substance abuse or dependence. (See Figure 3.4.)

Sedlak and Broadhurst note that the increase in illicit drug use since the Second National Incidence Study of Child Abuse and Neglect (1986) may have contributed to the increased child maltreatment incidence reported in NIS-3. Children whose parents are alcohol and substance abusers are at high risk of abuse and neglect because of the physiological, psychological, and sociological nature of addiction.

According to the U.S. Department of Health and Human Services, about one-third to two-thirds of substantiated child maltreatment reports (those having sufficient evidence to support the allegation of maltreatment)

FIGURE 3.4

Fathers and mothers living with one or more children age 17 or younger, by their own reports of past-year substance abuse or dependence, 2001

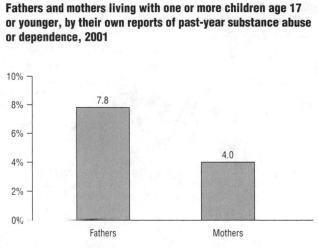

Note: Children include biological, step, adoptive, or foster.

SOURCE: "Figure 2. Percentage of Fathers and Mothers (Living with One or More Children Aged 17 or Younger) Reporting Past Year Substance Abuse or Dependence: 2001," in *Children Living with Substance-Abusing or Substance-Dependent Parents*, U.S. Department of Health and Human Services, Substance Abuse and Mental Health Services Administration, Office of Applied Studies, June 2, 2003, www.oas.samhsa.gov/2k3/children/children.pdf (accessed August 28, 2006)

TABLE 3.2

Illicit drug use in the past month among females by age, by pregnancy status, and by demographic characteristics, 2002–04

| | Total[a] | | Pregnancy status | | | |
| | | | Pregnant | | Not pregnant | |
Demographic characteristic	2002–2003	2003–2004	2002–2003	2003–2004	2002–2003	2003–2004
Total	**10.2**	**10.0**	**4.3**	**4.6**	**10.4**	**10.2**
Age						
15–17	16.5	16.1	12.8	16.0	16.5	16.0
18–25	16.4	16.0	7.5	7.8	16.9	16.4
26–44	6.8	6.7	1.6	2.1	7.0	6.9
Hispanic origin and race						
Not Hispanic or Latino	10.8	10.6	4.7	4.5	11.0	10.8
White	11.4	11.1	4.4	4.2	11.0	11.4
Black or African American	9.5	9.4	8.0	7.8	9.4	9.4
American Indian or Alaska native	15.4	17.8	*	*	16.3	18.6
Native Hawaiian or other Pacific Islander	12.6	*	*	*	12.8	*
Asian	4.3	3.5	*	*	4.4	3.6
Two or more races	15.4	20.3	*	*	15.9	20.8
Hispanic or Latino	7.2	6.9	3.0	5.0	7.4	7.0
Trimester[b]						
First	N/A	N/A	7.7	8.0	N/A	N/A
Second	N/A	N/A	3.2	3.8	N/A	N/A
Third	N/A	N/A	2.3	2.4	N/A	N/A

*Low precision; no estimate reported.
N/A: Not applicable.
Note: Illicit drugs include marijuana/hashish, cocaine (including crack), heroin, hallucinogens, inhalants, or prescription-type psychotherapeutics used nonmedically.
[a]Estimates in the total column are for all females aged 15 to 44, including those with unknown pregnancy status.
[b]Pregnant females aged 15 to 44 not reporting trimester were excluded.

SOURCE: "Table 7.71B. Illicit Drug Use in the Past Month among Females Aged 15 to 44, by Pregnancy Status and Demographic Characteristics: Percentages, Annual Averages Based on 2002–2003 and 2003–2004," in *National Survey on Drug Use and Health, 2004*, U.S. Department of Health and Human Services, Substance Abuse and Mental Health Services Administration, 2005, http://oas.samhsa.gov/nsduh/2k4nsduh/2k4tabs/Sect7peTabs70to77.pdf (accessed August 21, 2006)

involve substance abuse. Younger children, especially infants, are more likely to be victimized by substance-abusing parents, and the maltreatment is more likely to consist of neglect than abuse. Many children experience neglect when a parent is under the influence of alcohol or is out of the home looking for drugs. Even when the parent is at home, he or she may be psychologically unavailable to the children.

SUBSTANCE ABUSE AMONG PREGNANT WOMEN. Illicit drug use among pregnant women continues to be a national problem. Each year the National Survey on Drug Use and Health, formerly known as the National Household Survey on Drug Abuse, asks female respondents ages fifteen to forty-four about their pregnancy status and illicit drug use the month before the survey. According to the *NSDUH Report: Pregnancy and Substance Use* (January 2004, http://www.oas.samhsa.gov/2k3/pregnancy/pregnancy.pdf), in 2003–04 approximately 3% of pregnant women, compared with 9% of nonpregnant women, reported using illicit drugs during the past month. Table 3.2 shows that pregnant teens were much more likely to use illicit drugs while pregnant than were older women; 16% of pregnant women ages fifteen to seventeen reported illicit drug use the previous month, compared with just 2.1% of pregnant women ages twenty-six to forty-four. Among pregnant women, more African-Americans (7.8%) than whites (4.2%) and Hispanics (5%) reported using illicit drugs the previous month.

CHILDREN AT ILLICIT DRUG LABS. The rapid growth of methamphetamine use in the United States has resulted

in the establishment of clandestine methamphetamine laboratories (meth labs) in many places. Traditionally, large-scale operations, particularly in California and Mexico, produced large quantities of drugs, which were then distributed throughout various areas in the country. With more demand for methamphetamines, many small-scale businesses have started operating. Because meth-amphetamines can be produced almost anywhere using readily available ingredients, nearly anyone can set up a temporary laboratory, make a batch of drugs, then dismantle the apparatus. Authorities have found makeshift laboratories in places inhabited or visited by children, including houses, apartments, mobile homes, motel rooms, and storage lockers.

As more children are found living in or visiting home-based meth labs, child protection personnel have to deal with those children who have been exposed not only to potentially abusive people associated with the production of methamphetamines but also to such

TABLE 3.3

Children involved in methamphetamine lab incidents by selected demographics, 2000–02

Year	Number of meth lab-related incidents	Number of children					
		Present	Residing in seized meth labs[a]	Affected[b]	Exposed to toxic chemicals[c]	Taken into protective custody	Injured or killed
2002	15,353	2,077	2,023	3,167	1,373	1,026	26 injured, 2 killed
2001	13,270	2,191	976	2,191	788	778	14 injured
2000	8,971	1,803	216	1,803	345	353	12 injured, 3 killed

[a]Children included in this group were not necessarily present at the time of seizure.

[b]Includes children who were residing at the labs but not necessarily present at the time of seizure and children who were visiting the site; data for 2000 and 2001 may not show all children affected.

[c]Includes children who were residing at the labs but not necessarily present at the time of seizure.

SOURCE: Karen Swetlow, "Children Involved in Methamphetamine Lab-Related Incidents in the United States," in *Children at Clandestine Methamphetamine Labs: Helping Meth's Youngest Victims*, U.S. Department of Justice, Office of Justice Programs, Office for Victims of Crimes, June 2003, http://ojp.usdoj.gov/ovc/publications/bulletins/children/197590.pdf (accessed August 29, 2006)

dangers as fire and explosions. Melinda Hohman, Rhonda Oliver, and Wendy Wright report in "Methamphetamine Abuse and Manufacture: The Child Welfare Response" (*Social Work*, July 2004) that hazardous living conditions include unsafe electrical equipment, chemical ingredients that can cause respiratory distress and possibly long-term effects such as liver and kidney disease and cancers, syringes, and the presence of firearms and pornography. Police find meth homes with defective plumbing, rodent and insect infestation, and without heating or cooling. Children living in meth labs are also likely to be victims of severe neglect and physical and sexual abuse. A report by the El Paso Intelligence Center, a collaborative effort of more than fifteen federal and state agencies that track drug movement and immigration, shows that thousands of children were living in or visiting meth labs that were seized by law enforcement nationwide from 2000 to 2002. In 2002 more than one thousand children, or about half of the children present during lab-related incidents, were taken into protective custody. (See Table 3.3.)

Poverty and Unemployment

Even though NIS-3 finds a correlation between family income and child abuse and neglect, most experts agree that the connection between poverty and maltreatment is not easily explained. According to "The Extent and Consequences of Child Maltreatment" (*Protecting Children from Abuse and Neglect*, Spring 1998), Diana J. English finds that the stress that comes with poverty may predispose the parents to use corporal (physical) punishment, which may lead to physical abuse. English notes effects of poverty, such as stress, may influence other risk factors, including depression, substance abuse, and domestic violence. These risk factors, in turn, may predispose the parents to violent behavior toward their children.

Lawrence M. Berger argues in "Income, Family Characteristics, and Physical Violence toward Children" (*Child Abuse and Neglect*, February 2005) that several family factors make abuse of children more likely. He finds that in both single-parent and two-parent families, depression, maternal alcohol consumption, and a history of family violence put children at risk for abuse. Low income was significantly related to violence toward children, but only in single-parent families.

In *Depression, Substance Abuse, and Domestic Violence: Little Is Known about Co-occurrence and Combined Effects on Low-Income Families*, June 2004), Sharmila Lawrence, Michelle Chau, and Mary Clare Lennon show that the problems of depression, substance abuse, and domestic violence are interrelated and that these problems are more likely to be prevalent among low-income families. They note that federally funded and community-based programs, such as Early Head Start, which are designed to help low-income parents and their infants and toddlers, recognize the connection between poverty and parental and child well-being.

Violent Families

Child abuse is sometimes a reflection of other forms of severe family conflict. Violence in one aspect of family life often flows into other aspects. Straus and Smith find that parents who are in constant conflict are also more likely to abuse their children. They measured the level of husband-wife conflict over such issues as money, sex, social activities, housekeeping, and children. The child abuse rate for fathers involved in high marital conflict was thirteen per one hundred children, compared with 7.4 per one hundred children for other men. Mothers in high-conflict relationships reported an even higher child abuse rate: 13.6 per one hundred children versus eight per one hundred children among mothers in low-conflict homes.

Husbands and wives sometimes use verbal aggression to deal with their conflicts. Straus and Gelles find in their 1985 National Family Violence Resurvey that spouses who verbally attack each other are also more likely to abuse their children. Among verbally aggressive husbands, the child abuse rate was 11.2 per one hundred children, compared with 4.9 per one hundred children for other husbands. Verbally aggressive wives had a child abuse rate of 12.3 per one hundred children, compared with 5.3 per one hundred children for other wives. Straus and Smith believe that verbal attacks between spouses do not clear the air or resolve things but rather tend to both mask the reason for the dispute and create further conflict. The resulting additional tension makes it even harder to resolve the original source of conflict.

Parents who verbally abuse their children are also more likely to physically abuse their children. Respondents to Straus and Gelles's 1975 National Family Violence Survey who verbally abused their children reported a child abuse rate six times that of other parents (twenty-one per one hundred children versus 3.6 per one hundred children). The 1985 survey finds that verbally abusive mothers physically abused their children about nine times more than other mothers (16.3 per one hundred children versus 1.8 per one hundred children). Fathers who were verbally aggressive toward their children physically abused the children more than three times as much as other fathers (14.3 per one hundred children versus 4.2 per one hundred children).

SPOUSAL PHYSICAL AGGRESSION AND CHILD ABUSE. Straus and Smith report that one of the most distinct findings of the National Family Violence Resurvey is that violence in one family relationship is frequently associated with violence in other family relationships. In families in which the husband struck his wife, the child abuse rate was much higher (22.3 per one hundred children) than in other families (eight per one hundred children). Similarly, in families in which the wife hit the husband, the child abuse rate was also considerably higher (22.9 per one hundred children) than in families in which the wife did not hit the husband (9.2 per one hundred children).

Janet Carter, in *Domestic Violence, Child Abuse, and Youth Violence: Strategies for Prevention and Early Intervention* (2005, http://www.mincava.umn.edu/link/documents/fvpf2/fvpf2.shtml), reviews the research and finds that domestic violence and child abuse often occur in the same families. One study finds that 50% of the men who regularly assaulted their wives also assaulted their children; another finds that 55% of mothers of abused children have also been assaulted by their partners.

Although researchers and policy makers have studied the plight of battered women since the 1970s, no national data about children living in violent homes have ever been collected. The U.S. Department of Justice's report *Intimate Partner Violence, 1993–2001* (February 2003, http://www.ojp.usdoj.gov/bjs/pub/pdf/ipv01.pdf) by Callie Marie Rennison shows that in 2001, 588,490 women (85%, versus 103,220 men, or 15%) were victims of abuse by an intimate partner. (See Table 3.4.) The National Child Abuse and

TABLE 3.4

Violence by intimate partners, by type of crime and by gender of victims, 2001

	Intimate partner violence					
	Total		Female		Male	
	Number	Rate per 1,000 persons	Number	Rate per 1,000 females	Number	Rate per 1,000 males
Overall violent crime	**691,710**	**3.0**	**588,490**	**5.0**	**103,220**	**0.9**
Rape/sexual assault	41,740	0.2	41,740	0.4	—	—
Robbery	60,630	0.3	44,060	0.4	16,570	0.1
Aggravated assault	117,480	0.5	81,140	0.7	36,350	0.3
Simple assault	471,860	2.1	421,550	3.6	50,310	0.5

—Based on 10 or fewer sample cases.
Note: Categories used for "intimate" include spouses, former spouses, boyfriends, and girlfriends (including partners in homosexual relationships).

SOURCE: Callie Marie Rennison, "Table 1. Violence by Intimate Partners, by Type of Crime and Gender of Victims, 2001," in *Intimate Partner Violence, 1993–2001*, U.S. Department of Justice, Office of Justice Programs, Bureau of Justice Statistics, February 2003, http://www.ojp.usdoj.gov/bjs/pub/pdf/ipv01.pdf (accessed June 20, 2006)

Neglect Data System's *Child Maltreatment 2004* (2006, http://www.acf.hhs.gov/programs/cb/pubs/cm04/cm04.pdf) reports that an estimated 872,000 children were victims of child maltreatment in 2004. Experts believe that many of these abused children and battered women come from the same homes.

Some government data illustrate that children indeed live in households where domestic violence among adults occurs. Callie Marie Rennison and Sarah Welchans report in the U.S. Department of Justice's *Intimate Partner Violence* (July 2000, http://www.ojp.usdoj.gov/bjs/pub/pdf/ipv.pdf) that between 1993 and 1998 children younger than age twelve lived in 43% of households known to have intimate partner violence. In *Safe from the Start: Taking Action on Children Exposed to Violence* (November 2000, http://www.ncjrs.gov/pdffiles1/ojjdp/182789.pdf), the U.S. Department of Justice further reports that as many as half a million children may be present in homes where police make domestic violence arrests.

To determine the relationship among family stress, partner violence, caretaker distress, and child abuse, Suzanne Salzinger et al., in "Effects of Partner Violence and Physical Child Abuse in Child Behavior: A Study of Abused and Comparison Children" (*Journal of Family Violence*, March 2002), compared a sample of one hundred New York City children from grades four to six who experienced physical abuse with a control group of one hundred nonabused children. They questioned each caretaker concerning stressful events that had occurred in their family during the lifetime of the subject child. These stress factors included, among other things, separation or divorce, drug abuse, alcohol abuse, deaths, serious illness in the past year, and job loss in the past year. Salzinger et al. find that in households where partner violence and child maltreatment both occurred, the children suffered physical aggression from both the perpetrator and the victim. In addition, in these households the mothers who were typically the caretakers reported that they were more likely than the fathers to physically abuse the children. Interestingly, Salzinger et al. find that family stress, not partner violence, was responsible for caretaker distress, which in turn increased the risk for child abuse.

Even if children themselves are not battered, witnessing assaults on a mother is damaging to children. According to Jeffrey L. Edleson in *Should Childhood Exposure to Adult Domestic Violence Be Defined as Child Maltreatment under the Law?* (2004, http://www.mincava. umn.edu/link/documents/shouldch/shouldch.shtml), at least one state has defined exposure to domestic violence as a form of child maltreatment. In "Longitudinal Investigation of the Relationship among Maternal Victimization, Depressive Symptoms, Social Support, and Children's Behavior and Development" (*Journal of Interpersonal Violence*, December 2005), Catherine Koverola et al. find that maternal victimization is related to child behavior problems at age four and persists to at least age eight.

MOTHERS, FATHERS, AND SIBLINGS

A family's dynamics, stress levels, and overall situation are significant risk factors for child maltreatment, but there are other considerations as well. Many researchers have investigated how the background and temperament of the individual caregivers within a family influence the likelihood of child abuse.

Maltreatment by Mothers

Straus and Smith find that women are as likely, if not more likely, as men to abuse their children. They believe child abuse by women can be explained in terms of social factors rather than in psychological factors. Women are more likely to abuse their children because they are more likely to have much greater responsibility for raising the children, which means that they are more exposed to the trials and frustrations of child rearing.

Women spend more "time at risk" while tending to their children. "Time at risk" refers to the time a potential abuser spends with the victim. This would apply to any form of domestic violence, such as spousal abuse and elder abuse. For example, elderly people are more likely to experience abuse from each other, not from a caregiver, if one is present. This is not because elderly couples are more violent than caregivers, but because they spend more time with each other.

To determine the connection between psychological risk factors for child maltreatment and chronic maltreatment, Louise S. Ethier, Germain Couture, and Carl Lacharité, in "Risk Factors Associated with the Chronicity of High Potential for Child Abuse and Neglect" (*Journal of Family Violence*, February 2004), conducted interviews and tests of a group of abusive mothers in Quebec, Canada, on three separate occasions: during the initial recruitment for an intervention program; two years later at the end of the program; and four years after the initial recruitment as a follow-up. Fifty-six mothers were evaluated: twenty-one mothers whose files at the social agencies had been closed for at least four months (transitory problems group); and thirty-five mothers who were still abusive (chronic group). The risk factors were categorized into two general groups: the mother's history; and her characteristics as an adult. The mother's history included placement in foster care, childhood sexual abuse, running away from home in her teens, breakups with parental relationships, parental unavailability, neglect, and physical violence. The mother's adult characteristics included family unemployment, limited social support, past intimate partner violence, low level of intellectual functioning, low level of education, and high numbers of children and partners.

Ethier, Couture, and Lacharité find that mothers who reported a history of childhood sexual abuse, placement in foster care, and running away from home during adolescence were more likely to have chronic problems of child maltreatment. Overall, mothers exhibiting more than eight risk factors had about four times the risk for chronic child maltreatment. Those with a history of childhood sexual abuse had 3.75 times more risk of having chronic child maltreatment than those without this risk factor. The risk for chronic child maltreatment was 3.57 times greater for a childhood history of placement in foster care and 3.02 times greater for a history of running away from home in adolescence. Ethier, Couture, and Lacharité find that the following risk factors predisposed mothers to chronic child maltreatment: childhood neglect (0.58 times more likely than those without this risk factor), physical violence (0.69 times), and unavailability of and breakup with parental figures (0.92 and 1.54 times, respectively). Ethier, Couture, and Lacharité conclude that traumatic experiences of childhood sexual abuse (77.8% of mothers in the study), placement in foster care (80%), and running away from home during adolescence (77.3%) had adverse effects on the mothers' ability to parent their children.

Results also show that mothers with a low level of intelligence were 2.75 times more at risk for chronic child maltreatment. A total of 78.6% of the mothers showed such risk. However, Ethier, Couture, and Lacharité caution that some studies find that unless a parent's intelligence quotient (IQ) is below sixty, his or her low level of intelligence does not impair parenting abilities. Still other studies say IQ has nothing to do with parental competence. Mothers with a large family are found to have 3.13 times more risk for chronic maltreatment, with 80% of the sample displaying such risk.

In "Battered Mothers Who Physically Abuse Their Children" (*Journal of Interpersonal Violence*, August 2004), Carol Coohey compares mothers who were battered and who physically abused their children with one group of mothers who were neither battered nor who physically abused their children, another group of mothers who were battered but who did not physically abuse their children, and another group of mothers who were not battered but who did physically abuse their children. Coohey finds that women who were assaulted by their own mothers as children—not women who were battered by their partners—were the most likely to abuse their own children.

Maltreatment by Fathers

Katreena L. Scott and Claire V. Crooks, in "Effecting Change in Maltreating Fathers: Critical Principles for Intervention Planning" (*Clinical Psychology: Science and Practice*, Spring 2004), note that, although some fathers are perpetrators of child maltreatment, little research has been done on abusive fathers. According to Scott and Crooks, for interventions services to be effective, it is important to know the characteristics of abusive fathers. Abusive fathers tend to be controlling of their children. Being self-centered, they demand respect and unconditional love. They are insecure and are constantly looking for signs of defiance or disrespect. An abusive father may feel that a child has more power than he does and may misinterpret a child's action as misbehavior. He therefore inflicts physical abuse to regain control. An abusive father has a sense of entitlement, expecting his children to do as he says. Scott and Crooks point out that sexual abuse may result from the father's sense of entitlement.

An abusive father's involvement with his children is usually based on his own needs, focusing on activities that he likes instead of what the children may want to do. However, his interest in his children may come and go, depending on his emotional state. Some fathers maltreat their children because they believe in the stereotypical role of fathers as disciplinarians. Some also feel that they have to show others that they are doing a good job as parents. Refusing to acknowledge that they may be having a tough time as parents, they take out their frustrations on the children.

CHILD NEGLECT. One area of interest in the subject of child maltreatment involves the link between father involvement and child neglect. Howard Dubowitz et al., in "Fathers and Child Neglect" (*Archives of Pediatrics and Adolescent Medicine*, February 2000), examine this link in the first study of its kind. They find an overall range of 11% to 30% of child neglect in the households. The nature of father involvement, however, not the absence of the father, was associated with neglect. Dubo-

witz et al. find that less child neglect was associated with the following: a longer duration of father involvement in the child's life, the positive feelings the father had about his parenting skills, the father's greater involvement with household chores, and the father's less involvement with child care. Interestingly, the father's greater involvement with child care resulted in more child neglect. Dubowitz et al. explain that other studies show that fathers tend to be more involved in child care when the mothers are unavailable.

Maltreatment by Siblings

In *What Parents Need to Know about Sibling Abuse: Breaking the Cycle of Violence* (2002), Vernon R. Wiehe explores the reasons siblings hurt each other. Sibling abuse may stem from a desire to control another person to take advantage of that person. The sibling in control typically does not know how to empathize (be aware and sensitive to the feelings of others). Wiehe notes the reason most often given for sibling abuse is that an older sibling has been put in charge of younger siblings. Some parents may expect too much from older children, relegating parental responsibilities to them. Even if an older brother or sister is capable of babysitting his or her younger siblings, he or she lacks the knowledge or skills to parent. Wiehe also points out that sibling abuse may be a learned behavior. Children who grow up in households where they see their parents abusing each other or are the recipients of such abuse may in turn use aggression toward one another. Children may also learn abusive behavior from television programs, movies, videos, and computer games.

In "Sibling Abuse" (*Understanding Family Violence: Treating and Preventing Partner, Child, Sibling, and Elder Abuse*, 1998), Wiehe observes that abusive behavior between brothers and sisters is often considered sibling rivalry and is therefore not covered under mandatory reporting of abuse. Wiehe conducted a nationwide survey of survivors of sibling abuse who had sought professional counseling for problems resulting from physical, emotional, and sexual abuse by a brother or sister. The respondents were generally victims of more than one type of abuse—71% reported being physically, emotionally, and sexually abused. An additional 7% indicated being just emotionally abused, pushing the total of emotionally abused victims to 78%.

CONSEQUENCES OF CHILDHOOD MALTREATMENT
Cycle of Violence

In "Childhood Victimization: Early Adversity, Later Psychopathology" (*National Institute of Justice Journal*, January 2000), one of the most detailed longitudinal studies of the consequences of childhood maltreatment, Cathy Spatz Widom focuses on 908 children in a midwestern metropolitan area who were six to eleven years

TABLE 3.5

Childhood victimization and later criminality, 1986

	Abuse/neglect group (676) %	Control group (520) %
Arrest as juvenile	31.2	19.0
Arrest as adult	48.4	36.2
Arrest as juvenile or adult for any crime	56.5	42.5
Arrest as juvenile or adult for any violent crime	21.0	15.6

Note: Numbers in parentheses are numbers of cases.

SOURCE: Cathy Spatz Widom, "Table 1. Childhood Victimization and Later Criminality," in "Childhood Victimization: Early Adversity, Later Psychopathology," *National Institute of Justice Journal*, no. 242, January 2000, http://www.ncjrs.gov/pdffiles1/jr000242b.pdf (accessed July 24, 2006)

TABLE 3.6

Childhood victimization and later psychopathology, 1989

	Abuse/neglect group (676) %	Control group (520) %
Suicide attempt	18.8	7.7
Antisocial personality disorder	18.4	11.2
Alcohol abuse/dependence	54.5	51.0

Notes: Numbers in parentheses are numbers of cases. Diagnoses of antisocial personality disorder and alcohol abuse/dependence were determined by using the National Institute of Mental Health DIS-III-R diagnostic interview.

SOURCE: Cathy Spatz Widom, "Table 2. Childhood Victimization and Later Psychopathology," in "Childhood Victimization: Early Adversity, Later Psychopathology," *National Institute of Justice Journal*, no. 242, January 2000, http://www.ncjrs.gov/pdffiles1/jr000242b.pdf (accessed July 24, 2006)

TABLE 3.7

Childhood victimization and later psychopathology by gender, 1989

	Abuse/neglect group %	Control group %
Females	(338)	(224)
Suicide attempt	24.3	8.6
Antisocial personality disorder	9.8	4.9
Alcohol abuse/dependence	43.8	32.8
Males	(338)	(276)
Suicide attempt	13.4	6.9
Antisocial personality disorder	27.0	16.7
Alcohol abuse/dependence	64.4	67.0

Note: Numbers in parentheses are numbers of cases.

SOURCE: Cathy Spatz Widom, "Table 3. Childhood Victimization and Later Psychopathology, by Gender," in "Childhood Victimization: Early Adversity, Later Psychopathology," *National Institute of Justice Journal*, no. 242, January 2000, http://www.ncjrs.gov/pdffiles1/jr000242b.pdf (accessed July 24, 2006)

old when they were maltreated (between 1967 and 1971). A control group of 667 children with no history of childhood maltreatment was used for comparison. Each group has about two-thirds white and one-third African-American individuals and about an equal number of males and females. Widom examined the long-term consequences of childhood maltreatment on the subjects' intellectual, behavioral, social, and psychological development. When the two groups were interviewed for the study, they had a median age (half were older, half were younger) of about twenty-nine years.

Widom is widely known for her work on the "cycle of violence." The cycle of violence theory suggests that childhood physical abuse increases the likelihood of arrest and of committing violent crime during the victims' later years. Widom finds that, although a large proportion of maltreated children did not become juvenile delinquents or criminals, those who suffered childhood abuse or neglect were more likely than those with no reported maltreatment to be arrested as juveniles (31.2% versus 19%) and as adults (48.4% versus 36.2%) when surveyed in 1986. The maltreated victims (21%) were also more likely than those with no reported childhood maltreatment history (15.6%) to be arrested for a violent crime during their teen years or adulthood. (See Table 3.5.)

Widom notes that the victims' later psychopathology (psychological disorders resulting from the childhood maltreatment) manifested itself in suicide attempts, antisocial personality, and alcohol abuse and/or dependence. When surveyed in 1989, maltreatment victims were more likely than the control individuals to report having attempted suicide (18.8% versus 7.7%) and having manifested antisocial personality disorder (18.4% versus 11.2%). Both groups, however, did not differ much in the rates of alcohol abuse and/or dependence (54.5% for the abused or neglected group and 51% for the control group). (See Table 3.6.) In "Adult Psychopathology and Intimate Partner Violence among Survivors of Childhood Maltreatment" (*Journal of Interpersonal Violence*, October 2004), Ariel J. Lang et al. conducted research that also supports the association between childhood maltreatment and psychopathology in adulthood.

Widom finds that gender plays a role in the development of psychological disorders in adolescence and adulthood. In 1989 females (24.3%) with a history of childhood maltreatment reported being more likely to attempt suicide, compared with their male counterparts (13.4%). However, a significantly larger percentage of male victims (27%) than female victims (9.8%) developed an antisocial personality disorder. Although both male maltreated (64.4%) and control subjects (67%) had similar proportions of alcohol abuse or dependence, females who experienced abuse or neglect were more likely than the control group to have alcohol problems (43.8% versus 32.8%). (See Table 3.7.)

Another phase of Widom's cycle of violence research was conducted when the maltreated and control

TABLE 3.8

Involvement in criminality by race, 1994

[In percent]

Type of arrest	Abused and neglected group (sample size=900)	Comparison group (sample size=667)
Juvenile		
Black	40.6	20.9
White	21.8	15.2
Adult		
Black	59.8	43.6
White	33.8	26.6
Violent crime		
Black	34.2	21.8
White	11.0	9.7

SOURCE: Cathy S. Widom and Michael G. Maxfield, "Exhibit 4. Involvement in Criminality by Race, in Percent," in *Research in Brief: An Update on the "Cycle of Violence,"* U.S. Department of Justice, Office of Justice Programs, National Institute of Justice, February 2001, http://www.ncjrs.gov/pdffiles1/nij/184894.pdf (accessed August 29, 2006)

TABLE 3.9

Victims of child abuse arrested for violent crimes in later years, by type of abuse, 1994

Abuse group	Number of subjects	Percentage arrested for violent offense
Physical abuse only	76	21.1
Neglect only	609	20.2
Sexual abuse only	125	8.8
Mixed	98	14.3
Control	667	13.9

SOURCE: Cathy S. Widom and Michael G. Maxfield, "Exhibit 5. Does Only Violence Beget Violence?" in *Research in Brief: An Update on the "Cycle of Violence,"* U.S. Department of Justice, Office of Justice Programs, National Institute of Justice, February 2001, http://www.ncjrs.gov/pdffiles1/nij/184894.pdf (accessed August 29, 2006)

groups had a median age of 32.5 years. Aside from collecting arrest records from federal, state, and local law enforcement, Cathy S. Widom and Michael G. Maxfield, in *An Update on the "Cycle of Violence"* (February 2001, http://www.ncjrs.gov/pdffiles1/nij/184894.pdf), also conducted interviews in 1994 with the subjects. Overall, Widom and Maxfield find that childhood abuse or neglect increased the likelihood of arrest in adolescence by 59% and in adulthood by 28%. Childhood maltreatment also increased the likelihood of committing a violent crime by 30%.

While earlier analysis of the maltreated group found that most of the victims did not become offenders, Widom and Maxfield's study shows that nearly half (49%) of the victims had experienced a nontraffic offense as teenagers or adults. Comparison by race shows that, whereas both white and African-American maltreated children had more arrests than the control group, there was no significant difference among whites in the maltreated (21.8%) and control (15.2%) groups. Among African-American children, however, the maltreated group had higher rates of arrests. Maltreated African-Americans were nearly twice as likely as their counterparts in the control group to be arrested as juveniles (40.6% versus 20.9%). (See Table 3.8.)

Abigail A. Fagan's research in "The Relationship between Adolescent Physical Abuse and Criminal Offending: Support for an Enduring and Generalized Cycle of Violence" (*Journal of Family Violence*, October 2005) supports the cycle of violence theory. She demonstrates that adolescents who are physically abused are more likely to commit violent and nonviolent crimes, use drugs, and batter their partners. While this relationship holds steady across racial and class backgrounds, the frequency of this behavior is moderated by family income, area in which the adolescent lives, and family structure.

Widom and Maxfield also examined the type of childhood maltreatment that might lead to violence later in life. They find that physically abused children (21.1%) were the most likely to commit a violent crime in their teen or adult years and were closely followed by those who experienced neglect (20.2%). Although their study shows that just 8.8% of children who had been sexually abused were arrested for violence, Widom and Maxfield note that the victims were mostly females, and "females less often had a record of violent offenses." (See Table 3.9.)

Jennie G. Noll suggests in "Does Childhood Sexual Abuse Set in Motion a Cycle of Violence against Women?: What We Know and What We Need to Learn" (*Journal of Interpersonal Violence*, April 2005) that sexual abuse of females, rather than resulting in criminal behavior as the girl ages, instead sets in motion a cycle of violence against women. She argues that a girl who is sexually abused as a child is more likely than her peers to be physically or sexually assaulted in adolescence. Ultimately, these women are more likely to abuse their own children than are women who were not assaulted in childhood.

The Consequences of Neglect

When most people think of child maltreatment, they think of abuse and not neglect. Furthermore, research literature and conferences dealing with child maltreatment have generally overlooked child neglect. The congressional hearings that took place before the passage of the landmark Child Abuse Prevention and Treatment Act of 1974 focused almost entirely on examples of physical abuse. Barely three pages of the hundreds recorded pertained to child neglect.

Nonetheless, every year the federal government reports a high incidence of child neglect. According to *Child Maltreatment 2004*, in 2004 more than three times as many children were victims of neglect than of physical

FIGURE 3.5

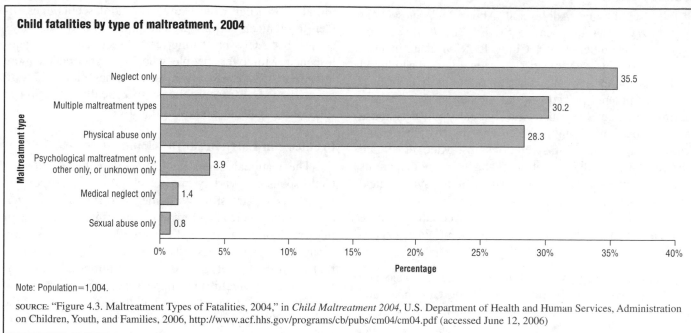

Child fatalities by type of maltreatment, 2004

Note: Population=1,004.

SOURCE: "Figure 4.3. Maltreatment Types of Fatalities, 2004," in *Child Maltreatment 2004*, U.S. Department of Health and Human Services, Administration on Children, Youth, and Families, 2006, http://www.acf.hhs.gov/programs/cb/pubs/cm04/cm04.pdf (accessed June 12, 2006)

abuse (7.4 versus 2.1 children per one thousand child population). It is important to note that these numbers pertain only to children reported to CPS, and whose cases had been substantiated. Experts believe these numbers are grossly underreported. Neglect does not necessarily leave obvious physical marks like abuse does, and it often involves infants and young children who cannot speak for themselves.

Severe neglect can have devastating consequences. For example, James M. Gaudin Jr., in "Child Neglect: Short-Term and Long-Term Outcomes" (Howard Dubowitz, ed., *Neglected Children: Research, Practice, and Policy*, 1999), reports that, compared with both nonmaltreated and physically abused children, neglected children have the worst delays in language comprehension and expression. Psychologically neglected children also score lowest in IQ tests.

Fully 35.5% of the children who died of child maltreatment in 2004 died of neglect alone. (See Figure 3.5.) Neglect can lead to death from such causes as malnourishment, lack of proper medical care, or abandonment. Emotional neglect, in its most serious form, can result in the "nonorganic failure to thrive syndrome," a condition in which a child fails to develop physically or even to survive. According to Gaudin, studies find that even with aggressive intervention the neglected child continues to deteriorate. The cooperation of the neglectful parents, which is crucial to the intervention, usually declines as the child's condition worsens. This shows that it is sometimes not that easy to change the parental attributes that have contributed to the neglect in the first place.

Maltreated Girls Who Become Offenders

In "Childhood Victimization and the Derailment of Girls and Women to the Criminal Justice System" (*Research on Women and Girls in the Justice System*, September 2000, http://www.ncjrs.gov/pdffiles1/nij/180973. pdf), Widom studied a group of girls who had experienced neglect and physical and sexual abuse from ages zero to eleven through young adulthood. Widom finds that abused and neglected girls were almost twice as likely (20%) to have been arrested as juveniles, compared with a matched control group of nonabused girls (11.4%), and almost twice as likely as the control group to be arrested as adults (28.5% versus 15.9%). Additionally, the maltreated girls were also more than twice as likely (8.2%) as the nonmaltreated girls (3.6%) to have been arrested for violent crimes. Widom notes, however, that although abused and neglected girls were at increased risk for criminal behavior, about 70% of the maltreated girls did not become criminals.

Cathy Spatz Widom, Daniel Nagin, and Peter Lambert find in "Does Childhood Victimization Alter Developmental Trajectories of Criminal Careers?" (paper presented at the annual meeting of the American Society of Criminology, Washington, DC, November 1998) that 8% of the maltreated girls developed antisocial and criminal lifestyles that carried over to adulthood. Among this group, nearly two out of five (38%) had been arrested for status offenses as juveniles, but a larger percentage had been arrested for violence (46%) and property crimes (54%). Almost another third (32%) had been arrested for drug crimes. None of the girls in the control group exhibited these tendencies.

Dating Violence

In "Child and Adolescent Abuse and Subsequent Victimization: A Prospective Study" (*Child Abuse and Neglect*, December 2005), Cindy L. Rich et al. investigate the possible relationship between abuse in childhood and abuse in adolescence. They find that early emotional abuse by parents put adolescent women at risk for later dating violence. They also find that early physical abuse by a father put female adolescents at risk for sexual violence in their dating relationships. Rich et al. are careful to note that emotional abuse by both parents was actually more predictive of subsequent psychological symptoms than was physical or sexual abuse. They write, "Thus, subtler forms of abuse can be equally or more traumatic and set the stage for subsequent abuse experiences."

On the contrary, Marie-Hélène Gagné, F. Lavoie, and M. Hebert find in "Victimization during Childhood and Revictimization in Dating Relationships in Adolescent Girls" (*Child Abuse and Neglect*, October 2005) that extrafamilial experiences with violence are a more important risk factor for subsequent dating violence than is abuse experienced at the hands of family members. In particular, young girls' experiences with violent or victimized peers, verbal sexual harassment by male peers, and previous dating violence all significantly contributed to the risk of subsequent dating violence.

Illicit Drug Use by Abused Children

It is recognized that illicit drug use is associated with behaviors leading to violence, sexually transmitted diseases, other health problems, and crime. In "Childhood Abuse, Neglect, and Household Dysfunction and the Risk of Illicit Drug Use: The Adverse Childhood Experiences Study" (*Pediatrics*, March 2003), Shanta R. Dube et al. study a population of 8,613 adult members of a health plan who filled out a questionnaire relating to their adverse childhood experiences (ACEs) during the first eighteen years of life. The intent of Dube et al.'s study was to determine the effects of related ACEs on various health outcomes and behaviors. ACEs included physical, emotional, or sexual abuse; physical or emotional neglect; and household dysfunction, such as a battered mother, parental separation or divorce, mental illness at home, substance abuse in the home, or an incarcerated household member.

Dube et al. find that each ACE increased two to four times the likelihood of initiation to illicit drug use by age fourteen and increased the risk of drug use into adulthood. They note that several ACEs usually occur together. Their cumulative effect on illicit drug use is strongest during early adolescence because the young teen has just been through those painful experiences and is at the same time undergoing the turmoil characteristic of that age group.

ACEs were also found to increase the likelihood of initiation to illicit drug use among adolescents ages fifteen to eighteen and people age nineteen and over. This shows that ACEs have long-term effects past early adolescence. Moreover, people who had experienced more than five ACEs were seven to ten times more likely to have illicit drug use problems, specifically addiction to illicit drugs and intravenous drug use.

Problems in Early Brain Development

The National Scientific Council on the Developing Child sponsors a variety of research projects that focus on the effects of "stressful environments" on children's developing brains. Increasing research shows that child abuse or neglect during infancy and early childhood affects early brain development ("Excessive Stress Disrupts the Architecture of the Developing Brain," Summer 2005, http://www.developingchild.net/papers/excessive_stress.pdf; and Dorian Friedman, "Stress and the Architecture of the Brain," 2005, http://www.developingchild.net/papers/stress_article.pdf).

Brain development, or learning, is the process of creating connections among neurons in the brain, called synapses. Neurons, or nerve cells, send signals to one another through synapses, which in turn form the neuronal pathways that enable the brain to respond to specific environments. An infant is born with very few synapses formed. These include those responsible for breathing, eating, and sleeping. During the early years of life the brain develops synapses at a fast rate. Scientists find that repeated experiences strengthen the neuronal pathways, making them sensitive to similar experiences that may occur later on in life. Unfortunately, if these early life experiences are of a negative nature, the development of the brain may be impaired. For example, if an infant who cries for attention constantly gets ignored, his or her brain creates the neuronal pathway that enables him or her to cope with being ignored. If the infant continually fails to get the attention he or she craves, the brain strengthens that same neuronal pathway.

Childhood abuse or neglect has long-term consequences on brain development. When children suffer abuse or neglect, their brains are preoccupied with reacting to the chronic stress. As the brain builds and strengthens neuronal pathways involved with survival, it fails to develop social and cognitive skills. Later on in life, maltreatment victims may not know how to react to kindness and nurturing because the brain has no memory of how to respond to those new experiences. They may also have learning difficulties because the brain has focused solely on the body's survival so that the thinking processes may not have been developed or may have been impaired.

Hyperarousal is another consequence of maltreatment on brain development. During the state of hyperarousal, the brain is always attuned to what it perceives as a threatening situation. The brain has "learned" that the world is a dangerous place and that it has to be constantly on the alert. The victim experiences extreme anxiety toward any perceived threat, or he or she may use aggression to control the situation. For example, children who have been physically abused may start a fight just so they can control the conflict and be able to choose their adversary. Males and older children are more likely to exhibit hyperarousal. As Friedman writes, "Childhood adversity shapes a stress system that has trouble flipping the 'off' switch."

Researchers find that, whereas males and older children tend to suffer from hyperarousal, younger children and females are more likely to show dissociation. In the dissociative state victims disconnect themselves from the negative experience. By "pretending" not to be there, their bodies and minds do not react to the abusive experience.

Childhood maltreatment can result in the disruption of the attachment process, which refers to the development of healthy emotional relationships with others. Under normal circumstances the first relationship that infants develop is with their caregivers. Such relationships form the basis for future emotional connections. In maltreated children the attachment process may not be fully developed, resulting in the inability to know oneself as well as to put oneself in another's position.

WHEN CHILDREN DIE FROM MALTREATMENT

Child fatality is the most severe result of abuse and neglect. In 2004 CPS and other state agencies, including coroners' offices and fatality review boards, reported an estimated 1,387 deaths from child maltreatment. The 2004 national fatality rate was 2.03 per one hundred thousand children in the general population. Indiana reported the highest rate (4.81 per one hundred thousand), followed by the District of Columbia (4.56 per one hundred thousand). New Hampshire and Vermont were the only two states that reported no deaths resulting from child maltreatment that year. (See Table 3.10.)

In 2004 children three years old and younger accounted for a majority (81%) of deaths. Almost half (45%) of the deaths were of children less than one year old. (See Figure 3.6.) *Child Maltreatment 2004* reports that infant boys had a fatality rate of eighteen per one hundred thousand boys of the same age and infant girls had a fatality rate of seventeen per one hundred thousand girls of the same age. Young children are more likely to be victims of child fatalities because of their small size, their dependency on their caregivers, and their inability to defend themselves.

TABLE 3.10

Child fatalities by state, 2004

[Per 100,000 children]

State	Child population	Child file and SDC fatalities	Agency file fatalities	Total child fatalities	Fatalities per 100,000 children
Alabama	1,094,533	11		11	1.00
Alaska					
Arizona	1,547,260	23	0	23	1.49
Arkansas	676,550	12		12	1.77
California	9,596,463		140	140	1.46
Colorado	1,178,889	35		35	2.97
Connecticut	838,788	9		9	1.07
Delaware	193,506	0	1	1	0.52
District of Columbia	109,547	5	0	5	4.56
Florida	4,003,290	86	0	86	2.15
Georgia	2,332,567	98		98	4.20
Hawaii	298,693	6		6	2.01
Idaho	372,411	4		4	1.07
Illinois	3,238,150	85	0	85	2.62
Indiana	1,600,295	77		77	4.81
Iowa	680,437	8	0	8	1.18
Kansas	683,491	8	0	8	1.17
Kentucky	980,187	38	0	38	3.88
Louisiana	1,164,961	18		18	1.55
Maine	282,129	0	2	2	0.71
Maryland	1,394,808		28	28	2.01
Massachusetts	1,464,189		12	12	0.82
Michigan					
Minnesota	1,240,280	10	0	10	0.81
Mississippi	749,569	19	0	19	2.53
Missouri	1,384,542	48		48	3.47
Montana	208,093	0	2	2	0.96
Nebraska	434,566	7	4	11	2.53
Nevada	603,596	2		2	0.33
New Hampshire	304,994		0	0	0.00
New Jersey	2,156,059	29	5	34	1.58
New Mexico	492,287	0	8	8	1.63
New York	4,572,363	71		71	1.55
North Carolina					
North Dakota	138,955	0		0	0.00
Ohio	2,779,212	61		61	2.19
Oklahoma	859,870	39	0	39	4.54
Oregon	852,357	8		8	0.94
Pennsylvania	2,837,009	38	4	42	1.48
Rhode Island	243,813	3	0	3	1.23
South Carolina	1,024,700	13	8	21	2.05
South Dakota	190,874	3		3	1.57
Tennessee	1,391,289	15		15	1.08
Texas	6,266,779	212	0	212	3.38
Utah	740,114	10	0	10	1.35
Vermont	134,894	0	0	0	0.00
Virginia	1,804,900		28	28	1.55
Washington	1,486,020		7	7	0.47
West Virginia	384,641	6	6	12	3.12
Wisconsin	1,307,986	11		11	0.84
Wyoming	116,932	4		4	3.42
Total	**68,437,838**	**1,132**	**255**	**1,387**	
Weighted rate					**2.03**
Number reporting	**48**	**42**	**29**	**48**	**48**

SOURCE: "Table 4.1. Child Fatalities, 2004," in *Child Maltreatment 2004*, U.S. Department of Health and Human Services, Administration on Children, Youth, and Families, 2006, http://www.acf.hhs.gov/programs/cb/pubs/cm04/cm04.pdf (accessed July 8, 2006)

According to *Child Maltreatment 2004*, neglect alone was responsible for more than one-third (35.5%) of maltreatment deaths. More than one-quarter (28.3%) of fatalities resulted from physical abuse. Another 30.2% of fatalities resulted from a combination of maltreatment

FIGURE 3.6

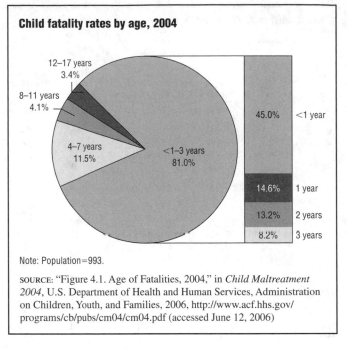

Child fatality rates by age, 2004

Note: Population=993.

SOURCE: "Figure 4.1. Age of Fatalities, 2004," in *Child Maltreatment 2004*, U.S. Department of Health and Human Services, Administration on Children, Youth, and Families, 2006, http://www.acf.hhs.gov/programs/cb/pubs/cm04/cm04.pdf (accessed June 12, 2006)

FIGURE 3.7

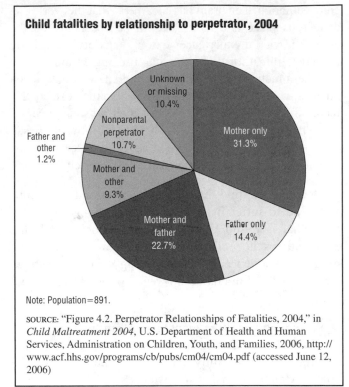

Child fatalities by relationship to perpetrator, 2004

Note: Population=891.

SOURCE: "Figure 4.2. Perpetrator Relationships of Fatalities, 2004," in *Child Maltreatment 2004*, U.S. Department of Health and Human Services, Administration on Children, Youth, and Families, 2006, http://www.acf.hhs.gov/programs/cb/pubs/cm04/cm04.pdf (accessed June 12, 2006)

types. The report also provides data on the victims' prior contact with CPS agencies. More than one in ten (12.4%) of the victims' families had received family preservation services during the five years before the deaths occurred; 1.7% had been in foster care and were reunited with their families in the past five years.

Perpetrators of Fatalities

Child Maltreatment 2004 shows that roughly three out of five maltreatment deaths (68.4%) were inflicted by one or both parents of the victims. Mothers alone accounted for about one-third (31.3%) of the deaths, whereas fathers were the perpetrators in 14.4% of the deaths. In about one-fifth (22.7%) of cases, both parents were responsible for causing their children's death. (See Figure 3.7.)

Family Composition and Maltreatment Deaths

In "Household Composition and Risk of Fatal Child Maltreatment" (*Pediatrics*, April 2002), Michael N. Stiffman et al. examined all information related to Missouri-resident children under five years old who died in that state within a three-year period to determine whether family composition might be a risk factor for fatal child maltreatment. They used the comprehensive data of child deaths (birth through age seventeen) collected by the Missouri Child Fatality Review Panel (CFRP) system between 1992 and 1994. The CFRP data contained information on all household members and their relationship to the deceased child. For comparison, Stiffman et al. used a control group consisting of children under age five who had died of natural causes. Of the 291 injury deaths that were examined, 175 children (60%) were determined to have died of maltreatment. Fifty-five (31%) of the deaths

resulted from injury caused by a parent or other caregiver. Of this group, thirty-nine of the children died from being shaken, hit, or dropped. Eleven children died from the use of physical objects, including guns. The cause of death for the remaining five children was unknown.

Stiffman et al. find that children living in households with one or more biologically unrelated adult males and boyfriends of the child's mother had the highest risk of death from maltreatment. These children were eight times more likely to die of maltreatment than children living with two biological parents with no other adults. Children residing with foster and adoptive parents, as well as with stepparents, were nearly five times as likely to suffer maltreatment deaths. Those living in households with other adult relatives present were twice as likely to die from maltreatment. However, children living with just one biological parent, with no other adult present, were not at increased risk for fatal maltreatment.

CORPORAL PUNISHMENT: ABUSE OR NOT?

Corporal Punishment by Parents

In the United States all fifty states allow parents to use corporal punishment for purposes of disciplining their children. As long as the child does not suffer injury, the parent may use objects such as belts and the more typical spanking with the hand. When states passed child abuse laws in the 1960s, provisions allowing parents to use corporal punishment helped facilitate passage of the

FIGURE 3.8

States banning corporal punishment in schools, August 2006

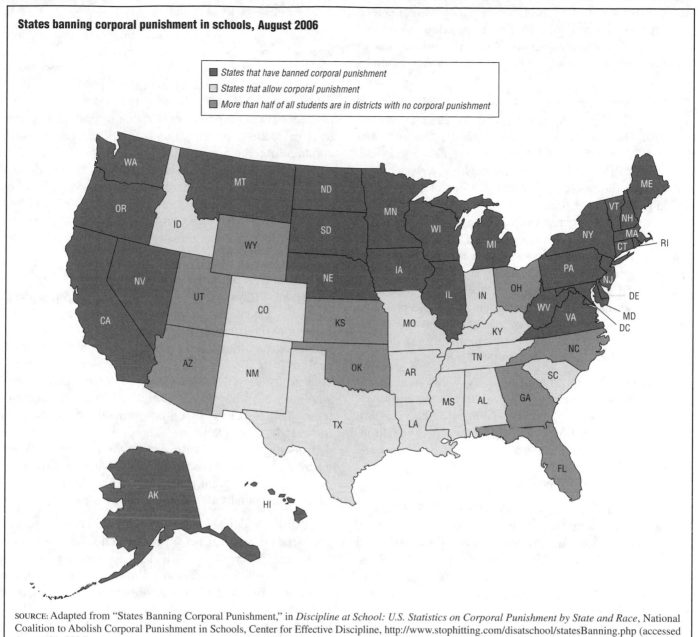

■ States that have banned corporal punishment
□ States that allow corporal punishment
■ More than half of all students are in districts with no corporal punishment

SOURCE: Adapted from "States Banning Corporal Punishment," in *Discipline at School: U.S. Statistics on Corporal Punishment by State and Race*, National Coalition to Abolish Corporal Punishment in Schools, Center for Effective Discipline, http://www.stophitting.com/disatschool/statesBanning.php (accessed August 21, 2006)

legislation. In sixteen countries around the world, corporal punishment by parents, caretakers, and teachers is completely banned. Since January 2003, Canada bans corporal punishment for children under two and over twelve years of age, as well as the use of any object, such as a paddle.

Corporal Punishment in Schools

As of 2006, among industrialized countries, only Australia (just Outback areas) and the United States allowed spanking in schools. Twenty-two U.S. states allowed corporal punishment in public schools, although in some schools parents could request that their children not be spanked. Most are southern states. (See Figure 3.8.) According to the U.S. Department of Education in "U.S. Statistics on Corporal Punishment by State and

Race" (November 2005, http://www.stophitting.com/disatschool/statesBanning.php), in 2002–03, the most recent school year for which figures are available, 301,016 children were subjected to physical punishment in public schools, a decrease of 12% from the previous year.

Prevalence and Chronicity of Corporal Punishment

In "Parents' Discipline of Young Children: Results from the National Survey of Early Childhood Health" (*Pediatrics*, June 2004), Michael Regalado et al. report on the parental use of corporal punishment for discipline in regard to the health and development of children under three years of age. Six percent of parents surveyed indicated they had spanked their children when they were four to nine months old. Twenty-nine percent spanked their children when they were ten to eighteen months old, and 64% spanked their children when they were nineteen to thirty-five months old. Frequent spankings were also administered by some parents (11%) of children ten to eighteen months old and nineteen to thirty-five months old (26%).

In another study Murray A. Straus and Julie H. Stewart, in "Corporal Punishment by American Parents: National Data on Prevalence, Chronicity, Severity, and Duration, in Relation to Child and Family Characteristics" (*Clinical Child and Family Psychology Review*, June 1999), find that more than a third (35%) of parents surveyed used corporal punishment on their infants, reaching a peak of 94% for parents of children who were three to four years old. The prevalence rate of parents using corporal punishment decreased after age five, with just over 50% of parents using it on children at age twelve, 33% at age fourteen, and 13% at age seventeen. Straus and Stewart also find that corporal punishment was more prevalent among African-Americans and parents in the low socioeconomic level. It was also more commonly inflicted on boys, by mothers, and in the South.

Chronicity refers to the frequency of the infliction of corporal punishment during the year. Corporal punishment was most frequently used by parents of two-year-olds, averaging eighteen times per year. After age two, chronicity declined, averaging six times per year for teenagers.

Effects of Corporal Punishment

BEHAVIOR PROBLEMS IN ELEMENTARY SCHOOL. Studies on the spanking of children have mostly used sample populations of children age two and older. In "Spanking in Early Childhood and Later Behavior Problems: A Prospective Study of Infants and Young Toddlers" (*Pediatrics*, May 2004), Eric P. Slade and Lawrence S. Wissow conducted the first study of its kind in the United States by following a group of 1,966 children younger than two years old to test the hypothesis that "spanking frequency before age two is positively associated with the probability of having significant behavior problems four years later."

Slade and Wissow collected data about 1,966 children and their mothers who participated in the National Longitudinal Survey of Mother-Child Sample, a large-scale national study of youth ages fourteen to twenty-one years old. Some of these young people were mothers with children. Data were collected on the mother-children groups when the children were under two years of age. Four years later, after the children had entered elementary school, Slade and Wissow interviewed the mothers to explore their hypothesis. Mothers were asked if they spanked their child the previous week and how frequently they spanked their children. They were also questioned about the child's temperament, mother-child interactions, and whether they had ever met with the child's teacher because of behavioral problems.

Slade and Wissow find that, compared with children who were never spanked, white non-Hispanic children who were frequently spanked (five times per week) before age two were four times more likely to have behavioral problems by the time they started school. No connection was found between spanking and later behavioral problems among African-American and Hispanic children. According to Slade and Wissow, the same results were found in studies involving children older than two years. They explain that the way white families and other ethnic groups view the spanking of children may influence the effects of spanking. For example, African-American families typically do not consider spanking as "harsh or unfair."

INCREASED RISK OF PHYSICAL ABUSE. Murray A. Straus, in "Physical Abuse" (Murray A. Straus with Denise A. Donnelly, *Beating the Devil out of Them: Corporal Punishment in American Families and Its Effects on Children*, 2001), presents a model called "path analysis" to illustrate how physical punishment could escalate to physical abuse. Straus theorizes that parents who have been physically disciplined as adolescents are more likely to believe that it is acceptable to use violence to remedy a misbehavior. These parents tend to be depressed and to be involved in spousal violence. When a parent resorts to physical punishment and the child does not comply, the parent increases the severity of the punishment, eventually harming the child.

Corporal punishment experienced in adolescence produces the same effect on males and females. Parents who were physically punished thirty or more times as adolescents (24%) were three times as likely as those who never received physical punishment (7%) to abuse their children physically. Straus notes, however, that his model also shows that three-quarters (76%) of parents who were hit many times (thirty or more) as adolescents did not, in turn, abuse their children.

EFFECTS ON COGNITIVE DEVELOPMENT. In "Corporal Punishment by Mothers and Child's Cognitive Development: A Longitudinal Study" (paper presented at the Fourteenth World Congress of Sociology, Montreal, Quebec, Canada, August 1998), Murray A. Straus and Mallie J. Paschall find that corporal punishment was associated with a child's failure to keep up with the average rate of cognitive development. Straus and Paschall followed the cognitive development of 960 children born to mothers who participated in the National Longitudinal Study of Youth. The women were fourteen to twenty-one years old in 1979, at the start of the study. In 1986, when the women were between the ages of twenty-one and twenty-eight, those with children were interviewed regarding the way they were raising their children. The children underwent cognitive, psychosocial, and behavioral assessments. Children ages one to four were selected, among other reasons, because "the development of neural connections is greatest at the youngest ages." The children were tested again in 1990.

About seven out of ten (71%) mothers reported spanking their toddlers in the past week, with 6.2% spanking the child during the course of their interview for the study. Those who used corporal punishment reported using it an average of 3.6 times per week. This amounted to an estimated 187 spankings per year.

Straus and Paschall find that the more prevalent the corporal punishment, the greater the decrease in cognitive ability. Considering other studies, which show that talking to children, including infants, is associated with increased neural connections in the brain and cognitive functioning, Straus and Paschall hypothesize that if parents are not using corporal punishment to discipline their child, they are very likely verbally interacting with that child, thus positively affecting cognitive development.

Corporal Punishment as Effective Discipline

Some experts believe nonabusive spanking can play a role in effective parental discipline of young children. According to Robert E. Larzelere, in "Child Outcomes of Nonabusive and Customary Physical Punishment by Parents: An Updated Literature Review" (*Clinical Child and Family Psychology Review*, December 2000), spanking can have beneficial results when it is "nonabusive (e.g., two swats to the buttocks with an open hand) and used primarily to back up milder disciplinary tactics with 2- to 6-year-olds by loving parents." Larzelere reviewed thirty-eight studies on corporal punishment to determine the effects of nonabusive and customary spanking. He describes research on customary spanking as "studies that measure physical punishment without emphasizing the severity of its use."

Generally, the thirty-eight studies were nearly equally divided in their reports of beneficial child outcomes, detrimental child outcomes, and neutral or mixed outcomes: 32%, 34%, and 34%, respectively. Larzelere examines seventeen studies he considers to be causally conclusive, that is, the research showed that nonabusive spanking was associated with the child outcomes. Nine studies in which children two to six years of age received nonabusive spankings after noncompliance with room time-out found beneficial child outcomes, such as subsequent compliance with parental orders. Of these nine studies, two studies in which parents used reasoning with the child followed by nonabusive spanking revealed a longer delay in between misbehaviors. A study involving extended disciplining by mothers showed that child compliance occurred at higher rates when the mothers used spanking as a final resort after other disciplinary measures had been tried.

Of the eight controlled longitudinal studies that examined spanking frequency, five reported negative child outcomes, such as low self-esteem. (Controlled studies refers to studies that excluded initial child misbehavior.) Larzelere notes that three of these studies showed that the detrimental effects were a result of frequent spankings.

Larzelere finds that the child's age was associated with the outcome of nonabusive spanking. Of twelve studies involving children with mean (average) ages under six, eleven reported beneficial outcomes. Among children ages seven-and-a-half to ten years, just one study reported beneficial outcomes, whereas six studies found detrimental outcomes.

Larzelere notes that confounding factors in some studies were responsible for a conclusion of detrimental child outcomes. In other words, studies that used opposing or unclear factors found negative outcomes. According to Larzelere, studies that did not show detrimental child outcomes shared three common factors: serious corporal punishment was not included in those studies, spanking was measured as a backup for other disciplinary practices and not in terms of frequency, and many children exhibited behavior problems at the start of the study.

CHAPTER 4
CHILD SEXUAL ABUSE

Many experts believe that sexual abuse is the most underreported type of child maltreatment. A victim, especially a young child, may not know what he or she is experiencing. In many cases the child was threatened to keep it secret. Adults who may be aware of the abuse sometimes get involved in a conspiracy of silence.

Child sexual abuse is the ultimate misuse of an adult's trust and power over a child. When the abuser is particularly close to the victim, the child feels betrayed and trapped in a situation where an adult who claims to care for the child is assaulting him or her. Familial abuse, or incest, involves the use of a child for sexual satisfaction by a family member—a blood relative who is too close to marry legally. Extrafamilial abuse involves a person outside the family. Extrafamilial predators may be strangers, but they may also be people in a position of trust, such as family friends, teachers, and spiritual advisers.

WHAT IS CHILD SEXUAL ABUSE?
Federal Definition

The Child Abuse Prevention and Treatment Act of 1974 (CAPTA) specifically identified parents and caretakers as the perpetrators of sexual abuse. Sexual molestation by other individuals was considered sexual assault. The 1996 amendments to this law, however, included a more comprehensive definition, one that also included sexually abusive behavior by individuals other than parents and caregivers.

The CAPTA Amendments of 1996 defined child sexual abuse as:

- The employment, use, persuasion, inducement, enticement, or coercion of any child to engage in, or assist any other person to engage in, any sexually explicit conduct or simulation of such conduct for the purpose of producing a visual depiction of such conduct

- The rape, and in cases of caretaker or interfamilial relationships, statutory rape, molestation, prostitution, or other form of sexual exploitation of children, or incest with children

State Definitions Vary

Whereas the federal government has established a broad definition of child sexual abuse, it leaves it up to state child abuse laws to specify detailed provisions. All states have laws prohibiting child sexual molestation and generally consider incest illegal. States also specify the age of consent, or the age at which a person can consent to sexual activity with an adult—generally between the ages of fourteen and eighteen. Sexual activity with children below the age of consent is considered statutory rape and is against the law. (See Table 4.1.)

HOW FREQUENT IS CHILD SEXUAL ABUSE?

Each year the National Child Abuse and Neglect Data System of the U.S. Department of Health and Human Services (HHS) collects child maltreatment data from child protective services (CPS) agencies in the fifty states and the District of Columbia, releasing the compiled information as *Child Maltreatment*. The federally mandated National Incidence Study of Child Abuse and Neglect (NIS) is another source that shows the extent of child sexual abuse. As of this writing, three national incidence studies had been conducted: NIS-1 (1980), NIS-2 (1986), and NIS-3 (1993). In 2003 the Keeping Children and Families Safe Act, which reauthorized CAPTA and authorized an additional $285 million for child abuse and neglect prevention programs, directed the collection of data for NIS-4, which was expected to be available by February 2008. A third source of sexual abuse data are retrospective studies, which are surveys

TABLE 4.1

Statutory rape laws by state, 2003

States	Statutory rape	Penalties
Alabama		
§ 13A-6-61	First-degree rape for someone age 16 or older to have sexual intercourse with someone under age 12	Life in prison or between 10 and 99 years
§ 13A-6-62	Second-degree rape for someone age 16 or older to have sexual intercourse with someone between age 12 and 16, when the actor is at least two years older	Two to 20 years in prison
Alaska		
§ 11. 41. 434	First-degree sexual abuse of a minor for someone age 16 or older to engage in sexual penetration with someone under age 13	Up to 30 years in prison
§ 11. 41. 436	Second-degree sexual abuse of a minor for someone age 16 or older to engage in sexual penetration with someone who is age 13, 14, or 15 and at least three years younger than the offender	Up to 10 years in prison
§ 11. 41. 440	Fourth-degree sexual abuse of a minor for someone under age 16 to engage in sexual penetration with someone under age 13 and at least three years younger	Up to one year in prison
Arizona		
§ 13-1405	Sexual conduct with a minor to engage in sexual intercourse with someone under age 18	(1) If the minor is under age 15, five years in prison; (2) if the offender is at least age 18 or is tried as an adult and the minor was age 12 or younger, life in prison and the offender is ineligible for release until serving 35 years; (3) if the offender is at least 18 or tried as an adult and the victim is age 12, 13, or 14, the presumptive sentence is 20 years; or (4) if the minor is at least age 15, it is punishable by one year in prison
Arkansas		
§ 5-14-103	Rape is engaging in sexual intercourse with someone under age 14 who is at least three years younger	10 to 40 years or life in prison
§ 5-14-127	Fourth-degree sexual assault if someone age 20 or older engages in sexual intercourse with someone under age 16	Up to one year in prison
California		
§ 261. 5(b)-(d)	Anyone who engages in an act of unlawful sexual intercourse with a person under age 18 and the actor is not more than three years older or three years younger, is guilty of a misdemeanor	Up to one year in county jail
	Anyone who engages in an act of unlawful sexual intercourse with a person under age 18 who is more than three years younger than the actor is guilty of either a misdemeanor or a felony	Up to one year in county jail or by imprisonment in the state prison (period unspecified)
	Any person 21 years of age or older who engages in an act of unlawful sexual intercourse with a minor who is under 16 years of age is guilty of either a misdemeanor or a felony	Up to one year in a county jail or by imprisonment in the state prison for two, three, or four years
Colorado		
§18-3-402	Sexual assault to knowingly inflict sexual intrusion or sexual penetration on a victim (1) under age 15 if the actor is at least four years older or (2) at least 15 years old but less than 17 years old and the actor is at least 10 years older	The former is punishable by two to six years' in prison and the latter by one to two years in prison
Connecticut		
§ 53a-70 (a)(2)	First-degree sexual assault to have sexual intercourse with a person under age 13 if the actor is more than two years older	10 to 25 years in prison with a mandatory minimum of five years if the victim is between age 10 and 16 and 10 years if the victim is under age 10. The combined sentence and special parole must equal at least 10 years
§ 53a-71 (a)(1)	Second-degree sexual assault to have sexual intercourse with a person between ages 13 and 16 if the actor is more than two years older	Up to 20 years in prison (nine months mandatory minimum)
Delaware		
§ 770	Fourth-degree rape to have sexual intercourse with (1) someone under age 16 or (2) someone under age 18 and the actor is at least 30 years older	Up to 10 years
§ 771	Third-degree rape to have sexual intercourse with a (1) victim under age 16 if the actor is at least 10 years older or (2) victim under age 14 if the actor is age 19 or older	Two to 20 years in prison
§772	Second-degree rape to sexually penetrate a person under age 12 if the actor is 18 or older	Two to 20 years in prison with a 10 year minimum
§ 773	First-degree rape to have sexual intercourse with a person under age 12 if the actor is age 18 or older	15 years to life in prison
Florida		
§ 794. 05	Unlawful sexual activity with certain minors if someone age 24 or older engages in sexual activity with someone age 16 or 17	Up to 15 years in prison

TABLE 4.1

Statutory rape laws by state, 2003 [CONTINUED]

States	Statutory rape	Penalties
Georgia		
§ 16-6-3	Statutory rape to have sexual intercourse with someone under age 16	One to 20 years in prison, but (1) 10 to 20 years if the offender is age 21 or older and (2) up to one year in prison if the victim is age 14 or 15 and the offender is no more than three years older
Hawaii		
§ 707-730	First-degree sexual assault to knowingly engage in sexual penetration (1) with someone under age 14 or (2) with someone between age 14 and 16 when the offender is more than five years older	An indeterminate term of 20 years in prison
Idaho		
§ 18-6101	Rape of a female under age 18	One year to life in prison
Illinois		
§ 730 ILCS 5/12-12 et seq	Aggravated sexual assault for sexual penetration by an offender under age 17 with a victim under age 9	Six to 30 years in prison
	Predatory criminal sexual assault of a child for sexual penetration by an offender age 17 or older and a victim under 13	Six to 30 years in prison
	Criminal sexual abuse is sexual penetration with (1) an offender under age 17 and a victim between ages 9 and 17 or (2) a victim between ages 13 and 17 and an offender less than five years older	Up to one year in prison
	Aggravated criminal sexual abuse is sexual penetration with a victim between age 13 and 17 by an offender at least five years older	Three to seven years in prison
Indiana		
§ 35-42-4-3	Child molesting is sexual intercourse with a child under age 14	(1) Fixed term of 10 years with up to 10 years added or four subtracted for aggravating and mitigating circumstances or (2) if the offender actor is at least age 21, a fixed term of 30 years, with up to 20 years added or 10 subtracted
§ 35-52-4-9	Sexual misconduct with a minor if a person at least age 18 engages in sexual intercourse with a child between ages 14 and 16	(1) Fixed term of four years with up to four added or two subtracted or (2) if the actor is at least age 21, a fixed term of 10 years with up to 10 years added or four subtracted
Iowa		
§ 709. 4	Third-degree sexual abuse to perform a sex act on another person, not his spouse, who is (1) age 12 or 13 or (2) age 14 or 15 if the actor is five or more years older	Up to 10 years in prison
Kansas		
§ 21-3504	Aggravated indecent liberties with a child is sexual intercourse with a child between age 14 and 16	These crimes are felonies subject to sentencing guidelines
§ 21-3522	Unlawful voluntary sexual relations is sexual intercourse with a child age 14 to 16 when the offender is under age 19 and less than four year older	
Kentucky		
§ 510. 020 et seq.	First-degree rape is sexual intercourse with someone under age 12	20 to 50 years in prison
	Second-degree rape is someone age 18 or older engaging in sexual intercourse with someone under 14	Five to 10 years in prison
	Third-degree rape is someone age 21 or older engaging in sexual intercourse with someone under 16	One to five years in prison
Louisiana		
§ 14-80	Felony carnal knowledge of a juvenile is sexual intercourse with consent between (1) someone age 19 or older and someone between age 12 and 17 or (2) someone age 17 or older and someone between age 12 and 15	Up to 10 years in prison (with or without hard labor)
§ 14. 80. 1	Misdemeanor carnal knowledge of a juvenile is sexual intercourse with consent between someone age 17 to 19 and someone age 15 to 17 when the difference in their ages is greater than two years	Up to six months in prison
Maine		
17-A § 253 (1)(B)	Gross sexual assault to have sexual intercourse with a person under age 14	Up to 40 years in prison
17-A § 254 (1)(A)	Sexual abuse of a minor for anyone to have sexual intercourse with someone, other than his spouse, who is either age 14 or 15 and the actor is at least five years older	Up to one year in prison. Up to five years in prison if the actor is at least 10 years older than the victim.
Maryland		
§ 3-306	Second-degree sexual offense to engage in a sexual act with a person under age 14 and the actor is at least four years older	Up to 20 years in prison
§ 3-307	Third-degree sexual offense for someone at least age 21 to engage in a sexual act, including vaginal intercourse, with someone age 14 or 15	Up to 10 years in prison
§ 3-304	Second-degree rape to have vaginal intercourse with a person under age 14 if the actor is at least four years older	Up to 20 years in prison

TABLE 4.1

Statutory rape laws by state, 2003 [CONTINUED]

States	Statutory rape	Penalties
Massachusetts		
272 § 4	Criminal inducement to get a person under age 18 of chaste life to have unlawful sexual intercourse	Up to three years in prison or up to two and one-half years in jail
Michigan		
§ 750. 520b et seq.	First-degree criminal sexual conduct is sexual penetration with someone under age 13	Up to life in prison
	Third-degree criminal sexual conduct is sexual penetration with someone between age 13 and 16	Up to 15 years in prison
Minnesota		
§ 609. 342 et seq.	First-degree criminal sexual conduct is sexual penetration with a victim under age 13 and an actor more than 36 months older	Up to 30 years in prison
	Third-degree criminal sexual conduct is sexual penetration with (1) a victim under age 13 and an actor no more than 36 months older or (2) a victim age 13 to 16 and an actor more than 24 months older	Up to 15 years in prison. But under the second part of the crime, if the actor is between 24 and 48 months older, up to five years in prison
Mississippi		
§ 97-3-95	Sexual battery to sexually penetrate a child (1) at least age 14 but under age 16 if the actor is at least 36 months older than the child or (2) under age 14 if the actor is at least 24 months older than the child	Up to 30 years in prison but (1) under the first part of the crime, if the actor is between age 18 and 21, up to five years and (2) under the second part of the crime, if the actor is 18 or older, then life or a term over 20 years
Missouri		
§ 566. 032 (1)	First-degree statutory rape to have sexual intercourse with another person who is less than fourteen years old	Five years to life in prison
§ 566. 034 (1)	Second-degree statutory rape for someone at least age 21 to have sexual intercourse with someone who is less than age 17	Up to seven years in prison
Montana		
§ 45-5-501 et seq.	Sexual intercourse with someone under age 16	Life imprisonment or between two and 100 years. If the victim is under age 16 and the offender is at least three years older, life imprisonment or four to 100 years.
Nebraska		
§ 28-319	First-degree sexual assault for a person age 19 or older to sexually penetrate a person under age 16	One to 50 years in prison
Nevada		
§§ 200. 364	Statutory sexual seduction for anyone age 18 or older to engage in sexual intercourse with a person under age 16	One to five years in prison if the actor is 21 years of age or older. Up to one year in prison if he is under age 21
New Hampshire		
§ 632-A: 3	Felonious sexual assault for anyone to engage in sexual penetration with a person, other than his spouse, who is under age 16	Up to seven years in prison
New Jersey		
§ 2C: 14-2	Aggravated sexual assault is sexual penetration with a victim under age 13	10 to 20 years in prison
	Sexual assault is sexual penetration with a victim between age 13 and 16 when the actor is at least four years older	Five to 10 years in prison
New Mexico		
§ 30-9-11	First-degree criminal sexual penetration to engage in sexual intercourse with a child less than age 13	Basic sentence of 18 years in prison
	Fourth-degree sexual penetration to engage in sexual intercourse with a child age 13 to 16 if the actor is at least age 18 and at least four years older than the child	Basic sentence of 18 months in prison
New York		
§§130. 25, 130. 30, and 130. 35	Third-degree rape for anyone age 21 or older to have sexual intercourse with someone under age 17	Up to four years in prison
	Second-degree rape for anyone age 18 or older to engage in sexual intercourse with someone under age 15. The fact that the offender was less than four years older than the victim at the time of the act is an affirmative defense	Up to seven years in prison
	First-degree rape to have sexual intercourse with someone (1) less than age 11 or (2) less than age 13 if the actor is age 18 or older	Five to 25 years in prison
North Carolina		
§ 14-27. 2 et seq.	First-degree rape is sexual intercourse with a victim under age 13 when the actor is at least age 12 and at least four years older	These crimes are felonies subject to the structured sentencing law with minimums and maximums depending on aggravating and mitigating factors and the offender's prior record
	Statutory rape or sexual offense of person age 13, 14, or 15 is intercourse with someone age 13, 14, or 15 when the actor is (1) at least six years older and (2) between four and six years older	

TABLE 4.1

Statutory rape laws by state, 2003 [CONTINUED]

States	Statutory rape	Penalties
North Dakota		
§ 12. 1-20-03	Gross sexual imposition is committing a sexual act with a victim under age 15	Up to 10 years in prison
	Corruption of minor is an adult engaging in sexual act with a minor	(1) Up to one year in prison if the victim is at least age 15 or (2) if actor is at least age 22 and the victim is a minor at least age 15, up to five years in prison
Ohio		
§ 2907. 04	Sexual assault for a person age 18 to engage in sexual conduct with a minor if the actor knows that the minor is between ages 13 and 16	(1) Six to 18 months in prison, (2) if the actor is less than four years older than the victim, a $1,000 fine, or (3) if the actor is 10 or more years older than the victim, one to five years in prison
Oklahoma		
§ 21-1114	First-degree rape for a person over age 18 to have sexual intercourse with a person under age 14	Five years in prison to death
	In all other cases rape is second-degree rape	One to 15 years in prison
Oregon		
§ 163. 355	Third-degree rape to have sexual intercourse with a person under age 16	Up to five years in prison
	Defense that the actor was less than three years older than the victim at the time of the offense	
§ 163. 365	Second-degree rape to have sexual intercourse with a person under age 14	Up to 10 years in prison
	Defense that the actor was less than three years older than the victim at the time of the offense	
§ 163. 375	First-degree rape to have sexual intercourse with a person under age 12	Up to 20 years in prison
Pennsylvania		
18 § 3121	Rape to engage in sexual intercourse with a complainant who is less than 13 years of age	Up to 20 years in prison
	Rape to engage in deviate sexual intercourse with a complainant who is less than (1) 13 years of age or (2) 16 years of age and the actor is four or more years older	
Rhode Island		
§ 11-37-6	Third-degree sexual assault for anyone over age 18 to engage in sexual penetration with someone over age 14 and under age 16	Up to five years in prison
South Carolina		
§ 16-3-655	First-degree criminal sexual conduct with a minor to have sexual intercourse with a person under age 11	Up to 30 years in prison
	Second-degree criminal sexual conduct with a minor to have sexual intercourse with a person between ages 11 and 14	Up to 20 years in prison
South Dakota		
§ 22-22-1	Rape to sexually penetrate a person under age 10	10 years in prison
	Rape to sexually penetrate a person between ages 10 and 16 if the actor is at least three years older than the victim	15 years in prison
Tennessee		
§ 39-13-506	Statutory rape to sexually penetrate a person at least age 13 but less than age 18 if the actor is at least four years older than the victim. Any actor under age 18 must be tried as a juvenile and cannot be transferred to adult court	Two to six years in prison
Texas		
§ 22. 011	Sexual assault for anyone to intentionally or knowingly penetrate a person under age 17, other than his spouse. The actor has an affirmative defense if he is not more than three years older than the victim, who is at least age 14	Two to 20 years in prison
Utah		
§ 76-5-401	Unlawful sexual activity with a minor to have sexual intercourse with someone age 14 or 15	Up to five years in prison, unless the actor is less than four years older than the victim
§ 76-5-401. 2	Unlawful sexual activity with a minor to have sexual intercourse with someone age 16 or 17 if the actor is 10 or more years older than the victim	Up to five years in prison
Vermont		
13 § 3252	Sexual assault to engage in a sexual act with a person under age 16, except where the actors are married and the act is consensual	Up to 20 years in prison
13 § 3253	Aggravated sexual assault for anyone age 18 or older to engage in a sexual act with someone under age 10	Up to life in prison

TABLE 4.1

Statutory rape laws by state, 2003 [CONTINUED]

States	Statutory rape	Penalties
Virginia		
§ 18. 2-61	Sexual intercourse with a child under the age of thirteen	Five years to life in prison
§ 18. 2-63	Carnal knowledge of a child between ages 13 and 15	Two to 10 years in prison
§ 18. 2-63	Carnal knowledge of a child between ages 13 and 15 when the actor is a minor and the victim is three or more years younger	One to five years in prison
§ 18. 2-63	Carnal knowledge of a child between ages 13 and 15 when the actor is a minor and the victim is less than three years younger	Maximum fine of $ 250
Washington		
§ 9A. 44. 073	First-degree rape of a child to have sexual intercourse with a person less than age 12 years and the actor is at least 24 months older	Five years to life in prison
§ 9A. 44. 076	Second-degree rape of a child to have sexual intercourse with a person who is at least 12 but less than 14 years old if the actor is at least 36 months older than the victim	Five years to life in prison
§ 9A. 44. 079	Third-degree rape of a child to have sexual intercourse with a person age 14 or 15 if the actor is at least 48 months older than the victim	Up to five years in prison
West Virginia		
§ 61-8B-3	First-degree sexual assault for a person age 14 or older to have sexual intercourse with a person age 11 or younger	15 to 35 years in prison
§ 61-8B-5	Third-degree sexual assault for a person age 16 or older to have sexual intercourse with a person under age 16 and at least four years younger than the actor	One to five years in prison
Wisconsin		
§ 948. 02	Sexual intercourse with a person under 13 years of age	Up to 40 years in prison
§ 948. 09	Sexual intercourse with a person under 16 years of age	Up to 25 years in prison
	Sexual intercourse with a minor at least age of 16	Up to nine months in prison
Wyoming		
§ 6-2-303	Second-degree sexual assault to inflict sexual intrusion upon a person under age 12 and the actor is at least four years older than the victim	Up to 20 years in prison
§ 6-2-304	Third-degree sexual assault if, under circumstances not constituting first- or second-degree sexual assault, the actor is at least four years older than the victim and inflicts sexual intrusion on a victim under age 16	Up to 15 years in prison

SOURCE: "Table 1. Statutory Rape Laws by State," in "Statutory Rape Laws by State," *OLR Research Report*, Office of Legislative Research, April 14, 2003, http://www.cga.ct.gov/2003/olrdata/jud/rpt/2003-R-0376.htm (accessed July 31, 2006)

of adults about their childhood experience of sexual abuse. Within this source type are periodic federal government surveys of jail inmates and prisoners regarding their experience of child sexual abuse.

According to the HHS, in 2000 the number of sexual abuse cases reported by CPS agencies in the United States was 87,770. In 2004 the number of sexual abuse cases was down to 84,398. (See Table 4.2.)

It is important to note that these numbers represent only cases that were reported and substantiated; unknown numbers of child sexual abuse cases are undiscovered. The secrecy surrounding child abuse makes it virtually impossible to count the cases perpetrated in the family. However, retrospective studies of adults are one attempt to get a true picture of the prevalence of child sexual abuse.

In "The Victimization of Children and Youth: A Comprehensive, National Survey" (*Child Maltreatment*, February 2005), a study of a nationally representative sample of one thousand children and youth ages two to seventeen, David Finkelhor et al. find that more than half of the children had been victimized in the previous year, either by a physical assault, a property offense, a form of child maltreatment, a sexual victimization, or a form of

indirect victimization, such as witnessing an act of violence. One youth out of twelve had been sexually victimized in the study year.

Determining the Extent of Child Sexual Abuse through Retrospective Studies

David Finkelhor is a national authority on child sexual abuse. In "Current Information on the Scope and Nature of Child Sexual Abuse" (*The Future of Children: Sexual Abuse of Children*, Summer–Fall 1994), Finkelhor notes that surveys of adults regarding their childhood experiences (called retrospective studies) probably give the most complete estimates of the actual extent of child sexual abuse. He reviews nineteen adult retrospective surveys and finds that the proportion of adults who indicated sexual abuse during childhood ranged widely, from 2% to 62% for females and from 3% to 16% for males.

Finkelhor observes that the surveys that reported higher levels of abuse were those that asked multiple questions about the possibility of abuse. Multiple questions are more effective because they provide respondents various "cues" about the different kinds of experiences the researchers are asking about. Multiple questions also give the respondents ample time to overcome their

TABLE 4.2

Rates of victimization by type of maltreatment, 2000–04

Maltreatment type	Child population	Victims	Rate*	No. of states
2000				
Physical abuse	70,984,343	167,713	2.4	50
Neglect	70,984,343	517,118	7.3	50
Medical neglect	54,042,346	25,498	0.5	40
Sexual abuse	70,984,343	87,770	1.2	50
Psychological maltreatment	69,407,948	66,965	1.0	49
Other abuse	51,761,974	143,406	2.8	33
Unknown	14,663,682	2,778	0.2	12
2001				
Physical abuse	72,603,552	168,510	2.3	51
Neglect	72,603,552	518,014	7.1	51
Medical neglect	54,118,412	17,670	0.3	39
Sexual abuse	72,603,552	86,857	1.2	51
Psychological maltreatment	70,901,061	61,776	0.9	49
Other abuse	54,577,834	175,979	3.2	34
Unknown	8,586,103	2,348	0.3	7
2002				
Physical abuse	72,846,774	167,168	2.3	51
Neglect	72,846,774	525,131	7.2	51
Medical neglect	55,060,453	18,128	0.3	40
Sexual abuse	72,846,774	88,688	1.2	51
Psychological maltreatment	71,139,086	58,029	0.8	49
Other abuse	51,580,777	169,465	3.3	31
Unknown	19,868,722	1,382	0.1	8
2003				
Physical abuse	73,043,506	164,689	2.3	51
Neglect	73,043,506	550,178	7.5	51
Medical neglect	55,032,613	17,945	0.3	39
Sexual abuse	73,043,506	87,078	1.2	51
Psychological maltreatment	71,331,202	57,391	0.8	49
Other abuse	44,951,148	133,172	3.0	29
Unknown	5,888,493	1,792	0.3	6
2004				
Physical abuse	73,089,769	152,250	2.1	50
Neglect	73,089,769	544,050	7.4	50
Medical neglect	53,639,843	17,968	0.3	38
Sexual abuse	73,089,769	84,398	1.2	50
Psychological maltreatment	69,893,907	61,272	0.9	47
Other abuse	40,000,786	126,856	3.2	26
Unknown	15,342,648	2,080	0.1	8

*Rates were based on the number of victims divided by the child population in the reporting states and multiplied by 1,000.

SOURCE: "Table 3.6. Victimization Rates by Maltreatment Type, 2000–2004," in *Child Maltreatment 2004*, U.S. Department of Health and Human Services, Administration on Children, Youth, and Families, 2006, http://www.acf.hhs.gov/programs/cb/pubs/cm04/cm04.pdf (accessed July 8, 2006)

FIGURE 4.1

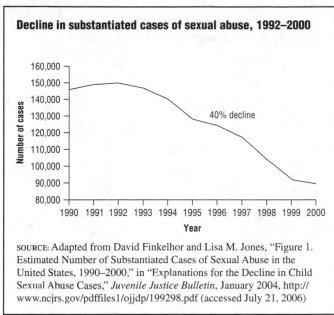

Decline in substantiated cases of sexual abuse, 1992–2000

SOURCE: Adapted from David Finkelhor and Lisa M. Jones, "Figure 1. Estimated Number of Substantiated Cases of Sexual Abuse in the United States, 1990–2000," in "Explanations for the Decline in Child Sexual Abuse Cases," *Juvenile Justice Bulletin*, January 2004, http://www.ncjrs.gov/pdffiles1/ojjdp/199298.pdf (accessed July 21, 2006)

had suffered incestuous and extrafamilial sexual abuse before their eighteenth birthday. About 16% had been abused by a family member.

Russell's study is still frequently cited by experts who believe that much more abuse occurs than is officially reported by government studies. They suggest the high results recorded in her study reflect the thoroughness of her preparation. While other studies ask one question concerning CSA, she asked fourteen different questions, any one of which might have set off a memory of sexual abuse.

In *The Epidemic of Rape and Child Sexual Abuse in the United States* (2000), Diana E. H. Russell and Rebecca M. Bolen revisit the prevalence rates reported in Russell's 1978 survey. Russell and Bolen believe those rates are underestimated. The 1978 survey subjects did not include two groups regarded to be highly probable victims of child sexual abuse: females in institutions and those not living at home. Russell and Bolen also find that some women were reluctant to reveal experiences of abuse to survey interviewers, whereas others did not recall these experiences.

Are Child Sexual Abuse Cases Declining?

According to CPS agencies across the United States, reported and substantiated cases of child sexual abuse have declined since 1992. Substantiated, or confirmed, cases of sexual abuse of children dropped from a peak of 150,000 in 1992 to less than 90,000 in 2000, a decrease of 40%. (See Figure 4.1.) Substantiated child abuse cases dropped to 84,398 victims in 2004, according to the HHS. (See Table 4.2.)

embarrassment. Many experts accept the estimate that one out of five (20%) American women and one out of ten (10%) American men have experienced some form of childhood sexual abuse (CSA).

One of the early landmark studies of child sexual abuse was conducted by the sociologist Diana E. H. Russell in 1978. Russell surveyed 930 adult women in San Francisco about their early sexual experiences and reported her findings in *The Secret Trauma: Incest in the Lives of Girls and Women* (1986). Russell noted that 38% of the women

FIGURE 4.2

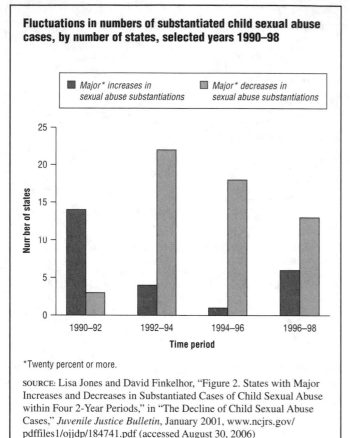

Fluctuations in numbers of substantiated child sexual abuse cases, by number of states, selected years 1990–98

*Twenty percent or more.

SOURCE: Lisa Jones and David Finkelhor, "Figure 2. States with Major Increases and Decreases in Substantiated Cases of Child Sexual Abuse within Four 2-Year Periods," in "The Decline of Child Sexual Abuse Cases," *Juvenile Justice Bulletin*, January 2001, www.ncjrs.gov/pdffiles1/ojjdp/184741.pdf (accessed August 30, 2006)

FIGURE 4.3

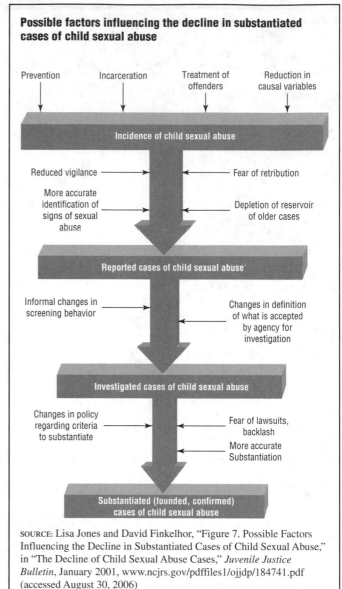

Possible factors influencing the decline in substantiated cases of child sexual abuse

SOURCE: Lisa Jones and David Finkelhor, "Figure 7. Possible Factors Influencing the Decline in Substantiated Cases of Child Sexual Abuse," in "The Decline of Child Sexual Abuse Cases," *Juvenile Justice Bulletin*, January 2001, www.ncjrs.gov/pdffiles1/ojjdp/184741.pdf (accessed August 30, 2006)

Lisa M. Jones and David Finkelhor examine in *The Decline in Child Sexual Abuse Cases* (January 2001, http://www.ncjrs.gov/html/ojjdp/jjbul2001_1_1/contents.html) the possible factors responsible for this decline. They find that between 1990 and 1992 just three states experienced a decrease in cases of substantiated child sexual abuse, compared with fourteen states reporting increases of 20% or more. The decreasing trend started between 1992 and 1994, with twenty-two states reporting a decline of 20% or more, followed by eighteen states reporting declines between 1994 and 1996. From 1996 to 1998 thirteen states showed decreases of substantiated child sexual abuse cases. (See Figure 4.2.)

According to Jones and Finkelhor, several factors may have influenced the decline in substantiated cases of child sexual abuse. (See Figure 4.3.) Since the 1990s the incidence of child sexual abuse may have been reduced by factors such as child victimization prevention programs, incarceration of sexual offenders, treatment programs for sex offenders, and other variables. These variables include female victimization by intimate partners and poverty. In other words, declining trends in these causal variables may play a role in the decreasing cases of child sexual abuse. Experts show a 30% to 60% overlap in the victimization of children and

the victimization of their mothers (Amy M. Slep and Susan G. O'Leary, "Parent and Partner Violence in Families with Young Children: Rates, Patterns, and Connections," *Journal of Consulting and Clinical Psychology*, June 2005; and Emiko A Tajima, "Correlates of the Co-occurrence of Wife Abuse and Child Abuse among a Representative Sample," *Journal of Family Violence*, December 2004).

Jones and Finkelhor suggest that the drop in reports of child sexual abuse from 1991 to 1998 might also be because of people's reluctance to report their suspicions because of widely publicized cases of false accusations. The public and mandated reporters, such as health care professionals, may also have learned accurate identification of the signs of abuse. In addition, the large numbers of sexual abuse cases that had surfaced as a result of increased vigilance starting in the 1980s may have been exhausted.

The investigation of child sexual abuse may have changed in scope. Jones and Finkelhor note that some CPS agencies may not be screening certain cases, such as sexual abuse by nonfamily members. Agencies with large caseloads may be investigating only cases they deem serious enough to warrant their time. These factors also affect the sexual abuse count. Changes in agency criteria of which investigated cases are substantiated may also affect the final count of substantiated cases.

Jones and Finkelhor point out that if declining numbers of child sexual abuse resulted from intimidation of child abuse reporters or changes in CPS investigative and substantiating policies, more research is needed. They suggest better training of professionals in identifying abuse. They also recommend exploring the cases that had not been investigated or substantiated and the changes in CPS procedures that may have caused the decline.

In the report *Explanations for the Decline in Child Sexual Abuse Cases* (January 2004, http://www.ncjrs.gov/pdffiles1/ojjdp/199298.pdf), Finkelhor and Jones revisit the factors possibly influencing the decline. They examine, among other things, four states (Illinois, Minnesota, Oregon, and Pennsylvania) with large decreases in substantiated child sexual abuse, as well as extensive information from the 1990s. Finkelhor and Jones find little or no evidence that the decline resulted from CPS agencies not investigating certain cases or the diminishing number of older cases. They cannot determine whether or not fear of repercussions, such as lawsuits, had contributed to the decline in mandated reporting by physicians because the states had mixed results in physician reports.

Although Finkelhor and Jones find "no solid and convincing explanation" for the decline of child sexual abuse in the 1990s, they offer two pieces of evidence for some true decline in sexual abuse cases. One piece of evidence was the results of two self-reports of sexual assault (by nonfamily members) and sexual abuse (by family members). The other piece of evidence cited by Finkelhor and Jones was the National Crime Victimization Survey (NCVS), an annual survey of eighty thousand people over age twelve, which found an overall 56% decline in self-reported sexual assault against twelve- to seventeen-year-old juveniles between 1993 and 2000, with a 72% decline by family members. (See Figure 4.4.) The Minnesota Student Survey, administered five times between 1989 and 2001 to students in grades six, nine, and twelve (to more than one hundred thousand individuals), found a slight increase in the sexual abuse trend from 1989 to 1992, then a 22%

FIGURE 4.4

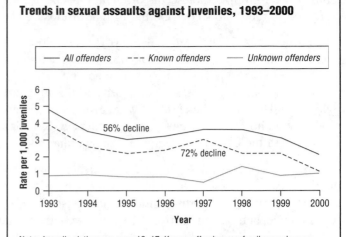

Trends in sexual assaults against juveniles, 1993–2000

Note: Juvenile victims are ages 12–17. Known offenders are family members or acquaintances, and unknown offenders are strangers or unidentified.

SOURCE: David Finkelhor and Lisa Jones, "Figure 12. Trends in Sexual Assaults against Juveniles," in "Explanations for the Decline in Child Sexual Abuse Cases," *Juvenile Justice Bulletin*, January 2004, http://www.ncjrs.gov/pdffiles1/ojjdp/199298.pdf (accessed July 21, 2006)

FIGURE 4.5

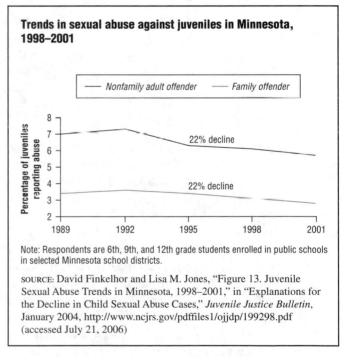

Trends in sexual abuse against juveniles in Minnesota, 1998–2001

Note: Respondents are 6th, 9th, and 12th grade students enrolled in public schools in selected Minnesota school districts.

SOURCE: David Finkelhor and Lisa M. Jones, "Figure 13. Juvenile Sexual Abuse Trends in Minnesota, 1998–2001," in "Explanations for the Decline in Child Sexual Abuse Cases," *Juvenile Justice Bulletin*, January 2004, http://www.ncjrs.gov/pdffiles1/ojjdp/199298.pdf (accessed July 21, 2006)

decline for sexual abuse by family and nonfamily members. (See Figure 4.5.)

WHAT MAKES A VICTIM DISCLOSE?

Rochelle F. Hanson et al., in "Correlates of Adolescent Reports of Sexual Assault: Findings from the National Survey of Adolescents" (*Child Maltreatment*, November 2003), report on the factors that contribute to the likelihood that an adolescent will disclose sexual abuse. They also examine whether, among the different ethnic/racial groups, adolescents differ in rates of disclosure and in the factors contributing to that disclosure.

Participants in the National Survey of Adolescents were a random sample of 4,023 U.S. adolescents ages twelve to seventeen. The sample was made up of 51.3% males and 48.7% females. A majority (70.2%) were white non-Hispanic. The children were grouped into several age cohorts. Interviews were conducted by telephone, with the consent of the parent or guardian.

A total of 326 adolescents (8.1%) indicated that they had experienced child sexual abuse. Approximately four out of five of those reporting child sexual abuse (78.1%) were female, and one out of five (21.9%) were male. Most (58.2%) were white, 23.6% were African-American, and 9.4% were Hispanic. Other ethnic groups made up the remaining 8.8% of child sexual abuse victims.

Of the 326 victims almost one-third (30.7%) had been raped, more than one-quarter (26.8%) reported fearing for their life during the assault, and about 10% had suffered physical injuries. Alcohol or drugs were involved in 6.7% of the incidents. Single incidents were reported by about two-thirds (64.1%) of the victims. Three-quarters (76.4%) knew the perpetrator. Specifically, 4.3% identified their father or stepfather as the abuser, 17.5% named another relative, 52.8% reported an unrelated acquaintance, and 1.8% knew the perpetrator but did not identify the person. Nearly one-quarter (23%) said the perpetrator was a stranger, and two victims did not name the perpetrator.

About two-thirds (68.1%) of the victims told interviewers they disclosed their sexual abuse to someone. Just 4.5% of those who disclosed first told a police officer or social worker. One-third (34.3%) told their mother or stepmother, and more than a third (39.3%) told a close friend. The other victims told another relative (6.1%), a teacher (1.8%), a father or stepfather (1.7%), or a doctor or other health professional (1.3%). About 3.4% indicated they disclosed the abuse to someone but did not say who it was. Another 3.9% would not say who they told of the abuse or could not remember who they first told. Overall, just one-third (33.6%) indicated they ever reported the abuse to police or other authorities.

More females (74%) than males (46.5%) disclosed to someone that they had been sexually abused. White victims (75.1%) were more likely than Hispanics (67.7%) and African-Americans (55.8%) to tell someone of their abuse. Those who feared for their lives during the assault were especially likely to disclose the abuse (80.7%). Other factors that were related to high levels of disclosure were having suffered physical injury (70.6%), having used substances (68.2%), having been assaulted once (67.9%), or having experienced a penetration assault (72%). The

likelihood of telling someone of the abuse was also influenced by the relationship between the victim and the perpetrator. Nearly nine out of ten victims (87.7%) who were sexually abused by a relative disclosed the incident, compared with those abused by a stranger (70.7%), an unrelated acquaintance (62.2%), or a father (57.1%).

The study shows that the gender of the adolescent is related to disclosure of sexual abuse, with girls more likely to do so. Hanson et al. reiterate previous findings that males might fear being thought of as gay if the abuser was male. Hanson et al. also note that other studies show that African-American females are reluctant to disclose sexual abuse because of fear of not being believed. Although no similar studies have been done of their male counterparts, Hanson et al. think the same reason might keep African-American male adolescents from reporting child sexual abuse. In this study African-American females were seven times more likely than their male counterparts to tell someone they had experienced sexual abuse. White adolescents did not differ in disclosure of abuse based on gender.

VICTIMS

Who Is Sexually Abused?

Most studies indicate that girls are far more likely than boys to suffer sexual abuse. Under the Harm and Endangerment Standards discussed by Andrea J. Sedlak and Diane D. Broadhurst in NIS-3, girls were sexually abused about three times more often than boys.

In "Childhood Sexual Abuse among Black Women and White Women from Two-Parent Families" (*Child Maltreatment*, August 2006), a retrospective study, Maryann Amodeo et al. examine 290 African-American and white women to determine differences in prevalence of CSA. Amodeo et al. used questionnaires and face-to-face interviews, as well as interviews with siblings, to determine whether child sexual abuse had occurred. African-American women showed a higher prevalence of child sexual abuse than did white women (34.1% and 22.8%, respectively).

Sarah E. Ullman and Henrietta Filipas find in "Ethnicity and Child Sexual Abuse Experiences of Female College Students" (*Journal of Child Sexual Abuse*, 2005) racial and ethnic differences in their retrospective study using a sample of 461 female college students. Analysis of their survey reveals that African-Americans reported more sexual abuse than other groups, followed by Hispanics, whites, and Asians.

Is Sexual Abuse of Boys Underreported?

William C. Holmes and Gail B. Slap claim that sexual abuse of boys is not only common but also underreported and undertreated. In "Sexual Abuse of Boys: Definition,

Prevalence, Correlates, Sequelae, and Management" (*Journal of the American Medical Association*, December 2, 1998), they review 149 studies of male sexual abuse. These studies, conducted between 1985 and 1997, included face-to-face interviews, telephone surveys, medical chart reviews, and computerized and paper questionnaires. The respondents included adolescents (ninth- through twelfth-graders, runaways, non-sex-offending delinquents, and detainees), college students, psychiatric patients, Native Americans, sex offenders (including serial rapists), substance-abusing patients, and homeless men. Holmes and Slap find that, overall, one out of five boys had been sexually abused.

Holmes and Slap note that boys younger than thirteen years of age, nonwhite, of low socioeconomic status, and not living with their fathers were at a higher risk for sexual abuse. Boys whose parents had abused alcohol, had criminal records, and were divorced, separated, or remarried were more likely to experience sexual abuse. Sexually abused boys were fifteen times more likely than boys who had never been sexually abused to live in families in which some members had also been sexually abused.

Start and Duration of Abuse

Kathleen A. Kendall-Tackett and Roberta Marshall, in "Sexual Victimization of Children: Incest and Child Sexual Abuse" (Raquel Kennedy Bergen, ed., *Issues in Intimate Violence*, 1998), report that studies find that the age of victims at the start of the abuse could be anywhere between seven and thirteen, although there had been cases of sexual abuse among children six years of age or younger. The sexual abuse may be a one-time occurrence or it may last for several years. Kendall-Tackett and Marshall find durations of abuse ranging from two and a half to eight years.

In the report *Sexual Assault of Young Children as Reported to Law Enforcement: Victim, Incident, and Offender Characteristics* (July 2000, http://www.ojp.usdoj. gov/bjs/pub/pdf/saycrle.pdf), Howard N. Snyder finds that 34.1% of all victims of sexual assault reported to law enforcement from 1991 to 1996 were under age twelve, with 14% under six years of age. (See Table 4.3.) (Some researchers distinguish between child sexual abuse as perpetrated by parents or caregivers and sexual assault as committed by other individuals. In this report, the term *sexual assault* included child sexual abuse.)

In *Extent, Nature, and Consequences of Rape Victimization: Findings from the National Violence against Women Survey* (January 2006, http://www.ncjrs.gov/pdffiles1/nij/210346.pdf), a study of rape using data from the National Violence against Women Survey, Patricia Tjaden and Nancy Thoennes find that 21.6% of women and 48% of men were under the age of twelve when they were first raped. Another 32.4% of women

TABLE 4.3

Victims of sexual assault by age and type of incident, 1991–96

Victim age	All sexual assault	Forcible rape	Forcible sodomy	Sexual assault with object	Forcible fondling
Total	100.0%	100.0%	100.0%	100.0%	100.0%
0 to 5	14.0%	4.3%	24.0%	26.5%	20.2%
6 to 11	20.1	8.0	30.8	23.2	29.3
12 to 17	32.8	33.5	24.0	25.5	34.3
18 to 24	14.2	22.6	8.7	9.7	7.7
25 to 34	11.5	19.6	7.5	8.3	5.0
Above 34	7.4	12.0	5.1	6.8	3.5

SOURCE: Howard N. Snyder, "Table 1. Age Profile of the Victims of Sexual Assault, 1991–96," in *Sexual Assault of Young Children As Reported to Law Enforcement: Victim, Incident, and Offender Characteristics*, NCJ 182990, U.S. Department of Justice, Bureau of Justice Statistics, July 2000, http://www.ojp.usdoj.gov/bjs/pub/pdf/saycrle.pdf (accessed August 4, 2006)

FIGURE 4.6

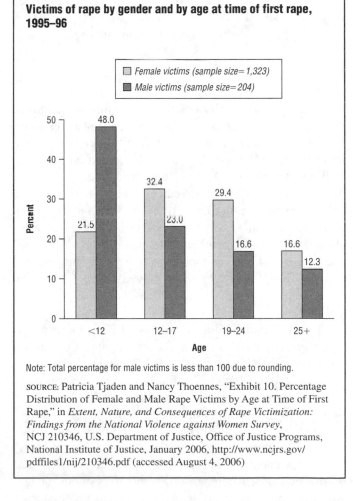

Victims of rape by gender and by age at time of first rape, 1995–96

Note: Total percentage for male victims is less than 100 due to rounding.

SOURCE: Patricia Tjaden and Nancy Thoennes, "Exhibit 10. Percentage Distribution of Female and Male Rape Victims by Age at Time of First Rape," in *Extent, Nature, and Consequences of Rape Victimization: Findings from the National Violence against Women Survey*, NCJ 210346, U.S. Department of Justice, Office of Justice Programs, National Institute of Justice, January 2006, http://www.ncjrs.gov/pdffiles1/nij/210346.pdf (accessed August 4, 2006)

and 23% of men were between ages twelve and seventeen. Therefore, more than half of all female rape victims and seven of ten male rape victims had been raped while children. (See Figure 4.6.)

In their research on male child victims, Holmes and Slap find that sexual abuse generally began before puberty. About 17% to 53% of the respondents reported

TABLE 4.4

Victim-offender relationship in sexual assault, 1991–96

	Offenders			
Victim age	Total	Family member	Acquaintance	Stranger
All victims	**100.0%**	**26.7%**	**59.6%**	**13.8%**
Juveniles	100.0%	34.2%	58.7%	7.0%
0 to 5	100.0	48.6	48.3	3.1
6 to 11	100.0	42.4	52.9	4.7
12 to 17	100.0	24.3	66.0	9.8
Adults	100.0%	11.5%	61.1%	27.3%
18 to 24	100.0	9.8	66.5	23.7
Above 24	100.0	12.8	57.1	30.1

SOURCE: Howard N. Snyder, "Table 6. Victim-Offender Relationship in Sexual Assault," in *Sexual Assault of Young Children As Reported to Law Enforcement: Victim, Incident, and Offender Characteristics*, NCJ 182990, U.S. Department of Justice, Bureau of Justice Statistics, July 2000, http://www.ojp.usdoj.gov/bjs/pub/pdf/saycrle.pdf (accessed August 4, 2006)

TABLE 4.5

Victim-offender relationship in sexual assault, by gender of victim, 1991–96

	Offenders			
Victim age	Total	Family member	Acquaintance	Stranger
Female victims	**100.0%**	**25.7%**	**59.5%**	**14.7%**
Juveniles	100.0%	33.9	58.7	7.5
0 to 5	100.0	51.1	45.9	3.0
6 to 11	100.0	43.8	51.4	4.8
12 to 17	100.0	24.3	65.7	10.0
Adults	100.0%	11.5	61.0	27.5
18 to 24	100.0	9.8	66.4	23.8
Above 24	100.0	12.9	56.9	30.2
Male victims	**100.0%**	**32.8%**	**59.8%**	**7.3%**
Juveniles	100.0%	35.8	59.2	5.0
0 to 5	100.0	42.4	54.1	3.5
6 to 11	100.0	37.7	57.7	4.6
12 to 17	100.0	23.7	68.7	7.6
Adults	100.0%	11.3	63.9	24.8
18 to 24	100.0	10.7	68.4	20.9
Above 24	100.0	11.8	60.3	27.9

SOURCE: Howard N. Snyder, "Table 7. Victim-Offender Relationship in Sexual Assault, by Victim Gender," in *Sexual Assault of Young Children As Reported to Law Enforcement: Victim, Incident, and Offender Characteristics*, NCJ 182990, U.S. Department of Justice, Bureau of Justice Statistics, July 2000, http://www.ojp.usdoj.gov/bjs/pub/pdf/saycrle.pdf (accessed August 4, 2006)

repeated abuse, with some victimization continuing over periods of less than six months and some victimization enduring for eighteen to forty-eight months.

PERPETRATORS

Snyder finds that the abusers of young victims were more likely than the abusers of older victims to be family members. Sexual abusers whose victims were children five years old and younger were family members nearly half the time (48.6%), a number that decreased for those ages six to eleven (42.4%), and further decreased for victims ages twelve to seventeen (24.3%). (See Table 4.4.) More female victims (51.1% of those age five years and younger and 43.8% of those ages six to eleven) were abused by family members, compared with their male counterparts (42.4% of those age five years and younger and 37.7% of those ages six to eleven). (See Table 4.5.)

Fathers

Linda Meyer Williams and David Finkelhor, in *The Characteristics of Incestuous Fathers* (1992, http://eric.ed.gov/ERICDocs/data/ericdocs2/content_storage_01/0000000b/80/25/10/cb.pdf), find that, generally, incestuous fathers had lonely childhoods (82%). Almost half (47%) had not lived with their own fathers and had changed living arrangements (43%), perhaps as a result of parental divorce or remarriage. Their own parents' alcohol problem, however, was no different from that of the nonabused comparison group. Incestuous fathers were far more likely to have been juvenile delinquents and to have been rejected by their parents. Williams and Finkelhor also find that the sex education of incestuous fathers while growing up did not come from friends or peers, but from being victims of sexual abuse. About 70% had a history of sexual abuse, with 45% having multiple abusers. Nearly three out of five were sexually abused by nonfamily adults.

Women Who Abuse

For many years, experts thought female sex abusers were uncommon. When women were involved in abuse, it was thought to be a situation in which a man had forced the woman to commit the abuse. Some experts postulate that women are more maternal and, therefore, less likely to abuse a child. Women are also thought to have different attitudes toward sex. While a man ties his feelings of self-worth to his sexual experiences, a woman is supposedly less concerned with sexual prowess and tends to be more empathetic toward others.

Some researchers propose that the abusive behavior of women is influenced by severe psychiatric disturbance, mental retardation, brain damage, or male coercion. In *A Comparative Analysis of Women Who Sexually Abuse Children* (1990), C. Allen studies female offenders and finds that their lives involved particularly harsh childhoods marked by instability and abuse.

Comparing male and female offenders, Allen finds that the women reported more severe incidents of physical and emotional abuse in their pasts, had run away from home more often, were more sexually promiscuous than male offenders, and had more frequent incidents of being paid for sex. Because they perceived child sexual abuse as a great social deviance, female offenders were less likely to admit guilt. They were less cooperative than men during the investigations and were angrier with informants and investigators. Following disclosure, they also appeared to experience less guilt and sorrow than male offenders.

MOTHERS. Sexual abuse by mothers may remain undetected because it occurs at home and is either denied or never reported. Mothers generally have more intimate contact with their children, and the lines between maternal love and care and sexual abuse are not as clear-cut as they are for fathers. Furthermore, society is reluctant to see a woman as a perpetrator of incest, portraying the woman as someone likely to turn her pain inward into depression, compared with the man who acts out his anger in sexually criminal behavior.

Siblings

Sibling incest is another form of abuse that has not been well studied. Some experts, however, believe that sibling sexual abuse is more common than father-daughter incest. Vernon R. Wiehe, in "Sibling Abuse" (*Understanding Family Violence: Treating and Preventing Partner, Child, Sibling, and Elder Abuse*, 1998), believes that the problem of sibling incest has not received much attention because of the families' reluctance to report to authorities that such abuse is happening at home, the parents' playing down the fact that "it" is indeed a problem, and the perception that it is normal for brothers and sisters to explore their sexuality. Wiehe believes that sexual abuse by a sibling should be considered a crime of rape because the perpetrator uses aggression, force, or threats. Moreover, the consequences to the victim are the same whether the sexual abuse takes the form of fondling or intercourse.

Mireille Cir et al. find in "Intrafamilial Sexual Abuse: Brother-Sister Incest Does Not Differ from Father-Daughter and Stepfather-Stepdaughter Incest" (*Child Abuse and Neglect*, September 2002) that there were few differences between sexual abuse perpetrated by fathers, stepfathers, or brothers in their survey of seventy-two sexually abused girls between the ages of five and sixteen. They find that penetration was much more frequent in the brother-sister incest group (70.8%) than in the stepfather-stepdaughter incest group (27.3%) or the father-daughter incest group (34.8%). They also find that nine out of ten girls abused by their brothers showed clinically significant traumatic stress. These findings show that sexual abuse perpetrated by a sibling should be taken seriously.

Educators

Sex between educators and students is nothing new. However, except for sensational cases, such as that of Washington teacher Mary Kay Letourneau who was charged with child rape of her twelve-year-old student and served a seven-and-a-half-year prison term, other cases have not received much attention. Some experts observe that there seems to be a double standard in cases involving a female teacher and a male student. They point to an example in New Jersey. In 2002 Superior Court judge Bruce A. Gaeta refused to sentence Pamela Diehl-Moore to prison for pleading guilty to sexual assault and instead ordered probation. The teacher admitted having sex for six months with a thirteen-year-old student. The judge claimed he saw no harm done to the student and that the relationship might have been a way for the boy to satisfy his sexual needs. Gaeta received public reprimand for his comments. Diehl-Moore was sentenced to three years in prison on appeal.

In 2004 Charol Shakeshaft reported that no national study of public school educators who have abused students had even been done. In compliance with the No Child Left Behind Act of 2001, the U.S. Department of Education commissioned Shakeshaft to conduct a national study of sexual abuse in schools. After identifying about nine hundred literature citations that discussed educator sexual misconduct and contacting over one thousand researchers, educators, and policy makers on the issue, Shakeshaft found just fourteen U.S. and five Canadian/British empirical studies on educator sexual misconduct. (Empirical studies are based on practical observations and not theory.) With scant empirical studies on hand, she based her conclusion on two American Association of University Women *Hostile Hallways* surveys conducted in 1993 and 2000 involving about 2,065 public school students in eighth and eleventh grades. Both were Shakeshaft's own work. In addition, Shakeshaft used her 2003 reanalysis of the surveys for additional data on educator sexual misconduct.

In the report *Educator Sexual Misconduct: A Synthesis of Existing Literature* (2004, http://www.ed.gov/rschstat/research/pubs/misconductreview/report.pdf), Shakeshaft projects the numbers in her surveys to the whole public school system. She concludes that 9.6% of public school children, accounting for 4.5 million students, experienced sexual misconduct—ranging from being told sexual jokes, to being shown pictures of a sexual nature, to sexual intercourse—by educators. Educators included teachers and other school officials, such as principals, coaches, counselors, substitute teachers, teacher's aides, security guards, bus drivers, and other employees.

The studies Shakeshaft analyzes do not reveal the number or proportion of educators who were perpetrators of sexual misconduct. However, Shakeshaft's surveys show that perpetrators of sexual misconduct against students in schools were 18% teachers, 15% coaches, and 13% substitute teachers. Principals accounted for 6%, and school counselors made up 5%. (See Table 4.6.) Shakeshaft observes that teachers whose jobs involve dealing with individual students, such as coaches and music teachers, are more likely than other educators to sexually abuse students. With regard to the gender of the perpetrators, the different studies Shakeshaft surveys show a range of 4% to 42.8% for female educators and a range of 57.2% to 96% for male educators.

TABLE 4.6

Perpetrators of sexual abuse of students in school by job title

Job title	Percent
Teacher	18
Coach	15
Substitute teachers	13
Bus driver	12
Teacher's aide	11
Other school employee	10
Security guard	10
Principal	6
Counselor	5
Total	**100**

SOURCE: Charol Shakeshaft, "Table 7. Percent of Student Targets by Job Title of Offender," in *Educator Sexual Misconduct: A Synthesis of Existing Literature*, U.S. Department of Education, Office of the Under Secretary, June 2004, http://www.ed.gov/rschstat/research/pubs/misconductreview/report.pdf (accessed August 4, 2006)

Babysitters

As more and more working parents depend on outside help to care for their children, the possibility of abuse by babysitters has grown. In *Crimes against Children by Babysitters* (September 2001, http://www.ncjrs.gov/pdffiles1/ojjdp/189102.pdf), David Finkelhor and Richard K. Ormrod examined 1,427 victimizations of children by babysitters. They used information from jurisdictions in seventeen states reported to the Federal Bureau of Investigation (FBI) in 1995 through 1998. (Nationwide data on babysitter abuse was not available.) In this study, "babysitter" referred to people who were paid to care for children on a temporary basis in their own home or in the home of the child. This definition purposely excluded family members and school or other day care programs.

Finkelhor and Ormrod report that about two-thirds (65%) of the babysitter offenses studied were sex offenses. Forcible fondling comprised 41% of the offenses, followed by 11% of sodomy and 9% of rape. Another 3% represented sexual assault with an object. (See Figure 4.7.) In comparison, simple assault accounted for approximately 25% of babysitter offenses, and aggravated assault accounted for another 9%. Finkelhor and Ormrod note that minor forms of abuse are less likely to have been reported to the police (and included in their data), and that older children are less likely to be cared for by babysitters.

Overall, 63% of babysitters reported for offenses against children were male and 37% were female. The high representation of male abusers is particularly noteworthy when the fact that male babysitters are less common than female babysitters is considered. Males were especially likely to be involved in sexual offenses, accounting for 77% of these cases. A majority (71%) of male sex offenders victimized females and more than half (54%) victimized children under six years of age. Female

FIGURE 4.7

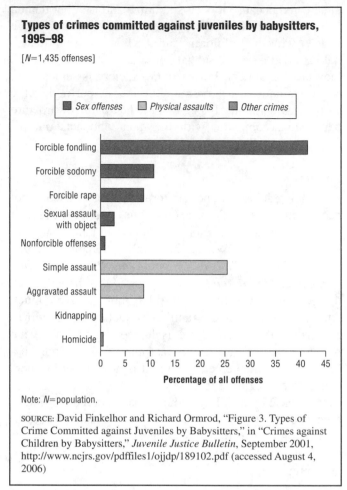

Types of crimes committed against juveniles by babysitters, 1995–98

[*N*=1,435 offenses]

Note: *N*=population.

SOURCE: David Finkelhor and Richard Ormrod, "Figure 3. Types of Crime Committed against Juveniles by Babysitters," in "Crimes against Children by Babysitters," *Juvenile Justice Bulletin*, September 2001, http://www.ncjrs.gov/pdffiles1/ojjdp/189102.pdf (accessed August 4, 2006)

sex offenders, however, nearly equally victimized female (46%) and male (54%) children, and more than two-thirds (68%) of their victims were younger children under age six. (See Figure 4.8.) Female sex offenders were most likely to be adolescents ages thirteen to fifteen (67%), male sex offenders tended to be adults (58%). Overall, more than 40% of all sexual abuse was perpetrated by babysitters between ages twelve and seventeen.

Sexual Abusers of Boys

Holmes and Slap find that more than 90% of the abusers of the sexually abused boys and young male adolescents in their study were male. Male abusers of older male teenagers and young male adults, however, made up 22% to 73% of perpetrators. This older age group also experienced abuse by females, ranging from 27% to 78%. Adolescent babysitters accounted for up to half of female sexual abusers of younger boys.

More than half of those who sexually abused male children were not family members but were known to the victims. Boys younger than six years old were more likely to be sexually abused by family and acquaintances, whereas those older than twelve were more likely to be victims of strangers. While male perpetrators used phys-

FIGURE 4.8

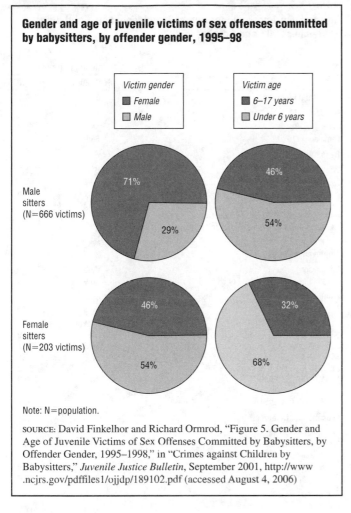

Gender and age of juvenile victims of sex offenses committed by babysitters, by offender gender, 1995–98

Victim gender
- ■ Female
- ▨ Male

Victim age
- ■ 6–17 years
- ▨ Under 6 years

Male sitters (N=666 victims)
- 71%
- 29%
- 46%
- 54%

Female sitters (N=203 victims)
- 46%
- 54%
- 32%
- 68%

Note: N=population.

SOURCE: David Finkelhor and Richard Ormrod, "Figure 5. Gender and Age of Juvenile Victims of Sex Offenses Committed by Babysitters, by Offender Gender, 1995–1998," in "Crimes against Children by Babysitters," *Juvenile Justice Bulletin*, September 2001, http://www.ncjrs.gov/pdffiles1/ojjdp/189102.pdf (accessed August 4, 2006)

ical force, with threats of physical harm increasing with victim age, female perpetrators used persuasion and promises of special favors. One study reviewed by Holmes and Slap found that up to one-third of boys participated in the abuse out of curiosity.

Priests

Public concern about sexual abuse by priests skyrocketed in the early twenty-first century as a result of a scandal surrounding abuse and cover-ups within the Catholic Church. On July 23, 2003, Massachusetts Attorney General Thomas F. Reilly released the report *The Sexual Abuse of Children in the Roman Catholic Archdiocese of Boston: A Report by the Attorney General* (http://www.ago.state.ma.us/filelibrary/archdiocese.pdf), describing the culture of secrecy involving the sexual abuse of an estimated one thousand minors in the archdiocese of Boston since 1940. Reilly's eighteen-month investigation finds that "there is overwhelming evidence that for many years Cardinal [Bernard] Law and his senior managers had direct, actual knowledge that substantial numbers of children in the Archdiocese had been sexually abused by substantial numbers of its priests."

Attorney General Reilly started the investigation in March 2002 soon after John Geoghan, a former priest in the Archdiocese of Boston, was sentenced to nine to ten years in prison for sexually abusing a ten-year-old boy. Reilly's investigators found that starting in 1979 the archdiocese had received complaints of child sexual abuse against Geoghan. Church documents, which had previously been sealed, revealed that the church not only moved him from parish to parish but had also paid settlements amounting to $15 million to the victims' families. Reilly reported that the archdiocese's own files showed that 789 people had brought sexual complaints against the Boston clergy. The attorney general believed the actual number of victims is higher. There were 237 priests and church workers who had been accused of rape and sexual assault.

EXTENT OF CHILD SEXUAL ABUSE BY PRIESTS. Responding to emerging allegations of sexual abuse by priests, in June 2002 the U.S. Conference of Catholic Bishops commissioned a study of the nature and scope of the problem of child sexual abuse in the Catholic Church. The John Jay College of Criminal Justice of the City University of New York conducted the study based on information provided by 195 dioceses, representing 98% of all diocesan priests in the United States. The researchers also collected data from 140 religious communities, accounting for about 60% of religious communities and 80% of all priests in the religious communities.

A report of the study was released in 2002. *The Nature and Scope of the Problem of Sexual Abuse of Minors by Catholic Priests and Deacons in the United States* (June 2002, http://www.usccb.org/nrb/johnjaystudy) covers the period from 1950 to 2002. Of the 109,694 priests and deacons (collectively referred to as priests) who served during this time period, 4,392 (4%) allegedly abused children under age eighteen. Most of these priests (55.7%) had a single allegation of abuse. Nearly 27% had two to three allegations, 13.9% had four to nine allegations, and 3.5% had ten or more allegations.

The report shows that 10,667 individuals made allegations of child sexual abuse by priests between 1950 and 2002. About 81% of the victims were male and 19% were female. About half (50.9%) were between the ages of eleven and fourteen. More than a quarter (27.3%) were fifteen to seventeen years old, 16% were ages eight to ten, and 6% were younger than seven. One survey question asked whether or not a sibling was also allegedly abused. Of the 6,350 individuals who provided this information, 1,842 answered "yes."

The largest number of allegations were made in the 1970s (35.3%) and the 1960s (26.1%). At the time of the allegations, most of the priests were serving in the capacity of pastors (25.1%), associate pastors (42.3%), and resident priests (10.4%). About 7.2% of the priests were teachers, 2.7% were chaplains, and 1.8% were seminary administrators or faculty members. The remaining 10.5% were bishops, vicars, cardinals, chancellors, deacons, seminarians, priests performing other functions, and priests who were relatives of the victims.

Most of the abuse occurred in the priest's home or parish residence (40.9%), in church (16.3%), and in the victim's home (12.4%). Nearly half (49.6%) of the priests socialized with the alleged victim's family, mostly (79.6%) in the family's home.

SEXUAL PREDATORS ON THE INTERNET

Many pedophiles find that the Internet gives them easy access to children. According to the report *Internet Crimes against Children* (February 2001, http://www.ojp.usdoj.gov/ovc/publications/bulletins/internet_2_2001/welcome.html) by the U.S. Department of Justice's Office for Victims of Crime, child predators who look for victims in places where children typically congregate, such as schoolyards, playgrounds, and shopping malls, now have cyberspace to commit their criminal acts. The Internet presents an even more attractive venue because predators can commit their crime anonymously and are able to contact the same child regularly. They may groom children online for the production of child pornography. They have been known to prey on vulnerable children, gaining their confidence online, and then meeting up with them for the purpose of engaging them in sex acts.

In October 2003 more than three-fourths (78.8%) of adolescents ages fourteen to seventeen used the Internet at some location. More than two-thirds (67.3%) of children ages ten to thirteen, 42% of children ages five to nine, and 19.9% of children ages three to four used the Internet. (See Table 4.7.)

Julian Fantino notes in "Child Pornography on the Internet: New Challenges Require New Ideas" (*The Police Chief*, December 2003) that more and more younger children are being used in child pornography, with a large proportion being infants and preschool children. Offenders form secret clubs, sharing modes of operation and protecting one another's identities. According to Fantino, in 2003 more than one hundred thousand Web sites contained child pornography.

National Survey on the Online Victimization of Children

In *Online Victimization: A Report on the Nation's Youth* (June 2000, http://www.missingkids.com/en_US/publications/NC62.pdf), the first national survey on the risks children face on the Internet, David Finkelhor, Kimberly J. Mitchell, and Janis Wolak find that nearly one out of five youths (19%) using the Internet in the past year had received an unwanted sexual solicitation or approach. Sexual solicitations involved requests to do sexual things

TABLE 4.7

Internet use from any location by individuals age 3 and older, September 2001 and October 2003

	Internet users (percent)	
	Sept. 2001	Oct. 2003
Total population	**55.1**	**58.7**
Gender		
Male	55.2	58.2
Female	55.0	59.2
Race/ethnicity[a]		
White[b]	61.3	65.1
White alone	n/a	65.1
Black[c]	41.1	45.6
Black alone	n/a	45.2
Asian American & Pacific Islander[d]	62.5	63.1
Asian American & Pacific Islander alone	n/a	63.0
Hispanic (of any race)	33.4	37.2
Employment status		
Employed[e]	66.6	70.7
Not employed (unemployed or NLF)[e]	38.0	42.8
Family income		
Less than $15,000	25.9	31.2
$15,000–$24,999	34.4	38.0
$25,000–$34,999	45.3	48.9
$35,000–$49,999	58.3	62.1
$50,000–$74,999	68.9	71.8
$75,000 & above	80.4	82.9
$75,000–$99,999[f]	n/a	79.8
$100,000–$149,999[f]	n/a	85.1
$150,000 & above[f]	n/a	86.1
Educational attainment[g]		
Less than high school	13.7	15.5
High school diploma/GED	41.1	44.5
Some college	63.5	68.6
Bachelor's degree	82.2	84.9
Beyond bachelor's degree	85.0	33.0
Age group		
Age 3–4	17.6	19.9
Age 5–9	41.0	42.0
Age 10–13	66.7	67.3
Age 14–17	76.4	78.8
Age 18–24	66.6	70.6
In school	85.4	86.7
Not in school	54.0	58.2
Age 25–49	65.0	68.0
In labor force	68.4	71.7
Not in labor force	47.1	49.7
Age 50+	38.3	44.8
In labor force	58.0	64.4
Not in labor force	22.2	27.6
Location of the person's household		
Rural	54.1	57.2
Urban	55.5	59.2
Urban not central city	58.8	62.5
Urban central city	50.3	54.0
Household type in which the individual lives[h]		
Married couple w/children <18 years old	63.5	65.3
Male householder w/children <18 years old	46.8	50.3
Female householder w/children <18 years old	46.6	51.4
Households without children	51.8	56.7
Non-family household	48.3	53.1
Location of Internet use		
Only at home	19.0	19.0
Only outside the home	11.8	11.6

TABLE 4.7

Internet use from any location by individuals age 3 and older, September 2001 and October 2003 [CONTINUED]

	Internet users (percent)	
	Sept. 2001	Oct. 2003
Disability status		
Between 25 and 60 and in the labor force		
Multiple disabilities	54.8	58.9
Blind or severe vision impairment	56.2	63.7
Deaf or severe hearing impairment	59.6	72.1
Difficulty walking	60.5	64.2
Difficulty typing	62.8	64.4
Difficulty leaving home	73.2	67.8
None of these disabilities	67.0	71.0
Between 25 and 60 and not in the labor force		
Multiple disabilities	25.5	27.9
Blind or severe vision impairment	40.3	40.0
Deaf or severe hearing impairment	30.9	47.9
Difficulty walking	26.3	33.1
Difficulty typing	28.8	34.3
Difficulty leaving home	24.0	26.1
None of these disabilities	47.0	52.5
Over age 60		
Multiple disabilities	6.7	8.3
Blind or severe vision impairment	9.6	23.0
Deaf or severe hearing impairment	18.7	23.6
Difficulty walking	17.3	20.7
Difficulty typing	13.5	26.1
Difficulty leaving home	7.5	10.5
None of these disabilities	26.4	34.2

n/a=Not applicable.
NLF=Not in the labor force.
[a]In 2003 respondents were able to choose multiple racial categories. Thus, 2003 race data are not strictly comparable with data from previous surveys.
[b]For 2003, "white" should be read as "white alone or in combination with other racial categories, non-Hispanic."
[c]For 2003, "black" should be read as "black alone or in combination with other racial categories, non-Hispanic."
[d]For 2003, "Asian American & Pacific Islander" should be read as "Asian American and Pacific Islander alone or in combination with other racial categories, non-Hispanic."
[e]Age 16 and older.
[f]The October 2003 current population survey had income categories above $75,000 that were not previously available.
[g]Age 24 and older.

SOURCE: Adapted from "Appendix Table 1. Internet Use from Any Location by Individuals Age 3 and Older, September 2001 and October 2003, and Living in a Home with Internet Broadband Age 3 and Older, October 2003," in *A Nation Online: Entering the Broadband Age*, U.S. Department of Commerce, September 2004, http://www.ntia.doc.gov/reports/anol/NationOnlineBroadband04.pdf (accessed August 4, 2006)

the children did not want to do, while sexual approaches involved incidents in which people tried to get children to talk about sex when they did not want to or asked them intimate questions. In addition, one out of four children (25%) reported at least one unwanted exposure to sexual material (pictures of naked people or people having sex) while surfing the Internet the past year. Michele L. Ybarra and Kimberly J. Mitchell, in "Exposure to Internet Pornography among Children and Adolescents: A National Survey" (*CyberPsychology & Behavior*, 2005, http://www.unh.edu/ccrc/pdf/jvq/CV76.pdf), show that 20% of youth between the ages of fourteen and seventeen and 8% of youth between the ages of ten and thirteen, primarily male, intentionally sought out pornographic materials on the Internet.

Teens Communicate with Strangers Online

In the report *Teenage Life Online: The Rise of the Instant-Message Generation and the Internet's Impact on Friendships and Family Relationships* (June 2001, http://www.pewinternet.org/pdfs/PIP_Teens_Report.pdf), Amanda Lenhart, Lee Rainie, and Oliver Lewis find that adolescents who have Internet access do communicate with strangers they meet online. About three out of five (60%) of online teens (ages twelve to seventeen) reported that they had received e-mails or instant messages from strangers. About 63% of those who had received e-mails or instant messages from strangers had answered such messages. Teens also said that they had lied about their age to get on a pornographic Web site. Boys (19%) were more likely than girls (11%) to have done so.

In 2006 parents, educators, and law enforcement officials sent out a warning about MySpace.com, a huge Web site designed to be an Internet chat room and hangout for teens and young adults, but which police say is attracting sexual predators. As many as fifty-eight million users post personal information on the site, including photos and Web logs (so-called blogs, containing journal-like postings from the user), sometimes with home addresses and phone numbers included. According to Jane Gordon, in "MySpace Draws a Questionable Crowd" (*New York Times*, February 26, 2006), in Connecticut police investigated several reports of sexual assaults of young girls between the ages of thirteen and fifteen that occurred after they met adult male suspects on the site. Anick Jesdanun reports in "MySpace Plans Adult Restrictions to Protect Teen Users" (*Washington Post*, June 21, 2006) that by June 2006 MySpace planned new restrictions on the interactions of adults over age eighteen and children under age sixteen on the site in response to criticisms.

EFFECTS OF CHILD SEXUAL ABUSE

According to the report *Understanding Child Sexual Abuse: Education, Prevention, and Recovery* (October 1999, http://www.apa.org/releases/sexabuse/), the American Psychological Association (APA) notes that children who have been sexually abused exhibit a range of symptoms. The immediate effects may include thumb sucking and/or bed wetting; sleep disturbances; eating problems; and school problems, including misconduct, problems with performing schoolwork, and failure to participate in activities.

The APA also details long-term effects of CSA. Adult victims of CSA may suffer from depression, sexual dysfunction, and anxiety. Anxiety may manifest itself in behaviors such as anxiety attacks, insomnia, and alcohol and drug abuse. Adult survivors of CSA also report revictimization, as rape victims or as victims of intimate physical abuse.

High-Risk Sexual Behaviors in Adolescent Girls

In "Sexual At-Risk Behaviors of Sexually Abused Adolescent Girls" (*Journal of Child Sexual Abuse*, 2003), a study of sexual at-risk behaviors of 125 female adolescents ages twelve to seventeen who had experienced sexual abuse, Caroline Cinq-Mars et al. administered a self-report questionnaire that asked about the subjects' sexual activities, not including sexual abuse experiences. Then the subjects were interviewed regarding their sexual abuse experiences, including information about the perpetrator (both family and nonfamily members), frequency and duration of abuse, severity of the abuse, and whether or not they told someone of the abuse.

Among offending family members, fathers were the perpetrators in 30.4% of incidents. Stepfathers and extended family members each were responsible for 28.8% of the sexual abuse, and brothers accounted for another 9.6% of abuse. The victims experienced more than one incident of sexual abuse, with the mean (average) number of perpetrators per victim being 1.8. The mean age for the start of abuse was 9.3 years. More than one-third (36.8%) of the victims experienced sexual abuse before age eleven.

More than half (55.3%) of the participants reported being sexually active. More than half (54.5%) had their first consensual intercourse before the age of fifteen. The rate of pregnancy was 15%. Cinq-Mars et al. find three sexual abuse characteristics that were associated with the adolescents' sexual at-risk behavior. Adolescents who experienced CSA involving penetration were more than thirteen times as likely to have been pregnant and twice as likely to have more than one consensual partner in the past year. Having been abused by more than one perpetrator (in one or more incidents) was also closely associated with at-risk behaviors—pregnancy (eight times as likely), more than one consensual sexual partner (four times as likely), and irregular condom use (three times as likely). Finally, physical coercion during abuse increased the odds of pregnancy (four times as likely), more than one consensual sexual partner (five times as likely), and irregular condom use (three times as likely).

Substance Abuse

Studies show that childhood abuse increases the risk for substance abuse later in life (see Christiane Brems et al., "Childhood Abuse History and Substance Use among Men and Women Receiving Detoxification Services," *American Journal of Drug and Alcohol Abuse*, November 2004; and Patricia B. Moran et al., "Associations between Types of Maltreatment and Substance Use during Adolescence," *Child Abuse and Neglect*, May 2004). Carl M. Anderson et al., in "Abnormal T2 Relaxation Time in the Cerebellar Vermis of Adults Sexually Abused in Childhood: Potential Role of the Vermis in

Stress-Enhanced Risk for Drug Abuse" (*Psychoneuroendocrinology*, January 2002), uncovered how this occurs. They find that the vermis, the region flanked by the cerebellar hemispheres of the brain, may play a key role in the risk for substance abuse among adults who have experienced child abuse. The vermis develops gradually and continues to produce neurons, or nerve cells, after birth. It is known to be sensitive to stress, so that stress can influence its development.

Anderson et al. compared young adults ages eighteen to twenty-two, including eight with a history of repeated CSA and sixteen others as the control group. Using functional magnetic resonance imaging technology, they measured the resting blood flow in the vermis. They find that the subjects who had been victims of CSA had diminished blood flow. Anderson et al. suggest that the stress experienced with repeated CSA may have caused damage to the vermis, which in turn could not perform its job of controlling irritability in the limbic system. The limbic system in the center of the brain, a collection of connected clusters of nerve cells, is responsible for, among other things, regulating emotions and memory. Therefore, the damaged vermis induces a person to use drugs or alcohol to suppress the irritability.

Because the CSA subjects had no history of alcohol or substance abuse, Anderson et al. wanted to confirm their findings, which linked an impaired cerebellar vermis and the potential for substance abuse in CSA victims. After analyzing test data collected from the 537 college students recruited for the study, they find that students who reported frequent substance abuse showed higher irritability in the limbic system. They also exhibited symptoms usually associated with drug use, including depression and anger.

A total of 1,478 noninjecting female sexual partners of male intravenous drug users were the subjects of a study by Robert C. Freeman, Karyn Collier, and Kathleen M. Parillo, in "Early Life Sexual Abuse as a Risk Factor for Crack Cocaine Use in a Sample of Community-Recruited Women at High Risk for Illicit Drug Use" (*American Journal of Drug and Alcohol Abuse*, February 2002). Nearly two-thirds (63.7%) of the women reported having used crack cocaine. Freeman, Collier, and Parillo find that an equal proportion of all women had suffered sexual abuse before age twelve (39.5%) and during adolescence (38.8%). Overall, nearly 22% were sexually abused during both childhood and adolescence.

While Freeman, Collier, and Parillo find a relationship between CSA and lifetime crack use, they find no direct link between sexual abuse during adolescence and lifetime crack use. They do find, however, some indirect connections between the two. Female teens who were victims of sexual abuse were more likely to run away, and these runaways were more likely to use crack because of the type of people with whom they associated.

Sexual Revictimization and Self-Harming Behaviors

In "Revictimization and Self-Harm in Females Who Experienced Childhood Sexual Abuse: Results from a Prospective Study" (*Journal of Interpersonal Violence*, December 2003), Jennie G. Noll et al. report on a longitudinal study that examines the impact of CSA on female development. This was the first prospective study that followed children from the time sexual abuse was reported through adolescence and into early adulthood. Referred by CPS agencies, the participants experienced sexual abuse by a family member before the age of fourteen. The median age at the start of sexual abuse was seven to eight years, and the median duration of abuse was two years. The group consisted of eighty-four abused children and a comparison group of eighty-two children. Two yearly interviews followed the first assessment of the group. A fourth interview was conducted four to five years after the third interview.

Noll et al. note that this study was the first to provide information about the revictimization of child sexual abuse survivors not long after their abuse (seven years after the abuse when the participants were in their adolescence and early adulthood). The study finds that participants who had been sexually abused during childhood were twice as likely as the comparison group to have experienced sexual revictimization, such as rape or sexual assault, and almost four times as likely to harm themselves through suicide attempts or self-mutilation. They also suffered about 1.6 times more physical victimization, such as domestic violence. Compared with the nonabused group, the abused group reported 20% more significant lifetime traumas subsequent to being sexually abused. Significant lifetime traumas reported by the participants included separation and losses (for example, having family or friends move away or die), emotional abuse and/or rejection by family, natural disasters, and witnessing violence.

Noll et al. observe that CSA is the "strongest predictor of self-harm," even when other types of abuse are present. They surmise that the victims may have negative feelings toward their own body and want to hurt it. Noll et al. write that some researchers believe victims may want to reveal internal pains through outward manifestation of self-harm. Others wish to reexperience feelings of shame in an attempt to resolve it.

Effects of Sexual Abuse by Women

Myriam S. Denov, in "The Long-Term Effects of Child Sexual Abuse by Female Perpetrators: A Qualitative Study of Male and Female Victims" (*Journal of Interpersonal Violence*, October 2004), conducted a qualitative study of the long-term effects of CSA by women. Unlike quantitative research, which involves collecting samples of quantitative data and performing some form of statistical analysis, qualitative research is based on a smaller sample of individuals and does not represent the general population. However, according to Denov, the qualitative approach "is particularly appropriate for a study of this nature as it can give depth and detail of phenomena that are difficult to convey with quantitative methods."

The study sample consisted of seven males and seven females, who ranged in age from twenty-three to fifty-nine years. The sexual abuse occurred when they were fourteen years old or younger. All participants reported at least one incident of sexual abuse by a lone female perpetrator. Five participants reported having been sexually abused by more than one lone perpetrator. Nine participants were abused by a female relative—six by their mother, two by their mother and grandmother, and one by his mother and sister. Four participants were abused by an unrelated person—three by a babysitter and one by a nun at a local church. While the study concerns abuse perpetrated by women, half (or seven) of the participants reported having also been sexually abused by a man (in a separate incident from the abuse by women)—four by their father, two by an unrelated male babysitter, and one by his older half-brother.

The sexual abuse started, on average, at age five and ended, on average, at age twelve. It lasted about six years. Five participants were abused more than once per week, three were abused once per week, and four were abused once per month. Two participants reported a single episode of abuse. All participants reported mild abuse (for example, kissing in a sexual way and sexual invitations). In addition, ten reported moderate abuse (genital contact or fondling [without penetration] and simulated intercourse). Nine participants experienced severe abuse (such as intercourse and penetration with fingers or objects).

Denov observes that while many effects of sexual abuse by females seem similar to that by males, female sexual abuse has long-term effects that are unique. Of the fourteen study participants, just one (a male) indicated he did not feel damaged by the sexual abuse by a woman. The other thirteen said they felt damaged by the abuse. All seven participants who were also abused by males reported that the sexual abuse by women was more damaging. The effects of child sexual abuse included substance abuse (used to "silence their rage and numb the pain"), self-injury, thoughts of suicide, depression, and rage. All victims reported a great mistrust of women and a discomfort with sexual intimacy. Most of the female victims were confused about their sense of identity and self-concept. Five out of seven said that, as young girls, they did not want to grow up to be women. Four women confessed that they continued to deny their femininity, one victim admitting that she dressed in an unwomanly fashion because she would be safest to herself and to others. Twelve participants feared they might sexually abuse their own children. In fact, two men and two women reported having sexually abused children. One man and three women decided not to have children.

Effects on Boys

MALE VICTIMS' PERCEPTION OF CSA AND CLINICAL FINDINGS. In their review of nearly 150 studies of male sexual abuse mentioned previously, Holmes and Slap find that only 15% to 39% of victims who responded to the studies thought that they were adversely affected by the sexual abuse. The victims stressed that the adverse effects were linked to the use of force, cases in which the perpetrator was much older than the victim, or cases where the victim was very young. Holmes and Slap note, however, that negative clinical results (in contrast to what the studies' subjects reported) included posttraumatic stress disorder, major depression, paranoia, aggressive behavior, poor self-image, poor school performance, and running away from home.

Holmes and Slap also find a connection between sexual abuse and subsequent substance abuse among male victims. Sexually abused males were more likely to have sex-related problems, including sexual dysfunction, hypersexuality, and the tendency to force sex on others. They surmise that the discrepancy between the respondents' perceptions of the negative consequences of their sexual victimization and those discovered in clinical outcomes may be because of several factors. Holmes and Slap observe that perhaps abused males believe they have failed to protect themselves as society expects them to do. Instead of owning up to their failure, they resort to not giving much gravity to their experiences. Moreover, if the victims had experienced pleasure while being abused, they may be confused by their feelings about it.

Sharon M. Valente finds in "Sexual Abuse of Boys" (*Journal of Child and Adolescent Psychiatric Nursing*, January 2005) that boys who have been sexually abused display a range of psychological consequences to the traumatic experience. She finds that common responses include anxiety, denial, dissociation, and self-mutilation. Boys who have been sexually abused are at risk for running away. Susan Rick, in "Sexually Abused Boys: A Vulnerable Population" (*Journal of Multicultural Nursing and Health*, Winter 2003), finds that sexually abused boys "had prominent symptoms such as fear, depression, guilt, self destructive behavior and hypersexuality."

Relationship between Male Child Sexual Abuse and Teen Pregnancy

Robert F. Anda et al., in "Abused Boys, Battered Mothers, and Male Involvement in Teen Pregnancy" (*Pediatrics*, February 2001), report on more than 4,100 men in a primary care setting who were interviewed regarding whether or not they had ever impregnated an adolescent girl. The study finds that men with a history of childhood sexual or physical abuse or of witnessing physical abuse of their mother were more likely to have been involved in teenage pregnancy. About 19% of the men reported ever getting a girl pregnant during adolescence and adulthood. The girls were between twelve and nineteen years old. About 59% of the men were age twenty or older at the time they impregnated the girls.

One-fourth (25.5%) of men who experienced CSA indicated having impregnated teen girls, compared with 17.8% of those who had not been sexually abused as children. Those whose sexual abuse was characterized by physical force or threat of harm were about twice as likely to have impregnated a teenage girl. Those who were abused at age ten and under showed an 80% increased risk of getting a teenage girl pregnant.

A Longitudinal Study of the Effects of Child Sexual Abuse

In "The Effects of Child Sexual Abuse in Later Family Life: Mental Health, Parenting, and Adjustment of Offspring" (*Child Abuse and Neglect*, May 2004), Ron Roberts et al. seek to determine the impact of child sexual abuse on adult mental health, parenting relationships, and the adjustment of the children of mothers who had been victims of CSA. They investigated 8,292 families, a subsample of the Avon Longitudinal Study of Parents and Children, a continuing study of women and their families in Avon, England. The participating women had self-reported experiences of sexual assault before adolescence. Four family groups were included:

- Single-mother families (9% of the study sample)— Consist of a nonmarried woman with no partner and her children

- Biological families (79.5%)—Consist of two parents and their biological children with no other children from previous relationships

- Stepmother/complex stepfamilies (4.6%)—Consist of fathers with at least one biological child (living in the household or visiting regularly) who is not the biological offspring of the mother

- Stepfather families (6.9%)—Consist of a mother and at least one biological child (living in the household or visiting regularly) who is not the biological offspring of the father

The study reveals that more than a quarter (26%) of survivors of child sexual abuse had teen pregnancies. These women were disproportionately likely to be currently living in a nontraditional family—single-mother families (3%) and stepfather families (2.9%)—than to be living in biological families (1.3%). Roberts et al. did not have a similar finding when it came to stepmother/complex stepfamilies. In this group just 0.8% reported child sexual abuse. They surmise that a woman who has experienced child sexual abuse tends to choose a partner without children because she might feel inadequate to take care of more children.

Child sexual abuse also has consequences on the adult survivors' mental health. Mothers who reported child sexual abuse were likely to report more depression and anxiety and lower self-esteem. These mental problems in turn affect the mothers' relationship with their children and the children's adjustment. Mothers with a history of child sexual abuse reported less self-confidence and less positive relationships with their children. The children were hyperactive and had emotional, peer, and conduct problems.

REPRESSED MEMORIES OF CHILD SEXUAL ABUSE

In the early 1900s the Austrian psychoanalyst Sigmund Freud first proposed the theory of repression, which hypothesizes that the mind can reject unpleasant ideas, desires, and memories by banishing them into the unconscious. Some clinicians believe that memory repression explains why a victim of a traumatic experience, such as childhood sexual abuse, may forget the horrible incident. Some also believe that forgotten traumatic experiences can be recovered later.

In 1988 Ellen Bass and Laura Davis published *The Courage to Heal: A Guide for Women Survivors of Child Sexual Abuse*. This book became controversial because it suggested that some women may not remember incidences of childhood abuse. Bass and Davis explain that in situations of overwhelming pain and betrayal, a child might dissociate, or separate, the memory of the experiences from conscious knowledge.

Some memory researchers do not agree, saying that children who have suffered serious psychological trauma do not repress the memory; rather, they can never forget it. They cite the examples of survivors of concentration camps or children who have witnessed the murder of a parent who never forget. Their explanation for recovered memories is that they are inaccurate. They point to studies that have demonstrated that memory is unreliable, and that it can be manipulated to "remember" events that never happened.

In the middle of this controversy are clinicians and memory researchers who believe that the workings of the mind have yet to be fully understood. They agree that, while it is possible for a trauma victim to forget and then remember a horrible experience, it is also possible for a person to have false memories.

Dissociative Amnesia for Childhood Abuse Memories

According to James A. Chu et al. in "Memories of Childhood Abuse: Dissociation, Amnesia, and Corroboration" (*American Journal of Psychiatry*, May 1999), although research shows that memories can be inaccurate and influenced by outside factors such as overt suggestions, most studies show that memory tends to be accurate when it comes to remembering the core elements of important events. Chu et al. conducted a study of ninety female patients ages eighteen to sixty who were undergoing treatment in a psychiatric hospital. Dissociative amnesia, which was discussed in this study, is a type of dissociation, or dissociative disorder.

A large proportion of patients reported childhood abuse: 83% experienced physical abuse, 82% were victims of sexual abuse, and 71% witnessed domestic violence. Those who had a history of any kind of abuse reported experiencing partial or complete amnesia. The occurrence of physical and sexual abuse at an early age accounted for a higher level of amnesia.

Contrary to the popular belief that recovered memory of childhood abuse typically occurs under psychotherapy or hypnosis, most of the patients who suffered complete amnesia of their physical and sexual abuse indicated first recalling the abuse when they were at home and alone. Most patients did not recover memory of childhood abuse as a result of suggestions during therapy. Just one or two participants (for each of the three types of abuse) reported first memory of abuse while in a therapy session. Nearly half (48% for physical abuse and 45% for sexual abuse) were not undergoing psychological counseling or treatment when they first remembered the abuse.

Critics of recovered memories note the lack of corroboration (confirmation that the abuse really occurred) in many instances of recovered memories. In this study Chu et al. find that, among patients who tried to corroborate their abuse, more than half found physical evidence such as medical records. Nearly nine out of ten of those who suffered sexual abuse found verbal validation of such abuse.

Betrayal Trauma Theory

In *Betrayal Trauma: The Logic of Forgetting Childhood Abuse* (1996), Jennifer J. Freyd proposes the betrayal trauma theory to explain how children who had experienced abuse may process that betrayal of trust by mentally blocking information about it. Freyd explains that people typically respond to betrayal by distancing themselves from the betrayer. Children, however, who have suffered abuse at the hands of a parent or a caregiver, might not be able to distance themselves from the betrayer. Children need the caregiver for their survival so they "cannot afford *not* to trust" the betrayer. Consequently, the children develop a "blindness" to the betrayal.

Jennifer J. Freyd, Anne P. DePrince, and Eileen L. Zurbriggen, in "Self-Reported Memory for Abuse Depends upon Victim-Perpetrator Relationship" (*Journal of Trauma and Dissociation*, 2001), report on their preliminary findings relating to the betrayal trauma theory. They find that people who had been abused by a trusted caregiver reported greater amnesia, compared with those whose abusers were not their caregivers. Greater amnesia was also more likely to be associated with the fact that the perpetrator was a caregiver than with the repeated trauma of abuse.

A Longitudinal Study of Memory and Childhood Sexual Abuse

In *Resolving Childhood Trauma: A Long-Term Study of Abuse Survivors* (2000), Catherine Cameron discusses a long-term study of child sexual abuse survivors she conducted between 1986 and 1998. Cameron interviewed seventy-two women, ages twenty-five to sixty-four, during a twelve-year period. The women comprised a group of sexual abuse survivors who sought therapy for the first time in the 1980s. On average, it had been thirty years since their first abuse occurred (thirty-six years for those who suffered amnesia). The women were in private therapy, were better educated, and were more financially well off than most survivors. Twelve imprisoned women were included in the survey. They came from a low socio-economic background, were serving long sentences, and had participated only in brief group therapy sessions, lasting less than a year.

Cameron sought to study amnesia as both an effect and a cause—what was it about the abuse that resulted in amnesia and how did the amnesia affect the victim later on in life? Twenty-five women were amnesic, having no awareness of the abuse until recently. Twenty-one were nonamnesic, unable to forget their abuse, and fourteen were partially amnesic about their abuse. The imprisoned women were not assigned a specific category because they were part of a therapy group.

About eight out of ten of the amnesic and partially amnesic women believed that they did not remember the sexual abuse because the memories were too painful to live with (82%) and they felt a sense of guilt or shame (79%). More than half of each group believed the amnesia served as a defense mechanism resulting from their desire to protect the family (58%) and love for, or dependence on, the perpetrator (53%). About three-quarters (74%) thought the amnesia occurred because they felt no one would believe them or help them. More than one-third (37%) thought the amnesia had come about because they needed to believe in a "safe" world.

During the years between the abuse and the recall of the abuse, the amnesics reported experiencing the same problems as the nonamnesics, including problems with relationships, revictimization, self-abuse, and dependency on alcohol. Because the amnesics, however, had no conscious knowledge of their childhood abuse, they could not find an explanation for their problems. Cameron theorizes that the conflict between the amnesia and memories that needed release left the amnesic victims depressed and confused.

Cameron addresses the allegations that some therapists implant false memories of sexual abuse in their clients. She notes that 72% of the amnesic women in her study had begun to recall their abuse before seeking therapy. Once the survivors in her study confronted their traumatic past, they took charge of how they wanted their therapy handled. Cameron also observes that, because it is evident that recovered memories of childhood abuse are common, they should not be labeled as "false memories" nor accepted as "flawless truth," but should instead be explored by proponents of the opposing views.

Research Supporting the Repression of Memory

The best study to date on amnesia for childhood abuse was conducted by Linda Meyer Williams. The strength of this study lies in the fact that she interviewed adults whose sexual abuse in childhood had been documented at the time that it happened. In "Recall of Childhood Trauma: A Prospective Study of Women's Memories of Child Sexual Abuse" (*Journal of Consulting and Clinical Psychology*, 1994), Williams reports on the detailed interviews she conducted with 129 women who, seventeen years previously, had been taken to the emergency room after being sexually abused. Williams finds that more than one out of three women did not report the sexual abuse during the interview. She concludes that most or all of these women did not remember the documented abuse. She also finds that the younger the child was at the time of the abuse, and the closer the relationship the child had with the perpetrator, the greater the likelihood that the abuse would not be remembered.

FALSE MEMORIES

In *The Myth of Repressed Memory: False Memories and Allegations of Sexual Abuse* (1994), psychologist Elizabeth F. Loftus, a leading opponent of the recovered-memory movement, claims that repression is not normal memory and that it is empirically unproven. She does not believe that the mind can block out experiences of recurrent traumas, with the person unaware of them, and then recover them years later. Her explanation for recovered memories is that they are false memories. While the people who experience them genuinely believe them, they did not actually happen. She and other critics of recovered memories believe that therapy to "recover" repressed memories can lead people to believe they remember things that never actually happened.

Loftus and other researchers have shown that false memories can be implanted fairly easily in the laboratory. In the *Myth of Repressed Memory*, Loftus recounts assigning a term project to students in her cognitive psychology class. The project involved implanting a false memory in someone's mind. One of the students chose his fourteen-year-old brother as his test subject. The student wrote about four events his brother had supposedly experienced. Three of the experiences really happened, but the fourth one was a fake event of his brother getting lost at the mall at age five. For the next five days the younger brother was asked to read about his experiences (written by his older brother) and then write down details that he could remember about them. The younger brother "remembered" his shopping mall experience quite well, describing details elaborately.

In "Make-Believe Memories" (*American Psychologist*, November 2003), Loftus notes that memories can be influenced by our imagination. "Imagination can not only make people believe they have done simple things that they have not done but can also lead people to believe that they have experienced more complex events," writes Loftus. She describes a study in which participants were told to imagine performing a common task with certain objects, such as flipping a coin. The second meeting consisted of imagining doing a task without using any object. In a subsequent meeting, participants were tested on their memory of the first day's task performance. Some participants "remembered" not only tasks they had not done but also unusual ones they had not performed.

In 1992 an organization called the False Memory Syndrome Foundation (FMSF) was formed. It is a network of people who have been accused of childhood sexual abuse by their adult children. They claim that the accusations of abuse, and their children's recovered memories, are false. The group coined the term False Memory Syndrome (not a recognized psychological disorder) and has worked to publicize the concept of false memories of childhood abuse.

CHAPTER 5

CHILD ABUSE AND THE LAW

BEGINNINGS OF INVOLVEMENT IN THE LAW: DISCLOSURE

What should parents do when their child says he or she has been abused? It may come as an offhand remark, as if the child is testing to see what the parents' reaction will be. Perhaps the child is engaged in sexual behavior, a common symptom of sexual abuse. For example, the child may go through the motions of sexual intercourse and then say that this is what a parent, stepparent, relative, or teacher at school has done. A major preschool sexual abuse case against Margaret Kelly Michaels, a teacher at the Wee Care Day Nursery in Maplewood, New Jersey, began when a boy who was having his temperature taken rectally at the pediatrician's office remarked that his teacher had been doing the same thing to him while he napped at school. The remark ultimately led to Michaels being charged with various forms of sexual abuse, and a nine-month trial ensued, at which several children testified.

Sometimes a parent realizes that something is wrong when the child's behavior changes. Some young children have an especially hard time expressing themselves verbally and may instead begin having sleep difficulties, such as nightmares and night terrors; eating problems; a fear of going to school (if that is the site of the abuse); regression; acting out, such as biting, masturbating, or sexually attacking other family members; and withdrawing. These behavior changes, however, do not necessarily mean that the child is being sexually abused. Children may also express themselves in their drawings.

The abuse may have occurred for a long time before children speak about it. Why do children keep the abuse a secret? Children who reveal their abuse through nonverbal ways may be afraid to speak out because they believe the threats of death or punishment made by their abuser. They may feel responsible for what has happened to them or fear that adults will not believe them. They may not know how to describe what has happened to them.

By contrast, children may tell about abuse when they come into contact with someone who feels safe, or who appears to already know about the abuse. Or they may tell when they are physically injured or pregnant. Sometimes children tell when they believe that if the abuse continues it will be unbearable.

If parents believe their child, particularly if the abuser is not a family member, their first reaction may be to file charges against the alleged perpetrator. Parents rarely realize how difficult and painful the process can be. Some experts claim that children psychologically need to see their abuser punished, whereas others feel children are victimized by the court process, only this time by the people who are supposed to protect them.

Is a Child's Account Reliable?

Some experts believe children do not lie about abuse. They point out that children cannot describe events unfamiliar to them. For example, the average six-year-old has no concept of how forced penetration feels or how semen tastes. Experts also note that children lie to get themselves out of trouble, not into trouble, and reporting sexual abuse is definitely trouble. Children sometimes recant, or deny that any abuse has happened, after they have disclosed it. Perhaps the reaction to the disclosure was unfavorable, or the pain and fear of talking about the experience were too great. The child's recanting under interrogation in a court of law may prove damaging to the case and may encourage claims that the child has made false accusations.

Kenneth V. Lanning, in "Criminal Investigation of Sexual Victimization of Children" (John E. B. Myers et al., eds., *The APSAC Handbook on Child Maltreatment*, 2002), claims that children rarely lie about sexual abuse. Some children, however, may recount what they believe in their minds to be the truth, although their accounts may turn out to be inaccurate. Lanning gives the following explanations for these inaccuracies:

- The child may be experiencing distorted memory because of trauma.
- The child's story might be a reflection of normal childhood fears and fantasy.
- The child may have been confused by the abuser's use of trickery or drugs.
- The child's testimony may be influenced by the suggestive questions of investigators.
- The child's account might reflect urban legends and cultural mythology.

JUVENILE COURT SYSTEM: INNOVATIONS TO HELP CHILD WITNESSES

In 2006 all fifty states had authorized juvenile family courts to intervene in child abuse cases, and all fifty states considered child abuse of any kind to be a felony and a civil crime. A felony (a serious crime) could result in a prison term; a loss in a civil suit (a noncriminal case involving private parties) could result in the payment of a fine or in losing custody of the child. While many states have distinct and separate juvenile courts, some states try juvenile or family cases in courts of general jurisdiction, where child protection cases are given priority over other cases on the court's docket.

Government child protective services (CPS) initiates a civil court proceedings (after consultation with CPS lawyers) if it seeks to remove the child from the home, provide in-home protective services, or require the abuser to get treatment. Criminal proceedings are initiated by a government prosecutor if the abuser is to be charged with a crime, such as sexual abuse.

In civil child protection cases the accused has the right to a closed trial (a hearing with no jury and closed to the public) in which court records are kept confidential, although a few states permit jury trials. In criminal child protection cases, however, the person charged with abuse is entitled to the Sixth Amendment right to an open trial (a jury trial opened to the public), which can be waived only by the defendant.

In 1967 *In re Gault* substantially changed the nature of juvenile courts. Initially, children were not subject to constitutional due process rights or legal representation, and judges presiding over these courts were given unlimited power to protect children from criminal harm. The U.S. Supreme Court decided *In re Gault* that children—whether they have committed a crime or are the victims of a crime—are entitled to due process and legal representation. These rights, however, are interpreted differently among the states.

Court-Appointed Special Advocates

The federal Victims of Child Abuse Act of 1990 requires that a court-appointed special advocate (CASA) volunteer be provided to every child maltreatment victim who needs such an advocate. A CASA volunteer serves as the guardian *ad litem* (guardian at law) of the child during legal proceedings. Their duty is to ensure that the legal system serves the best interests of the child.

According to the National CASA Association (August 2006, http://www.nationalcasa.org/about_us/history.html), 948 CASA programs, with more than fifty thousand volunteers, have been established in all fifty states. Typically, the judge appoints a CASA volunteer, who then reviews all records pertaining to the maltreated child, including CPS reports and medical and school records. The volunteer also meets with the child, parents and family members, social workers, health care providers, school officials, and other people who may know of the child's history. The research compiled by the CASA volunteer helps the child's lawyer in presenting the case. It also helps the court in deciding what is best for the child. Each trained volunteer works with one or two children at a time, enabling the volunteer to research and monitor each case thoroughly.

Anatomically Detailed Dolls

Many legal professionals use dolls with sexual organs made to represent the human anatomy to help sexually abused children explain what has happened to them in court. Advocates of the use of dolls report that they make it easier to get a child to talk about things that can be difficult to discuss. Even when children know the words, they may be too embarrassed to say them out loud to strangers. The dolls allow these children to point out and show things difficult or even impossible for them to say. Some experts claim dolls work because children find them easier to use, as they are age appropriate and familiar to them.

Lori S. Holmes notes in "Using Anatomical Dolls in Child Sexual Abuse Forensic Interviews" (*American Prosecutors Research Institute Update*, 2000) that the use of anatomical dolls helps the child demonstrate internal consistency. A child who has made allegations of abuse can show the interviewer exactly what happened to him or her, thus confirming the oral disclosure. In "Anatomical Dolls: Their Use in Assessment of Children Who May Have Been Sexually Abused" (*Journal of Child Sexual Abuse*, 2005), Kathleen Coulborn Faller also finds that the selective use of the dolls to help children who have trouble speaking about sexual abuse is warranted.

Potential problems, however, exist in using dolls. According to the "affordance phenomenon," children will experiment with any opportunities provided by a new experience. Some experts believe that what might appear to be sexual behavior, such as putting a finger in a hole in the doll, may have no more significance than a child putting a finger through the hole in a doughnut.

Such exploratory play can have disastrous effects when it is misinterpreted as the re-creation of a sexual act. In addition, some researchers who compare children's verbal details of sexual abuse with their enactments with anatomical dolls find that children under age six using the dolls often contradicted the verbal details provided without the dolls. They also find that children from three to twelve years old produced more fantastic details with the dolls than without them (Karen L. Thierry et al., "Developmental Differences in the Function and Use of Anatomical Dolls during Interviews with Alleged Sexual Abuse Victims," *Journal of Consulting and Clinical Psychology*, December 2005).

Videotaped Testimony and Closed-Circuit Television Testimony: Does It Violate the Confrontation Clause?

It is difficult for children to deal with the fear and intimidation of testifying in open court. The person who has allegedly abused and threatened them may be sitting before them, while the serious nature of the court can be intimidating to them. Videotaped testimony and closed-circuit television testimony have become common methods used to relieve the pressure on the child who must testify. According to the National Center for Prosecution of Child Abuse in "Legislation Regarding the Use of Closed-Circuit Television Testimony in Criminal Child Abuse Proceedings" (September 2002, http://www.ndaa-apri.org/pdf/closed_circuit_tv_testimony.pdf), the federal government and thirty-seven states allow the use of closed-circuit television testimony instead of in-court testimony for children under age eighteen. States vary in their requirements regarding the use of closed-circuit television testimony. In some states the jury stays in the courtroom while the child, the judge, the prosecutor, the defendant, and the defense attorney are in a different room. In some states the child is alone in a room separate from the jury and other participants.

Furthermore, the National Center for Prosecution of Child Abuse notes in "Legislation Regarding the Admissibility of Videotaped Interviews/Statements in Criminal Child Abuse Proceedings" (July 2004, http://www.ndaa-apri.org/pdf/statute_admissibility_videotaped_interviews_statements.pdf) that the federal government and seventeen states recognize the right to use videotaped testimony taken at a preliminary hearing or deposition (testimony given under oath to be used in court at a later date) for children under age eighteen. A videotape of the pretrial interviews shows the jury how the child behaved and whether the interviewer prompted the child. Often prepared soon after the abuse, videotaped interviews preserve the child's memory and emotions when they are still fresh. Because a videotaped interview presents an out-of-court statement, which the alleged abuser cannot refute face to face, it can be admitted only as a hearsay

exception. (Hearsay is considered secondhand information; hearsay evidence and exceptions are further discussed below). Some state laws also say that, even with the videotaped testimony, the child may still be called to testify and be cross-examined.

Videotaping can cut down on the number of interviews the child must undergo, and prosecutors indicate that this method encourages guilty pleas. Videotapes can be powerful tools to deal with the problem of the child who recants his or her testimony when put on the witness stand. The case can still be prosecuted, with the jury witnessing the child's opposing statements. Experts believe that a videotape statement containing sufficient details from the child and elicited through nonleading questions makes for compelling evidence.

Depositions, however, can be as demanding and difficult as a trial. They often take place in small rooms, forcing the child and defendant closer together than they might have been in a courtroom. The judge might not be there to control the behavior of the defendant or his or her attorney. Individuals who might offer the child support, such as victim advocates, may not be permitted to attend.

Furthermore, if the prosecutor claims the child is unable to handle the emotional trauma of the witness stand, the child may have to undergo medical or psychiatric tests by the state or defense attorney to permit videotaped testimony. This could be as traumatic as going through with a personal appearance at the trial. Some states permit the child to sit behind a one-way mirror so that the defendant can see the child and communicate with the defense attorney, but the child is shielded from direct confrontation with the defendant.

Critics of videotaping suggest other possible problems:

- It is possible that people "perform" for the camera instead of communicating.

- Victims are placed under subjective scrutiny by juries when every gesture, change in voice or speech pattern, and eye movement are judged.

- There is no accountability for the videotapes. Multiple copies of tapes are sometimes made and given to various attorneys and witnesses. Some tapes are used at training sessions, often without concealing the victims' names.

Use of closed-circuit television testimony or videotape testimony has been challenged on the grounds that the defendant's Sixth Amendment constitutional right permits him or her to confront an accuser face to face. The Confrontation Clause of the Sixth Amendment states, "In all criminal prosecutions, the accused shall enjoy the right ... to be confronted with the witnesses against him."

Several court rulings in the 1990s upheld the introduction of closed-circuit television, but only when it was used carefully and with full recognition of the rights of the accused. Those who disagree with these rulings claim that this method unfairly influences the jury to think that the accused is guilty simply because the procedure is permitted, and, worse, it deprives the defendant of his or her constitutional right to confront the accuser face to face.

COY V. IOWA. The use of closed-circuit television to help child witnesses in abuse cases has been repeatedly challenged in the courts. In one such case an Iowa trial court, pursuant to a state law enacted to protect child victims of sexual abuse, allowed a screen to be placed between the two child witnesses and the alleged abuser. The lighting in the courtroom was adjusted so that the children could not see the defendant, Coy, through the screen. Coy, however, was able to see the children dimly and hear them testify. The trial judge cautioned the jury that the presence of the screen was not an indication of guilt. Coy was convicted.

In *Coy v. Iowa* (1986), Coy appealed to the Iowa Supreme Court, arguing that the screen denied him the right to confront his accusers face to face as provided by the Sixth Amendment. In addition, he claimed that due process was denied because the presence of the screen implied guilt. The Iowa Supreme Court, however, upheld the conviction of the trial court, ruling that the screen had not hurt Coy's right to cross-examine the child witnesses, nor did its presence necessarily imply guilt.

The U.S. Supreme Court, however, in a 6–2 decision, reversed the ruling of the Iowa Supreme Court and remanded the case to the trial court for further proceedings. In *Coy v. Iowa* (1988) the Court maintained that the right to face-to-face confrontation was the essential element of the Sixth Amendment's Confrontation Clause. It held that any exceptions to that guarantee would be allowed only if needed to further an important public policy. The Court found no specific evidence in this case that these witnesses needed special protection that would require a screen.

MARYLAND V. CRAIG. In another case in June 1990, in a 5–4 decision, the U.S. Supreme Court upheld the use of one-way closed-circuit television. In *Maryland v. Craig* a six-year-old child alleged that Sandra Craig had committed perverted sexual practices and assault and battery on her in the prekindergarten run by Craig. In support of its motion to permit the child to testify through closed-circuit television, the state presented expert testimony that the child "wouldn't be able to communicate effectively[,] would probably stop talking and . . . would withdraw and curl up" if required to testify in the courtroom.

The Supreme Court decision, written by Justice Sandra Day O'Connor, noted that the Sixth Amendment Confrontation Clause does not guarantee "absolute" right to a face-to-face meeting with the witness. The closed-circuit television does permit cross-examination and observation of the witness's demeanor. Justice O'Connor declared, "We are therefore confident that use of the one-way closed-circuit television procedure, where necessary to further an important state interest, does not impinge upon the truth-seeking or symbolic purposes of the Confrontation Clause."

Hearsay Evidence

With the Sixth Amendment Confrontation Clause, the hearsay rule is intended to prevent the conviction of defendants by reports of evidence offered by someone other than the witness. With a few exceptions, hearsay is inadmissible as testimony because the actual witness cannot be cross-examined and his or her demeanor cannot be assessed for credibility of testimony. Whether or not to accept the hearsay evidence from a child's reports of abuse to a parent has been frequently debated.

Some courts consider spontaneous declarations or excited utterances made by a person right after a stressful experience as reliable hearsay. Courts also allow statements individuals have made to physicians and other medical personnel for purposes of medical treatment or diagnosis. In this case it is generally assumed that people who consult with physicians are seeking treatment and, therefore, tell the physicians the truth about their illness.

Hearsay evidence is especially important in cases of child sexual abuse. Cases often take years to come to trial, by which time a child may have forgotten the details of the abuse or may have made psychological progress in dealing with the trauma. The parents may be reluctant to plunge the child back into the anxious situation suffered earlier. Hearsay evidence can be crucial in determining the validity of sexual abuse charges in custody cases. In these cases juries need to know when the child first alleged abuse, to whom, under what circumstances, and whether the child ever recanted.

In *Ohio v. Roberts* (1980), a case that was not about child abuse, the U.S. Supreme Court established the basis for permitting hearsay evidence: the actual witness has to be unavailable and his or her statement has to be reliable enough to permit another person to repeat it to the jury. Many judges have chosen to interpret unavailability on physical standards rather than on the emotional unavailability that children who are afraid to testify may exhibit. Furthermore, legal experts insist that the reliability of a statement does not refer to whether the statement appears to be truthful, but only that it has sufficient reliability for the jury to decide whether it is true.

WHITE V. ILLINOIS. In *White v. Illinois* (1992), the U.S. Supreme Court dealt with both the hearsay rules and the Confrontation Clause of the Sixth Amendment.

Randall White was charged with sexually assaulting a four-year-old girl, S. G., in the course of a residential burglary. The child's screams attracted the attention of her babysitter, who witnessed White leaving the house. S. G. related essentially the same version of her experience to her babysitter, her mother (who returned home shortly after the attack), a police officer, an emergency room nurse, and a doctor. All these adults testified at the trial. S. G. did not testify, being too emotional each time she was brought to the courtroom.

White was found guilty and appealed on the grounds that, because the defendant had not been able to face the witness who had made the charges of sexual assault, her hearsay testimony was invalid under the Confrontation Clause. The Court, in a unanimous decision, rejected linking the Confrontation Clause and the admissibility of hearsay testimony.

S. G.'s statements fulfilled the hearsay requirements in that they were either spontaneous declarations or made for medical treatment and, therefore, in the eyes of the Supreme Court, "may justifiably carry more weight with a [court] than a similar statement offered in the relative calm of a courtroom." The Court concluded that whether the witness appeared to testify had no bearing on the validity of the hearsay evidence. Furthermore, because the hearsay statements in this case fit the "medical evidence" and "spontaneous declaration" exceptions, its decision upheld hearsay evidence as valid.

BUGH V. MITCHELL. Richard Bugh was convicted of sexually molesting his four-year-old daughter in 1989. He was convicted based on hearsay testimony. The girl had told four people in out-of-court statements about the sexual abuse: her mother, a counselor, a county social services supervisor, and a medical doctor. Fourteen years later, having gone through a series of appeals, Bugh petitioned the U.S. Court of Appeals for the Sixth Circuit, challenging the hearsay testimony. Bugh claimed that the trial court's admission of hearsay testimony violated his Sixth Amendment confrontation rights.

On May 13, 2003, in *Bugh v. Mitchell,* the appeals court ruled that the hearsay testimonies were admissible. The court added that the defendant's confrontation rights had not been violated because he had the chance to cross-examine the child and the four witnesses. The court rejected Bugh's argument that the child's statements to her mother were not excited utterances because when she told her mother of the alleged molestation "there was no startling event which would have produced nervous excitement." The court noted that the hearsay exception applied in this case, relying on *State v. Wagner* (1986), "in which the Ohio appeals court noted the 'limited reflective powers' of a three-year-old and the lack of motive or reflective capacities to prevaricate [lie about]

the circumstances of an attack, as supporting the trust-worthiness of a child's communications to others."

COURT REJECTS HEARSAY EVIDENCE. In *Carpenter v. State* (2003) the Indiana Supreme Court heard an appeal by William Carpenter, who had been found guilty of sexually molesting his three-year-old daughter, A. C., in 2000. Among the evidence presented at the trial were out-of-court statements made by the child to her mother and grandfather. Relying on its decision in *Pierce v. State* (1997), the state supreme court noted that in *Pierce* the child's statements were spontaneous and took place soon after the alleged molestation. On the contrary, in Carpenter's case the state could not establish the precise time of alleged molestation or whether the child's statements occurred immediately after the alleged molestation. The court observed:

> We find that the testimony recounting A. C.'s statements to her mother and grandfather and her videotape interview failed to exhibit sufficient indications of reliability as the protected person statute requires because of the combination of the following circumstances: there was no indication that A. C.'s statements were made close in time to the alleged molestations, the statements themselves were not sufficiently close in time to each other to prevent implantation or cleansing, and A. C. was unable to distinguish between truth and falsehood.

CRAWFORD V. WASHINGTON **OVERRULES** *OHIO V. ROBERTS.* On March 8, 2004, the U.S. Supreme Court, in *Crawford v. Washington,* overturned its 1980 ruling in *Ohio v. Roberts,* which held that the Sixth Amendment right of confrontation does not prohibit hearsay evidence if a judge deems that evidence reliable and trustworthy. *Crawford* was not a child abuse case. In 1999 Michael Crawford stabbed a man who allegedly attempted to rape his wife. During the trial the state introduced an out-of-court, tape-recorded statement to police by his wife, who was present during the assault. The state wanted to show that Crawford did not stab the man in self-defense as he had told police. His wife did not testify during the trial because of Washington's spousal privilege, which prohibits one spouse from testifying against the other without the other's consent. The trial court found the wife's statement to be reliable and trustworthy and accepted it as evidence. Crawford was convicted of assault with a deadly weapon.

On Crawford's appeal, the Washington Court of Appeals reversed the trial court ruling. The Washington Supreme Court subsequently reinstated the conviction. The U.S. Supreme Court agreed to hear the case to determine whether the state's use of the wife's statement violated the Confrontation Clause. In reversing the judgment of the Washington Supreme Court, the Court held that when a hearsay statement is "testimonial," the Confrontation Clause bars the state from using that statement against a criminal defendant unless the person who made the statement is available to testify at trial, or the defendant had a prior opportunity to cross-examine that person.

Although the Court stated, "We leave for another day any effort to spell out a comprehensive definition of 'testimonial,'" it gave as an example of a testimonial statement that which is made during police interrogations (for example, the pretrial statement of Crawford's wife). The Court added that its *Crawford* ruling holds regardless of whether or not the statement is a hearsay exception or is judged reliable, thus overruling *Ohio v. Roberts*. The case was sent back to the Washington Supreme Court for further proceedings. Although *Crawford* was not a child abuse case, it has major implications in child abuse cases.

CRAWFORD V. WASHINGTON **IS INTERPRETED BY A CALIFORNIA COURT.** In a California case defendant Seum Sisavath was convicted of, among other things, several child sexual abuse charges involving two sisters, ages four and eight. The younger child was not at trial because she was found incompetent to testify. Based on the hearsay testimonies of an officer who responded to the mother's call to police and of an investigator from the district attorney's office who attended a videotaped interview of the younger child, the court admitted the statements. Sisavath was found guilty of most of the sexual charges and sentenced to thirty-two years to life. The defendant petitioned the California Court of Appeals.

While the appeal was pending, the U.S. Supreme Court decided *Crawford v. Washington*. Consequently, the appeals court ruled in *People v. Sisavath* that the "testimonial" hearsay statements against the defendant were inadmissible under *Crawford* because they violated the Confrontation Clause of the Sixth Amendment. Because the U.S. Supreme Court did not define "testimonial," the appeals court observed:

> It is more likely that the Supreme Court meant simply that if a statement was given under circumstances in which its use in a prosecution is reasonably foreseeable by an objective observer, then the statement is testimonial. . . . We have no occasion here to hold, and do not hold, that statements made in every MDIC [Multidisciplinary Interview Center] interview are testimonial under *Crawford*. We hold only that Victim 2's [younger victim's] statements in the MDIC interview in this case were testimonial. [The MDIC is a facility specially designed and staffed for interviewing children suspected of being victims of abuse.]

EFFECT ON CHILD ABUSE CASES. Because child abuse cases typically rely on evidence such as videotaped testimony, statements to physicians, parents, counselors, and other adults in the aftermath of an assault, the impact of *Crawford* may be substantial. Although children cannot be expected to understand that their statements to physicians and counselors will be used at trial, Myrna Raeder argues in "Remember the Ladies and the Children Too: Crawford's

Impact on Domestic Violence and Child Abuse Cases" (*Brooklyn Law Review*, Fall 2005) that courts, in the aftermath of *Crawford*, have interpreted statements as testimonial using an "objective standard." In other words, if an adult could reasonably be expected to understand that statements made would be used at trial, they have been ruled as inadmissible unless the child is present. Raeder argues that statements made to physicians, counselors, and even parents are all being interpreted by courts as testimonial, and therefore not acceptable as evidence under *Crawford*. Videotaped interviews by forensic teams have also generally been found to be testimonial, and therefore may fall into disuse as a result of *Crawford*. Raeder concludes that "post-Crawford, if a child does not testify, the chances of winning at trial plummet."

In fact, many child sexual abuse convictions were overturned after the *Crawford v. Washington* decision. According to Erin Thompson in "Child Sex Abuse Victims: How Will Their Stories Be Heard after *Crawford v. Washington*?" (*Campbell Law Review*, Spring 2005), convictions in *People v. Espinoza*, *People v. Vigil*, *In the Interest of R.A.S.*, and *Snowden v. State* were all overturned because the perpetrators had been convicted based on videotaped testimony, with no opportunity for cross-examination of the child witnesses. The reversal of these convictions reflects the difficulty faced by prosecutors in child abuse cases in the aftermath of *Crawford*.

Expert Witnesses

Videotaping and closed-circuit television permit juries to see and hear child witnesses but do not mean that the juries will understand or believe them. Prosecutors often request permission to bring in an expert witness to clarify an abused child's behavior, particularly to explain why a child might have waited so long to make an accusation or why the child might withdraw an accusation made earlier.

The danger of bringing in an expert witness is that the expert often lends an unwarranted stamp of authenticity to the child's truthfulness. If an expert states that children rarely lie about sex abuse, that expert might be understood by the jury to be saying that the defendant must be guilty, when the expert has no way of knowing if this is the case. In some highly contested cases, expert witnesses swayed the jurors in their decision.

The states have their own rules when it comes to expert testimony. Federal courts, however, follow the Federal Rules of Evidence. On December 1, 2000, the Federal Rules of Evidence were amended because of concerns that experts in the past had lacked the proper qualifications. The new rule requires that before the jury can hear expert testimony, the trial judge first has to determine that the expert has the proper "knowledge, skill, experience, training, or education" to help the jury understand the evidence.

For expert testimony to be acceptable in court, the statements made must be general and explain only psychological tendencies, never referring specifically to the child witness. The U.S. Court of Appeals for the Eighth Circuit, in *United States v. Azure* (1986), reversed the conviction of the defendant because an expert's testimony was too specific. During trial an expert witness had testified that the alleged victim was believable. According to the court, by "putting his stamp of believability on [the young girl's] entire story, [the expert] essentially told the jury that [the child] was truthful in saying that [the defendant] was the person who sexually abused her. No reliable test for truthfulness exists and [the expert witness] was not qualified to judge the truthfulness of that part of [the child's] story."

DIFFICULTIES IN PROSECUTING CHILD ABUSERS

For the prosecutor's office, child abuse can present many problems. The foremost is that the victim is a child. This becomes an even greater problem when the victim is young (from birth to age six), because the question of competency arises. More and more studies have examined children's reliability in recalling and retelling past events. Researchers find that different settings and interview techniques may result in children remembering different details at different times.

The prosecutor may also worry about the possible harm the child may suffer in having to relive the abuse and in being interrogated by adversarial defense attorneys. For instance, if the child is an adolescent making accusations of sexual abuse, the defendant's attorney may accuse the teenage victim of seducing the defendant or having willingly taken part in the acts.

Other factors that prosecutors must consider include the slowness of the court process and the possibility that the case may be delayed, not just once, but several times. This is hard enough for adults to tolerate, but it is particularly difficult for children. The delay prolongs the child's pain. Children may become more reluctant to testify or may no longer be able to retell their stories accurately. There is a far greater difference between a thirty-one-year-old testifying about something that happened when he or she was twenty-six and an eleven-year-old retelling an event that happened at six years of age. Prosecutors are also obliged to keep the child's best interests in mind and to try and preserve the family.

Prosecuting Child Sexual Abuse

Prosecuting a child sexual abuse case is particularly challenging. A child who has been physically abused will often display unmistakable signs of the abuse, such as broken bones. Sexual abuse does not necessarily leave such visible marks. So the abuse is less likely to have been noticed by others and is more difficult to verify once an accusation has been made.

Many other difficulties exist. For example, physical abusers will sometimes admit to having "disciplined" their children by striking them or have actually been seen committing abusive acts in public. Sexual abusers almost never admit to their actions when confronted, and their abuse always takes place in secret. Another major difficulty is that young children who have little or no knowledge of sex may have trouble understanding, let alone explaining in a court room, what was done to them.

The willingness of people to believe children's accusations of sexual abuse has varied greatly since the mid-twentieth century. At one time people were simply unwilling to believe that sexual abuse of children was happening or happening with any frequency. Once society accepted the fact that child sexual abuse was occurring, responses to accusations of child sexual abuse went from disbelief to almost total acceptance by the public. In the 1980s and 1990s, when day care workers were prosecuted for alleged child and ritual abuses, some experts, claiming children do not lie about these things, further contributed to the belief that predators were everywhere. In the aftermath of the many convictions of abusers, some of which have been overturned and others have not been resolved, medical and legal experts have learned many things. They acknowledge that child sexual abuse indeed occurs and children may not tell for various reasons. Experts have also found that some child witnesses are reliable, whereas others are not. Authorities have since developed better interviewing techniques of child witnesses.

Are Children Competent Witnesses?

Traditionally, judges protected juries from incompetent witnesses, which in the early years of the United States were considered to include women, slaves, and children. Children in particular were believed to live in a fantasy world, and their inability to understand such terms as *oath*, *testify*, and *solemnly swear* denied them the right to appear in court. In 1895 the U.S. Supreme Court, in *Wheeler v. United States*, established the rights of child witnesses. The Court explained:

> There is no precise age which determines the question of competency. This depends on the capacity and intelligence of the child, his appreciation of the difference between truth and falsehood, as well as of his duty to tell the former. The decision of this question rests primarily with the trial judge, who sees the proposed witness, notices his manner, his apparent possession or lack of intelligence, and may resort to any examination which will tend to disclose his capacity and intelligence, as well as his understanding of the obligations of an oath.

. . . To exclude [a child] from the witness stand . . . would sometimes result in staying the hand of justice.

As a result of this ruling, the courts formalized the *Wheeler* decision, requiring judges to interview all children to determine their competency. It was not until 1974 that the revised Federal Rules of Evidence abolished the competency rule so that children may testify at trial in federal courts regardless of competence.

In state courts judges sometimes still apply the competency rule regardless of state laws that may have banned it. In the 1987 Margaret Kelly Michaels case, the judge chatted with each child witness before he or she testified, holding a red crayon and asking questions such as, "If I said this was a green crayon, would I be telling the truth?"

CHILDREN CAN BE UNRELIABLE WITNESSES IF SUBJECTED TO SUGGESTED EVENTS. In "Children's Eyewitness Reports after Exposure to Misinformation from Parents" (*Journal of Experimental Psychology: Applied*, March 2001), Debra Ann Poole and D. Stephen Lindsay examine children's eyewitness reports after the children were given misinformation by their parents and show that children may not be able to distinguish fact from fiction when subjected to suggested events before formal interviews.

A total of 114 children ages three to eight participated, on a one-to-one basis, in four science activities with a man called "Mr. Science." Three interviews were conducted afterward. The first interview occurred right after the science activities in which an interviewer asked each child nonsuggestive questions about the activities. About three and a half months later the children's parents read them a story, in three instances, about their science experience. The story included two science activities they had experienced and two others that they had not experienced. The story also included an event in which the child experienced unpleasant touching by Mr. Science. In reality this event did not happen. The children were then interviewed. The final step in the interview consisted of a source-monitoring procedure, in which the children were reminded of their actual experiences, as well as the story, to help them distinguish fact from fiction. A final interview was conducted after another month. This time the children were not given any misinformation.

The interview conducted soon after the science activities showed that the children recalled their experiences, with the amount of events reported increasing with the age of the child. When prompted for more information, the amount of new information reported also increased with age. The reports resulting from the promptings remained accurate.

In the interview that occurred soon after the children were read the storybook with misleading suggestions, 35% (forty of the 114 children) reported fifty-eight sug-

gested events in free recall (without prompting from the interviewer), including seventeen events relating to the unpleasant touching by Mr. Science. In the last interview a month later, with no additional misinformation given the children, 21% (twenty-four children) reported twenty-seven suggested events, including nine suggested events that involved unpleasant touching. Even when the children were prompted to provide more information about their experiences, they continued to report false events. Poole and Lindsay conclude that, because children's credibility as eyewitnesses depends on their ability to distinguish their memories from other sources, interviewers will have to develop better procedures to help them do so.

STATUTE OF LIMITATIONS AND RECOVERED MEMORY

Suing Alleged Abusers

According to Anita Lipton, in "Recovered Memories in the Courts" (Sheila Taub, ed., *Recovered Memories of Child Sexual Abuse: Psychological, Social, and Legal Perspectives on a Contemporary Mental Health Controversy*, 1999), between 1983 and 1998 many individuals who had "recovered" memories of childhood sexual abuse sued their alleged abusers. During those years a total of 589 lawsuits based on repressed memory were filed, of which 506 were civil and eighty-three were criminal. Following a sharp rise in 1992, the year the False Memory Syndrome Foundation was created, the number of lawsuits dropped rapidly after 1994.

While the courts readily accepted some early cases of child sexual abuse, courts in more and more states have become increasingly suspicious of accounts of outrageous abuse. Therapists are being held liable for malpractice not only by their patients but also by third parties (usually the accused parents of someone who has allegedly recovered memories of sexual abuse).

EXCEPTION TO STATUTE OF LIMITATIONS IN CASES OF REPRESSED MEMORY. A statute of limitations is a law that sets the time within which criminal charges or civil claims can be filed and after which one loses the right to sue or make a claim. Most states provide for extensions of the statute of limitations, either through state law or judicial tolling doctrines. A tolling doctrine is a rule that suspends the date from which a statutory period starts to run. An example is the minority tolling doctrine, which provides that a statutory period does not begin to run until the child becomes an adult. For instance, in 2003, in response to revelations of clergy abuse, Illinois extended the statute of limitations in cases of childhood sexual abuse, allowing prosecutors twenty years from the time the victim turns eighteen to bring criminal charges. Victims wishing to bring a civil suit have up to ten years from the time they discover abuse and its connection to their injuries.

One of the legal issues contested in cases of childhood sexual abuse of repressed memory is how long the statute of limitations should run. In 1991 Paula Hearndon sued her stepfather, Kenneth Graham, for sexually abusing her from 1968 to 1975 (when she was between the ages of eight and fifteen). According to Hearndon, the traumatic amnesia she experienced because of the abuse lasted until 1988. Because of Florida's four-year statute of limitations, the lawsuit did not proceed.

In September 2000, however, the Florida Supreme Court, in a 5–2 decision, ruled in *Hearndon v. Graham* that memory loss resulting from the trauma of childhood sexual abuse should be considered an exception to the statute of limitations. The court, while observing that disagreements about recovered memory exist, stated: "It is widely recognized that the shock and confusion resultant from childhood molestation, often coupled with authoritative adult demands and threats for secrecy, may lead a child to deny or suppress such abuse from his or her consciousness."

U.S. SUPREME COURT RULES ON CALIFORNIA'S RETROACTIVE CHANGE IN STATUTE OF LIMITATIONS. In 2003 the U.S. Supreme Court heard arguments in a case that involved California's statute of limitations. In 1998 Marion Stogner was charged with the alleged sexual molestation of his two daughters between 1955 and 1973. Although the statute of limitations had expired, prosecutors brought criminal charges under a 1994 state law that had removed the statute of limitations for the time the crime was committed. In the trial court Stogner claimed that the *Ex Post Facto* Clause of the U.S. Constitution forbids revival of prosecution that was previously time-barred. The trial court agreed, but the California Court of Appeals, in *People v. Stogner v. California* (1999), reversed the ruling, saying that the 1994 law was not unconstitutional as an *ex post facto* law. (Article 1 of the U.S. Constitution forbids the passing of an *ex post facto* law—that is, a law that applies retroactively.)

On the defendant's second appeal, the California Court of Appeals, in *Stogner v. Superior Court*, held that the 1994 law allows the prosecution of Stogner's alleged crimes committed between 1955 and 1973. On June 26, 2003, the U.S. Supreme Court ruled on *Stogner v. California*. By a 5–4 vote the Court reversed the appeals court decision, concluding that "a law enacted after expiration of a previously applicable limitations period violates the *Ex Post Facto* Clause when it is applied to revive a previously time-barred prosecution."

LEGAL PROTECTIONS FOR CHILDREN

Child Pornography

Although the First Amendment protects pornography, it does not protect child pornography. Under the definition established in *Miller v. California* (1973), pornography may be banned if it is deemed legally obscene. To be considered obscene, material "taken as a whole" must:

- Appeal to a prurient interest in sex
- Be patently offensive in light of community standards
- Lack serious literary, artistic, political, or scientific value

Since 1982 child pornography has been banned by the U.S. Supreme Court ruling *New York v. Ferber*, which held that pornography depicting children engaged in sexually explicit acts can be banned, whether or not it is obscene, because of the state's interest in protecting children from sexual exploitation. In other words, such images are not protected by the First Amendment.

CHILD PORNOGRAPHY PREVENTION ACT. The Child Pornography Prevention Act of 1996 (CPPA) attempted to legally define child pornography. The CPPA, in part, bans any visual depiction that "is, or appears to be, of a minor engaging in sexually explicit conduct." The "appears to be" portion of the law was intended to combat virtual child pornography, which includes computer-generated images and images using youthful-looking adults. The CPPA also prohibits the advertisement or promotion of any sexually explicit image that "conveys the impression" that children are performing sexual acts.

On April 16, 2002, the U.S. Supreme Court ruled that CPPA is unconstitutional, because it prohibits free speech that is neither obscene based on *Miller* nor child pornography based on *Ferber*.

The Supreme Court, in *Ashcroft v. Free Speech Coalition et al.*, ruled 6–3 that banning virtual child pornography is unconstitutional because, unlike *Ferber*, actual children are not used in its production. Moreover, the Court claimed that the government cannot prohibit material fit for adults just because children might get hold of it. The Court also struck down the government's argument that child pornography whets the appetites of pedophiles and encourages them to commit unlawful acts. As to that part of the law that bans material that "conveys the impression" it contains children performing sexual acts, the justices noted that anyone found in possession of such "mislabeled" material could be prosecuted.

Protecting Children on the Internet

In October 1998, in an effort to further protect children from sexual predators who target minors through the Internet, Congress enacted the Protection of Children from Sexual Predators Act. The legislation provides punishment for any individual who knowingly contacts, or tries to contact, children under eighteen to engage in criminal sexual activity, or who knowingly transfers obscene material to children.

The Deleting Online Predators Act of 2006 proposes to amend the Communications Act of 1934 to require publicly supported schools and libraries to monitor children's use of the Internet. The bill is intended to restrict access to child pornography, material deemed obscene, or anything "harmful to minors." It would also require schools and libraries to restrict children's access to chat rooms or social networking Web sites, because in these places they "may easily access or be presented with obscene or indecent material" or "may easily be subject to unlawful sexual advances." The bill was passed by the House on July 26, 2006, and was referred to a Senate committee.

Ending the "Incest Exception"

In "Closing the Loopholes for Incestuous Offenders" (May 18, 2003, http://www.protect.org/articles/belleville_nd. shtml), Elizabeth Donald notes that about forty states have an "incest exception" in their criminal codes and sentencing guidelines. This means that a person who commits incest (sexual abuse of a biological family member, sometimes one's own child) legally can receive a lighter sentence, if any at all, compared with a person who sexually abuses an unrelated child. In some states a family member who commits incest with a child is charged with a misdemeanor. In other states the molester can get off with probation and therapy. Often, the offender is not required to stay away from the child he or she abused. Andrew Vachss first brought up the incest exception issue in "Our Endangered Species: A Hard Look at How We Treat Children" (*Parade*, March 29, 1998). Vachss is an advisory board member of the National Association to Protect Children, which is an organization working to change incest laws in different states.

In 1999 a bill was introduced in Congress that would have banned states from treating rape committed by a biological relative as a lesser crime than the rape of a stranger. That legislation was not enacted, and, as of 2006, no such federal law had been passed. In the meantime, the National Association to Protect Children decided to fight the incest exception one state at a time. In 2002 the association was instrumental in changing North Carolina's archaic incest law of 1879. Before the new legislation, a father who raped his child was found guilty of minor felony, punishable by probation, and an uncle who raped his niece was required to perform forty-five days of community service for the misdemeanor offense of incest. In April and May 2003 Arkansas and Illinois, respectively, reformed their incest laws to impose stricter penalties for offenders. Under Arkansas's old incest laws an adult who raped a child in his or her own family was considered guilty of incest and was either fined or put under probation. In Illinois the laws had been deliberately revised in 1981 with a view to keeping families together, imposing a punishment of probation or two years of counseling rather than jail time for incestuous offenders.

Protecting Fetuses and Infants

In November 1997 the South Carolina Supreme Court, in *Whitner v. South Carolina*, held that pregnant women who use drugs can be criminally prosecuted for child maltreatment. The court found that a viable fetus (potentially capable of surviving outside the womb) is a person covered by the state's child abuse and neglect laws. The ruling was handed down in a case appealed by Cornelia Whitner, who was sentenced to eight years in prison in 1992 for pleading guilty to child neglect. This was the first time the highest court of any state upheld the criminal conviction of a woman charged with such an offense. Whitner's newborn tested positive for cocaine.

In March 1998 Malissa Ann Crawley, charged with the same criminal offense, began serving a five-year prison sentence in South Carolina. In June 1998 the U.S. Supreme Court refused to hear appeals by Whitner and Crawley.

Whitner's lawyer had argued that if a woman could be prosecuted for child abuse for having used drugs while pregnant, what was to keep the law from prosecuting her for smoking or drinking alcohol or even for failing to obtain prenatal care? Other critics of the law argued that women who are substance abusers, fearing prosecution, might not seek prenatal care and counseling for their drug problems, which would further endanger the child.

In another South Carolina case Regina McKnight, a crack cocaine addict, was arrested in 1999 after giving birth to a stillborn. In 2001 she was convicted of homicide by child abuse and was sentenced to twelve years in prison. The jury found her guilty of killing a viable fetus, considered a child under South Carolina law. In January 2003 the South Carolina Supreme Court ruled in *State v. Regina D. McKnight* against McKnight. The court pointed out that the state legislature amended the homicide by child abuse statute in 2000, about three years after the court held in *Whitner v. South Carolina* that the term *child* includes a viable fetus. The court added, "The fact that the legislature was well aware of this Court's opinion in *Whitner*, yet failed to omit 'viable fetus' from the statute's applicability, is persuasive evidence that the legislature did not intend to exempt fetuses from the statute's operation." In October 2003 the U.S. Supreme Court refused to hear McKnight's case.

The Child Abuse Prevention and Treatment Act requires that all states have ways to address the needs of drug-addicted infants or infants suffering from symptoms resulting from prenatal drug exposure. As of 2004 twelve states had specific reporting procedures in their laws, and twelve states and the District of Columbia included prenatal drug exposure as a form of child abuse or neglect. The District of Columbia and twenty-three states had laws requiring the mandatory reporting of drug-exposed infants. After receiving a report of a drug-exposed infant, CPS typically visits the mother, sometimes removing the infant from her custody on a temporary or permanent basis. South Dakota mandates the reporting of substance-ingesting pregnant women for child abuse to law enforcement instead of to social services. Failure to report such cases of child abuse is a crime punishable by up to six months in prison.

In "Punishment of Pregnant Women" (2006, http://advocatesforpregnantwomen.org/issues/punishment_of_pregnant_women/), the National Advocates for Pregnant Women reports that since the Supreme Court's refusal to consider McKnight's case, South Carolina has led the way in the prosecution of pregnant women for behaviors that harmed their unborn children. In 2006 alone, Jennifer Lee Arrowood was arrested for "homicide by child abuse" after giving birth to a stillborn son, which was attributed to her drug use; Carolyn Michelle Wright was charged with "unlawful neglect" after testing positive for cocaine when she was in the hospital giving birth; Betty L. Staley was charged with "unlawful neglect" after her newborn tested positive for cocaine; and Hannah Lauren Jolly was charged with "unlawful neglect" after her newborn tested positive for marijuana and cocaine.

In 2004 President George W. Bush signed the Unborn Victims of Violence Act into law, making it a crime to harm a fetus in the commission of federal crimes. In 2005 six states passed laws making it a crime to kill a viable fetus. NARAL Pro-Choice America notes in "Who Decides?: The Status of Women's Reproductive Rights in the United States" (2006, http://www.prochoiceamerica.org/choice-action-center/in_your_state/who-decides/nationwide-trends/key-findings-threats-to.html) that in 2005 states considered sixty-eight measures that would create a separate legal status for embryos and fetuses. In "States Grapple with Fetal-Protection Legislation" (*Lexington Herald-Ledger*/Kentucky.com, July 10, 2006), Rick Montgomery states that in 2006 Arkansas lawmakers were debating making smoking a crime for pregnant women.

Critics of fetal-rights legislation argue that these laws disregard the rights of women. They believe such legislation may lead to greater and greater restrictions on the activities and decisions of pregnant women—for example, could it become a crime to fail to take prenatal vitamins, to play sports, or to make informed medical decisions contrary to a doctor's advice? Quoted by Montgomery, Lynn M. Paltrow, the executive director of the National Advocates for Pregnant Women, said, "What we're seeing is a political trend in which the fetuses are coming first, and the rights of women . . . are coming last."

DRUG TESTING OF PREGNANT WOMEN. In 1989 a public hospital in Charleston, South Carolina, run by the Medical University of South Carolina, offered to work with the city officials and police to test pregnant women suspected of drug use. The women were not told they were being screened for drugs or that they would be turned over to police if they tested positive. Many of the women were prosecuted and subsequently imprisoned for child abuse.

In 1993 ten women who had been subjected to the "search and arrest" policy of the hospital and police filed a lawsuit, charging that "warrantless and nonconsensual drug tests conducted for criminal investigatory purposes were unconstitutional searches" prohibited by the Fourth Amendment. In 1997, in *Ferguson v. City of Charleston*, the U.S. District Court upheld the policy. In 1999 on appeal, the U.S. Court of Appeals for the Fourth Circuit affirmed the judgment of the district court, saying that the searches constitute a "special needs" exception to the Fourth Amendment, which justifies searches done for non-law enforcement ends, in this case, the medical interests of the mothers and infants, even though law enforcement means were used.

The U.S. Supreme Court reviewed the ruling by the Fourth Circuit Court to determine whether the policy involved searches justified by "special needs." On March 21, 2001, the Court ruled 6–3 that the policy was unconstitutional, noting:

> While the ultimate goal of the program may well have been to get the women in question into substance abuse treatment and off drugs, the immediate objective of the searches was to generate evidence for law enforcement purposes in order to reach that goal. Given that purpose and given the extensive involvement of law enforcement officials at every stage of the policy, this case simply does not fit within the closely guarded category of "special needs."

The Court remanded the case to the U.S. Court of Appeals for the Fourth Circuit to determine whether or not the women gave informed consent to the hospital to test them for drugs. On October 17, 2002, the appellate court noted that eight of the women did not provide informed consent to the drug testing; therefore, the "search and arrest" policy violated their Fourth Amendment rights. The city of Charleston appealed to the U.S. Supreme Court, but the Court declined to rehear the case.

Child Abuse Laws Relating to Domestic Violence

Some local laws impose penalties for domestic violence when children are present. For example, Salt Lake County, Utah, and Houston County, Georgia, enacted statutes creating a new crime of child maltreatment when domestic violence is witnessed by a child. Multnomah County, Oregon, passed legislation upgrading some assault offenses to felonies when a child is present during domestic violence. In "Prosecutors, Kids, and Domestic Violence Cases" (*National Institute of Justice Journal*, March 2002), Debra Whitcomb reports on a study she conducted involving a survey of prosecutors to determine their responses to cases where children witness domestic violence.

The survey asked 128 prosecutors across the country how they would respond to three domestic violence cases in which children were present. A majority of prosecutors (94%) stated they would report a battered mother to CPS if she were found abusing the child. All indicated they would prosecute the abusing mother. Prosecutors would more likely report a battered mother if she failed to protect her child from abuse (63%) than if she failed to protect the child from witnessing the domestic violence (40%). More than three times as many prosecutors would charge the mother with a crime for the child's abuse (77.5%) than for exposure to family violence (25%). (See Table 5.1.)

COURT SIDES WITH BATTERED WOMEN WHOSE CHILDREN ARE REMOVED. Battered women with children are often further traumatized by CPS's removal of their children. On December 21, 2001, Jack B. Weinstein, a federal judge, ruled that New York City's Administration for Children's Services (ACS) violated the constitutional rights of mothers and their children by removing the children simply because the mothers were victims of domestic violence. In this first case of its kind, fifteen

TABLE 5.1

Action taken by prosecutors in cases of children and domestic violence, by scenario

Scenario	Would report at least sometimes	Would prosecute at least sometimes
Mom abuses children	94% (n=90)	100% (n=82)
Mom fails to protect from abuse	63% (n=87)	77.5% (n=80)
Mom fails to protect from exposure	40% (n=86)	25% (n=73)

Note: n=sample size.

SOURCE: Debra Whitcomb, "Table 1. Prosecutors' Responses to Scenarios Involving Children and Abuse," in "Prosecutors, Kids, and Domestic Violence Cases," *National Institute of Justice Journal*, no. 248, March 2002, http://www.ncjrs.gov/pdffiles1/ji000248.pdf (accessed July 26, 2006)

battered women had brought the class action suit *Nicholson v. Scoppetta*.

On January 3, 2002, the judge issued an injunction ordering ACS to stop separating a child from his or her battered mother unless the child "is in such imminent danger." The injunction asserted that the government "may not penalize a mother, not otherwise unfit, who is battered by her partner, by separating her from her children; nor may children be separated from the mother, in effect visiting upon them the sins of their mother's batterer."

CHAPTER 6
THE PREVALENCE OF DOMESTIC VIOLENCE

WHO IS ABUSED?

In the past domestic violence was viewed as a phenomenon exclusively affecting the lower classes. However, when researchers began investigating the causes of family violence in the 1970s, they noticed that although lower-class women at first appeared to make up most victims, domestic violence, in reality, spanned all social and economic groups.

Middle- and upper-class women were also abused, the researchers found, but they often did not turn to hospital emergency rooms and shelters for help. Instead, they used private facilities and remained largely unknown, unreported, and uncounted by the public agencies that attempt to measure the rates of domestic violence and aid victims.

While women of any social class may be victims of abuse, general population studies find that women with lower incomes and less education, as well as minority women, are more likely to be the primary victims of domestic violence. Still, researchers note, classification is not exclusive. Just about anyone, rich or poor, male or female, may be a victim of domestic violence.

WHO ARE THE ABUSERS?

Like victims of domestic abuse, batterers come from all socioeconomic groups and all ethnic backgrounds. They may be male or female, young or old, but by definition they share one common characteristic: they all have a personal relationship with their victims.

During 2004 men were equally likely to be victimized by a stranger (50.2%) or nonstranger (48.1%), whereas women were more likely to be victimized by someone they knew (64.1%) as opposed to a stranger (34.3%). Nearly two-thirds of rape and sexual assault victims knew their assailant (65.1%). (See Table 6.1.) Rates of violent victimization by an intimate partner

toward women increase as household incomes go down, according to Callie Marie Rennison and Sarah Welchans in *Intimate Partner Violence* (July 2000, http://www.ojp.usdoj.gov/bjs/pub/pdf/ipv.pdf).

Single people were victimized by violent crime much more often than married or widowed people in 2004. Never-married people experienced violent crime at a rate of 39.4 per one thousand people, and divorced or separated people experienced violent crime at a rate of thirty-three per one thousand people. These rates were more than three times higher than the rates of violent crime experienced by married and widowed people. Married people experienced violent crime at a rate of 9.7 per one thousand people, whereas widowed people (who tend to be older, on average) experienced violent crime at a rate of four per one thousand people. (See Table 6.2.)

Women as Abusers

As Amy Holtzworth-Munroe points out in "Female Perpetration of Physical Aggression against an Intimate Partner: A Controversial New Topic of Study" (*Violence and Victims*, April 2005), until the early twenty-first century, "it was politically incorrect to even consider studying female aggression when conducting research on marital violence." However, as surveys reveal, a substantial minority of perpetrators of intimate partner violence are women. Intimate partner violence has traditionally been understood as a method to gain power and control in a relationship. Research indicates, however, that that model may be useful mainly for understanding male batterers. By contrast, Poco Kernsmith notes in "Exerting Power or Striking Back: A Gendered Comparison of Motivations for Domestic Violence Perpetration" (*Violence and Victims*, April 2005) that female batterers "appear more motivated by the desire to maintain personal liberties in a relationship where they have been victimized."

TABLE 6.1

Victim population by personal characteristics, by type of crime, and by victim/offender relationship, 2004

Characteristic	Total victimizations	Percent of all victimizations					
		Nonstrangers				Stranger	Don't know relationship
		Total	Intimate	Other relative	Friend or acquaintance		
Both genders							
Crimes of violence	**100.0%**	**55.0%**	**11.2%**	**7.0%**	**36.9%**	**43.3%**	**1.6%**
Rape/sexual assault[a]	100.0	65.1	16.8	2.7*	45.6	33.5	1.5*
Robbery	100.0	41.0	13.4	2.6*	25.0	56.4	2.6*
Assault	100.0	56.1	10.6	7.7	37.8	42.3	1.5
Aggravated	100.0	49.9	8.1	8.7	33.1	47.5	2.6*
Simple	100.0	58.0	11.4	7.4	39.2	40.8	1.2
Male							
Crimes of violence	100.0	48.1	3.8	5.6	38.7	50.2	1.7
Rape/sexual assault[a]	100.0*	0.0*	0.0*	0.0*	0.0*	100.0*	0.0*
Robbery	100.0	34.8	5.0*	1.7*	28.0	62.0	3.2*
Assault	100.0	49.9	3.7	6.1	40.2	48.6	1.5
Aggravated	100.0	44.2	2.9*	6.5	34.7	53.8	2.0*
Simple	100.0	52.0	3.9	5.9	42.2	46.7	1.3*
Female							
Crimes of violence	100.0	64.1	20.8	8.8	34.5	34.3	1.5
Rape/sexual assault[a]	100.0	67.0	17.4	2.7*	46.9	31.4	1.5*
Robbery	100.0	53.6	30.3	4.5*	18.8*	45.0	1.4*
Assault	100.0	64.7	20.3	9.9	34.5	33.7	1.6*
Aggravated	100.0	61.2	18.2	13.1	29.8	35.0	3.9*
Simple	100.0	65.5	20.8	9.2	35.6	33.4	1.0*
All races							
Crimes of violence	100.0	55.0	11.2	7.0	36.9	43.3	1.6
Rape/sexual assault[a]	100.0	65.1	16.8	2.7*	45.6	33.5	1.5*
Robbery	100.0	41.0	13.4	2.6*	25.0	56.4	2.6*
Assault	100.0	56.1	10.6	7.7	37.8	42.3	1.5
Aggravated	100.0	49.9	8.1	8.7	33.1	47.5	2.6*
Simple	100.0	58.0	11.4	7.4	39.2	40.8	1.2
White only							
Crimes of violence	100.0	54.3	10.8	7.1	36.4	44.5	1.2
Rape/sexual assault[a]	100.0	69.4	22.7	3.6*	43.1	28.6	2.0*
Robbery	100.0	37.2	11.9	3.7*	21.6	61.2	1.6*
Assault	100.0	55.3	10.2	7.6	37.5	43.6	1.1
Aggravated	100.0	49.3	8.2	8.4	32.6	47.7	3.0*
Simple	100.0	57.0	10.7	7.4	38.9	42.4	0.6*
Black only							
Crimes of violence	100.0	59.4	13.7	5.0	40.7	37.0	3.7*
Rape/sexual assault[a]	100.0	58.2*	0.0*	0.0*	58.2*	41.8*	0.0*
Robbery	100.0	58.7	18.9*	0.0*	39.8	34.6	6.8*
Assault	100.0	59.6	13.9	6.2	39.5	37.0	3.4*
Aggravated	100.0	53.8	9.0*	8.1*	36.7	44.6	1.6*
Simple	100.0	62.4	16.2	5.3*	40.8	33.3	4.3*
Other race only[b]							
Crimes of violence	100.0	47.8	4.0*	6.2*	37.7	48.2	3.9*
Rape/sexual assault[a]	0.0*	0.0*	0.0*	0.0*	0.0*	0.0*	0.0*
Robbery	100.0*	8.1*	8.1*	0.0*	0.0*	91.9*	0.0*
Assault	100.0	58.1	3.0*	7.8*	47.3	37.0	4.9*
Aggravated	100.0*	25.6*	0.0*	15.4*	10.3*	74.4*	0.0*
Simple	100.0	65.2	3.6*	6.1*	55.5	28.8*	6.0*
Two or more races[c]							
Crimes of violence	100.0	64.2	17.8*	17.1*	29.3	35.8	0.0*
Rape/sexual assault[a]	100.0*	0.0*	0.0*	0.0*	0.0*	100.0*	0.0*
Robbery	100.0*	100.0*	26.6*	0.0*	73.4*	0.0*	0.0*
Assault	100.0	64.6	18.0*	19.4*	27.2*	35.4	0.0*
Aggravated	100.0*	72.7*	0.0*	26.4*	46.2*	27.3*	0.0*
Simple	100.0	63.5	20.5*	18.5*	24.6*	36.5*	0.0*
Ethnicity							
Crimes of violence	100.0	55.0	11.2	7.0	36.9	43.3	1.6
Rape/sexual assault[a]	100.0	65.1	16.8	2.7*	45.6	33.5	1.5*
Robbery	100.0	41.0	13.4	2.6*	25.0	56.4	2.6*
Assault	100.0	56.1	10.6	7.7	37.8	42.3	1.5
Aggravated	100.0	49.9	8.1	8.7	33.1	47.5	2.6*
Simple	100.0	58.0	11.4	7.4	39.2	40.8	1.2

Motivation for battering is important to consider; so, too, is the impact and pattern of abuse. L. Kevin Hamberger addresses these issues in "Men's and Women's Use of Intimate Partner Violence in Clinical Samples: Toward a Gender-Sensitive Analysis" (*Violence and Victims*, April 2005). While some surveys find that women initiate domestic violence nearly as often as men, Hamberger argues that in evaluating those results, research

TABLE 6.1

Victim population by personal characteristics, by type of crime, and by victim/offender relationship, 2004 [CONTINUED]

Characteristic	Total victimizations	Percent of all victimizations					
		Nonstrangers				Stranger	Don't know relationship
		Total	Intimate	Other relative	Friend or acquaintance		
Hispanic							
Crimes of violence	100.0	51.5	16.4	5.6*	29.5	47.7	0.8*
Rape/sexual assault[a]	100.0*	39.7*	12.0*	0.0*	27.6*	60.3*	0.0*
Robbery	100.0	29.4*	15.8*	0.0*	13.6*	70.6	0.0*
Assault	100.0	56.1	16.6	6.9*	32.6	42.9	1.0*
Aggravated	100.0	40.7	5.6*	0.0*	35.1	54.5	4.8*
Simple	100.0	60.3	19.6	8.8*	31.9	39.7	0.0*
Non-Hispanic							
Crimes of violence	100.0	55.7	10.6	7.2	37.9	42.7	1.6
Rape/sexual assault[a]	100.0	67.6	17.3	2.9*	47.3	30.8	1.6*
Robbery	100.0	42.9	13.0	3.2*	26.7	53.9	3.2*
Assault	100.0	56.4	10.0	7.8	38.6	42.1	1.4
Aggravated	100.0	51.3	8.4	9.7	33.1	46.3	2.4*
Simple	100.0	58.0	10.5	7.2	40.3	40.9	1.1

Note: Detail may not add to total shown because of rounding.
*Estimate is based on about 10 or fewer sample cases.
[a]Includes verbal threats of rape and threats of sexual assault.
[b]Includes American Indian, Eskimo, Asian Pacific Islander if only one of these races is given.
[c]Includes all persons of any race, indicating two or more races.

SOURCE: "Table 43a. Personal Crimes of Violence, 2004: Percent Distribution of Victimizations, by Characteristics of Victims, Type of Crime, and Victim/Offender Relationship," in *Criminal Victimization in the United States, 2004*, U.S. Department of Justice, Office of Justice Programs, Bureau of Justice Statistics, June 2006, http://www.ojp.usdoj.gov/bjs/pub/pdf/cvus04.pdf (accessed July 8, 2006).

must also assess the impact and context of intimate partner violence. In his review, he used a model that included gender differences in key elements of partner violence, including the initiation of the pattern of violence in the relationship, how often each partner initiates violence, the physical and mental health impacts of domestic violence, behavioral and emotional responses to being victimized by violence, and the motivations of the batterer. He concludes that, even in relationships in which women also use violence against their partners, "women are disproportionately victimized by partner violence compared to men."

ESTIMATES OF DOMESTIC VIOLENCE

Because domestic violence is often unreported, it is impossible to be certain exactly how many domestic assaults occur each year. Variations in definitions of violence and abuse, the types of questions posed by researchers, and the context in which they are asked compound the difficulty. For example, when victims are questioned in the presence of their abusers, or even other family members, they are often more reluctant to report instances of violence. Studies on the subject are sometimes contradictory, but most show that domestic violence remains a growing concern. Many researchers fear that available data represent only the tip of the iceberg of a problem of glacial proportions.

To understand why there are so many varying estimates of domestic violence, it is necessary to consider the surveys, studies, and reports themselves. Richard J. Gelles

notes in "Estimating the Incidence and Prevalence of Violence against Women" (*Violence against Women*, July 2000) that the source and purpose of the research, the definition of abuse used, the population surveyed, and the survey setting, as well as the political agendas of the surveyors and researchers, may elicit different data and varying interpretations of these data.

According to *World Report on Violence and Health* (2002, http://www.who.int/violence_injury_prevention/violence/world_report/en/full_en.pdf), Etienne G. Krug et al. find that in countries where large-scale studies are conducted, between 10% and 69% of women report they have suffered physical abuse at the hands of an intimate partner (intimates include spouses, former spouses, boyfriends, and girlfriends). One-third to one-half of these women have also been sexually assaulted by their partners. Krug et al. also observe that prostitution and trafficking for sex, activities strongly linked to violence against women and girls, appeared to be on the rise during the late 1990s and early twenty-first century.

The 1975 National Family Violence Survey and the 1985 National Family Violence Resurvey are among the most analyzed and cited data in the literature about intimate partner violence. The strength of these surveys lies in their ability to measure violent behavior that respondents might not classify as criminal. Using data from both surveys, Murray A. Straus and Richard J. Gelles estimate in "Societal Change and Change in Family Violence from 1975 to 1985 as Revealed by Two National Surveys" (*Journal of Marriage and the Family*, August

TABLE 6.2

Victims age 12 and over by type of crime and by marital status, 2004

| Type of crime | Rate per 1,000 persons age 12 and over | | | |
	Never married	Married	Widowed	Divorced or separated
All personal crimes	**40.9**	**10.2**	**4.7**	**34.0**
Crimes of violence	39.4	9.7	4.0	33.0
Completed violence	14.0	2.1	0.7*	14.5
Attempted/threatened violence	25.4	7.6	3.3	18.5
Rape/sexual assault	1.6	0.2*	0.0*	2.3
Rape/attempted rape	0.7	0.1*	0.0*	1.1*
Rape	0.5	0.0*	0.0*	0.7*
Attempted rape[a]	0.3*	0.1*	0.0*	0.4*
Sexual assault[b]	0.9	0.1*	0.0*	1.2*
Robbery	4.0	0.8	0.6*	3.0
Completed/property taken	2.3	0.5	0.1*	2.2
With injury	0.7	0.2*	0.1*	1.2*
Without injury	1.5	0.4	0.0*	1.0*
Attempted to take property	1.8	0.3	0.5*	0.9*
With injury	0.6	0.1*	0.2*	0.4*
Without injury	1.1	0.2*	0.3*	0.4*
Assault	33.8	8.7	3.3	27.6
Aggravated	7.9	1.9	1.2*	6.6
With injury	3.0	0.4	0.2*	3.5
Threatened with weapon	4.9	1.4	1.0*	3.2
Simple	25.9	6.8	2.1*	21.0
With minor injury	7.4	1.0	0.4*	7.0
Without injury	18.4	5.8	1.8*	14.0
Purse snatching/pocket picking	1.5	0.6	0.8*	1.1*
Population age 12 and over	77,809,950	121,607,250	14,356,700	26,046,520

Note: Detail may not add to total shown because of rounding. Excludes data on persons whose marital status was not ascertained.

*Estimate is based on about 10 or fewer sample cases.

[a]Includes verbal threats of rape.

[b]Includes threats.

SOURCE: "Table 11. Personal Crimes, 2004: Victimization Rates for Persons Age 12 and Over, by Type of Crime and Marital Status of Victims," in *Criminal Victimization in the United States, 2004*, U.S. Department of Justice, Office of Justice Programs, Bureau of Justice Statistics, June 2006, http://www.ojp.usdoj.gov/bjs/pub/pdf/cvus0401.pdf (accessed August 22, 2006)

TABLE 6.3

Definition of an intimate partner by source of report, 1998

Intimate partner relationships involve current spouses, former spouses, current boy/girlfriends, or former boy/girlfriends. Individuals involved in an intimate partner relationship may be of the same gender. The FBI does not report former boy/girlfriends in categories separate from current boy/girlfriends. Rather, they are included in the boy/girlfriend category during the data collection process.

	National Crime Victimization Survey categories	Supplementary Homicide Reports categories
Intimate	Spouse	Husband/wife
	Ex-spouse	Common-law husband or wife
	Boyfriend/girlfriend	Ex-husband/ex-wife
	Ex-girlfriend/ex-boyfriend	Boyfriend/girlfriend
		Homosexual relationship
Friend/ acquaintance	Friend/ex-friend	Acquaintance
	Roommate/boarder	Friend
	Schoolmate	Neighbor
	Neighbor	Employee
	Someone at work/customer	Employer
	Other non-relative	Other known
Other family	Parent or step parent	Mother/father
	Own child or stepchild	Son/daughter
	Brother/sister	Brother/sister
	Other relative	In-law
		Stepfather/stepmother
		Stepson/stepdaughter
		Other family
Stranger	Stranger	Stranger
	Known by sight only	

SOURCE: Callie Marie Rennison and Sarah Welchans, "Definitions of *Intimate Partner*," in *Intimate Partner Violence*, U.S. Department of Justice, Office of Justice Programs, Bureau of Justice Statistics, May 2000, http://www.ojp.usdoj.gov/bjs/pub/pdf/ipv.pdf (accessed July 8, 2006)

1986) that about 1.6 million women were severely beaten by their partners in 1985, down from 2.1 million in 1975.

The National Crime Victimization Surveys (NCVS; published by the Bureau of Justice Statistics) and the Uniform Crime Reports (UCR; published by the Federal Bureau of Investigation) are valuable sources of information on crime, including violent crime by intimate partners such as rape and sexual assault. Both studies measure the amount and prevalence of crime in the United States. The NCVS is a national survey that asks Americans about crimes they have personally suffered, including those that were not reported to the police. By its nature it cannot include coverage of murder. The UCR is a compilation of crime statistics reported by law enforcement agencies across the United States. Crimes that were not reported to the police are not included.

Since they are based on different sources of data, the surveys give different results, and neither can be assumed to measure the true amount of intimate partner violence since some people will not report that it is occurring. One advantage of these surveys, however, is that they enable researchers to observe trends in interpersonal violence over time. For example, NCVS data show that the rate of nonfatal intimate violence against females declined by nearly half between 1993 and 2001 before leveling off.

A joint effort of the National Institute of Justice and the Centers for Disease Control and Prevention, the National Violence against Women Survey (NVAWS) collected data about intimate and nonintimate partner violence during the 1990s. The NVAWS and NCVS are considered the most reliable sources of data about intimate partner violence, even though their differing approaches make data comparisons difficult. For example, the NCVS is a survey about crime, and because some victims do not consider instances of intimate partner violence as a crime, they are less likely to disclose them in the NCVS.

The NCVS defines an intimate partner as a spouse, former spouse, or a current or former boyfriend or girlfriend, either of the same sex or the opposite sex. (See Table 6.3.) In *Criminal Victimization in the United States, 2004* (2006), the NCVS finds that in 2004, 11.2% of all violent crimes, including rape, sexual

FIGURE 6.1

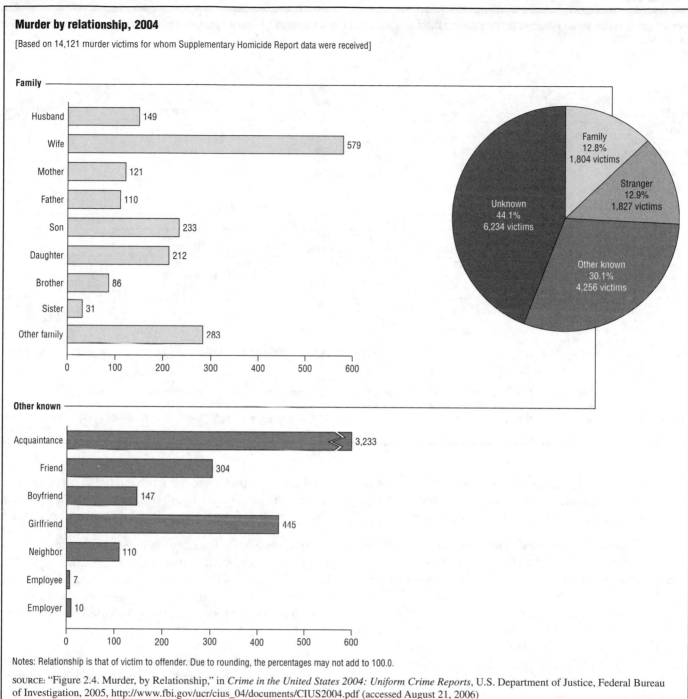

Murder by relationship, 2004

[Based on 14,121 murder victims for whom Supplementary Homicide Report data were received]

Notes: Relationship is that of victim to offender. Due to rounding, the percentages may not add to 100.0.

SOURCE: "Figure 2.4. Murder, by Relationship," in *Crime in the United States 2004: Uniform Crime Reports*, U.S. Department of Justice, Federal Bureau of Investigation, 2005, http://www.fbi.gov/ucr/cius_04/documents/CIUS2004.pdf (accessed August 21, 2006)

assault, aggravated assault (assault with a weapon), and simple assault victimizations (assault without a weapon and resulting in minor injuries), were committed against intimate partners. However, women were disproportionately likely to be victimized by their intimate partners. More than one out of five (20.8%) violent crimes against women were committed by intimate partners, whereas only 3.8% of violent crimes against men were committed by intimates. (See Table 6.1.)

Far more women than men are murdered by their intimate partners, as well. *Crime in the United States,* *2004*, an annual survey, finds that in 2004, 12.8% of murders were committed by family members. In that year, 579 wives were killed by their husbands; 149 husbands were killed by their wives. In addition, 445 girlfriends were killed by their boyfriends; 147 boyfriends were killed by their girlfriends. (See Figure 6.1.)

National Violence against Women Survey

The NVAWS collected information from interviews with eight thousand men and eight thousand women to assess their experiences as victims of various types of

TABLE 6.4

Persons victimized by an intimate partner during their lifetime and/or in a selected 12–month period, by type of violent act and by gender of victim, 1988

	In lifetime			
	Percent		Number[a]	
Type of victimization	Women (*n*=8,000)	Men (*n*=8,000)	Women (100,697,000)	Men (92,748,000)
Rape	7.7	0.3	7,753,669	278,244
Physical assault	22.1	7.4	22,254,037	6,863,352
Rape and/or physical assault	24.8	7.6	24,972,856	7,048,848
Stalking	4.8	0.6	4,833,456	556,488
Total victimized	25.5	7.9	25,677,735	7,327,092

	In previous 12 months			
	Percent		Number[a]	
Type of violence	Woman (*n*=8,000)	Men (*n*=8,000)	Women (100,697,000)	Men (92,748,000)
Rape	0.2	—[b]	201,394	—[b]
Physical assault	1.3	0.9	1,309,061	834,732
Rape and/or physical assault	1.5	0.9[c]	1,510,455	834,732
Stalking	0.5	0.2	503,485	185,496
Total victimized	1.8	1.1	1,812,546	1,020,228

[a]Based on estimates of women and men 18 years of age and older.
[b]Estimates not calculated on fewer than five victims.
[c]Because only three men reported being raped by an intimate partner in the previous 12 months, the percentage of men physically assaulted and physically assaulted and/or raped is the same.
Note: *n*=sample size.

SOURCE: Patricia Tjaden and Nancy Thoennes, "Exhibit 1. Persons Victimized by an Intimate Partner in Lifetime and in Previous 12 Months, by Type of Victimization and Gender," in *Extent, Nature, and Consequences of Intimate Partner Violence: Findings from the National Violence against Women Survey*, National Institute of Justice and Centers for Disease Control and Prevention, July 2000, http://www.ncjrs.org/pdffiles1/nij/181867.pdf (accessed August 28, 2006)

violence, including domestic violence. The NVAWS asked survey respondents about physical assaults and rape, but excluded other sexual assaults, murders, and robberies.

In *Extent, Nature, and Consequences of Intimate Partner Violence: Findings from the National Violence against Women Survey* (July 2000, http://www.ncjrs.gov/pdffiles1/nij/181867.pdf), Patricia Tjaden and Nancy Thoennes find that intimate violence is pervasive in American society, with women suffering about three times as much of this violence as men. They estimate that in 1998, 22.1% of women (22.3 million) have been physically assaulted by a loved one during the course of their lifetime, whereas 7.4% of men (6.9 million) have been physically assaulted by intimates over their lifetime. (See Table 6.4.) Women were also more likely to become victims of rape, stalking, and physical assault by intimates than their male counterparts at some time during their lifetime. Furthermore, women physically assaulted by their partners averaged 6.9 assaults by the same person, as opposed to men, who averaged 4.4 assaults.

During the twelve months that preceded the interview, women also reported higher rates of rape, stalking, and physical assault than did men. Tjaden and Thoennes estimate based on NVAWS data that about 1.5% of the surveyed women (1.5 million) and 0.9% of the men (834,732) reported they had been raped and/or physically

assaulted by a partner in the twelve months preceding the survey. In other words, approximately 4.8 million women and 2.9 million men are assaulted by a partner every year.

The rates of violence between intimate partners varied by race. Asian and Pacific Islanders reported lower rates of violence than men and women from other minority groups, and African-Americans and Native American and Alaskan Natives reported higher rates. (See Table 6.5.)

Tjaden and Thoennes conclude that most partner abuse and violence is not reported to the police. Women reported about one-fifth of rapes, one-quarter of physical assaults, and one-half of stalking incidents to police, whereas men who had been victimized reported abuse to police even less frequently. Table 6.6 shows the reasons victims did not report their abuse to the police. Many victims said they felt the police would not or could not do anything on their behalf. These expressions of helplessness and hopelessness—feeling that others in a position to assist would be unwilling or unable to do so—is a common characteristic shared by many victims of intimate partner violence.

STATISTICS FOR VIOLENCE IN SAME-SEX COUPLES ARE PROBLEMATIC. Tjaden and Thoennes also find that same-sex couples who lived together reported experiencing far more intimate violence in their lifetime than

TABLE 6.5

Persons victimized by an intimate partner, by gender, by type of victimization, and by race of victim, 1996

Victim gender/ type of victimization	Persons victimized in lifetime (%)				
	White	African-American	Asian/ Pacific Islander	America Indian/ Alaska Native	Mixed race
Women	(*n*=6,452)	(*n*=780)	(*n*=133)	(*n*=88)	(*n*=397)
Rape[a]	7.7	7.4	3.8[b]	15.9	8.1
Physical assault[c, d]	21.3	26.3	12.8	30.7	27.0
Stalking	4.7	4.2	—[e]	10.2[b]	6.3
Total victimized[c]	24.8	29.1	15.0	37.5	30.2
Men	(*n*=6,424)	(*n*=659)	(*n*=165)	(*n*=105)	(*n*=406)
Rape	0.2	0.9[b]	—[e]	—[e]	—[e]
Physical assault	7.2	10.8	—[e]	11.4	8.6
Stalking	0.6	1.1[b]	—[e]	—[e]	1.2[b]
Total victimized	7.5	12.0	3.0[b]	12.4	9.1

[a]Estimates for American Indian/Alaska Native women are significantly higher than those for white and African-American women.
[b]Estimates not included in statistical testing.
[c]Estimates for Asian/Pacific Islander women are significantly lower than those for African-American, American Indian/Alaska Native, and mixed-race women.
[d]Estimates for African-American women are significantly higher than those for white women.
[e]Estimates not calculated on fewer than five victims.
Note: *n*=sample size.

SOURCE: Patricia Tjaden and Nancy Thoennes, "Exhibit 6. Persons Victimized by an Intimate Partner in Lifetime, by Victim Gender, Type of Victimization, and Victim Race," in *Extent, Nature, and Consequences of Intimate Partner Violence: Findings from the National Violence against Women Survey*, National Institute of Justice and Centers for Disease Control and Prevention, July 2000, http://www.ncjrs.org/pdffiles1/nij/181867.pdf (accessed July 24, 2006)

TABLE 6.6

Rape, physical assault, and stalking victims who failed to report their victimization to the police, by reasons for not reporting and by gender[a], 1996

Reason for not reporting[b]	Rape victims (%)	Physical assault victims (%)		Stalking victims (%)	
	Women (*n*=311)	Women (*n*=2,062)	Men (*n*=468)	Women (*n*=165)	Men (*n*=30)
Police couldn't do anything	13.2	99.7	100.0	100.0	100.0
Police wouldn't believe me	7.1	61.3[c]	45.1	98.2	93.3
Fear of perpetrator	21.2	11.7[c]	1.9[d]	38.2[c]	16.7[d]
Minor, one-time incident	20.3	37.9[c]	58.5	33.9	36.7[d]
Ashamed, wanted to keep incident private	16.1	10.4[c]	7.1	61.8	76.7
Wanted to handle it myself	7.7	7.3	5.8	7.9	—[e]
Victim or attacker moved away	—[e]	2.4	—[e]	12.1	—[e]
Attacker was a police officer	—[e]	4.7	3.8	7.9	—[e]
Too young, a child	3.5	2.2	1.5[d]	—[e]	—[e]
Reported to the military or someone else	—[e]	0.8[d]	—[e]	—[e]	—[e]
Didn't want police, court involvement	5.8	32.0[c]	24.6	35.2	40.0
Wanted to protect attacker, relationship, or children	8.7	34.8[c]	29.5	45.5	43.3

[a]Estimates are based on the most recent intimate partner victimization since age 18. Estimates not calculated for male rape victims because there were fewer than five victims when stratified by variables.
[b]Estimates exceed 100 percent because some victims gave multiple responses.
[c]Differences between women and men are statistically significant.
[d]Statistical tests not performed.
[e]Estimates not calculated for fewer than five victims.

SOURCE: Patricia Tjaden and Nancy Thoennes, "Exhibit 17. Distribution of Rape, Physical Assault, and Stalking Victims Who Did Not Report Their Victimization to the Police, by Reasons for Not Reporting and Gender," in *Extent, Nature, and Consequences of Intimate Partner Violence: Findings from the National Violence against Women Survey*, National Institute of Justice and Centers for Disease Control and Prevention, July 2000, http://www.ncjrs.org/pdffiles1/nij/181867.pdf (accessed July 24, 2006)

---

heterosexual cohabitants. Among women, 39.2% of the same-sex cohabitants and 21.7% of the opposite-sex cohabitants reported being raped, physically assaulted, or stalked by a partner during their lifetime. Among men, the comparative figures were 23.1% and 7.4%, respectively.

Although survey findings indicated that members of same-sex couples have experienced more intimate partner violence than have members of heterosexual couples, the reported violence does not necessarily occur within the same-sex relationship. When comparing intimate partner victimization rates among same-sex and opposite-sex cohabitants by the gender of the perpetrator, Tjaden and Thoennes find that in 1996, 30.4% of the same-sex women cohabitants reported being victimized by a male partner sometime in their lifetime, whereas 11.4%

FIGURE 6.2

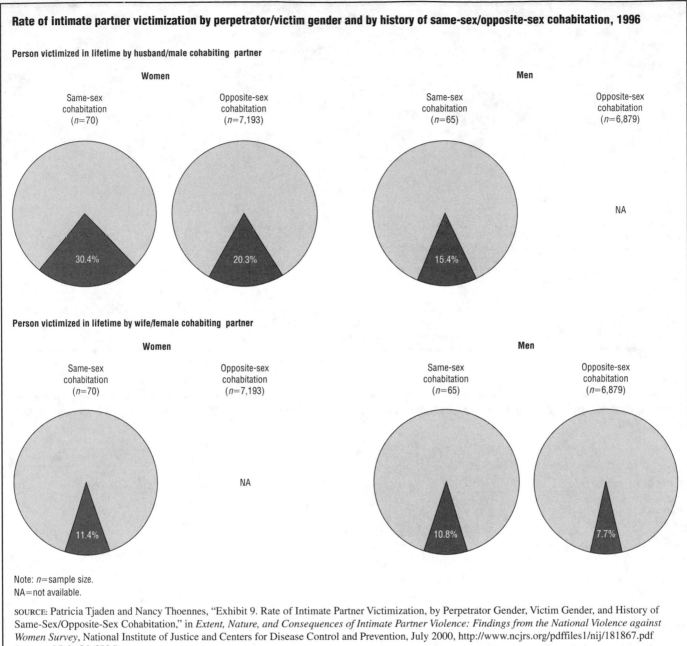

Rate of intimate partner victimization by perpetrator/victim gender and by history of same-sex/opposite-sex cohabitation, 1996

Person victimized in lifetime by husband/male cohabiting partner

Women

Same-sex cohabitation (*n*=70)

Opposite-sex cohabitation (*n*=7,193)

Men

Same-sex cohabitation (*n*=65)

Opposite-sex cohabitation (*n*=6,879)

30.4%

20.3%

15.4%

NA

Person victimized in lifetime by wife/female cohabiting partner

Women

Same-sex cohabitation (*n*=70)

Opposite-sex cohabitation (*n*=7,193)

Men

Same-sex cohabitation (*n*=65)

Opposite-sex cohabitation (*n*=6,879)

11.4%

NA

10.8%

7.7%

Note: *n*=sample size.
NA=not available.

SOURCE: Patricia Tjaden and Nancy Thoennes, "Exhibit 9. Rate of Intimate Partner Victimization, by Perpetrator Gender, Victim Gender, and History of Same-Sex/Opposite-Sex Cohabitation," in *Extent, Nature, and Consequences of Intimate Partner Violence: Findings from the National Violence against Women Survey*, National Institute of Justice and Centers for Disease Control and Prevention, July 2000, http://www.ncjrs.org/pdffiles1/nij/181867.pdf (accessed July 24, 2006)

reported being victimized by a female partner. Tjaden and Thoennes conclude that same-sex cohabiting women were three times more likely to report being victimized by a male partner than by a female partner. In comparison, women who lived with men were nearly twice as likely to report being victimized by a male than same-sex cohabiting women were to report being victimized by a female partner. (See Figure 6.2.)

According to Tjaden and Thoennes, male same-sex partners reported more partner violence than men who lived with women. About 23% of men who lived with men said they had been raped, sexually assaulted, or stalked by a male cohabitant, as opposed to just 7.4%

of men who reported comparable experiences with female cohabitants. This finding confirms the widely held observation that violence and abuse in intimate partner relationships is primarily inflicted by men, whether the victimized partner is male or female.

In comparison with the research on intimate partner violence between men and women, the literature about same-sex violence is sparse, in part because many respondents may consider disclosing same-sex relationships risky and revealing partner violence within them even more sensitive. Furthermore, not all people who engage in same-sex relationships identify themselves as homosexual, leading to more questions about the quality

TABLE 6.7

Victim-offender relationship, 2004

Relationship with victim	Violent crime Number	Violent crime Percent	Rape/sexual assault Number	Rape/sexual assault Percent	Robbery Number	Robbery Percent	Aggravated assault Number	Aggravated assault Percent	Simple assault Number	Simple assault Percent
Male victims										
Total	2,937,250	100%	6,200	100%	335,520	100%	683,440	100%	1,912,090	100%
Nonstranger	1,412,860	48%	0	0%*	116,670	35%	301,940	44%	994,250	52%
Intimate	111,750	4	0	0*	16,860	5*	20,160	3*	74,730	4
Other relative	163,700	6	0	0*	5,720	2*	44,430	7	113,550	6
Friend/acquaintance	1,137,410	39	0	0*	94,100	28	237,350	35	805,960	42
Stranger	1,475,230	50%	6,200	100%*	208,160	62%	367,760	54%	893,110	47%
Relationship unknown	49,150	2%	0	0%*	10,680	3%*	13,740	2%*	24,740	1%*
Female victims										
Total	2,245,420	100%	203,680	100%	166,310	100%	346,650	100%	1,528,790	100%
Nonstranger	1,439,430	64%	136,550	67%	89,100	54%	212,030	61%	1,001,750	66%
Intimate	466,600	21	35,340	17	50,410	30	63,250	18	317,600	21
Other relative	198,590	9	5,600	3*	7,470	5*	45,440	13	140,080	9
Friend/acquaintance	774,250	35	95,610	47	31,220	19*	103,340	30	544,070	36
Stranger	771,230	34%	64,040	31%	74,810	45%	121,220	35%	511,160	33%
Relationship unknown	34,760	2%	3,090	2%*	2,400	1%*	13,400	4%*	15,880	1%

Note: Percentages may not total to 100% because of rounding.
*Based on 10 or fewer sample cases.

SOURCE: Shannan M. Catalano, "Table 9. Victim and Offender Relationship, 2004," in *National Crime Victimization Survey: Criminal Victimization, 2004*, U.S. Department of Justice, Bureau of Justice Statistics, September 2005, http://www.ojp.usdoj.gov/bjs/pub/pdf/cv04.pdf (accessed August 21, 2006)

of data gathered. The research that examines same-sex partner violence reveals that it is quite similar to heterosexual partner violence—abuse arises in the attempts of one partner to exert control over the other and it escalates throughout the course of the relationship.

National Crime Victimization Surveys

The NCVS are ongoing federal surveys that interview eighty thousand people from a representative sample of households biannually to estimate the amount of crime committed against people over age twelve in the United States. While the surveys cover all types of crime, they were extensively redesigned in 1992 to produce more accurate reports of rape, sexual assault, and other violent crimes committed by intimates or family members.

In *National Crime Victimization Survey: Criminal Victimization, 2004* (September 2005, http://www.rain-n.org/docs/statistics/ncvs2004.pdf), Shannan M. Catalano finds that the rate of violent crime was 21.1 per one thousand population in 2004. Although the 2004 NCVS's criminal victimization estimates are the lowest since the NCVS began in 1973, the numbers are still staggering: 5.1 million violent crimes were committed in 2004 (rape/sexual assault, robbery, aggravated assault, and simple assault). Over half a million (578,350) violent crimes were committed against intimate partners. (See Table 6.7.)

More than one out of ten people (11.2%) who were victims of violent crimes in 2004 were victimized by intimate partners. (See Table 6.1.) Women were victimized by intimate partners at a greater rate than were men—20.8% of female victims named an intimate

partner as the offender, compared with only 3.8% of men. In rape and sexual assault cases, 17.4% of women reported that the rapist was an intimate partner, 2.7% of female rape victims reported another relative was the perpetrator, and 46.9% reported a friend or acquaintance was the perpetrator.

Women identified offenders as an intimate, friend, other relative, or acquaintance in about two-thirds of violent crimes (64.1%), whereas more than half of male victims identified the offender as a stranger (50.2%). Women were also more likely to report that their offender was another relative (8.8%) than men were (5.6%). (See Table 6.1.)

Although men continued to experience higher rates of violent victimizations than women, the rates for both genders declined from 1993 to 2004. Rates among people from most racial, ethnic, and socioeconomic groups also declined from 1993 to 2004. The most significant annual declines in violent crime rates were observed among males and Hispanics. (See Table 6.8.)

According to *Criminal Victimization in the United States, 2004*, almost half (49.9%) of all violent victimizations were reported to the police in 2004—35.8% of rape and sexual assaults, 64.2% of aggravated assaults, and 44.9% of simple assaults. (See Table 6.9.) Female victims were more likely to report violent offenses than male victims. Two-thirds of African-American women (66.9%) and Hispanic women (65.1%) and about one-half (52.1%) of white women reported the violent crimes they suffered; 45.1% of African-American men, 41.6% of

TABLE 6.8

Violent victimization rates by demographic characteristics, 1993–2004

Demographic category of victim	Number of violent crimes per 1,000 persons age 12 or older												Percent change, 1993–2004
	1993	1994	1995	1996	1997	1998	1999	2000	2001	2002	2003	2004	
Gender													
Male	59.8	61.1	55.7	49.9	45.8	43.1	37.0	32.9	27.3	25.5	26.3	25.0	−58.2%
Female	40.7	43.0	38.1	34.6	33.0	30.4	28.8	23.2	23.0	20.8	19.0	18.1	−56.5
Race													
White	47.9	50.5	44.7	40.9	38.3	36.3	31.9	27.1	24.5	22.8	21.5	21.0	−56.2%
Black	67.4	61.3	61.1	52.3	49.0	41.7	41.6	35.3	31.2	27.9	29.1	26.0	−61.4
Other race	39.8	49.9	41.9	33.2	28.0	27.6	24.5	20.7	18.2	14.7	16.0	12.7	−68.1
Two or more races	—	—	—	—	—	—	—	—	—	—	67.7	51.6	—
Hispanic origin													
Hispanic	55.2	61.6	57.3	44.0	43.1	32.8	33.8	28.4	29.5	23.6	24.2	18.2	−67.0%
Non-Hispanic	49.5	50.7	45.2	41.6	38.3	36.8	32.4	27.7	24.5	23.0	22.3	21.9	−55.8
Annual household income													
Less than $7,500	84.7	86.0	77.8	65.3	71.0	63.8	57.5	60.3	46.6	45.5	49.9	38.4	−54.7%
$7,500–$14,999	56.4	60.7	49.8	52.1	51.2	49.3	44.5	37.8	36.9	31.5	30.8	39.0	−30.9
$15,000–$24,999	49.0	50.7	48.9	44.1	40.1	39.4	35.3	31.8	31.8	30.0	26.3	24.4	−50.2
$25,000–$34,999	51.0	47.3	47.1	43.0	40.2	42.0	37.9	29.8	29.1	27.0	24.9	22.1	−56.7
$35,000–$49,999	45.6	47.0	45.8	43.0	38.7	31.7	30.3	28.5	26.3	25.6	21.4	21.6	−52.6
$50,000–$74,999	44.0	48.0	44.6	37.5	33.9	32.0	33.3	23.7	21.0	18.7	22.9	22.1	−49.8
$75,000 or more	41.3	39.5	37.3	30.5	30.7	33.1	22.9	22.3	18.5	19.0	17.5	17.0	−58.8

Notes: Annual rates are based on interviews conducted during the calendar year. Beginning in 2003 the racial categories are white/black/other "only" and "two or more races." "Other race" includes American Indians/Alaska Natives, Asians, and Native Hawaiians/other Pacific Islanders identifying a single racial background. The collection of racial and ethnic categories in 2003 changed from that of previous years; however, because about 0.9% of survey respondents identified two or more races, the impact on the victimization rates for each race is small.
—Not available.

SOURCE: Shannan M. Catalano, "Table 4. Violent Victimization Rates of Selected Demographic Categories, 1993–2004," in *National Crime Victimization Survey: Criminal Victimization, 2004*, U.S. Department of Justice, Bureau of Justice Statistics, September 2005, http://www.ojp.usdoj.gov/bjs/pub/pdf/cv04.pdf (accessed August 21, 2006)

Hispanic men, and 45.8% of white men reported violent crimes. However, as mentioned earlier, women are known to seriously underreport sexual assaults and rapes. (See Table 6.10.)

National Family Violence Survey

The 1985 National Family Violence Resurvey, considered by many to be the source of the most important research on family violence, was originally conducted in 1975 for the Family Research Laboratory at the University of New Hampshire, Durham. In the 1985 study Murray A. Straus and Richard J. Gelles found that the rate of assaults by husbands on wives had dropped slightly during the decade, from 121 instances per one hundred thousand couples in 1975 to 113 instances per one hundred thousand couples in 1985. The rate of severe violence, such as hitting, kicking, or using a weapon, however, had declined sharply, from thirty-eight to thirty per one hundred thousand couples—a 21% drop.

The study's most controversial finding indicated that women were initiating domestic violence at a rate equal to men. The 1985 study reported that in half of the cases, the abuse was mutual. After reassessing their data in 1990 and again in 1993, Straus and Gelles concluded that although there were similar levels of abuse between men and women, men were six times more likely to inflict serious injury.

In "Changes in Spouse Assault Rates from 1975 to 1992: A Comparison of Three National Surveys in the United States" (paper presented at the Thirteenth World Congress of Sociology, Bielefeld, Germany, July 1994), Murray A. Straus and Glenda Kaufman Kantor compare the rates of abuse from the 1975 National Family Violence Survey and the 1985 National Family Violence Resurvey and a 1992 survey conducted by Kantor. When the researchers reclassified "minor assault" to include pushing, grabbing, shoving, and slapping, and "severe assault" to include behavior likely to cause serious injury, such as kicking, punching, beating, and threatening with a weapon, they found some startling results.

The rates of reclassified minor assaults, which were considered less likely to cause injuries requiring medical treatment, decreased for husbands between the 1975 and 1985 surveys, yet remained constant for wives. The researchers find the same trend held true for severe assaults by husbands versus those by wives. While the rate of severe assaults by men against their wives declined 50% in the seventeen years from 1975 to 1992, severe assaults by women remained fairly steady. Straus and Kantor conclude that the reason for the decline in severe assaults by husbands was that over time men became increasingly aware that battering was a crime and grew reluctant to admit the abuse. At the same time,

TABLE 6.9

Victimizations by type of crime and by victims' decision to report or not report the incident to police, 2004

Sector and type of crime	Number of victimizations	Percent of victimizations reported to the police			
		Total	Yes[a]	No	Not known and not available
All crimes	**24,061,140**	**100.0%**	**41.4%**	**57.5%**	**1.1%**
Personal crimes	**5,406,740**	**100.0%**	**49.5%**	**49.2%**	**1.2%**
Crimes of violence	5,182,670	100.0	49.9	48.8	1.2
Completed violence	1,737,000	100.0	62.1	36.5	1.4[b]
Attempted/threatened violence	3,445,670	100.0	43.8	55.1	1.1
Rape/sexual assault	209,880	100.0	35.8	62.9	1.3*
Rape/attempted rape	101,000	100.0	46.6	53.4	0.0*
Rape	58,780	100.0	56.8	43.2*	0.0*
Attempted rape[b]	42,220	100.0	32.4*	67.6*	0.0*
Sexual assault[c]	108,880	100.0	25.7*	71.7	2.6*
Robbery	501,820	100.0	61.1	38.9	0.0*
Completed/property taken	299,240	100.0	73.0	27.0	0.0*
With injury	110,200	100.0	71.0	29.0*	0.0*
Without injury	189,040	100.0	74.2	25.8	0.0*
Attempted to take property	202,580	100.0	43.4	56.6	0.0*
With injury	70,650	100.0	57.0	43.0*	0.0*
Without injury	131,940	100.0	36.1	63.9	0.0*
Assault	4,470,960	100.0	49.4	49.3	1.4
Aggravated	1,030,080	100.0	64.2	35.3	0.5*
With injury	377,840	100.0	70.6	29.4	0.0*
Threatened with weapon	652,240	100.0	60.4	38.8	0.7*
Simple	3,440,880	100.0	44.9	53.5	1.6
With minor injury	898,120	100.0	59.6	38.0	2.4*
Without injury	2,542,760	100.0	39.7	58.9	1.4
Purse snatching/pocket picking	224,070	100.0	40.5	58.4	1.1*
Completed purse snatching	27,980*	100.0*	73.5*	26.5*	0.0*
Attempted purse snatching	14,840*	100.0*	17.5*	82.5*	0.0*
Pocket picking	181,250	100.0	37.3	61.3	1.4*
Property crimes	**18,654,400**	**100.0%**	**39.0%**	**59.9%**	**1.1%**
Household burglary	3,427,690	100.0	53.0	46.0	0.9*
Completed	2,909,160	100.0	54.6	44.6	0.8*
Forcible entry	1,095,560	100.0	76.1	23.2	0.7*
Unlawful entry without force	1,813,600	100.0	41.6	57.5	0.9*
Attempted forcible entry	518,530	100.0	44.4	54.1	1.5*
Motor vehicle theft	1,014,770	100.0	84.8	14.7	0.5*
Completed	779,220	100.0	94.8	4.8	0.4*
Attempted	235,560	100.0	51.8	47.3	0.9*
Theft	14,211,940	100.0	32.3	66.5	1.2
Completed	13,583,940	100.0	32.1	66.7	1.2
Less than $50	4,114,020	100.0	18.8	79.9	1.4
$50–$249	4,846,570	100.0	27.4	71.7	0.9
$250 or more	3,259,970	100.0	54.9	44.3	0.8*
Amount not available	1,363,380	100.0	34.9	62.7	2.5
Attempted	628,000	100.0	37.2	61.8	1.0*

Note: Detail may not add to total shown because of rounding.
*Estimate is based on about 10 or fewer sample cases.
[a]Figures in this column represent the rates at which victimizations were reported to the police, or "police reporting rates."
[b]Includes verbal threats of rape.
[c]Includes threats.

SOURCE: "Table 91. Personal and Property Crimes, 2004: Percent Distribution of Victimizations, by Type of Crime and Whether or Not Reported to the Police," in *Criminal Victimization in the United States, 2004*, U.S. Department of Justice, Office of Justice Programs, Bureau of Justice Statistics, June 2006, http://www.ojp.usdoj.gov/bjs/pub/pdf/cvus04.pdf (accessed July 8, 2006)

women had been encouraged not to tolerate abuse and to report it, accounting for an increase in the reporting of even minor instances of abuse.

When abuse was measured based on separate reports by men and women, Straus and Kantor find that minor assaults by husbands decreased from 1975 to 1985. Based on the husbands' reports, these rates continued to decline from 1985 to 1992, but wives reported an increase over the same period. Men also reported a decrease in the rate of severe abuse between 1975 and 1985, whereas women reported no change. In contrast, between 1985 and 1992 men reported a slight increase in the rate of severe abuse, whereas women reported a sharp drop of 43%. These findings appear to contradict Straus and Kantor's hypothesis that the rate change was a result of men's reluctance to report abuse and women's greater freedom to report it.

According to women, minor abuse perpetrated by wives against their husbands declined from 1975 to 1985 but increased substantially from 1985 to 1992. Men, however, said the rate of minor abuse by their

TABLE 6.10

Victimizations reported to police by type of crime, by gender, and by race or ethnicity of victims, 2004

Characteristic	Percent of all victimizations reported to the police	
	Crimes of violence[a]	Property crimes
Total	**49.9**	**39.0**
Male		
White only	45.8	38.6
Black only	45.1	42.9
Other race only[b]	49.9	31.8
Two or more races[c]	49.3	26.5*
Female		
White only	52.1	38.8
Black only	66.9	42.6
Other race only[b]	71.9	35.2
Two or more races[c]	67.9^	37.6
Male		
Hispanic	41.6	39.2
Non-Hispanic	46.3	38.7
Female		
Hispanic	65.1	34.4
Non-Hispanic	53.8	40.1

*Estimate is based on about 10 or fewer sample cases.
Note: Excludes data on persons whose ethnicity was not ascertained.
[a]Includes data on rape and sexual assault, not shown separately.
[b]Includes American Indian, Eskimo, Asian Pacific Islander if only one of these races is given.
[c]Includes all persons of any race, indicating two or more races.

SOURCE: "Table 91b. Violent Crimes, 2004: Percent of Victimizations Reported to the Police, by Type of Crime and Gender and Race or Ethnicity of Victims," in *Criminal Victimization in the United States, 2004*, U.S. Department of Justice, Office of Justice Programs, Bureau of Justice Statistics, June 2006, http://www.ojp.usdoj.gov/bjs/pub/pdf/cvus04.pdf (accessed July 8, 2006)

TABLE 6.11

Intimate homicide victims by gender, 1976–2004

	Male	Female
1976	1,347	1,596
1977	1,288	1,430
1978	1,193	1,480
1979	1,260	1,506
1980	1,217	1,546
1981	1,268	1,567
1982	1,135	1,480
1983	1,112	1,461
1984	988	1,439
1985	956	1,546
1986	979	1,584
1987	927	1,486
1988	848	1,578
1989	895	1,411
1990	853	1,493
1991	773	1,503
1992	718	1,448
1993	698	1,571
1994	684	1,403
1995	544	1,315
1996	506	1,310
1997	445	1,209
1998	502	1,310
1999	418	1,204
2000	425	1,238
2001	392	1,194
2002	378	1,193
2003	371	1,163
2004	385	1,159

SOURCE: James Alan Fox and Marianne W. Zawitz, "Intimate Homicide Victims by Gender, 1976–2004," in *Homicide Trends in the United States*, U.S. Department of Justice, Office of Justice Programs, Bureau of Justice Statistics, June 2006, http://www.ojp.usdoj.gov/bjs/pub/pdf/htius.pdf (accessed July 8, 2006)

wives increased over both periods. Women also reported that the rate of severe assaults against their husbands remained steady during the first decade but increased between 1985 and 1992. Husbands reported a steady decrease in severe assaults by their wives during both periods.

DRAWING CONCLUSIONS FROM THE DATA. Straus and Kantor observe that the large decrease in severe assaults by husbands was supported by Federal Bureau of Investigation (FBI) statistics showing an 18% drop in the number of women killed by their husbands during that period. Straus and Kantor speculate that strides made over several years, such as justice system interventions to punish abusive husbands, along with the greater availability of shelters and restraining orders, played a role in the decline of severe abuse. The lack of change in minor assaults by husbands may reflect the emphasis that has been placed on severe assaults, which could allow men to mistakenly assume that an occasional slap or shove did not constitute abusive behavior.

To explain the increase in minor assaults by women, Straus and Kantor suggest that there had been no effort to condemn assaults by wives, and with increasing gender equality, women might feel entitled to hit as often as their male partners. The decrease in severe abuse by wives as reported by their husbands, which is inconsistent with the wives' responses, might have reflected men's reluctance to admit they have been victims of abuse.

ABUSED TO DEATH

In 2004, 1,159 women and 385 men were killed by an intimate partner. (See Table 6.11.) Although these statistics sound alarming, they reflect a positive trend in domestic homicides. Since 1976, when the FBI began keeping statistics on intimate murders, the number of men and women killed by an intimate partner has dropped significantly. The number of men killed by an intimate declined from 1,347 in 1976 to 385 in 2004, a decrease of 71%, and the number of women killed was stable until 1993, when it began to decline. (See Figure 6.3.)

Although the number of white females killed by an intimate increased during the 1980s, it declined after 1987. In 1997 it reached its lowest point in two decades. This decline, however, did not hold true across all relationship categories. The intimate homicide rate for white girlfriends in 2004 was about the same as it was in 1976,

FIGURE 6.3

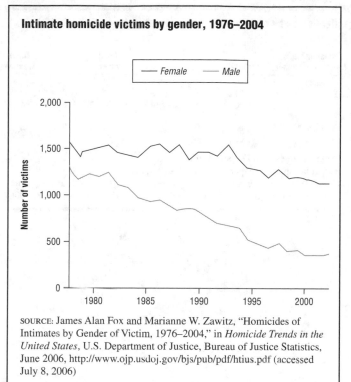

Intimate homicide victims by gender, 1976–2004

SOURCE: James Alan Fox and Marianne W. Zawitz, "Homicides of Intimates by Gender of Victim, 1976–2004," in *Homicide Trends in the United States*, U.S. Department of Justice, Bureau of Justice Statistics, June 2006, http://www.ojp.usdoj.gov/bjs/pub/pdf/htius.pdf (accessed July 8, 2006)

FIGURE 6.4

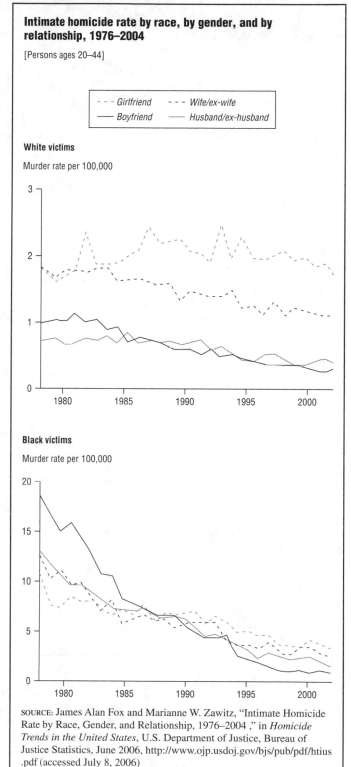

Intimate homicide rate by race, by gender, and by relationship, 1976–2004

[Persons ages 20–44]

SOURCE: James Alan Fox and Marianne W. Zawitz, "Intimate Homicide Rate by Race, Gender, and Relationship, 1976–2004 ," in *Homicide Trends in the United States*, U.S. Department of Justice, Bureau of Justice Statistics, June 2006, http://www.ojp.usdoj.gov/bjs/pub/pdf/htius.pdf (accessed July 8, 2006)

and while the homicide rate for white wives and former wives had declined somewhat, it had not declined as much as that for white husbands and former husbands. The intimate homicide rates among African-Americans dropped more dramatically for all relationship categories, with the steepest decline experienced by boyfriends and the most modest decrease experienced by girlfriends. (See Figure 6.4.)

Of all intimate homicides committed during this period, guns were used in a majority of the murders, although other weapons such as knives were also used. In the period between 1990 and 2004 more than two-thirds of all victims of murder at the hands of spouses and former spouses were killed by guns. However, almost half (45%) of the boyfriends murdered by their partners and one out of five (20%) of the girlfriends murdered by their partners were killed with knives. (See Figure 6.5 and Table 6.12.)

In "How Can Practitioners Help an Abused Woman Lower Her Risk of Death?" (*National Institute of Justice Journal*, November 2003), Carolyn Rebecca Block investigates what factors present in abusive relationships might indicate a threat of the violence escalating to homicide. She finds that certain types of past violence directed against female intimates indicate an increased risk of homicide, especially choking. She also finds that recently abused women are more likely to be killed—half

of women who were killed in 1995 and 1996 by their partners had experienced violence in the previous thirty days before the survey. Increasingly frequent violent incidents posed a higher risk of homicide.

FIGURE 6.5

Intimate homicide victims killed by gun or by another type of weapon, 1976–2004

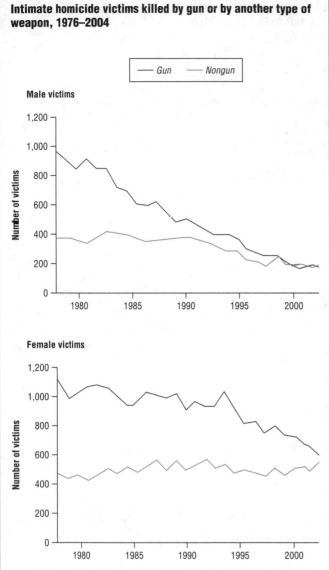

SOURCE: James Alan Fox and Marianne W. Zawitz, "Intimate Homicide Victims by Type of Weapon, 1976–2004 ," in *Homicide Trends in the United States,* U.S. Department of Justice, Bureau of Justice Statistics, June 2006, http://www.ojp.usdoj.gov/bjs/pub/pdf/htius.pdf (accessed July 8, 2006)

TABLE 6.12

Homicides by relationship and by weapon type, 1990–2004

Relationship of victim to offender	Total	Gun	Knife	Blunt object	Force	Other weapon
Husband	100%	69%	26%	2%	1%	2%
Ex-husband	100	87	9	1	0	2
Wife	100	68	14	5	10	4
Ex-wife	100	77	12	2	6	3
Boyfriend	100	46	45	3	3	3
Girlfriend	100	56	20	5	14	5

SOURCE: James Alan Fox and Marianne W. Zawitz, "Homicides by Relationship and Weapon Type, 1990–2004," in *Homicide Trends in the United States*, U.S. Department of Justice, Bureau of Justice Statistics, June 2006, http://www.ojp.usdoj.gov/bjs/pub/pdf/htius.pdf (accessed July 8, 2006)

CHAPTER 7
CAUSES, EFFECTS, AND PREVENTION OF DOMESTIC VIOLENCE

SOCIOLOGICAL THEORIES ON THE CAUSES OF DOMESTIC VIOLENCE

Researchers have studied domestic violence for about thirty years. While scholars from different intellectual traditions have varying theories on the causes of domestic violence, sociological explanations have gained wide acceptance. Some sociological models are examined in this chapter.

General Systems Theory

The general systems theory views violence as a system rather than as a result of individual mental disturbance. It describes a system of violence that operates at the individual level, the family level, and the societal level.

In "A General Systems Theory Approach to a Theory of Violence between Family Members" (*Social Science Information*, June 1973), Murray A. Straus provides eight concepts to illustrate the general systems theory:

- Violence between family members has many causes and roots, and personality, stress, and conflicts are only some of the causes of domestic violence.

- More family violence occurs than is reported.

- Most family violence is either denied or ignored.

- Stereotyped family-violence imagery is learned in early childhood from other family members.

- The family-violence stereotypes are continually reaffirmed through ordinary social interactions and the mass media.

- Violent acts by violent people may generate positive feedback; that is, these acts may produce desired results.

- Use of violence, when contrary to family norms, creates additional conflict.

- People who are labeled violent may be encouraged to play out a violent role, either to live up to the expectations of others or to fulfill their own self-concepts of being violent or dangerous.

Resource Theory

The second theory in sociological models used to explain domestic violence is known as the resource theory. According to this theory, the more resources—social, personal, and economic—a person can command, the more power he or she can potentially call on. The individual who is rich in terms of these resources has less need to use force in an open manner. In contrast, a person with little education, low job prestige and income, or poor interpersonal skills may use violence to compensate for a real or perceived lack of resources and to maintain dominance.

EFFECTS OF POVERTY. Straus finds that serious physical acts of wife abuse are more likely to occur in poorer homes. His research shows that for lower levels of violence, such as shoving or slapping, the differences in socioeconomic status are small. For more serious types of violence, the rates increase dramatically as the socioeconomic status drops.

The 1985 National Family Violence Survey, based on 6,002 households, provided researchers with the primary data to test their observations against a database large enough to produce statistically significant, valid findings. In the survey, families living at or below the poverty level had a rate of marital violence 500% greater than more affluent families.

In "Neighborhood Environment, Racial Position, and Domestic Violence Risk: Contextual Analysis" (*Public Health Reports*, January–February 2003), Deborah N. Pearlman et al. present the findings of an analysis of police-reported domestic violence in relation to variables including socioeconomic conditions, age, race, and ethnicity. They find a complex but strong relationship between poverty and domestic violence. Pearlman et al. speculate that one explanation for the increased risk of domestic violence in poorer neighborhoods might be differences in law enforcement availability and practices—economically deprived communities might have less police notification, attention, and documentation.

The desire to dominate one's partner may be manifested using methods other than violence, such as attempts at financial, social, and decision-making control. Some researchers theorize that men of lower socioeconomic status are more likely to batter because they do it to assert the power that they lack economically. Violence becomes the tactic that compensates for the control, power, independence, and self-sufficiency these men lack in other areas.

Exchange/Social Control Theory

The exchange/social control theory argues that violence can be explained by the principle of costs and rewards. The private nature of the family, the reluctance of social institutions to intervene, and the low risk of other interventions reduce the risk of negative consequences from abuse. This theory maintains that cultural sanction and approval of violence increase the potential rewards for violence.

LEARNED GENDER ROLES. Pointing to history, some researchers see wife abuse as a natural consequence of women's second-class status in society. Among the first to express this viewpoint were R. Emerson Dobash and Russell E. H. Dobash in *Violence against Wives: A Case against the Patriarchy* (1979). Dobash and Dobash argue that men who assaulted their wives were actually living up to roles and qualities expected and cherished in Western society—aggressiveness, male dominance, and female subordination—and that they used physical force as a means to enforce these roles. Many sociologists and anthropologists believe that men are socialized to exert power and control over women. Some men may use both physical and emotional abuse to attain the position of dominance in the spousal relationship. In "Gendering Violence: Masculinity and Power in Men's Accounts of Domestic Violence" (*Gender and Society*, June 2001), a study of thirty-three male batterers, Kristin L. Anderson and Debra Umberson state that "violence is...an effective means by which batterers reconstruct men as masculine and women as feminine."

Subculture of Violence Theory

Another sociological theory explaining domestic violence posits that there is a subculture of violence in which some groups within society hold values that permit, and even encourage, the use of violence. This theory is offered as an explanation of why some segments of society and some cultures are more violent than others. This theory is perhaps the most widely accepted theory of violence.

ATTITUDES TOWARD VIOLENCE. Some researchers believe attitudes about violence are shaped early in life, long before the first punch is thrown in a relationship. In "The Attitudes towards Violence Scale: A Measure for Adolescents" (*Journal of Interpersonal Violence*, November 1999), Jeanne B. Funk et al. asked junior high and high school students attending an inner-city public school in a midwestern city about their attitudes toward violence. Some students identified themselves as victims of violence and others completed the survey before and after participating in a violence awareness program.

Using the responses of 638 students who took the survey before the violence awareness program, Funk et al. examined the correlation of violence with gender, grade level, and ethnicity. They find that males endorsed more pro-violence attitudes independent of age, grade level, and ethnicity, as did those students who identified themselves as victims of violence. African-American teenagers endorsed "reactive violence," or violence used in response to actual or perceived threats, at higher levels than other groups. Endorsement of reactive violence was linked to having violent behaviors in one's repertoire, willingness to act in a violent manner, and supporting the actual choice of a violent response. Hispanics endorsed "culture of violence" measures, reflecting a pervasive identification with violence as a valued activity, at slightly higher levels than the teenagers as a group. "Culture of violence" measures included the belief that the world is a dangerous place where the best way to ensure survival is to be vigilant and prepared to take the offensive. European-Americans scored lower on measures of "reactive violence" as well as on "total pro-violence attitudes."

Funk et al. find that gender, ethnicity, and self-identification as a victim of violence were all related to pro-violence attitudes. Males, regardless of cultural background, were more likely than females to endorse pro-violence attitudes. Funk et al. conclude that a combination of biological, environmental, and social influences were responsible for these findings.

Feminist Theory

Feminist theories of violence against women emphasize that societal patriarchal structures of gender-based inequalities of power are at the root of the problem. That is, the violence, rather than being an individual psychological problem, is instead an expression of male domination of females. Violence against women, in the feminist view, includes a variety of "control tactics" meant to control women.

DOES A PATRIARCHAL SOCIETY BREED VIOLENCE?

Donald G. Dutton questions the role of male domination in wife battering and offers alternative explanations for violence in "Patriarchy and Wife Assault: The Ecological Fallacy" (*Violence and Victims*, 1994). According to the patriarchal model, societies that place a high value on male dominance should have high rates of abuse. However, Dutton and other investigators cite studies that contradict this premise. For example, Diane Coleman and Murray A. Straus, in "Marital Power, Conflict, and Violence in a Nationally Representative Sample of American Couples" (*Violence and Victims*, 1986), find that in marriages where spouses agreed that the husband should be dominant, violence levels were low.

Other research discounts the weight of the patriarchal theory of abuse. David B. Sugarman and Susan Frankel, in "Patriarchal Ideology and Wife-Assault: A Meta-analytical Review" (*Journal of Family Violence*, 1996), examine studies for evidence of a relationship between patriarchy and violence. They measure whether violent husbands had a higher acceptance of violence than nonviolent men and whether they believed that women should exhibit traditional gender roles of obedience, loyalty, and deference. Sugarman and Frankel also measure whether assaultive men were more likely to possess a traditional "gender schema," an internal perception of an individual's own levels of masculinity, femininity, or androgyny. They also consider whether assaulted wives held more traditional gender attitudes than wives who were not battered and whether battered wives held more traditional feminine gender schemas.

Overall, Sugarman and Frankel's analysis finds support for only two of the five hypotheses. Predictably, assaultive husbands found marital violence more acceptable than nonviolent husbands, and battered wives were more likely to be classified as having "traditional" feminine gender schemas than wives who were not assaulted. Sugarman and Frankel conclude that their findings offer only partial support for the patriarchy theory.

In contrast, Donna Chung, in "Violence, Control, Romance, and Gender Equality: Young Women and Heterosexual Relationships" (*Women's Studies International Forum*, November–December 2005), concludes that patriarchal belief systems combine with heterosexual norms and sometimes result in violence. She examines dating violence with a view to discerning the "structural factors" that influence the violent actions of young people within relationships. She argues that the "micropractices" of heterosexual relationships embody power relations between the genders. This inequality in power relationships at times results in intimate partner violence.

In "Girlfriend Abuse as a Form of Masculinity Construction among Violent, Marginal Male Youth" (*Men and Masculinities*, July 2003), a study of thirty male adolescents,

primarily gang members, Mark Totten finds another link between patriarchy and violence. He concludes that underprivileged males in society use violence toward women in response to their lack of access to the traditional benefits of patriarchy. Totten posits that the ideals of patriarchy—and the inability of these disenfranchised boys to wield any patriarchal power outside of their gangs or family groups—leads them to be violent toward their girlfriends as one way to define their masculinity. He states that "violence was one of the few resources over which they had control." However, he also suggests that "men with more resources can commit different, less visible forms of abuse."

Structure of Interpersonal Relationships Theory

Joseph H. Michalski, in "Making Sociological Sense out of Trends in Intimate Partner Violence" (*Violence against Women*, June 2004), argues that many of the insights of other theories need to be integrated into a more comprehensive theory of the impact of the structure of relationships on domestic violence. He suggests that key risk factors of domestic violence include:

- Social isolation of the couple
- Separate peer support networks
- Inequality between partners
- Lack of relational distance, or a high degree of intimacy within a couple
- The centralization of authority—in other words, patriarchal dominance within a family
- Exposure to violence and violent networks

DOES SUBSTANCE ABUSE CAUSE DOMESTIC VIOLENCE?

The role of alcohol and drug abuse in family violence features in many studies, and it is a factor in physical violence and stalking, according to researchers such as Pam Wilson et al., who examine this issue in "Severity of Violence against Women by Intimate Partners and Associated Use of Alcohol and/or Illicit Drugs by the Perpetrator" (*Journal of Interpersonal Violence*, September 2000). Although researchers generally do not consider alcohol and drug use to be the cause of violence, they find that it can contribute to, accelerate, or increase aggression. A variety of data sources establish a correlation (a complementary or parallel relationship) between substance abuse and violence, but a correlation does not establish a causation. In theory, and possibly even in practice, substance abuse may promote or provoke domestic violence, but both may also be influenced by other factors, such as environmental, biological, and situational stressors. Based on available research, it remains unclear whether substance abuse is a key factor in most domestic violence incidents.

TABLE 7.1

Victimizations by offenders who appeared to be under the influence of drugs and/or alcohol, 2004

				Assault		
				Percent of victimizations		
Perceived drug or alcohol use by offender	Crimes of violence	Rape/ sexual assault[a]	Robbery	Total	Aggravated	Simple
Total victimizations	**100.0%**	**100.0%**	**100.0%**	**100.0%***	**100.0%**	**100.0%**
Total (perceived to be under the influence of drugs or alcohol)	30.0	44.4	22.4	30.2*	34.5	28.9
Under the influence of alcohol	18.4	34.1	6.9	18.9*	21.7	18.1
Under the influence of drugs	5.0	4.1*	9.2	4.5*	3.4	4.9
Under the influence of both drugs and alcohol	5.0	6.1*	4.0*	5.0*	7.1	4.4
Under the influence of one, not sure which	1.1	0.0*	1.7*	1.1*	0.9*	1.2
Not available whether drugs or alcohol	0.6*	0.0*	0.6*	0.6*	1.5*	0.3*
Not on alcohol or drugs	26.9	11.9*	20.5	28.3*	23.2	29.8
Don't know or not ascertained	43.1	43.7	57.1	41.5*	42.4	41.3

Note: Detail may not add to total shown because of rounding.
*Estimate is based on about 10 or fewer sample cases.
[a]Includes verbal threats of rape and threats of sexual assault.

SOURCE: "Table 32. Personal Crimes of Violence, 2004: Percent Distribution of Victimizations by Perceived Drug or Alcohol Use by Offender," in *Criminal Victimization in the United States, 2004*, U.S. Department of Justice, Office of Justice Programs, Bureau of Justice Statistics, June 2006, http://www.ojp.usdoj.gov/bjs/pub/pdf/cvus04.pdf (accessed July 8, 2006)

In 2004, 18.4% of victims of violent assaults believed their offenders had been using alcohol, 5% believed offenders had been using both alcohol and drugs, 5% believed offenders had been using drugs only, and 1.1% believed offenders had used either alcohol or drugs. Only 26.9% of victims believed the offender had not used any drugs or alcohol, whereas another 43.1% reported they did not know. (See Table 7.1.)

While anecdotal evidence suggests that alcohol and drugs appear to be linked to violence and abuse, in controlled studies the connection is not as clear. For example, some research finds that heavy binge drinking is more predictive of abuse than daily consumption of alcohol. Other research reveals little evidence that drug use directly causes people to become aggressive or violent, and some investigators believe that the substance abuse-violence link varies across individuals, over time within an individual's life, and even in response to environmental influences, such as epidemics of drug use and changing law enforcement policies. In *Alcohol and Intimate Partner Violence* (March 2005, http://pubs.niaaa.nih.gov/publications/Social/Module8IntimatePartnerViolence/Module8.html), the National Institute on Alcohol Abuse and Alcoholism states that "alcohol is not a clearly identified direct cause of IPV [intimate partner violence], though it clearly is a correlate and may be a contributing factor."

Richard J. Gelles, in "Alcohol and Other Drugs Are Not the Cause of Violence" (Gelles and Donileen R. Loseke, eds., *Current Controversies on Family Violence*, 1993), argues that substance abuse is not a cause of family violence—rather, it is often used as an excuse for family violence. Gelles argues that although substantial evidence has linked alcohol and drug use to violence, there is little scientific evidence that alcohol or other drugs, such as cocaine, have pharmacological properties that produce violent and abusive behavior. Although amphetamines have been proven to generate increased aggression, there is no evidence that such aggression is routinely expressed as family or intimate partner violence. Gelles maintains that although alcoholism may be associated with intimate violence, it is not a primary cause of the violence. He cites experiments using college students as subjects that have found that when the students thought they were consuming alcohol, they acted more aggressively than if they were told they had been given nonalcoholic drinks. According to Gelles, it is the expectation of the effects of alcohol that influences behavior, not the actual liquor consumed.

In "Risky Mix: Drinking, Drug Use, and Homicide" (*National Institute of Justice Journal*, November 2003), a study of patterns of alcohol and drug use in murders and attempted murders of women by their partners, Phyllis Sharps et al. show a relationship between substance use and violence. They find that in the year before the violent incident, female victims used alcohol and drugs less frequently and consumed smaller amounts than did their male partners. (See Table 7.2.) Sharps et al. also find that during the homicide or attempted homicide, 31.3% of perpetrators consumed alcohol, 12.6% of perpetrators used drugs, and 26.2% used both. Less than one out of three perpetrators (29.9%) used neither alcohol nor drugs. (See Table 7.3.) By contrast, perpetrators who abused their partners without attempting to kill them consumed alcohol 21% of the time, drugs 6.7% of the time, and both drugs and alcohol 5.8% of the time. Nearly two-thirds (65.8%) of perpetrators used neither alcohol nor drugs. Sharps et al. conclude that increased substance use results in more serious violence.

TABLE 7.2

Rate of alcohol and drug use by victims and their partners in the year prior to selected violent acts against women, 1996

Substance	Homicide/attempted homicide %		Abused %		Nonabused %	
	Women	Partners	Women	Partners	Women	Partners
Alcohol						
Drunk every day	—	35.1	—	11.6	—	1.2
Problem drinker	13.0	49.2	7.0	31.1	1.7	6.2
Drinks per episode						
1–2	64.6	24.4	61.4	35.1	77.7	65.8
3–4	22.9	17.1	27.9	27.2	18.2	25.5
5–6	8.9	24.8	7.9	18.2	3.8	4.8
7+	3.7	33.7	2.9	19.5	3.0	3.9
Ever been in alcohol treatment	27.7	13.5	13.3	18.1	57.1	19.2
Drugs						
Use drugs	18.4	54.2	13.4	25.0	6.7	4.3
Ever been in drug treatment	20.6	11.3	3.5	12.4	14.3	21.4

SOURCE: Phyllis Sharps, Jacquelyn C. Campbell, Doris Campbell, Faye Gary, and Daniel Webster, "Table 1. Alcohol and Drug Use by Victims and Their Partners in the Year Prior to the Killing or Attempted Killing of Women or the Worst Violent Incident," in "Risky Mix: Drinking, Drug Use, and Homicide," *National Institute of Justice Journal*, no. 250, November 2003, http://www.ncjrs.gov/pdffiles1/jr000250d.pdf (accessed July 2006)

Does Treatment Help?

Timothy J. O'Farrell and Christopher M. Murphy, in "Marital Violence before and after Alcoholism Treatment" (*Journal of Consulting and Clinical Psychology*, April 1995), examine whether behavioral marital therapy was helpful in reducing violence in abusive relationships. They find the percentage of couples who experienced violent acts decreased from about 65% before treatment to about 25% after treatment. Severe violence dropped from between 30% and 35% before to about 10% after treatment.

According to O'Farrell and Murphy, following treatment, recovering alcoholics no longer had elevated violence levels, but alcoholics who relapsed did. Based on women's reports of their partners' violence, 2.5% of non-drinking alcoholics, compared with 12.8% of the non-alcoholic sample, were violent. In contrast, 34.7% of the relapsed alcoholics were violent. O'Farrell and Murphy warn that the data do not permit drawing the conclusion that drinking caused the continued violence because other factors may have influenced behavior. They do conclude, however, that their findings support the premise that recovery from alcoholism can reduce the risk of marital violence.

According to Gregory L. Stuart et al. in "Reductions in Marital Violence following Treatment for Alcohol Dependence" (*Journal of Interpersonal Violence*, October 2003), after intensive inpatient treatment of male batterers for alcoholism, both alcohol consumption and levels of violence within families decreased. Not only did the frequency of husband-to-wife physical and psychological abuse

TABLE 7.3

Rate of substance use during the commission of selected violent acts against women, 1996

Substance use	Homicide/attempted homicide		Abuse	
	Victims (N=456) %	Perpetrators (N=456) %	Victims (N=427) %	Perpetrators (N=427) %
Alcohol	14.6	31.3	8.9	21
Drugs	3.3	12.6	1.6	6.7
Both	4.7	26.2	0.9	5.8
None	77.4	29.9	88.5	65.8

Note: N=population.

SOURCE: Phyllis Sharps, Jacquelyn C. Campbell, Doris Campbell, Faye Gary, and Daniel Wester, "Table 2. Substance Use During the Killing or Attempted Killing of Women or the Worst Violent Incident," in "Risky Mix: Drinking, Drug Use, and Homicide," *National Institute of Justice Journal*, no. 250, November 2003, http://www.ncjrs.gov/pdffiles1/jr000250d.pdf (accessed July 2006)

decrease, but the frequency of wife-to-husband marital violence also decreased significantly.

DOES PREGNANCY EXACERBATE DOMESTIC VIOLENCE?

Research about intimate partner violence reveals that violence does not stop when women become pregnant. The Division of Reproductive Health at the Centers for Disease Control and Prevention (CDC) gathers data about the health of expectant mothers using its Pregnancy Risk Assessment Monitoring System (PRAMS). An analysis of PRAMS data reveals that between 2.9% to 5.7% of women report being abused by their husbands or partners in the year before they gave birth. Jana L. Jasinski states in "Pregnancy and Domestic Violence: A Review of the Literature" (*Trauma, Violence, and Abuse*, January 2004) that this estimate is too low because PRAMS asks limited questions about domestic violence and asks about abuse rather than about particular behaviors. Still, she argues, pregnancy does not appear to increase the risk of domestic violence, although more research into this question is needed.

Studies estimating higher rates of abuse of pregnant women—as many as 324,000 women per year and rates as high as 20% of pregnant women—have been reported (Julie Gazmararian et al., "Prevalence of Violence against Pregnant Women," *International Journal of Gynecology and Obstetrics*, December 1996; and Julie Gazmararian et al., "Violence and Reproductive Health: Current Knowledge and Future Research Directions," *Maternal and Child Health Journal*, June 2000). According to Gazmararian et al. in "Prevalence of Violence against Pregnant Women," higher abuse rates were reported later in pregnancy, with 7.4% to 20% of that violence occurring in the third trimester. The lowest rates were reported in a study of women with a higher socioeconomic status who were treated in a private clinic. The assailants were mainly intimate or former intimate partners, parents, or other family members. Two studies that also examined violence in the period after birth found that violence was more prevalent after birth than during pregnancy.

Jasinski suggests that violence directed toward pregnant women is usually part of an ongoing pattern of domestic violence. Some factors, however, do seem to increase the risk of violence for pregnant women. In "Prevalence of Violence against Pregnant Women," Gazmararian et al. find that women with unwanted pregnancies had 4.1 times the risk of experiencing physical violence by a husband or boyfriend during the months before delivery than did women with desired pregnancies. Loraine Bacchus, Gill Mezey, and Susan Bewley, in "A Qualitative Exploration of the Nature of Domestic Violence in Pregnancy" (*Violence against Women*, June 2006), find that abuse of pregnant women centered around financial worries, the woman's inability to be as physically and emotionally available during pregnancy, the lack of support of a male partner, and doubts about paternity. In "Police-Reported Intimate Partner Violence during Pregnancy: Who Is at Risk?" (*Violence and Victims*, February 2005), Sherry Lipsky et al. find that certain factors put pregnant women at risk for police-reported intimate partner violence, including unmarried status, public health program use, smoking or alcohol use while pregnant, and having previously been pregnant or given birth.

EXPERIENCING VIOLENCE AS A CHILD

Research demonstrates a relationship between having been a victim of violence and becoming violent in future relationships. In fact, a 1996 report prepared by the American Psychological Association Task Force on Violence and the Family concluded that children's exposure to their father abusing their mother is the single strongest risk factor for passing violence down from one generation to the next. Shelby A. Kaura and Craig M. Allen find in "Power and Dating Violence Perpetration by Men and Women" (*Journal of Interpersonal Violence*, May 2004), a study of 352 male and 296 female undergraduate college students, that witnessing parental violence was the strongest predictor of perpetrating dating violence.

According to Erika L. Lichte and Laura A. McCloskey, in "The Effects of Childhood Exposure to Marital Violence on Adolescent Gender-Role Beliefs and Dating Violence" (*Psychology of Women Quarterly*, December 2004), adolescents who were exposed to domestic violence during their childhoods were in fact more likely to justify being violent in dating relationships. However, Lichte and McCloskey find that even more important in predicting dating violence was an adolescent's belief in traditional models of male-female relationships and the belief that violence was sometimes justified.

Along this line, Straus cautions against jumping to the conclusion that once violence occurs in a family it will inevitably or automatically be transmitted to the next generation. Not all men who grow up in violent families end up abusing their spouses, and not all abused children or abused wives will abuse others. Conversely, some violent individuals grow up in nonviolent families.

Dating Violence in Adolescence

Dating violence encompasses physical, sexual, or psychological violence in a dating relationship. Experiencing dating violence puts victims at a greater risk for engaging in risky sexual behavior, anorexia or bulimia, substance abuse, and suicide. It can also be an indicator that a person is at risk for victimization in intimate relationships in adulthood. The CDC's Youth Risk Behavior Surveillance system surveyed students in grades nine to twelve on their experience of dating violence. Students were asked: "During the past twelve months, did your boyfriend or girlfriend ever hit, slap, or physically hurt you on purpose?" Almost one out of ten students answered yes. Experience of dating violence was similar for male teens (8.9%) and female teens (8.8%). It was higher for African-Americans (13.9%) than for whites (7%) or Hispanics (9.3%). (See Table 7.4.)

AGE AND DOMESTIC VIOLENCE

Intimate Partner Violence Declines with Increasing Age

Jill Suitor, Karl Pillemer, and Murray A. Straus, in "Marital Violence in a Life Course Perspective" (Murray A. Straus and Richard J. Gelles, eds., *Physical Violence in American Families: Risk Factors and Adaptations to Violence in 8,145 Families*, 1990), find that both marital conflict and verbal aggression consistently decline with age over every ten-year period. Analysis of the 1975 National Family Violence Survey and 1985 National Family Violence Resurvey data reveals that the rate of violence in the age eighteen- to twenty-nine-year-old group dropped when its members entered the age thirty- to thirty-nine-year-old group. The rate dropped even further when the older group became the age forty- to forty-nine-year-old group. The consistent decline applied to both men and women in all age groups between ages eighteen and sixty-five.

Suitor, Pillemer, and Straus conclude that marital conflict and verbal aggression decrease with age. They considered several different possible explanations for this observation, including greater pressure to conform (perhaps because of a greater stake in society), the greater cost of deviating from accepted patterns—having "more to lose"—and greater expectations.

TABLE 7.4

Prevalence of physical dating violence among high school students by sex and by selected characteristics, 2003

Characteristic	Total %	Male %	Female %
Overall	8.9	8.9	8.8
Grade level			
9	8.1	7.8	8.6
10	8.8	9.3	8.2
11	8.1	7.9	8.2
12	10.1	10.1	10.2
Race/ethnicity			
White, non-Hispanic	7.0	6.6	7.5
Black, non-Hispanic	13.9	13.7	14.0
Hispanic	9.3	9.2	9.2
Geographic region*			
Northeast	10.6	10.8	10.4
Midwest	7.5	8.3	6.5
South	9.6	9.3	9.9
West	6.9	6.1	7.8
Self-reported grades			
Mostly A's	6.1	6.6	5.7
Mostly B's	7.7	7.4	8.0
Mostly C's	11.2	10.4	12.3
Mostly D's or F's	13.7	13.0	14.9

Note: Victimization is defined as a response of "yes" to a single question: "During the past 12 months, did your boyfriend or girlfriend ever hit, slap, or physically hurt you on purpose?"

* Northeast: Connecticut, Maine, Massachusetts, New Hampshire, New Jersey, New York, Pennsylvania, Rhode Island, and Vermont. *Midwest:* Illinois, Indiana, Iowa, Kansas, Michigan, Minnesota, Missouri, Nebraska, North Dakota, Ohio, South Dakota, and Wisconsin. *South:* Alabama, Arkansas, Delaware, District of Columbia, Florida, Georgia, Kentucky, Louisiana, Maryland, Mississippi, North Carolina, Oklahoma, South Carolina, Tennessee, Texas, Virginia, and West Virginia. *West:* Alaska, Arizona, California, Colorado, Hawaii, Idaho, Montana, Nevada, New Mexico, Oregon, Utah, Washington, and Wyoming.

SOURCE: "Table 1. Prevalence of Physical Dating Violence Victimization among High School Students, by Sex and Selected Characteristics—United States, 2003," in "Physical Dating Violence among High School Students—United States, 2003," *MMWR Weekly,* vol. 55, no. 19, May 19, 2006, http://www.cdc.gov/mmwr/preview/mmwrhtml/mm5519a3.htm (accessed August 4, 2006)

Subsequent studies confirm that intimate partner violence declines with advancing age. Analyzing National Crime Victimization Survey data, Callie Marie Rennison, in *Intimate Partner Violence and Age of Victim, 1993–99* (October 2001, http://www.ojp.usdoj.gov/bjs/pub/pdf/ipva99.pdf), finds married women ages twenty to twenty-four had eight victimizations per one thousand women, compared with just one per one thousand among married women age fifty or older. In "Nonlethal Intimate Partner Violence against Women: A Comparison of Three Age Cohorts" (*Violence against Women*, December 2003), Callie Marie Rennison and Michael Rand also find lower rates of intimate partner violence in women over age fifty-four in their study. They believe lower rates might be because of several factors, such as homicides of younger women, earlier divorces from abusive partners, or the turning of older perpetrators to other forms of victimization, such as psychological abuse or economic domination.

Effects of Abuse among Older Adults

In "The Nature and Impact of Domestic Violence across Age Cohorts" (*Affilia*, Fall 2005), a study of the nature and extent of domestic violence among women of different age groups, Dina J. Wilke and Linda Vinton find that there were no differences among abused women of different ages in the severity of the abuse, the kind of injuries received, substance abuse at the time of the incidents, the likelihood that women would report the violence, or the rates of childhood abuse or depression. However, older women, on average, had endured abuse for a longer time. They were also more likely to currently be in violent relationships and to have health and mental health problems than were younger women.

SIGNS OF POTENTIAL VIOLENCE

Can a woman expect to see certain signs of potential violence in a man she is dating or living with before she becomes a victim of abuse? Some researchers focus on risk markers, which may indicate an increased propensity for violence. These include:

- An unemployed male
- A male who uses illegal drugs
- Males and females with different religious backgrounds
- A male who saw his father hit his mother
- Male and female unmarried cohabitants
- Males with blue-collar occupations
- Males who did not graduate from high school
- Males between eighteen and thirty years of age
- Males or females who use severe violence toward children in the home
- Total family income below the poverty level

In "Men Who Batter: The Risk-Markers" (*Violence Update*, 1994), Richard Gelles, Regina Lackner, and Glen Wolfner find that in families where two risk markers are present, there is twice as much violence as those with none. In homes with seven or more of those factors, the violence rate is a staggering forty times higher.

A separate analysis by Gerald T. Hotaling and David B. Sugarman surveys risk markers present in more than four hundred studies. In "A Risk Marker Analysis of Assaulted Wives" (*Journal of Family Violence*, March 1990) and in "Prevention of Wife Assault" (Robert T. Ammerman and Michel Hersen, eds., *Treatment of Family Violence*, 1990), Hotaling and Sugarman use the analysis of risk markers to test the theory that there is a continuum (progression) of aggression in husband-to-wife violence that is linked to some of the risk markers. The risk markers considered were marital conflict, depressive symptoms, alcohol use, attitude toward interpersonal violence, violence in the family in which the individuals grew up, nonfamily violence level, and socioeconomic status. Hotaling and Sugarman find that an increase in the severity of husband-to-wife violence is associated with an increase in depressive symptoms in the husband, along with his greater acceptance of marital violence and a higher likelihood that he experienced and witnessed violence in his family as a child. In addition, greater alcohol use and higher levels of nonfamily violence by the couple are linked to more severe violence.

Hotaling and Sugarman's conclusions are consistent with other research: people who engage in minor violence do not necessarily progress to severe violence, but those who use severe violence almost always began with minor violence. The most important implication of this finding is that early intervention (at the stage of minor abuse) may prevent more severe abuse. Most treatment programs are only initiated after a woman has suffered severe battering. Prevention programs that emphasize the importance of seeking treatment for low-level abuse before it escalates to serious violence might encourage women to escape abuse before it claims their health or their lives.

In "The Utility of Male Domestic Violence Offender Typologies: New Directions for Research, Policy, and Practice" (*Journal of Interpersonal Violence*, February 2005), Mary M. Cavanaugh and Richard J. Gelles review the literature on battering and identify three types of batterers: a low, moderate, and high-risk offender. Cavanaugh and Gelles find that most male batterers do not escalate over time from low to high levels of risk.

Jacquelyn C. Campbell et al., in "Assessing Risk Factors for Intimate Partner Homicide" (*National Institute of Justice Journal*, November 2003), evaluate the risk factors among abused women for being killed by their intimate partners. Campbell et al. find that abused women whose abusers owned guns and who had threatened to kill them were at a high risk of being killed by their intimate partners. (See Figure 7.1.) Other high-risk factors for homicide include extreme jealousy, attempts to choke, and marital rape. Campbell et al. hope that the "danger assessment" tool they use may assist women and advocates for battered women to better assess the level of risk in abusive relationships.

WHY DOES SHE STAY?

Why don't battered women leave? This question does not have a single answer but, rather, many answers. Even the question has many connotations. For battered women, the question is not uniformly "How can I leave him?" but "How can I get the violence to stop?" or "How can I get my relationship to be happy and fulfilling?" For women who want to leave, the question may become "Can I support myself and the children by

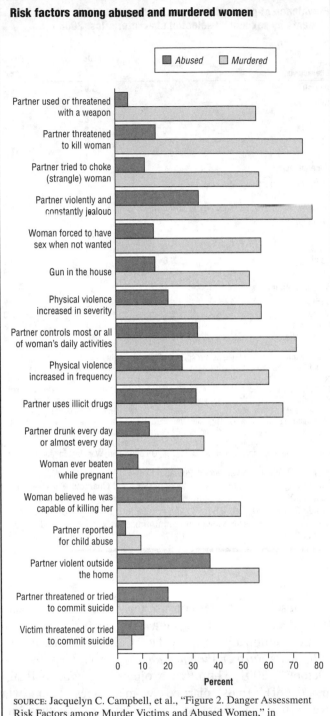

FIGURE 7.1

Risk factors among abused and murdered women

SOURCE: Jacquelyn C. Campbell, et al., "Figure 2. Danger Assessment Risk Factors among Murder Victims and Abused Women," in "Assessing Risk Factors for Intimate Partner Homicide," *National Institute of Justice Journal*, no. 250, November 2003, http://www.ncjrs .gov/pdffiles1/jr000250e.pdf (accessed July 17, 2006)

myself?" "How can I escape?" "Will he kill me if I try?" or "How will my children fare without a father?" For clinicians working with battered women, the question might be "How can she make any decisions when she is so emotionally traumatized?"

—Ola W. Barnett, "Why Battered Women Do Not Leave, Part 1" (*Trauma, Violence, and Abuse*, October 2000)

One of the most frequently asked questions about abused women is: Why do they stay? Some authors and advocates argue that the relevant questions for battered women themselves are different. They believe that the very question implies there is something wrong with the woman for staying, rather than placing the blame where it belongs: on the batterer. Better questions, Ola W. Barnett argues, might be: "Why does he beat her?" or "Why does society let him get away with it?" or "What can be done to stop him?"

However, not all women stay in abusive relationships. Many leave abusive relationships and situations without turning to the police or support organizations. While their number is unknown, most women who leave without asking for help usually have strong personal support systems of friends and family or employment and earnings that enable them to live economically independent of their abusive partners. Yet, there can be little question that a large percentage of women remain with their abusers. There are as many reasons women stay as there are consequences and outcomes of abusive relationships.

Women's Reasons to Stay

Women stay in abusive relationships for a variety of reasons. A major reason women stay is their economic dependency on their batterers. Many women feel they are better off with a violent husband than facing the challenge of raising children on their own. Some harbor deep feelings for their abusive partners and believe that over time they can change their partner's behavior. Others mistakenly interpret their abuser's efforts to control their life as expressions of love. Some frequently reported practical considerations include:

- Most women have at least one dependent child who must be cared for.

- Many are unemployed.

- Their parents are either distant, unable, or unwilling to help.

- The women may fear losing mutual friends and the support of family, especially in-laws.

- Many have no property that is solely their own.

- Some lack access to cash, credit, or any financial resources.

- If the woman leaves, then she risks being charged with desertion and losing her children and joint assets.

- She may face a decline in living standards for herself and her children, and the children, especially older ones, may resent this reduced living standard.

- The woman and/or children may be in poor health.

- The abuser may have threatened or harmed her pets, as noted by Catherine A. Faver and Elizabeth B. Strand in

"To Leave or to Stay? Battered Women's Concern for Vulnerable Pets" (*Journal of Interpersonal Violence*, December 2003).

Some battered women hold values and beliefs that experts term *traditional ideology*. These patriarchal beliefs, often reinforced by clergy, mental health professionals, and physicians, tend to normalize violence against women. This ideology may include:

- A belief that divorce is not a viable alternative and that marriage is a permanent commitment

- A belief that having both a mother and father is crucial for children

- An emotional dependence on her husband, and a feeling she needs someone to take care of her

- Feelings of helplessness and a belief that she is dependent on a man and unable to take the initiative to escape her situation

- A belief that a "successful marriage" depends on her, leading her to assume responsibility or to blame herself for the abuse

- Feelings of low self-esteem and self-worth

- The rationalization that her situation is caused by heavy stress, alcohol, problems at work, or unemployment

- A cycle of abuse that includes periods when her husband is exceedingly romantic, leading her to believe that she still loves him or that he is basically good

- A feeling of isolation from friends and family that may have been forced on her by a jealous and possessive husband who does not allow her any freedom

Some social isolation may be self-imposed by a woman who is ashamed and neither wishes to admit that the person she loves is an abuser, nor wants visible signs of beating to be seen by friends or family.

In her article "'We Don't Have Time for Social Change': Cultural Compromise and the Battered Woman Syndrome" (*Gender and Society*, October 2003), Bess Rothenberg argues that women are victimized and coerced into staying in violent relationships by a combination of different forces. According to Rothenberg, women are victimized first and foremost by violent abusers; second, by a society that sanctions the right of men to hit women and socializes women into staying in abusive relationships; third, by representatives of institutions who are in a position to help but who instead ignore the plight of battered women (for example, doctors, police, the criminal justice system, clergy, and therapists); and fourth, by the everyday realities of being a woman in a patriarchal system that expects women to raise children and denies them access to education, job skills, and good employment.

Similarly, April L. Few and Karen H. Rosen, in "Victims of Chronic Dating Violence: How Women's Vulnerabilities Link to Their Decisions to Stay" (*Family Relations*, April 2005), examine why women stay in abusive dating relationships and describe a combination of "relational" and "situational" vulnerabilities that work together to influence a woman's decision to stay. They define relational vulnerabilities as one's beliefs about what behaviors and interactions are normal in an intimate relationship. Situational vulnerabilities refer to the degree to which a woman was experiencing stress at the beginning of the abusive relationship (either as a consequence of life changes or as a consequence of feeling like one is getting too old for marriage or parenthood). Few and Rosen find that an accumulation of vulnerabilities, combined with lacking protective factors such as high self-esteem, a social support system, and healthy coping skills, made it more likely a woman would stay in a chronically abusive dating relationship.

The Role of Self-Blame

Some researchers find that battered women often hold distorted beliefs and perceptions that tend to keep them in abusive relationships. Some women blame themselves for the violence; they believe that they cause the abuse and that they should be able to prevent it by changing their behavior. Others see the abuse as normal and rationalize the violence as "not that bad."

Ola W. Barnett, Tomas E. Martinez, and Mae Keyson, in "The Relationship between Violence, Social Support, and Self-Blame in Battered Women" (*Journal of Interpersonal Violence*, June 1996), find that battered women have higher levels of self-blame and perceive less availability of social support than women who are not battered. They also found that women who return to abusive relationships have higher levels of self-blame than women who permanently leave their abusers.

Escalating levels of violence in a relationship often lead to greater use of violence by the woman as a means of self-defense or retaliation. This can result in still more self-blame, because the woman feels she is at fault for the violence. It also may deter her from seeking help and prompt her to believe no help is available. External sources of support may be less inclined to help a woman who presents the problem as her fault; as a result, the self-blaming woman may receive less assistance from health and social service agencies and organizations. To break this vicious cycle requires counselors or advisers who can help the woman shift the blame to her abusive mate. In fact, some researchers, such as Kate Cavanagh in "Understanding Women's Responses to Domestic Violence" (*Qualitative Social Work*, September 2003), suggest that while women may blame themselves when the abuse begins, as the frequency and severity of violence increases, they do eventually begin to assign the blame to the perpetrators.

The Role of Fear

Many women fear that attempting to end an abusive relationship will lead to even worse violence. Research has shown that this fear of reprisal is well founded. As Lenore E. Walker explains in *Terrifying Love: Why Battered Women Kill and How Society Responds* (1989), batterers often panic when they think women are going to end the relationship. In the personal stories women told Walker, they repeatedly related that after calling the police or asking for a divorce, their partners' violence escalated.

Walker observes that in an abusive relationship it is often the man who is desperately dependent on the relationship. Battered women are likely to feel that the batterers' sanity and emotional stability is their responsibility—that they are their men's only link to the normal world. Walker alleges that almost 10% of abandoned batterers committed suicide when their women left them.

It appears, however, that more batterers become homicidal than suicidal. Angela Browne, in "When Battered Women Kill," and Kirk Williams, in "Resource Availability for Women at Risk and Partner Homicide" (both published in *Law and Society Review*, 1989), find that more than 50% of all female homicide victims were murdered by former abusive male partners. Barnett emphasizes that evidence consistently demonstrates that after women leave abusive partners they often continue to be assaulted, stalked, and threatened and that leaving provokes some batterers to kill their partners. In "How Can Practitioners Help an Abused Woman Lower Her Risk of Death?" (*National Institute of Justice Journal*, November 2003), Carolyn Rebecca Block concurs that an attempt to leave can escalate domestic violence. She finds that 45% of homicides of a woman by a man were in response to women trying to leave abusive partners.

The Battered Woman Syndrome

In *The Battered Woman* (New York; Harper & Row, 1979), Lenore E. Walker claims that abused women suffer from a constellation of symptoms—"the battered woman syndrome"—that keeps them from leaving abusive partners. As part of her book, Walker argues that a psychological condition known as learned helplessness plays a significant role in keeping women in abusive relationships. While Walker recognizes, as do other multiple-victimization theorists, that women are victims of a patriarchal society and institutions that fail to advocate for abused women, she emphasizes the psychological problems women develop in response to abuse.

The concept of learned helplessness was discovered by researcher Martin E. P. Seligman. In *Helplessness: On*

Depression, Development and Death (1975), Seligman describes how he conducted an experiment in which he taught dogs to fear the sound of a bell. He did so by restraining a dog, ringing the bell, and then subjecting the dog to a painful (but not dangerous) shock. This process was repeated many times.

Next, to test the effectiveness of the training, Seligman placed the dog in a cage with a floor that could be electrified. One wall of the cage was low enough that the dog could jump over it if it wished. Seligman then rang the bell and administered shocks through the floor. He expected that the dog would jump out of the cage. However, most of the dogs did not. Seligman theorized this was because their earlier experience, where they had been shocked with no possibility of escape, had taught them that they were helpless.

Seligman called this learned helplessness. He and other psychologists theorize that it also occurs in humans, with similar effects. In *The Battered Woman* Walker contends that battered women have learned through their life experiences that they are helpless to escape or avoid violence. These battered women are conditioned to believe that they cannot predict their safety and that nothing can be done to fundamentally change their situations. They become passive, submissive, depressed, overwhelmingly fearful, and psychologically paralyzed. Walker emphasizes that although they do not respond with total helplessness, they narrow their choices, choosing the ones that seem to have the greatest likelihood of success.

Based on her research, much of which focused on severely abused women who killed their husbands, Walker identifies five factors in childhood and seven factors in adulthood that contribute to learned helplessness. The childhood factors include physical or sexual abuse, the learning of traditional sex roles, health problems, and episodes during childhood when a child loses control of events, such as in frequent moves or the death of a family member. Adult factors include patterns of physical and sexual abuse, jealousy and threats of death from a batterer, psychological torture, seeing other abuse committed by the batterer, and drug or alcohol abuse by either partner.

In "The Battered Woman Syndrome Is a Psychological Consequence of Abuse" in *Current Controversies on Family Violence*, Walker claims that battered woman syndrome is common among severely abused women and that it is part of the recognized pattern of psychological symptoms called posttraumatic stress disorder (PTSD). Normally, fear and the responses to fear abate once the feared object or circumstance is removed. People who have suffered a traumatic event, however, often continue to respond to the fear with flashbacks and violent thoughts long after the event has passed. Symptoms

of PTSD may include difficulty in thinking clearly and a pessimistic outlook, memory distortions, intrusive memories, sleep and eating disorders, and medical problems associated with persistent high levels of stress. Over time, the more aggressive symptoms diminish and are replaced by more passive, constrictive symptoms, making the affected women appear helpless. The abused woman's outlook often improves, however, when she regains some degree of power and control in her life.

Women Are Not Helpless

Beginning in the 1980s a number of critics emerged who argued that the emphasis on psychological problems of abuse victims was an inadequate explanation of domestic violence. Lee H. Bowker argues in "A Battered Woman's Problems Are Social, Not Psychological" in *Current Controversies on Family Violence* that women remain trapped in violent marriages because of conditions in the social system rather than because they suffer from psychological problems. According to Bowker, battered women are not as passive as they are portrayed in abuse literature and routinely take steps to make their lives safer or to escape abuse. Bowker views husbands' unwillingness to stop being dominant and a lack of support from traditional social institutions as the factors that delay battered women in escaping from abuse.

To support these findings, Bowker analyzes survey questionnaires completed by one thousand women and finds that women used several major strategies to end abuse. They tried to extract promises from their partners that the battering would stop, threatened to call police or file for divorce, avoided their partners or certain topics of conversation, hid or ran away, tried to talk the men out of violent behavior, covered their bodies to deflect the blows, and, in some cases, tried to hit back. Of these strategies, extracting a promise to change helped most often (54% of the time), whereas self-defense proved the least effective strategy.

Because the effectiveness of these strategies was limited, most women turned to outside sources for help. First, they contacted family or friends. However, for most women, family and friends did not help stop the violence. Generally, these women then turned to organized or institutional sources of aid, such as police, physicians, clergy, lawyers, counselors, women's groups, and shelters. Calling a lawyer or prosecutor proved the most effective way to end the battering, followed by seeking assistance from women's groups and social service agencies offering referral to shelters or counselors.

Bowker does not find that loss of self-esteem inevitably paralyzes women, leading them to remain in abusive relationships. While battered women do lose self-esteem for a time, many still escape from their abusers. This suggests that when all seems hopeless, an innate need to save themselves propels abused women to escape from their situations. Bowker theorizes that the reason women's groups and shelters are effective is that they counter the effects of abuse by supporting personal growth and nurturing the women's strength.

Bowker concludes that because women recover from their feelings of helplessness as they gain strength, battered woman syndrome symptoms are fundamentally different from the long-lasting symptoms that characterize most psychiatric disorders. In Bowker's interpretation, battered woman syndrome refers to the social, economic, psychological, and physical circumstances that keep women in abusive relationships for long periods. The abusive relationship engenders feelings of learned helplessness that are difficult to escape. Conditioned by their batterers to feel helpless, some women have not yet learned how to resist this type of brainwashing and how to compel their abusers to retreat without having to leave or kill the batterer.

External Barriers to Leaving

Barnett argues that battered women face many obstacles to leaving abusive relationships. She states that many of these barriers are external—in other words, not because of an individual or psychological problem with the abused woman. Barnett outlines many external obstacles to an abused woman's quest to leave her partner, including:

- The patriarchal structure of society—When men control all of a family's resources, women may be economically powerless.

- Problems with the criminal justice system—The U.S. criminal justice system is underfunded and tends not to enforce legislation prohibiting the abuse of women. The lack of adequate funding keeps battered women from getting legal assistance. Police decisions to arrest or not arrest batterers tend to be inconsistent; when police do not arrest, it impedes women's attempts to leave and leaves them vulnerable to further abuse. Barnett notes that only one-quarter of batterers are arrested, about one-third of those arrested are prosecuted, and only 1% of those prosecuted serve jail time beyond the time served at arrest. Orders of protection are ineffective because most judges will not enforce them.

- Child custody and visitation—Women fear losing their children if they report intimate partner violence. A report of domestic violence can trigger an investigation by child protective services. When women do retain custody of their children, judges usually do not take intimate partner violence into account when writing visitation orders. Court-ordered visitation is often used by abusers as an opportunity for further battering.

Internal and Psychological Barriers to Leaving

In "Why Battered Women Do Not Leave, Part 2" (*Trauma, Violence, and Abuse*, January 2001), Ola W. Barnett outlines several internalized socialization beliefs—normal, learned beliefs about how society and relationships work—as well as psychological factors induced by trauma that serve as obstacles to battered women leaving their abusers. Barnett emphasizes that many of these beliefs are detrimental to all women—but battered women are particularly vulnerable. Among them are:

- Gender-role socialization—Society values male traits more than female traits and often devalues female gender roles. As girls age into adolescents, they begin to lose self-confidence as they turn to romantic relationships for a sense of self-worth. When an adult woman values her ability to form a relationship with a male partner over other characteristics, losing the relationship may seem worse than staying and enduring the abuse.

- Distorted beliefs and perceptions—As previously mentioned, battered women tend to hold some distorted beliefs that keep them in abusive relationships. Common distorted thought patterns among battered women include a belief that violence is commonplace and not abusive, a belief that they caused the abuse, a lack of recognition that children are harmed more by witnessing intimate partner violence than by living with a single parent, and a belief that they can and should help the abuser to change.

- PTSD—This is a prolonged psychological reaction to a traumatic event. The level of psychological distress abused women experience can keep them from being able to escape the violence.

- Impaired problem-solving abilities—Many factors can impede the problem-solving abilities of battered women, including postconcussion syndrome resulting from head injuries and the cognitive distortions of PTSD.

- Prior victimization effects—Women who have been abused during their childhoods have an increased risk of becoming involved with an abusive intimate partner in adulthood. This may be because these women have difficulty judging how trustworthy people are, or they hold a distorted belief that they cannot escape violence.

WHAT CAN A WOMAN DO?

Cavanagh gathered qualitative data from interviews with the female partners of violent men to illustrate that battered women try to end the violence in their relationships in many ways, even if they stay—complicating the notion of the battered woman as passive and helpless. She finds that women worked to stop the violence by talking with their partners about the violence, developing strategies for avoiding the violence (for example, being affectionate or feigning agreement with the abuser), challenging the violence (for example, fighting back, verbally or physically), telling other people about the violence, and leaving (usually temporarily) the relationship. Cavanagh argues that abused women almost always actively fight the abuse: "At some points in time the struggle to change took second place to the struggle to survive but not even women subjected to the extremes of abuse totally 'gave up.'"

Avoidance

For their landmark book *Intimate Violence* (1988), Richard J. Gelles and Murray A. Straus interviewed 192 women who suffered minor violence and 140 who suffered severe violence, and asked which long-range strategies they used to avoid violence. Fifty-three percent of the minor-violence victims and 69% of the severe-violence victims learned to avoid issues they thought would anger their partners. Others learned to read a change in their partners' facial expressions as one of the first signs of impending abuse. "I have learned what gets him mad. I also know just by looking at him, when he gets that kind of weird, screwed-up expression on his face, that he is getting ready to be mad. Most of the time I figure I just have to walk on eggshells," one woman said. Avoidance worked for about 68% of those women who suffered minor abuse, but this tactic was successful for less than one-third of the more severely abused victims.

Leaving

Some battered women do leave their husbands. Straus and Gelles find that 70% had left their spouses in the year preceding the interview. Only about half of those who left, however, reported that this was a "very effective" method of ending the abuse. In fact, for one out of eight women it only made things worse. Batterers put incredible pressure on their partners to return. Often, when the women returned they were abused more severely than before—as revenge or because the men learned that, once again, they could get away with this behavior. Women who returned also risked losing the aid of personal and public support systems, because these people perceived that their help or advice was useless or ignored.

Just Say "No"

Many researchers believe that there is real truth to the statement that men abuse because they can. A wife who will not permit herself to be beaten from the first act of minor abuse, such as a slap or push, is the most successful in stopping it. Straus and Gelles find that simply eliciting a promise to stop was by far the most effective strategy women could undertake—especially in cases of minor violence. Threatening to divorce or leave the home worked in about 40% of the minor-abuse cases, but this strategy worked in less than 5% of the severe-abuse situations. Physically fighting back was the most unsuccessful method. It worked in fewer than 2% of the minor-abuse cases and in less than 1% of the severe-abuse cases.

HEALTH EFFECTS OF DOMESTIC VIOLENCE

There are often urgent and long-term physical and health consequences of domestic violence. Short-term physical consequences include mild to moderate injuries, such as broken bones, bruises, and cuts. More serious medical problems include sexually transmitted diseases, miscarriages, premature labor, and injury to unborn children, as well as damage to the central nervous system sustained as a result of blows to the head, including traumatic brain injuries, chronic headaches, and loss of vision and hearing. The medical consequences of abuse are often unreported or underreported because women are reluctant to disclose abuse as the cause of their injuries, and health professionals are uncomfortable inquiring about it. In fact, in "Violence against Women" (Dawn Misra, ed., *The Women's Health Data Book*, December 2001, http://www.kff.org/women shealth/6004-index.cfm), Nancy Berglas and Dawn Misra find that while more than half of abused women are physically injured by their abusers, only four out of ten seek professional medical care.

Abused women are also at risk for health problems not directly caused by the abuse. In "Intimate Partner Violence and Physical Health Consequences" (*Archives of Internal Medicine*, May 2002), Jacquelyn Campbell et al. compare the physical health problems of abused women to a control group of women who had never suffered abuse. Campbell et al. find that abused women suffered from 50% to 70% more gynecological, central nervous system, and stress-related problems. Examples of stress-related problems included chronic fear, headaches, back pain, gastrointestinal disorders, appetite loss, and increased incidence of such viral infections as colds. Although women who most recently suffered physical abuse reported the most health problems, Campbell et al. find evidence that abused women remain less healthy over time.

Hospitalization of Battered Women

The hospital emergency department is often the first contact the health care system has with battered women and offers the first opportunity to identify victims, refer them to support services and safe shelters, and otherwise intervene to improve their situations.

In "Rates and Relative Risk of Hospital Admission among Women in Violent Intimate Partner Relationships"

(*American Journal of Public Health*, September 2000), Mary A. Kernic, Marsha E. Wolf, and Victoria L. Holt report on hospitals and battered women. They find that women who had filed for protection orders against male intimate partners had an overall increased risk for earlier hospitalization than women who had not been abused. Abused women had a 50% increase in hospitalization rates for any diagnosis, compared with nonabused women, and the risk of hospitalization was highest in the younger age groups of abused women. Abused women were hospitalized much more frequently for injuries resulting from assaults, suicide attempts, poisonings, and digestive system disorders than the nonabused women and were almost four times as likely to be hospitalized with a psychiatric diagnosis. Kernic, Wolf, and Holt reaffirm the observation that intimate partner violence has a significant impact on women's health and their utilization of health care services.

WHEN WOMEN KILL THEIR PARTNERS

According to the Federal Bureau of Investigation's *Crime in the United States, 2004: Uniform Crime Reports* (2005, http://www.fbi.gov/ucr/cius_04/documents/CIUS 2004.pdf), in 2004, 7.1% of all known murder offenders were female. Their victims were often their spouses or intimate partners. A 1994 U.S. Department of Justice study on "murder in families" analyzed ten thousand cases and determined that women made up more than 41% of those charged in familial murders, but only 10.5% of those charged with murder overall. In 2004, 1,159 women and 385 men were killed by an intimate partner. (See Table 6.11 in Chapter 6.) CDC researchers also report in *Morbidity and Mortality Weekly Report Surveillance Summaries* (October 12, 2001, http://iier.isciii.es/mmwr/PDF/ss/ss5003.pdf) that the risk of intimate partner homicide increases with population size—rates in metropolitan areas with more than 250,000 people are two to three times higher than rates in cities with fewer than ten thousand residents.

Figure 6.3 in Chapter 6 shows that the number of males killed by intimate partners dropped substantially (by 71%) between 1976 and 2004. Researchers and advocates for battered women attribute this dramatic decline to the widespread availability of support services for women, including shelters, crisis counseling, hotlines, and legal measures such as protection and restraining orders. These services offer abused women options for escaping violence and abuse other than taking their partners' lives. Other factors that may have contributed to the decline are the increased ease of obtaining divorce and the generally improved economic conditions for women.

Spousal Murder Defendants

In the report *Spouse Murder Defendants in Large Urban Counties* (September 1995, http://www.ojp.usdoj.gov/bjs/pub/pdf/spousmur.pdf), Patrick A. Langan and John M. Dawson report on their examination and analysis of 540 spouse homicide cases in the nation's seventy-five largest counties—59% of the killers were husbands and 41% were wives. Even though Langan and Dawson analyzed data from crimes and court decisions that took place more than a decade ago, they explain that "the Bureau of Justice Statistics knows from long experience with surveying courts that changes in case processing are quite gradual. The report's results are therefore likely to be applicable today."

In 44% of wife defendant cases there was evidence that the wife had acted in response to a violent attack from her husband at the time of the killing. In contrast, just 10% of the husbands claimed that their victims had assaulted them at the time of the murder. Female spouses in this study were more likely to be acquitted than were male spouses (31% versus 6%). According to the Bureau of Justice Statistics (October 1995, http://www.ojp.usdoj.gov/bjs/pub/pdf/spousfac.pdf), Langan observes that "in many instances in which wives were charged with killing their husbands, the husbands had assaulted the wife, and the wife then killed in self-defense."

In fact, with strong legal defense and detailed documentation of abuse, many women are able to successfully argue that after suffering years of mental and/or physical abuse at the hands of their abusers, they suffer from battered woman syndrome and killed in self-defense. Battered woman syndrome has become a recognized defense in courtrooms throughout the country. At least some scholars, however, advocate relying on evidence of "battering and its effects" rather than on testimony of a "syndrome" that reduces the issues facing battered women to a psychological problem and does not fit every victim's circumstances. Kathleen J. Ferraro explores this issue in "The Words Change, but the Melody Lingers: The Persistence of the Battered Woman Syndrome in Criminal Cases Involving Battered Women" (*Violence against Women*, January 2003).

Factors That Influence the Murder of Husbands by Wives

In *When Battered Women Kill* (1987), one of the first studies of wives who murdered their abusive partners, Angela Browne compares forty-two women charged with murdering or seriously injuring their spouses with 205 abused women who had not killed their husbands. Wondering why some women were unable to see that their partners were dangerously violent, she finds that some of the personal characteristics of men inclined to violent, abusive behavior were the same qualities that initially attracted the women to them. For example, a woman might initially perceive a man who always wanted to know where she had been as intensely romantic. Only later, when she was unable to act or move without her partner's supervision, might she realize that she had become a virtual prisoner of her controlling mate.

Browne's findings suggest a link between homicide potential and three things: marital rape, murder and suicide threats, and drug use. In her study, more than 75% of women who had committed homicide claimed they were forced to have sexual intercourse with their husbands, compared with 59% in the group of women who had not killed their husbands. Some 39% of the former group had been raped more than twenty times, compared with 13% of the latter group. One woman Browne interviewed said, "It was as though he wanted to annihilate me . . . ; as though he wanted to tear me apart from the inside out and simply leave nothing there."

In addition, men murdered by their spouses had often threatened to kill their partners. In Browne's study 83% of the men killed by their wives had threatened to kill someone, compared with 59% of the men whose wives did not kill them. Men killed by their wives had used guns to frighten their spouses and were sometimes killed with their own weapons. Nearly two-thirds (61%) of this group also threatened to kill themselves. Many of the threats were made when women tried to leave the relationship or when the men were depressed. Browne questioned whether the suicide threats were genuine expressions of wishes to die or whether they were used to manipulate the women in efforts to make them feel guilty and prevent them from leaving.

When Browne compared abused women who had murdered their spouses and women who had not, she found that in the homicide group, 29% of the men had used drugs daily or almost daily versus only 7.5% of the men in the other group. There were even sharper differences in reported alcohol use. Twice as many (80%) of the men killed by their wives were reportedly drunk every day, compared with 40% of the abusive men not killed by their spouses.

Legal Defense

In legal cases involving battered women who kill their abusers, the defendants often admit to the murder and reveal a history of physical abuse. The charge is usually first- or second-degree murder, which is murder with malicious intent either with or without premeditation. The outcome of these trials depends on three main issues: self-defense, equal force, and imminent versus immediate danger (all three of which are explained in detail below). Expert witnesses are crucial in an abused woman's trial to explain how these issues are different for cases involving battered women than for other homicide cases.

SELF-DEFENSE. Women often plead that they killed in self-defense, a plea that requires proof that the woman used such force as was necessary to avoid imminent bodily harm. Self-defense was originally intended to cover unexpected attacks by strangers and did not take into account a past history of abuse or a woman's fear of renewed violence. Traditionally applied, a self-defense plea does not exonerate a woman who kills during a lull in the violence, for example, when the drunken abuser passes out.

Many observers feel that self-defense law is problematic, inadequate, and/or not appropriate for use in self-defense cases of battered women, according to Diane Follingstad et al. in "The Impact of Elements of Self-Defense and Objective versus Subjective Instructions on Jurors' Verdicts for Battered Women Defendants" (*Journal of Interpersonal Violence*, October 1997). Traditionally, self-defense permits an individual to use physical force when he or she reasonably believes it is necessary to counteract imminent or immediate danger of serious bodily harm. Furthermore, a person must use only a reasonable amount of force to stop the attack and cannot be the one who provoked the encounter or initiated the violence. To justify the use of reciprocal deadly force, most jurisdictions require that the defendant reasonably believes the attacker is using or is about to use deadly force. Some jurisdictions further require that before resorting to deadly force, the defendant must make an effort to retreat, although this is not required in most courts if the attack took place in the defendant's own home.

Advocates of battered women have succeeded in convincing many courts to accept a subjective standard of determining whether a battered woman who killed her husband was protecting her own life. This concession allows the court to judge the circumstances of the crime in relation to the special needs of battered women and not according to the strict definition of self-defense. This looser definition is especially important for women who killed during a lull in the violence, because a strict interpretation of imminent danger does not provide legal justification for their actions.

According to Gena Rachel Hatcher in "The Gendered Nature of Battered Woman Syndrome: Why Gender Neutrality Does Not Mean Equality" (*New York University Annual Survey of American Law*, March 2003), for this modified definition of self-defense to work, the court must first be subjective in understanding the woman's circumstances. Next, it must be objective in deciding that, given the situation, she truly did act in a reasonable manner. Courts have already accepted the notion that self-defense does not require perfect judgment in a violent situation, only reasonableness. In *Brown v. United States* (1921), Justice Oliver Wendell Holmes said: "Detached reflection cannot be demanded in the presence of an uplifted knife." Battered women and their advocates have asked the courts to revise their definitions of imminent danger and appropriate force in cases involving domestic violence.

EQUAL FORCE. Self-defense permits the use of equal force, which is defined as the least amount of force necessary to prevent imminent bodily harm or death. Women, however, who are generally physically weaker than men and who know the kind of physical damage their batterers can inflict, may justifiably feel that they are protecting their lives when shooting unarmed men. In *State v. Wanrow* (1977), the Washington Supreme Court ruled that it was permissible to instruct the jury that the objective standard of self-defense does not always apply.

Yvonne Wanrow was sitting up at night fearful that a male neighbor, who she thought had molested the child in her care, was going to make good on his threats to break into the house where she was staying. When the large, intoxicated man did enter, Wanrow, who was incapacitated with a broken leg, shot him. The court ruled, "The respondent was entitled to have the jury consider her actions in the light of her own perceptions of the situation, including those perceptions which were the product of our nation's 'long and unfortunate history of sex discrimination.' Until such time as the effects of that history are eradicated, care must be taken to assure that our self-defense instructions afford women the right to have their conduct judged in light of the individual physical handicaps which are the product of sex discrimination. To fail to do so is to deny the right of individual women involved to trial by the same rules which are applicable to male defendants."

IMMINENT VERSUS IMMEDIATE DANGER. Traditionally, self-defense required that the danger be immediate, meaning that the danger was present at the moment the decision to respond was made, to justify the use of force, as noted by Kimberly Kessler Ferzan in "Defending Imminence: From Battered Women to Iraq" (*Arizona Law Review*, Summer 2004). Accepting imminent danger, or danger that is about to occur, as justification for action permits the jury to understand the motivations and dynamics of a battered woman's behavior. A history of abuse may explain why a defendant might react to the threat of violence more quickly than a stranger would in the same circumstances. In *Wanrow*, the Washington Supreme Court found that "it is clear that the jury is entitled to consider all of the circumstances surrounding the incident in determining whether the defendant had reasonable grounds to believe grievous bodily harm was about to be inflicted."

LEGAL OUTCOMES. Whether a woman will be convicted depends largely on the jury's attitude, or the judge's disposition when it is not a jury trial, and the amount of background and personal history of abuse that the judge or jury is permitted to hear. Juries that have not heard expert witnesses present the battered woman defense are often unsympathetic to women who kill their abusive partners.

In "Jurors' Decisions in Trials of Battered Women Who Kill: The Role of Prior Beliefs and Expert Testimony" (*Journal of Applied Psychology*, February 1994), Regina Schuller, Vicki L. Smith, and James M. Olson find that jurors who learned about battered woman syndrome from expert testimony were more likely to believe the defendant feared for her life, that she was in danger, and that she was trapped in the abusive relationship. Equipped with knowledge and understanding of battering and its effects, jurors handed down fewer murder convictions than were issued by a control group of jurors who were not given this specialized information.

PREVENTION OF DOMESTIC VIOLENCE
Empowerment of Battered Women

Researchers and advocates find that one of the most effective ways to deal with partner violence is by giving the victim the power, encouragement, and support to stop it. In "Estrangement, Interventions, and Male Violence toward Female Partners" (*Violence and Victims*, Spring 1997), Desmond Ellis and Lori Wight assert that abused women want the violence to stop and most, if not all, attempt to do something to stop it. They find evidence showing that empowerment of abused women is related to a decrease in the likelihood of further violence. The interventions Ellis and Wight recommend to promote gender equality include:

- Social service agencies such as counselors or shelters to provide information and support

- Mediation to facilitate a woman's control over the process

- Prosecution with an option to drop the charges, which also facilitates control by female victims

- Separation, which indicates the woman's strength in decision making

Ellis and Wight find that separation or divorce is one of the most effective strategies for ending abuse. Levels of violence after separation, according to Ellis and Wight, vary with the type of legal separation or divorce proceedings. Women who participate in mediation before separation are less likely to be harmed, either physically or emotionally, than women whose separation is negotiated by lawyers. Ellis and Wight find that other legal proceedings, such as restraining orders and protection orders, were relatively ineffective in protecting female abuse victims.

Interventions to Help Battered Women

Throughout the United States, voluntary health and social service agencies and institutions, such as hospitals, mental health centers, clinics, and shelters, have developed programs that aim to help abused women break free physically, economically, and emotionally from their violent partners. Still, many abused women do not seek help from these specialized programs and services as a result of fear, shame, or lack of knowledge about how to gain access to available services. Instead, many injured women seek medical care from physicians, nurses, and other health professionals. For this reason, medical professional organizations, such as the American Medical Association and the American College of Obstetricians and Gynecologists, exhort physicians to advocate on behalf of abused women. They offer guidelines to help professionals detect and intervene in cases of domestic violence.

Despite the ambitious objectives of professional societies and the widespread distribution of guidelines, many health professionals most likely to encounter victims of abuse remain untrained, fearful, and unable even to question patients about domestic violence. Barbara Gerbert et al. interviewed physicians to determine how they have overcome these and other barriers to help patients who are victims of domestic violence. Their findings were published in "Interventions That Help Victims of Domestic Violence: A Quantitative Analysis of Physicians' Experiences" (*Journal of Family Practice*, October 2000).

Although physician respondents reported feeling overwhelmed, frustrated, and often inadequately prepared to tackle these problems, they nonetheless felt it was their responsibility to help battered women improve their situations. The technique they believed most effective was validation—expressing concern by compassionately communicating to the woman that the abuse was undeserved. Other strategies they considered effective were:

- Overcome denial and plant seeds of change—Physicians helped the women to appreciate the seriousness of their situations and to understand that the abusers' actions were wrong and criminal. Some physicians used photographs of injuries to remind patients who denied the extent of their abuse about the severity of the injuries they had sustained.

- Nonjudgmental listening—To build trust, physicians listened without rushing to judgment or criticizing women for not fleeing their abusers.

- Document, refer, and help prepare a plan—Physicians documented abuse with photographs and detailed descriptions in the patients' medical records for use in medical and mental health treatment as well as in court proceedings. They offered ongoing, confidential referrals to hotlines, shelters, and other community resources; advised patients about when to call police; and assisted them to develop escape plans.

- Use a team approach—Physicians felt it was valuable to be able to immediately refer abused women to on-site professionals, such as counselors, nurses, social workers, or psychologists, who were able to take advantage of the medical visit as a "window of opportunity," that is, an occasion to detect and intervene to stop abuse.

- Make domestic violence a priority—Given time constraints of busy medical practices, many physicians advocated forgoing all but the most urgent medical treatment and instead used the appointment time to address the issue of abuse. They also encouraged colleagues and personnel in their practices to obtain continuing education about domestic violence, child, and elder abuse.

The author of "How Can Practitioners Help an Abused Woman Lower Her Risk of Death?," mentioned previously, Carolyn Rebecca Block makes recommendations to nurses, doctors, and other service professionals likely to come in contact with battered women on what to look for as indications that the violence may soon escalate to deadly violence. She finds that practitioners should evaluate three aspects of the violence:

- The type of past violence—Women who had experienced at least one serious or life-threatening incident (for example, being choked, burned, or threatened with weapons) in the past year were at the greatest risk of being killed by their partners. Being choked, burned, or threatened with weapons also indicated a higher risk.

- The number of days since the last incident—No matter how severe the incident of past abuse, women who have been abused within the past thirty days are at greatest risk for being killed.

- The frequency, or increasing frequency, of violence—If violent episodes are increasing, women are at high risk of deadly violence.

AN INNOVATIVE PROGRAM TO HELP BATTERED WOMEN. Collaboration between law enforcement and hospital emergency department personnel produced a novel program to prevent and intervene in domestic violence. This program was developed in Richmond, Virginia, in response to a challenge issued by Mark Rosenberg, the director of the National Center for Injury Prevention and Control at the CDC. The program, called Cops and Docs, involves participation of law enforcement personnel working "handcuff in glove" with emergency and trauma nurses. The program is described by Colleen McCue in "Cops and Docs Program Brings Police and ED Staff Together to Address the Cycle of Violence" (*Journal of Emergency Nursing*, December 2001).

Program personnel are trained together in a variety of techniques, including interviewing victims, collecting and preserving forensic evidence, and gathering and documenting information. Besides helping to safeguard victims and apprehend and prosecute offenders, the program offers other health benefits to the community it serves. For example, shared emergency department data about substance abuse gives law enforcement personnel additional information to use in efforts to combat drug-related violence and crime.

CHAPTER 8

RAPE AND STALKING

Historically, because women have been viewed as the possessions of their fathers and husbands, sexual abuse of a woman has been considered a violation of a man's property rights rather than a violation of a woman's human rights. However, primarily through the efforts of women's advocacy groups worldwide, rape is no longer viewed as a violation of family honor but as an abuse and violation of women. In most countries rape is now considered a crime. The United Nations' Declaration on the Elimination of Violence against Women (December 1993, http://www.unhchr.ch/huridocda/huridoca.nsf/(Symbol)/A.RES.48.104.En?Opendocument) specifically names marital rape, sexual abuse of female children, selling women into slavery or prostitution, and other acts of sexual violence against women in its condemnation of "any act of gender-based violence that results in, or is likely to result in, physical, sexual or psychological harm or suffering to women, including threats of such acts, coercion or arbitrary deprivation of liberty, whether occurring in public or in private life."

RAPE IN THE UNITED STATES

In the report *Extent, Nature, and Consequences of Rape Victimization: Findings from the National Violence against Women Survey* (January 2006, http://www.ncjrs.gov/pdffiles1/nij/210346.pdf), an analysis of data from the National Violence against Women Survey (NVAWS), Patricia Tjaden and Nancy Thoennes estimate that more than 302,000 women are raped each year and that 17.7 million women have been raped in their lifetime, compared with almost 93,000 men who are raped each year and 2.8 million men who have been raped in their lifetime. (See Table 8.1.) Native American and Alaskan Native women have the highest rate of having been raped in their lifetime (34.1%), followed by African-American women (18.8%), non-Hispanic white women (17.9%), and Hispanic women (11.9%). (See Table 8.2.)

Tjaden and Thoennes find that most female victims of rape had been raped by a current or former intimate partner. One out of five (20.2%) had been raped by a spouse or ex-spouse, 4.3% by a cohabiting partner or ex-partner, and 21.5% by a date or former date. Male victims tended to be raped by acquaintances. Only 4.1% of males had been raped by a spouse or ex-spouse, 3.7% by a current or former cohabiting partner, and 2.7% by a date or former date. (See Figure 8.1.) In fact, 7.7% of all women, but only 0.4% of all men, had ever been raped by a current or former intimate partner. (See Table 8.3.)

Justice System Outcomes

Tjaden and Thoennes find that the overwhelming majority of rapes are unreported to police, and women raped by intimate partners are even less likely to report rapes to the police than were women raped by nonintimate partners. Only 18% of women raped by intimates reported the rape, compared with 20.9% of women raped by nonintimates. (See Table 8.4.) Of women who did not report to the police, 22.1% said they were too afraid of the rapist, 18.1% said they were too ashamed, 17.7% said it was a minor incident, 12.6% said the police could not do anything, and 11.9% said the police would not believe them. Almost one out of ten (8.6%) said it was because the perpetrator was a husband, family member, or friend. (See Table 8.5.)

When women did report to the police, police took a report only 79.8% of the time, and in 8.3% of the cases, the police did nothing. In 46.4% of the cases the perpetrator was arrested or detained. The perpetrator was prosecuted in only 32.1% of reported cases; only 36.4% of those prosecutions resulted in a conviction. Of those convicted rapists, 33.3% did not go to jail. (See Table 8.4.)

MARITAL RAPE

It was very clear to me. He raped me. He ripped off my pajamas, he beat me up. I mean, some scumbag

TABLE 8.1

Women and men raped during their lifetime and/or in a selected 12–month period in 1995–96

| | Percentage | | Number[a] | |
| | | | Women | Men |
Rape timeframe	Women[b]	Men[b]	(100,697,000)	(92,748,000)
Raped in lifetime[c]	17.6	3.0	17,722,672	2,782,440
Raped in previous 12 months	0.3	0.1	302,091	92,748

[a]Estimates are based on women and men age 18 and older.
[b]Sample size=8,000.
[c]Difference between women and men is statistically significant.
Notes: Lifetime prevalence rates for women in this exhibit are based on survey records of 6,999 women who were administered a version of the survey questionnaire that contains separate questions about attempted rape and completed rape. The remaining 1,001 women were administered versions of the questionnaire that combine questions about attempted rape and completed rape. Because it is impossible to distinguish attempted rape and completed rape from the combined questions, the corresponding 1,001 survey records were excluded when attempted rape and completed rape rates for women were calculated. The 1,001 survey records also were excluded when the total lifetime rape rate for women presented here was calculated.

SOURCE: Patricia Tjaden and Nancy Thoennes, "Exhibit 1. Percentage and Number of Women and Men Who Were Raped in Lifetime and Previous 12 Months," in *Extent, Nature, and Consequences of Rape Victimization: Findings from the National Violence against Women Survey*, NCJ 210346, U.S. Department of Justice, Office of Justice Programs, National Institute of Justice, January 2006, http://www.ncjrs.gov/pdffiles1/nij/210346.pdf (accessed August 4, 2006)

TABLE 8.2

Women and men who were raped in their lifetime, by race/ethnicity, 1995–96

Victims' gender	Non-Hispanic white (%)	Hispanic white (%)	African-American (%)	American Indian/Alaska Native (%)	Mixed race (%)	Asian/Pacific Islander (%)
Women[a]	17.9 (n=6,217)	11.9 (n=235)	18.8 (n=780)	34.1 (n=88)	24.4 (n=397)	6.8 (n=133)
Men	2.8 (n=6,250)	—[b] (n=174)	3.3 (n=659)	—[b] (n=105)	4.4 (n=406)	—[b] (n=165)

[a]Difference between Hispanic white and mixed-race women and between American Indian/Alaska Native and all other non-Asian/Pacific Islander women is statistically significant.
[b]Estimates were not calculated on five or fewer victims
Notes. Rates for women in this exhibit are based on 8,000 records of survey data. n=sample size.

SOURCE: Patricia Tjaden and Nancy Thoennes, "Exhibit 8. Percentage of Women and Men Who Were Raped in Lifetime by Race/Ethnicity," in *Extent, Nature, and Consequences of Rape Victimization: Findings from the National Violence against Women Survey*, NCJ 210346, U.S. Department of Justice, Office of Justice Programs, National Institute of Justice, January 2006, http://www.ncjrs.gov/pdffiles1/nij/210346.pdf (accessed August 4, 2006)

FIGURE 8.1

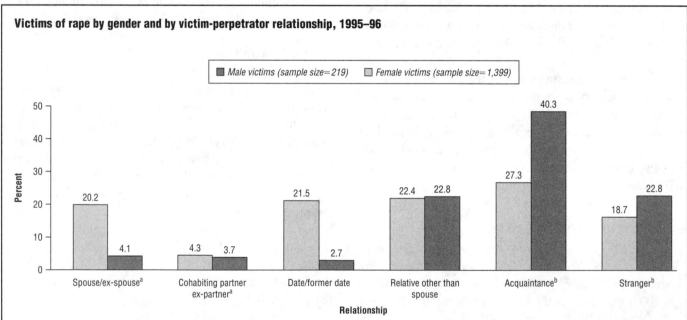

Victims of rape by gender and by victim-perpetrator relationship, 1995–96

Note: Percentages by victim gender exceed 100 because some victims were raped by more than one person.
[a]The number of male victims is too small to conduct statistical tests.
[b]Difference between male and female victims is statistically significant.

SOURCE: Patricia Tjaden and Nancy Thoennes, "Exhibit 13. Percentage Distribution of Female and Male Victims by Victim-Perpetrator Relationship," in *Extent, Nature, and Consequences of Rape Victimization: Findings from the National Violence against Women Survey*, NCJ 210346, U.S. Department of Justice, Office of Justice Programs, National Institute of Justice, January 2006, http://www.ncjrs.gov/pdffiles1/nij/210346.pdf (accessed August 4, 2006)

down the street would do that to me. So to me, it wasn't any different because I was married to him, it was rape—real clear what it was. It emotionally hurt worse. I mean you can compartmentalize it as stranger rape—you were at the wrong place at the wrong time. You can manage to get over it differently.

However, here, you're at home with your husband and you don't expect that. I was under constant terror [from then on] even if he didn't do it.

—A victim of marital rape (Raquel Kennedy Bergen, *Wife Rape: Understanding the Response of Survivors and Service Providers*, 1996)

TABLE 8.3

Women and men who were raped in their lifetime, by victim-perpetrator relationship, 1995–96

Victim-perpetrator relationship[a]	Raped in lifetime (%)	
	Women[b]	Men[b]
Intimate partner	7.7	0.4
Relative other than spouse	3.9	0.6
Acquaintance	4.8	1.4
Stranger	2.9	0.6

[a]Difference between women and men is statistically significant.
[b]Sample size=8,000.

SOURCE: Patricia Tjaden and Nancy Thoennes, "Exhibit 14. Percentage of Women and Men Who Were Raped in Lifetime by Victim-Perpetrator Relationship," in *Extent, Nature, and Consequences of Rape Victimization: Findings from the National Violence against Women Survey*, NCJ 210346, U.S. Department of Justice, Office of Justice Programs, National Institute of Justice, January 2006, http://www.ncjrs.gov/pdffiles1/nij/210346.pdf (accessed August 4, 2006)

TABLE 8.4

Female rape cases by justice system outcomes and by victims' level of intimacy with rapist, 1995–96

Outcome	Intimate (%)	Nonintimate (%)	Total
Rape was reported to police	(n=461)	(n=273)	(n=734)
Yes	18.0	20.9	19.1
No	82.0	79.1	80.9
Identity of reporter[a, b]	(n=84)	(n=57)	(n=141)
Victim	78.3	59.6	70.2
Other	21.7	40.4	29.8
Police response	(n=84)	(n=57)	(n=141)
Took report	79.8	73.7	75.9
Arrested/detained perpetrator	46.4	40.4	43.3
Referred case to prosecutor/court[b]	40.5	24.6	33.3
Referred victim to victim services[b]	39.3	29.8	34.8
Gave victim advice[b]	42.9	19.2	32.6
Did nothing	8.3	12.2	9.9
Perpetrator was prosecuted[a]	(n=81)	(n=54)	(n=135)
Yes	32.1	44.4	37.0
No	67.9	55.6	63.0
Perpetrator was convicted[b,c]	(n=33)	(n=21)	(n=54)
Yes	36.4	61.9	46.2
No	63.6	38.1	53.8
Perpetrator was sentenced to jail[d]	(n=12)	(n=13)	(n=25)
Yes	66.7	84.6	76.0
No	33.3	15.4	24.0
Victim obtained restraining order[b]	(n=452)	(n=257)	(n=709)
Yes	17.7	4.7	13.0
No	82.3	95.3	87.0
Perpetrator violated restraining order[e]	(n=80)	(n=11)	(n=91)
Yes	68.8	45.5	65.9
No	31.3	54.5	34.1

Note: Estimates are based on the most recent rape since age 18.
n=sample size.
[a]Estimates are based on responses from victims whose rape was reported to the police.
[b]Difference between intimates and nonintimates is statistically significant.
[c]Estimates are based on responses from victims whose rapist was prosecuted.
[d]Estimates are based on responses from victims whose rapist was convicted.
[e]Estimates are based on responses from victims who obtained a restraining order.

SOURCE: Patricia Tjaden and Nancy Thoennes, "Exhibit 21. Percentage Distribution of Female Rape Victims by Justice System Outcomes and Whether Rapist Was Intimate or Nonintimate," in *Extent, Nature, and Consequences of Rape Victimization: Findings from the National Violence against Women Survey*, NCJ 210346, U.S. Department of Justice, Office of Justice Programs, National Institute of Justice, January 2006, http://www.ncjrs.gov/pdffiles1/nij/210346.pdf (accessed August 4, 2006)

TABLE 8.5

Women's failure to report rape to the police by reason for not reporting, 1995–96

Reason	Percent
Reported to someone else	1.5
One-time incident, last incident	2.9
Did not want perpetrator arrested	2.9
Did not want police or court involved	3.5
Too young to understand	4.4
Handled it myself	7.7
Perpetrator was husband, family member, friend	8.6
Police would not believe me or would blame me	11.9
Police could not do anything	12.6
Minor incident; not a crime or police matter	17.7
Too ashamed or embarrassed	18.1
Fear of rapist	22.1

Notes: Estimates are based on the most recent rape since age 18. Total percentages exceed 100 because some victims had multiple responses.

SOURCE: Patricia Tjaden and Nancy Thoennes, "Exhibit 22. Percentage Distribution of Female Victims Who Did Not Report Rape to the Police by Reason for Not Reporting," in *Extent, Nature, and Consequences of Rape Victimization: Findings from the National Violence against Women Survey*, NCJ 210346, U.S. Department of Justice, Office of Justice Programs, National Institute of Justice, January 2006, http://www.ncjrs.gov/pdffiles1/nij/210346.pdf (accessed August 4, 2006)

Rape has little to do with the sexual relations associated with love and marriage. Rape is an act of violence by one person against another. It is an act of power that aims to hurt at the most intimate level. Rape is a violation, whether it occurs at the hands of a stranger or within the home at the hands of an abusive husband or partner.

State laws on marital rape vary in the United States. On July 5, 1993, marital rape became a crime in all fifty states. In thirty-three states, however, there are exemptions from prosecution if, for example, the husband did not use force or if the woman is legally unable to consent because of a severe disability. There is still a tendency in the legal system to consider marital rape far less serious than either stranger or acquaintance rape.

It is vitally important to recognize the limitations of available data about marital rape and intimate partner violence in general. In *Intimate Partner Violence and Age of Victim, 1993–99* (October 2001, http://www.ojp.usdoj.gov/bjs/pub/pdf/ipva99.pdf), Callie Marie Rennison cautions that marital status may relate directly to a survey respondent's willingness to reveal violence at the hands of an intimate partner or spouse. For example, a married woman may be afraid to report her husband as the offender or she may be in a state of denial—unable to admit to herself or others that her husband has victimized her.

In her landmark study *Rape in Marriage* (1990), Diana E. H. Russell reports on interviews with a random sample of 930 women in the San Francisco area. Of all the women who had been married, 14% had been raped by their spouses at least once. Of this number, one-third reported being raped once; one-third reported between

FIGURE 8.2

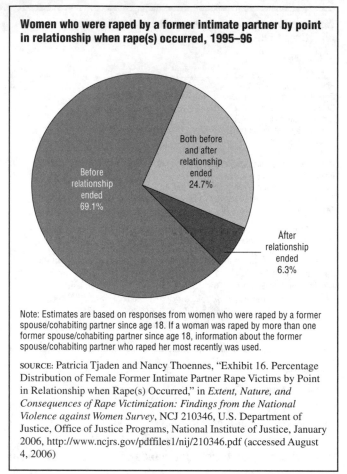

Women who were raped by a former intimate partner by point in relationship when rape(s) occurred, 1995–96

- Before relationship ended 69.1%
- Both before and after relationship ended 24.7%
- After relationship ended 6.3%

Note: Estimates are based on responses from women who were raped by a former spouse/cohabiting partner since age 18. If a woman was raped by more than one former spouse/cohabiting partner since age 18, information about the former spouse/cohabiting partner who raped her most recently was used.

SOURCE: Patricia Tjaden and Nancy Thoennes, "Exhibit 16. Percentage Distribution of Female Former Intimate Partner Rape Victims by Point in Relationship when Rape(s) Occurred," in *Extent, Nature, and Consequences of Rape Victimization: Findings from the National Violence against Women Survey*, NCJ 210346, U.S. Department of Justice, Office of Justice Programs, National Institute of Justice, January 2006, http://www.ncjrs.gov/pdffiles1/nij/210346.pdf (accessed August 4, 2006)

two and twenty incidents; and one-third said they had been raped by their spouses more than twenty times.

According to Russell, the first incident of rape usually occurred in the first year of marriage. Data from the NVAWS confirms that most rapes perpetrated against women by intimate partners occur in ongoing, not terminated, relationships. Only 6.3% of rapes by intimate partners occur exclusively after the end of the relationship; 69.1% occur before the relationship has ended; and 24.7% occur both before and after a relationship has ended. (See Figure 8.2.) Although marital rape occurred more frequently in spousal relationships where emotional and physical abuse were present, it could also happen in marriages where there was little other violence.

How Is Aggression Related to Marital Rape?

Because marital rape frequently occurs in relationships plagued by other types of abusive behavior, some researchers view it as just another expression of intimate partner violence. Support for this idea comes from research documenting high rates of forced sex, ranging from 34% to 57%, reported by married women in battered women's shelters. Still, research has not conclusively demonstrated whether husbands who engage in physical and psychological violence will be more likely to use threatened or forced sex.

Amy Marshall and Amy Holtzworth-Munroe investigated the relationship between two forms of sexual aggression—coerced sex (persuading or pressuring the victim into having sex) and threatened/forced sex—and husbands' physical and psychological aggressiveness. They report their findings in "Varying Forms of Husband Sexual Aggression: Predictors and Subgroup Differences" (*Journal of Family Psychology*, September 2002).

Marshall and Holtzworth-Munroe interviewed 164 couples and evaluated husbands using their own self-reports and their wives' reports on three measures: the revised Conflict Tactics Scale, a questionnaire called the Sexual Experiences Survey, and the Psychological Maltreatment of Women Inventory, a fifty-eight-item measure of psychological abuse. Marshall and Holtzworth-Munroe find that "husbands' physical and psychological aggression predicted husbands' sexual coercion, but only physical aggression predicted threatened/forced sex." Husbands who were rated as generally violent and antisocial engaged in the most threatened and forced sex. Interestingly, even the subtype of physically nonviolent men was found to have engaged in some sexual coercion in the year preceding the study.

Marshall and Holtzworth-Munroe conclude that their findings underscore the need to consider sexual aggression as a form of intimate partner abuse. They also call for research to determine the extent to which sexual coercion precedes and predicts threatened and forced sex and whether this association holds true for all relationships or only for those relationships in which there are other forms of marital violence.

Effects of Marital Rape

Contrary to the traditional belief that victims of marital rape suffer few or no consequences, research reveals that women may suffer serious long-term medical and psychological consequences from this form of abuse. In *Marital Rape* (March 1999, http://www.vawnet.org/DomesticViolence/Research/VAWnetDocs/AR_mrape.pdf), a review of the relevant research, Raquel Kennedy Bergen reports rape-related genital injuries, such as lacerations (tears), soreness, bruising, torn muscles, fatigue, vomiting, unintended pregnancy, and infection with sexually transmitted diseases. Victims who had been battered before, during, or after the rape suffered broken bones, black eyes, bloody noses, and knife wounds, as well as injuries sustained when they were kicked, punched, or burned.

The short-term psychological effects are similar to those experienced by other victims of sexual assault and include anxiety, shock, intense fear, suicidal thinking, depression, and posttraumatic stress disorder (PTSD). However, marital rape victims reportedly suffer higher rates of anger and depression than women raped by strangers, perhaps because the violence was perpetrated

TABLE 8.6

Change in marital status among married women who were violently victimized by an intimate, by six-month interval between interviews

Marital status over 6 months	Women married at the time of the earlier interview	
	Experienced intimate violence	Experienced non-intimate violence
Total	100%	100%
Still married	62	97
Divorced	8	1
Separated	30	1

Note: Percentages may not add to 100% due to rounding. Percentages exclude women who did not complete two consecutive interviews. Among married female respondents reporting having experienced a violent victimization, those who reported that an intimate had victimized them were substantially more likely to also report a change in their marital status.

SOURCE: Callie Marie Rennison, "Among Married Female Respondents Reporting Having Experienced a Violent Victimization, Those Who Reported That an Intimate Had Victimized Them Were Substantially More Likely to Also Report a Change in Their Marital Status," in *Intimate Partner Violence and Age of Victim, 1993–1999*, NCJ 187635, U.S. Department of Justice, Bureau of Justice Statistics, October 2001, http://www.ojp.usdoj.gov/bjs/pub/pdf/ipva99.pdf (accessed August 4, 2006)

by a person they had loved and trusted to not harm them. Long-term consequences include serious depression, sexual problems, and emotional pain that lasts years after the abuse. Jennifer A. Bennice et al. find in "The Relative Effects of Intimate Partner Physical and Sexual Violence on PTSD Symptomatology" (*Violence and Victims*, February 2003) that marital rape survivors were more likely than other battered women to suffer the debilitating effects of PTSD, even when controlling for the severity of the beatings.

As is true with other violent acts, marital rape prompts some women to leave their husbands. Bergen reports that women from selected ethnic groups, such as Hispanics, appeared less likely to characterize forced sex as rape and consequently were less likely to accuse or flee their spouses. The fact that married women do leave their abusers, however, was confirmed by an analysis of National Crime Victimization Surveys data that compared marital status of survey respondents from one survey with the next. Table 8.6 shows that 30% of the female victims of intimate partner violence who were married during the previous survey interview when they had reported being victimized had separated from their husbands, and an additional 8% had divorced their husbands.

Attitudes about Marital Rape

Historically, wives were considered the property of the husband, and therefore rape of a wife was viewed as impossible. No husband still living with his wife was prosecuted for marital rape in the United States until 1978—and at that time, marital rape was a crime in only five states, as reported by Jennifer A. Bennice and Patricia A. Resick in "Marital Rape: History, Research, and Practice" (*Trauma, Violence, and Abuse*, July 2003). By 1993 marital rape under some conditions was recognized in all fifty states.

However, public attitudes toward rape in marriage have been slow to change, with many people believing that marital rape is not "real rape." Kathleen C. Basile, in "Attitudes toward Wife Rape: Effects of Social Background and Victim Status" (*Violence and Victims*, June 2002), examines variables that might predict specific attitudes about wife rape: beliefs about the occurrence and frequency of forced sex by a husband on his wife and whether respondents would classify various scenarios as constituting rape. Basile chose to analyze data from a nationally representative telephone survey of 1,108 adults to produce more widely applicable findings.

Basile hypothesized that social background variables and victim status would predict how survey respondents felt about marital rape. Based on earlier research, she believed that males, African-Americans, and other racial minorities would express opinions more supportive of wife rape (and would be less likely to believe that wife rape occurs). Similarly, Basile expected that supportive attitudes would increase with age. She felt that victims and people with higher educational attainment would hold less supportive views of wife rape.

Survey respondents were asked whether they "think husbands ever use force, like hitting, holding down, or using a weapon, to make their wives have sex when the wife doesn't want to" to find out if they thought wife rape occurs. Respondents who answered "yes" to this question were asked how often they thought this occurs to gauge their perceptions of the frequency of wife rape. They also listened to descriptions of three scenarios of forced sex: two scenarios involved forced sex between husband and wife and the other was a woman forced to have sex with someone with whom she was previously intimate. The respondents were asked whether they considered each scenario to be an instance of rape.

Basile finds that 73% of respondents believed that wife rape occurs, 18% thought it does not occur, and 5% were unsure. Among those who thought wife rape occurs, 38% said it happens often, and an additional 40% felt it happens somewhat often. Fifteen percent felt wife rape is infrequent and 4% said it is a rare occurrence.

Basile finds support for nearly all her of hypotheses. The older the respondents, the less likely they were to believe that wife rape occurs, and white respondents were 2.5 times more likely to believe that wife rape occurs than African-Americans and other minorities. Women thought wife rape occurs more frequently than did men and, predictably, victims were more than twice as likely as nonvictims to feel that wife rape occurs.

Although Basile finds that, overall, Americans were more likely than not to recognize forced sex upon a wife by her husband as rape, the variations she discovered in attitudes toward the two marital rape scenarios prompted her to observe that many Americans still feel victims play some part in their own victimization.

Mark A. Whatley, in "The Effect of Participant Sex, Victim Dress, and Traditional Attitudes on Causal Judgments for Marital Rape Victims" (*Journal of Family Violence*, June 2005), also investigates attitudes toward whether marital rape victims "deserved" to be raped. Participants in the study read a fiction account of a marital rape in which the victim was dressed either somberly or seductively. Male participants in the study rated the victim more "deserving" of the attack than did female participants. The seductively dressed victim was rated more responsible for the attack by all participants. Participants who held more traditional attitudes toward marriage were more likely to hold the victim responsible than were participants with more egalitarian attitudes toward marriage.

ACQUAINTANCE RAPE

According to a number of widely publicized studies, young women are at high risk of sexual assault by acquaintances or boyfriends. Studies find rates ranging from a low of 15% for rape to a high of 78% for unwanted sexual aggression. For example, in "Rates and Risk Factors for Sexual Violence among an Ethically Diverse Sample of Adolescents" (*Archives of Pediatrics and Adolescent Medicine*, December 2004), Vaughn I. Rickert et al. find that of their sample of 689 adolescents and young adults, 30% reported having had an unwanted sexual experience in the past year, including verbal sexual coercion, rape, or attempted rape by a date or acquaintance. Other studies, such as Victoria L. Banyard et al. in "Revisiting Unwanted Sexual Experiences on Campus: A 12-Year Follow-Up" (*Violence against Women*, April 2005), find that the number of rapes on college campuses has remained fairly steady since the late 1980s. Researchers surmise that acquaintance rape is especially underreported because the victims believe that nothing can or will be done, feel unsure about how to define the occurrence, or are uncertain about whether the action qualified as abuse.

Date rape is considered a form of acquaintance rape (as opposed to intimate partner rape), especially if the perpetrator and victim have not known one another for long and the abuse begins early in the relationship. In "Adolescent Dating Violence and Date Rape" (*Current Opinion in Obstetrics and Gynecology*, October 2002), a review of the current research and literature about date rape, Vaughn I. Rickert, Roger D. Vaughan, and Constance

TABLE 8.7

Extent of rape among college women by number of victims, number of incidents, and type of victimization incident, August 1996–February 1997

Type of victimization	Victims			Incidents	
	Number of victims in sample	Percentage of sample	Rate per 1,000 female students	Number of incidents	Rate per 1,000 female students
Completed rape	74	1.7	16.6	86	19.3
Attempted rape	49	1.1	11.0	71	16.0
Total	**123**	**2.8**	**27.7***	**157**	**35.3**

*Total has been rounded (from 27.665 to 27.7).

SOURCE: Bonnie S. Fisher, Francis T. Cullen, and Michael G. Turner, "Exhibit 3. Extent of Rape, by Number of Victims, and Number of Incidents, by Type of Victimization Incident," in *The Sexual Victimization of College Women*, NCJ 182369, U.S. Department of Justice, Bureau of Justice Statistics, December 2000, http://www.ncjrs.org/pdffiles1/nij/182369.pdf (accessed August 4, 2006)

M. Wiemann observe that female teens ages sixteen to nineteen years old and young adult women ages twenty to twenty-four are not only four times as likely to be raped as women of other ages but also that teens who have experienced rape or attempted rape during adolescence are twice as likely to experience an additional assault when they are college age.

Rickert, Vaughan, and Wiemann also focus on high-risk subgroups of adolescents that, although less often studied, appear to experience high rates of date rape and other dating violence. They cite academically underperforming teens as at high risk, with 67% of female students and 33% of male students in a high school dropout prevention program admitting to having experienced or perpetrated dating violence, including sexual abuse and rape.

College Rape

In *Sexual Victimization of College Women* (December 2000, http://www.ncjrs.gov/pdffiles1/nij/182369.pdf), Bonnie S. Fisher, Francis T. Cullen, and Michael G. Turner find a disturbingly high rate of rapes among college women. Their study was based on a national telephone survey of 4,446 randomly selected women attending colleges and universities in the fall of 1996. Respondents were asked between late February and early May 1997 if they had experienced sexual victimization "since school began in fall 1996."

Fisher, Cullen, and Turner find that in that period of almost seven months, 2.8% of the women had experienced either an attempted or completed rape. (See Table 8.7.) They suggest that the data show that nearly 5% of women college students are victimized in a given calendar year and that the percentage of attempted or completed rape victimizations of college women during their college careers approaches one in four. Fisher, Cullen,

TABLE 8.8

Extent of sexual victimization among college women by number of victims, number of incidents, and type of victimization incident, August 1996–February 1997

	Victims			Incidents	
Type of victimization	Number of victims in sample	Percentage of sample	Rate per 1,000 female students	Number of incidents	Rate per 1,000 female students
Completed or attempted					
Completed sexual coercion	74	1.7	16.6	107	24.1
Attempted sexual coercion	60	1.3	13.5	114	25.6
Completed sexual contact with force or threat of force	85	1.9	19.1	130	29.2
Completed sexual contact without force	80	1.8	18.0	132	29.7
Attempted sexual contact with force or threat of force	89	2.0	20.0	166	37.6
Attempted sexual contact without force	133	3.0	29.9	295	66.4
Threats					
Threat of rape	14	0.31	3.2	42	9.5
Threat of contact with force or threat of force	8	0.18	1.8	50	11.3
Threat of penetration without force	10	0.22	2.3	50	11.3
Threat of contact without force	15	0.34	3.4	75	16.9
Total	**568**			**1,161**	

SOURCE: Bonnie S. Fisher, Francis T. Cullen, and Michael G. Turner, "Exhibit 5. Extent of Sexual Victimization," in *The Sexual Victimization of College Women*, NCJ 182369, U.S. Department of Justice, Bureau of Justice Statistics, December 2000, http://www.ncjrs.org/pdffiles1/nij/182369.pdf (accessed August 4, 2006)

FIGURE 8.3

Victimization of college women by type of incident, August 1996–February 1997

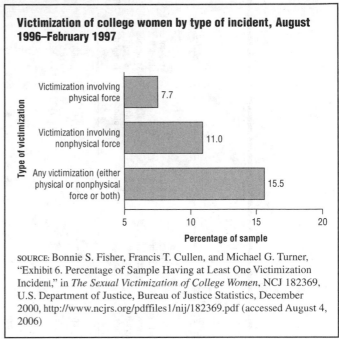

SOURCE: Bonnie S. Fisher, Francis T. Cullen, and Michael G. Turner, "Exhibit 6. Percentage of Sample Having at Least One Victimization Incident," in *The Sexual Victimization of College Women*, NCJ 182369, U.S. Department of Justice, Bureau of Justice Statistics, December 2000, http://www.ncjrs.org/pdffiles1/nij/182369.pdf (accessed August 4, 2006)

11% had experienced sexual victimization involving nonphysical force, and 15.5% had experienced any victimization since the start of the academic year.

Fisher, Cullen, and Turner also find that fewer than 5% of the rapes and attempted rapes had been reported to police, and even lower percentages of other types of sexual victimization were reported. (See Table 8.9.)

These numbers demonstrating that students overwhelmingly do not report acquaintance rapes or attempted rapes confirm other researchers' findings, including those of Bonnie S. Fisher et al. in "Reporting Sexual Victimization to the Police and Others: Results from a National-Level Study of College Women" (*Criminal Justice and Behavior*, February 2003). According to the Centers for Disease Control and Prevention, the term *hidden rape* has been used to describe this finding of widespread unreported and underreported sexual assault. Anecdotal reports from college and university administrators suggest that many female students who have been raped not only fail to report the offense but also drop out of school.

In "Acquaintance Rape and the College Social Scene" (*Family Relations*, January 1991), Sally K. Ward et al. examine men's and women's perceptions of what constitutes sexual assault. Ward et al. surveyed 518 women and 337 men at a large university. Thirty-four percent of the female respondents had experienced unwanted sexual contact, such as attempted or actual kissing, fondling, or touching; 20% had experienced unwanted attempted sexual intercourse; and 10% had unwanted intercourse, which was defined as any form of sexual penetration, including vaginal, anal, and oral. Most incidents were party related,

and Turner conclude that although the 2.8% figure might "seem" low, "from a policy perspective, college administrators might be disturbed to learn that for every 1,000 women attending their institutions, there may well be 35 incidents of rape in a given academic year. . . . For a campus with 10,000 women, this would mean the number of rapes would exceed 350."

Fisher, Cullen, and Turner also asked respondents about other types of sexual victimization. They find that 1.7% of their sample had been victims of completed sexual coercion (unwanted sexual penetration with the threat of punishment or promise of reward), 1.3% had been victims of attempted sexual coercion, 1.9% had been victims of unwanted completed sexual contact with force or the threat of force, and 1.8% had been victims of completed sexual contact without physical force. Smaller percentages of women had been sexually threatened. Table 8.8 shows these additional types of sexual victimization. Figure 8.3 displays the data slightly differently, showing that 7.7% of college women surveyed had experienced sexual victimization involving physical force,

TABLE 8.9

College women's reasons for not reporting sexual victimization to police, by type of incident, 1996

Type of incident	Incident was not reported %	Reason for not reporting incident*											
		Did not want family to know %	Did not want other people to know %	Lack of proof that incident happened %	Fear of being treated hostilely by police %	Fear of being treated hostilely by other parts of justice system %	Not clear it was a crime or that harm was intended %	Did not know how to report %	Police wouldn't think it was serious enough %	Police wouldn't want to be bothered %	Afraid of reprisal by assailant or other %	Did not think it was serious enough to report %	Other %
Completed or attempted													
Completed rape	95.2	44.4	46.9	42.0	24.7	6.2	44.4	13.6	27.2	25.9	39.5	65.4	7.4
Attempted rape	95.8	32.4	32.4	30.9	8.8	1.5	39.7	7.4	33.8	13.2	25.0	76.5	1.5
										(9)	(17)	(52)	(1)
Completed sexual coercion	100.0	41.9	43.8	33.3	8.6	1.9	58.1	14.3	24.8	21.9	31.4	71.4	1.9
Attempted sexual coercion	100.0	21.2	19.5	15.9	2.7	2.7	46.9	6.2	28.3	18.6	11.5	86.7	0
Completed sexual contact with force or threat of force	99.2	19.5	16.4	21.9	9.4	0	37.5	7.0	37.5	30.5	22.7	81.3	3.1
Completed sexual contact without force	98.5	4.7	11.7	18.0	4.7	1.6	43.0	5.5	29.7	18.8	12.5	91.4	0.8
Attempted sexual contact with force or threat of force	97.0	13.8	21.9	23.1	8.8	6.3	37.5	10.0	31.3	22.5	23.8	80.0	2.5
Attempted sexual contact without force	99.3	7.2	10.2	18.1	4.4	1.4	39.6	6.1	22.9	18.4	10.9	88.4	2.7
Threats													
Threat of rape	90.5	26.3	34.2	31.6	13.2	7.9	39.5	13.2	34.2	31.6	26.3	65.8	2.6
Threat of contact with force or threat of force	90.0	22.2	20.0	20.0	8.9	4.4	51.1	13.3	37.8	26.7	17.8	68.9	4.4
Threat of penetration without force	100.0	20.0	22.0	24.0	4.0	4.0	46.0	6.0	30.0	30.0	12.0	88.0	2.0
Threat of contact without force	98.7	6.8	8.1	21.6	8.1	6.8	31.1	2.7	21.6	9.5	13.5	83.8	0

*Percentages may be greater than 100 because a respondent could give more than one response.

SOURCE: Bonnie S. Fisher, Francis T. Cullen, and Michael G. Turner, "Exhibit 12. Reasons for Not Reporting Incident to the Police, by Type of Victimization," in *The Sexual Victimization of College Women*, NCJ 182369, U.S. Department of Justice, Bureau of Justice Statistics, December 2000, http://www.ncjrs.org/pdffiles1/nij/182369.pdf (accessed August 30, 2006)

Child Abuse and Domestic Violence

and most involved alcohol, with 75% of the males and over half the females reporting alcohol consumption at the time of the incident. Women reported that most of the perpetrators initiated the acts without warning. The percentage of cases involving force by men ranged from 8% for sexual contact to 21% for completed intercourse. Most of the women verbally protested, although 20% of victims said they were too frightened to protest. Victims most frequently chose to confide in a roommate or close friend, although 41% of the women told no one about the rape. Counselors were almost never told of the incidents.

The men reported a different picture of unwanted sexual behavior on campus. Only 9% reported committing either unwanted sexual contact or attempted intercourse, and 3% admitted to incidents of unwanted sexual intercourse. Ward et al. propose that the reason for the different results is that men and women read sexual cues and form sexual expectations differently. V. J. Willan and Paul Pollard, in "Likelihood of Acquaintance Rape as a Function of Males' Sexual Expectations, Disappointment, and Adherence to Rape-Conducive Attitudes" (*Journal of Social and Personal Relationships*, 2003), find that men are far more likely than women to interpret a woman's behavior as sexual and misconstrue it as an invitation to sexual intimacy. They write:

> In conjunction with the finding that males significantly misperceived the female's sexual intent to engage in sexual intercourse, following the initial contact, this suggests that males, in a bid to calculate the probability of obtaining sexual intercourse, overestimate the predictive value of the female's initial consent to "attend a party together." This consequently leads to greater goal expectation, which, combined with hostile beliefs about women, might result in a greater likelihood of nonconsensual sexual intercourse.

Influence of Alcohol on Sexual Assault

Alcohol reduces inhibitions and, in some cases, enhances aggression, so it is not surprising that researchers examine the link between alcohol and sexual assault. In "Alcohol and Sexual Assault in a National Sample of College Women" (*Journal of Interpersonal Violence*, June 1999), Sarah E. Ullman, George Karabatsos, and Mary P. Koss examine how drinking before an assault influenced the severity of the attack.

They administered a questionnaire to 3,187 college-age women, more than half of whom had been victims of rape, attempted rape, unwanted sexual contact, or sexual coercion. They measured the participants' alcohol use, the severity of the sexual attack, the social context in which the assault occurred, and the victims' familiarity with the offenders. As expected, victims who reported getting drunk more often also reported more severe assaults ("more severe" meaning, for example, the completion of the rape but not necessarily a more aggressive,

forceful, or violent attack) than those who were drunk less often. Neither the victim's family income nor how well the victim knew the offender was related to the severity of the attack, although older women experienced more severe victimization.

Ullman, Karabatsos, and Koss also find that alcohol's role in predicting the severity of an attack did not vary according to how well the victim knew her attacker or whether a social situation, such as a party, was the setting for the assault—with one exception. Unplanned social situations were associated with more severe assaults when offenders were not drinking before the assault than when they were drinking. The victim's use of alcohol was related to the severity of the attack in cases where the rapist was not drinking. According to Ullman, Karabatsos, and Koss, this finding suggests that intoxicated victims may be targeted by offenders, who perceive an opportunity to engage in sex without having to use coercive behaviors.

As anticipated, Ullman, Karabatsos, and Koss find that victims who abused alcohol or offenders and victims who used alcohol before the attack suffered higher rates of severe assaults (completion of the rape). They also find that offender drinking was related to more aggressive offender behavior and more severe victimization, suggesting that more violent assaults occurred when assailants had been drinking. Conversely, victim drinking was related to less offender aggression and violence, possibly because force was not needed to complete the rape of intoxicated victims.

Not all researchers find that the use of alcohol by offenders increases the severity of sexual assaults. Leanne R. Brecklin and Sarah E. Ullman find in "The Role of Offender Alcohol Use in Rape Attacks: An Analysis of National Crime Victimization Survey Data" (*Journal of Interpersonal Violence*, January 2001) that alcohol use of offenders did not affect victim physical injury or need for medical attention. They also find that alcohol use was related to less completed rape. They suggest, however, that alcohol use might be indirectly associated with injury outcomes, because offenders using alcohol were more likely to assault in more dangerous situations (assaulting at night and outdoors, and attacking strangers).

According to Ullman, Karabatsos, and Koss, of the 54.2% of women who had experienced some sexual victimization, 53.4% reported that their assailants were using alcohol at the time of the incident, and 42% reported that they themselves were using alcohol. Over a third of the assaults (39.7%) occurred during dates with men that the women knew well or moderately well. Most assaults were committed without weapons, although 40% of the men used physical force. More than 90% of the victims said they attempted to resist the assault.

Overall, Ullman, Karabatsos, and Koss's findings indicate that alcohol use by victims and offenders before an assault plays direct and indirect roles in the severity of assaults, but generally the woman's drinking behavior contributes less strongly to the outcome of the attack.

Sexual Coercion

Sexual coercion is generally considered any situation where one person uses verbal or physical methods to obtain sex or sexual activity without consent of the other. Lisa K. Waldner-Haugrud and Brian Magruder find in "Male and Female Sexual Victimization in Dating Relationships: Gender Differences in Coercion Techniques and Outcomes" (*Violence and Victims*, Fall 1995) that a "phenomenal" amount of sexual coercion was reported by 422 college students. Only 17% of the females and 27% of the males reported never experiencing any coercion. The most common coercion techniques experienced by both sexes were persistent touching and the use of alcohol and drugs. Together, these methods comprised more than half the reported incidents of coercion. Women were more likely to experience unwanted detainment, persistent touching, lies, and being held down.

In another study, Michele Poitras and Francine Lavoie questioned 644 adolescents between fifteen and nineteen years of age and published their results in "A Study of Prevalence of Sexual Coercion in Adolescent Heterosexual Dating Relationships in a Quebec Sample" (*Violence and Victims*, Winter 1995). The most frequently occurring unwanted sexual experiences reported by the adolescents were kissing, petting, and fondling. Verbal coercion was the most frequently used technique. Two out of five girls reported sexual contact resulting from verbal coercion, and one out of five reported intercourse resulting from verbal coercion. Approximately one out of ten females reported intercourse resulting from the use of force, alcohol, or drugs. Boys rarely reported the use of force, although 2.3% reported that they had had sex after giving their partners drugs or alcohol, and 2.9% reported intercourse as a result of verbal coercion. Poitras and Lavoie speculate that some of the differences in the reported rates of girls as the recipients of coercion and boys inflicting it may be attributed to the fact that adolescent girls often date older men, who may be more likely than boys to engage in coercive behaviors.

In "College Women's Experiences of Sexual Coercion: A Review of Cultural, Perpetrator, Victim, and Situational Variables" (*Trauma, Violence, and Abuse*, April 2004), Leah E. Adams-Curtis and Gordon B. Forbes complicate the view of sexual coercion in their review of research. They argue that coercive sexual behavior must be understood within prevalent sexual values on college campuses, including attitudes toward women, beliefs about sexual behavior, rape-supporting beliefs, coercion-supporting peer groups such as fraternities and athletic teams, gender concepts of both victims and perpetrators, and sexual promiscuity and its link with alcohol.

Adams-Curtis and Forbes posit that sexual coercion has its roots in traditional sex roles and expectations. Perpetrators of sexual coercion are not psychopaths, but men not particularly different from other men. Instead, Adams-Curtis and Forbes write, "We view sexual coercion as a complex, multiply determined, social behavior that has its origins in normal heterosexual interactions.... The factors influencing the progression from normal sexual negotiations to coercive sexuality are often commonplace elements of college life." They recommend that work be done to change traditional concepts of masculinity and femininity that result in the large percentages of college women being coerced into unwanted sexual activity.

Debra L. Oswald and Brenda L. Russell agree. They argue in "Perceptions of Sexual Coercion in Heterosexual Dating Relationships: The Role of Aggressor Gender and Tactics" (*Journal of Sex Research*, February 2006) that college students do not perceive coercive behaviors (verbal pressure, purposeful intoxication, or physical force) as "highly problematic." Instead, men who coerce women are viewed as sexually aggressive; women who coerce men are viewed as promiscuous.

Fraternities and Athletics

A national discussion about athletes on campus and rape was set in motion in 2006, when a stripper hired for a team party accused three Duke University lacrosse players of raping her in a bathroom on March 13 of that year. The university's president canceled the rest of the lacrosse team's season. The case set off racial tensions in Durham, North Carolina, as the woman accuser was a student of North Carolina Central University, a historically black college.

The relationship between athletics, fraternities, and rape is not a new dynamic. Several studies find that peer support of violence and social ties with abusive peers are predictors of abuse against women. In addition, training for violent occupations such as athletics and the military can "spill over" into personal life. Athletic training is sex-segregated, promotes hostile attitudes toward rivals, and rewards athletes for physically dominating others. Todd W. Crosset et al., in "Male Student-Athletes and Violence against Women: A Survey of Campus Judicial Affairs Offices" (*Violence against Women*, June 1996), report on data that they gathered from the judicial affairs offices of the ten Division I schools with the largest athletic programs. Although male student athletes made up just 3% of the student population, they accounted for 35% of the reported perpetrators.

Gordon B. Forbes et al., in "Dating Aggression, Sexual Coercion, and Aggression-Supporting Attitudes among College Men as a Function of Participation in Aggressive High School Sports" (*Violence against Women*, May 2006), find that participation in aggressive male sports in high school was a risk factor in perpetrating dating violence in college. In a study of 147 men, Forbes et al. find that men who had been involved in aggressive sports in high school engaged in more psychological and physical aggression and sexual coercion in their dating relationships. They were also more accepting of violence, caused their partners more physical injury, and were more hostile toward women. Forbes et al. state that the results indicate "that participation in aggressive high school sports is one of the multiple developmental pathways leading to relationship violence."

Mary Koss and Hobart H. Cleveland, in "Athletic Participation, Fraternity Membership, and Date Rape: The Question Remains—Self-Selection or Different Causal Processes?" (*Violence against Women*, June 1996), try to determine whether date rape is more likely to be perpetrated by athletes and fraternity members. They speculate that a fraternity-sponsored party draws acquaintances of the same social network together, whereas the fraternity controls the limited physical space with little supervision. Together, these circumstances create an environment that legitimizes the actions of the members, thereby minimizing the chance of reporting as well as the credibility of women who do report sexual misconduct. Koss and Cleveland conclude that there is low reporting of fraternity rape.

Fraternity members are frequently blamed as perpetrators of college rapes. In "Fraternity Membership, Rape Myths, and Sexual Aggression on College Campus" (*Violence against Women*, June 1996), Martin D. Schwartz and Carol A. Nogrady think this characterization is false. They argue that men who are most likely to rape in college are fraternity pledges and postulate that fraternity members are more likely to have a narrow conception of masculinity, espouse group secrecy, and sexually objectify women. Schwartz and Nogrady assert that alcohol is the crucial variable, and because fraternity members are often heavy drinkers, researchers mistakenly link these men and sexually aggressive behavior.

Stephen E. Humphrey and Arnold S. Kahn examine in "Fraternities, Athletic Teams, and Rape: Importance of Identification with a Risky Group" (*Journal of Interpersonal Violence*, December 2000) the question of whether fraternity members and male athletes are more likely to perpetrate sexual assaults than other college males. They argue that one reason that previous studies have yielded conflicting results is that they treat all sports teams and fraternities as the same, but that "there is evidence that fraternities vary widely in their attitudes toward women and their behavior toward them." They conclude that some "high-risk groups" had higher levels of sexual aggression and hostility toward women, as well as more support for sexual violence than did other "low-risk groups." In other words, the members of some fraternities and athletic teams *are* more likely to perpetrate sexual assault, whereas others are not.

Rohypnol—The "Date Rape Drug"

While alcohol abuse remains a significant problem on college campuses, other drugs, such as Rohypnol, have made resistance to attacks practically impossible. A hypnotic sedative ten times more powerful than Valium, Rohypnol (known as "Roofies," "Roches," and "Ropies") has been used to obtain nonconsensual sex from many women. Mixed in a drink, it causes memory impairment, confusion, and drowsiness. A woman may be completely unaware of a sexual assault until she wakes up the next morning. The only way to determine if a victim has been given Rohypnol is to test for the drug within two or three days of the rape, and few hospital emergency departments routinely screen for this drug. Health educators, high school guidance counselors, resident advisers at colleges, and scores of newspaper and magazine articles advise women not to accept drinks at parties or to leave drinks sitting unattended.

Although Rohypnol is legally prescribed outside of the United States for short-term treatment of severe sleep disorders, it is neither manufactured nor approved for sale in the United States. The importation of the drug was banned in March 1996, and the U.S. Customs and Border Patrol began seizing quantities of Rohypnol at U.S. borders. In response to reported abuse, the manufacturers reformulated the drug as green tablets that can be detected in clear liquids and are visible in the bottom of a cup. Anyone convicted of slipping a controlled substance, including Rohypnol, to an individual with intent to commit a violent act, such as rape, faces a prison term of up to twenty years and a fine as high as $2 million.

According to *Monitoring the Future*, an annual survey of illicit drug, alcohol, and tobacco use among the nation's youth, Rohypnol has a low prevalence rate that generally declined between 2004 and 2005. Less than 1% of eighth and tenth graders had used the drug within the past year; 1.2% of twelfth graders had used it. (See Table 8.10.) Still, given the drug's association with committing crime, even the use of the drug by one in one hundred high schoolers is cause for concern.

Two other drugs are also used as date rape pills. Gamma hydroxybutyric acid (GHB, also known as "liquid ecstasy") enhances the effects of alcohol, which reduces the drinker's inhibitions. It also causes a form of amnesia. Ketamine hydrochloride (also known as "Special K") is an animal tranquilizer used to impair a person's natural resistance impulses. Table 8.10 shows that annual prevalence of use of both of these drugs ranged

TABLE 8.10

Trends in annual use of "date rape drugs" by grade, 1991–2005

	1991	1992	1993	1994	1995	1996	1997	1998	1999	2000	2001	2002	2003	2004	2005	'04–'05 change
								Annual								
Any illicit drug																
8th grade	11.3	12.9	15.1	18.5	21.4	23.6	22.1	21.0	20.5	19.5	19.5	17.7	16.1	15.2	15.5	+0.3
10th grade	21.4	20.4	24.7	30.0	33.3	37.5	38.5	35.0	35.9	36.4	37.2	34.8	32.0	31.1	29.8	−1.3
12th grade	29.4	27.1	31.0	35.8	39.0	40.2	42.4	41.4	42.1	40.9	41.4	41.0	39.3	38.8	38.4	−0.4
MDMA (ecstasy)																
8th grade	—	—	—	—	—	2.3	2.3	1.8	1.7	3.1	3.5	2.9	2.1	1.7	1.7	−0.1
10th grade	—	—	—	—	—	4.6	3.9	3.3	4.4	5.4	6.2	4.9	3.0	2.4	2.6	+0.2
12th grade	—	—	—	—	—	4.6	4.0	3.6	5.6	8.2	9.2	7.4	4.5	4.0	3.0	−0.9
Rohypnol																
8th grade	—	—	—	—	—	1.0	0.8	0.8	0.5	0.5	0.7	0.3	0.5	0.6	0.7	+0.1
10th grade	—	—	—	—	—	1.1	1.3	1.2	1.0	0.8	1.0	0.7	0.6	0.7	0.5	−0.3
12th grade	—	—	—	—	—	1.1	1.2	1.4	1.0	0.8	0.9‡	1.6	1.3	1.6	1.2	−0.4
GHB																
8th grade	—	—	—	—	—	—	—	—	—	1.2	1.1	0.8	0.9	0.7	0.5	−0.2
10th grade	—	—	—	—	—	—	—	—	—	1.1	1.0	1.4	1.4	0.8	0.8	0.0
12th grade	—	—	—	—	—	—	—	—	—	1.9	1.6	1.5	1.4	2.0	1.1	−0.9
Ketamine																
8th grade	—	—	—	—	—	—	—	—	—	1.6	1.3	1.3	1.1	0.9	0.6	−0.3
10th grade	—	—	—	—	—	—	—	—	—	2.1	2.1	2.2	1.9	1.3	1.0	−0.3
12th grade	—	—	—	—	—	—	—	—	—	2.5	2.5	2.6	2.1	1.9	1.6	−0.3

SOURCE: Adapted from L. D. Johnston, P. M. O'Malley, J. G. Bachman, and J. E. Schulenberg, "Table 2. Trends in Annual Prevalence of Use of Various Drugs for Eighth, Tenth, and Twelfth Graders," in *Monitoring the Future: National Survey Results on Drug Use, 1975–2005, Volume 1: Secondary School Students*, NIH Publication No. 06-5883, National Institute on Drug Abuse, 2006, http://www.monitoringthefuture.com (accessed August 24, 2006)

from .5% to 1.6% for eighth, tenth, and twelfth graders in 2005. During 2002 anecdotal reports about another dangerous drug surfaced—a combination of 3,4-methylene-dioxymethamphetamine (known as "Ecstasy," "MDMA," or "crystal methamphetamine") and Viagra (a prescription drug used to treat erectile dysfunction); this combination was dubbed "Sextasy." According to media reports, the drugs are taken together by male teens because Viagra offsets impotence, a potential side effect of methamphetamine use. Public health officials are alarmed by this "off-label" use of Viagra and fear that it may contribute to increased rates of sexually transmitted diseases and sexual assault. In 2005, 1.7% of eighth graders, 2.6% of tenth graders, and 3% of twelfth graders had used Ecstasy in the past twelve months. (See Table 8.10.)

RAPE AMONG LESBIANS AND GAY MEN

Lesbians and gay men have been victims of rape and sexual abuse at rates comparable to or higher than rates in the heterosexual community. In "Comparing Violence over the Lifespan in Samples of Same-Sex and Opposite Sex Cohabitants" (*Violence and Victims*, 1999), Patricia Tjaden, Nancy Thoennes, and Christine J. Allison find that cohabiting lesbians were nearly twice as likely as women living with male partners to have been forcibly raped as a minor (16.5% versus 8.7%) and nearly three times as likely to report being raped as an adult (25.3%

versus 10.3%). They also find that 15.4% of cohabiting gay men were raped as minors, whereas 10.8% were raped as adults. The rate of rape for heterosexual men living with female partners was insignificant.

Tjaden, Thoennes, and Allison find that cohabiting gay men usually had been raped by strangers and acquaintances, whereas cohabiting females usually had been raped by intimate partners. A vast majority of the rape victims, regardless of gender or sexual preference, were raped by men.

Gay and lesbian cohabitants were also significantly more likely to report being physically assaulted as a child by an adult caretaker. Among gay men, 70.8% reported such violence, compared with 50.3% of heterosexual cohabitants. Among women, the figures were 59.5% and 37.5%, respectively. Gay and lesbian cohabitants also experienced higher levels of physical assault in adulthood.

Tjaden, Thoennes, and Allison found that same-sex cohabiting partners reported significantly more intimate partner violence than did cohabiting heterosexuals. About 32% of gay respondents said they had been raped or physically assaulted by a spouse or cohabiting partner at some point in their life, compared with just 7.7% of heterosexual men. Among lesbian cohabitants, 39.2% reported having been physically assaulted by a spouse or cohabiting partner, compared with 20.3% of women living with a male partner. Tjaden, Thoennes, and Allison note that lesbian cohabitants were also more than twice as likely to report having been victimized by male intimate partners than by female intimate partners, with 30.4% of the lesbian cohabitants raped or physically assaulted by male intimates. Only 11.4% of that group said they were raped or physically assaulted by female intimate partners. The same group reported less violence by their female partners than did heterosexual women living with males, which leads Tjaden, Thoennes, and Allison to conclude that women are far more likely to be assaulted by male intimate partners than by female intimate partners.

STALKING

Many abused women who leave their partners feel threatened and remain in physical danger of further attacks. One form of threatening behavior—stalking—is generally defined as harassment that involves repeated visual or physical proximity; nonconsensual communication; oral, written, or implied threats; or a combination of these acts that would cause a reasonable person fear. Stalking is a series of actions, usually escalating from legal but annoying acts, such as following or repeatedly phoning the victim, to violent or even fatal actions.

Not all stalking incidents involve abusive couples or intimate relationships. A stalker may fixate on an acquaintance or a stranger as the object of obsession. Celebrity stalking cases have been highly publicized, but they account for a small percentage of stalking incidents. Stalking most often involves intimates or former intimates and starts or continues after a victim leaves the relationship. It is a widespread problem. In "Stalking in the United States: Recent National Prevalence Estimates" (*American Journal of Preventive Medicine*, August 2006), Kathleen C. Basile et al. estimate that nearly one in twenty-two adults, or almost ten million, have been stalked in their lifetimes. Four out of five stalking victims are women.

According to the report *Stalking in America: Findings from the National Violence against Women Survey* (April 1998, http://www.ncjrs.gov/pdffiles/169592.pdf), Patricia Tjaden and Nancy Thoennes estimate that one out of twelve American women and one out of forty-five American men had been stalked at some point in their lives. An estimated 1% of all women respondents and 0.4% of all male respondents were stalked in the twelve months before the NVAWS. These percentages represent more than one million women and 370,000 men who are stalked annually in the United States.

Stalkers: Who Are They?

No data have been collected since the 1996 NVAWS on the details of stalking incidents. However, Basile et al.'s study demonstrates that prevalence rates remain

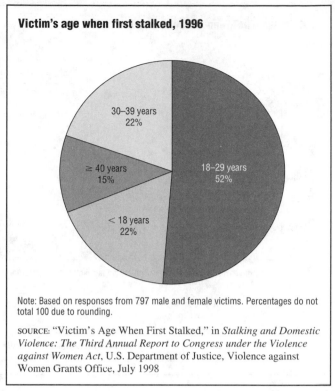

FIGURE 8.4

Victim's age when first stalked, 1996

Note: Based on responses from 797 male and female victims. Percentages do not total 100 due to rounding.

SOURCE: "Victim's Age When First Stalked," in *Stalking and Domestic Violence: The Third Annual Report to Congress under the Violence against Women Act*, U.S. Department of Justice, Violence against Women Grants Office, July 1998

virtually unchanged. As such, the NVAWS detailed findings are valid and worth studying in the absence of more recent detailed data.

Although stalking is considered a "gender-neutral" crime, most victims are women and the main perpetrators are men. Young adults are the primary targets—52% of victims were between the ages of eighteen and twenty-nine. Another 22% were between ages thirty and thirty-nine when the stalking began, and 15% were forty years old or older. (See Figure 8.4.) Recent data backs up the assertion that stalking victims are primarily younger adults; Basile et al. report that 6.5% of adults ages eighteen to twenty-four reported ever having been stalked, compared with 5.7% of those ages twenty-five to thirty-four, 5.5% of those ages thirty-five to forty-four, 5.2% of those ages forty-five to fifty-four, and 1.7% of those ages fifty-five and older.

As suspected, the NVAWS found that most victims knew their stalker. Only 23% of female victims and 36% of male victims were stalked by strangers. (See Figure 8.5.) Most women were stalked by intimate partners. Overall, 62% of female and 32% of male victims were stalked by current or former intimates. Figure 8.5 shows the relationship between stalkers and victims—female victims were stalked by spouses and former spouses nearly three times as often as male victims.

Most stalkers follow or spy on their victims, place unwanted phone calls, and send unwanted letters or other items. Tjaden and Thoennes note in *Stalking in America*

FIGURE 8.5

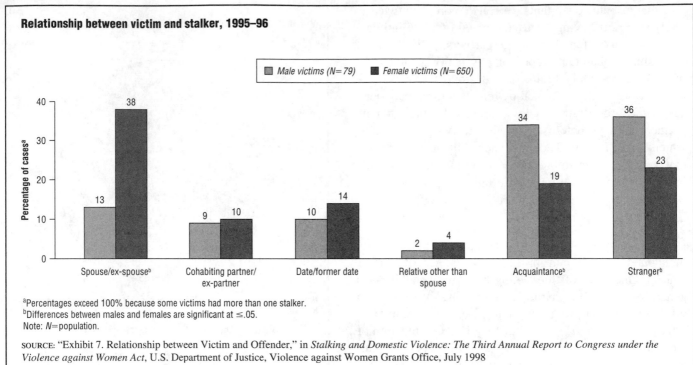

Relationship between victim and stalker, 1995–96

■ Male victims (N=79)   ■ Female victims (N=650)

[a]Percentages exceed 100% because some victims had more than one stalker.
[b]Differences between males and females are significant at ≤.05.
Note: N=population.

SOURCE: "Exhibit 7. Relationship between Victim and Offender," in *Stalking and Domestic Violence: The Third Annual Report to Congress under the Violence against Women Act*, U.S. Department of Justice, Violence against Women Grants Office, July 1998

that the pattern of harassment is similar whether the victim is male or female. Eighty-two percent of all female stalking victims and 72% of all male stalking victims reported being followed or spied on or found the stalker standing outside their home or workplace. Sixty-one percent of the females and 42% of the males reported receiving phone calls from the stalker. Twenty-nine percent of the women and 30% of the men reported property damage by the stalker, and 9% of the women and 6% of the male victims said the stalker either killed or threatened to kill their family pet.

When the Violence Occurs

Victims' advocates and counselors have long held that women are at the greatest risk of violence when they end a relationship with a batterer. This assumption is based on findings that divorced or separated women report more intimate partner violence than married women. In addition, interviews conducted with men who killed their wives reveal that the violence escalated or was precipitated by separation or threats of separation from their partners.

Many female stalking victims (43%) reported that they were stalked after ending their relationship with intimate partners, although 36% said they were stalked both before and after the breakup. Twenty-one percent of the victims said the stalking began before they terminated their relationships. (See Figure 8.6.)

According to findings released in *Extent, Nature, and Consequences of Intimate Partner Violence: Findings from the National Violence against Women Survey* (July 2000,

FIGURE 8.6

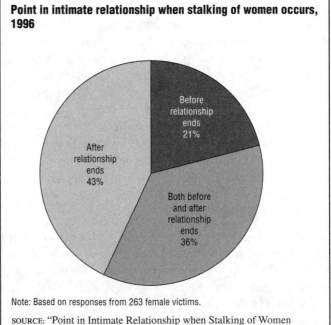

Point in intimate relationship when stalking of women occurs, 1996

Note: Based on responses from 263 female victims.

SOURCE: "Point in Intimate Relationship when Stalking of Women Occurs," in *Stalking and Domestic Violence: The Third Annual Report to Congress under the Violence against Women Act*, U.S. Department of Justice, Violence against Women Grants Office, July 1998

http://www.ncjrs.gov/pdffiles1/nij/181867.pdf), Tjaden and Thoennes find that separated women are nearly four times more likely to report rape, physical assault, or being stalked by their spouses than women who live with their husbands. In comparison, men who live apart from their spouses are nearly three times as likely to report being victimized by

FIGURE 8.7

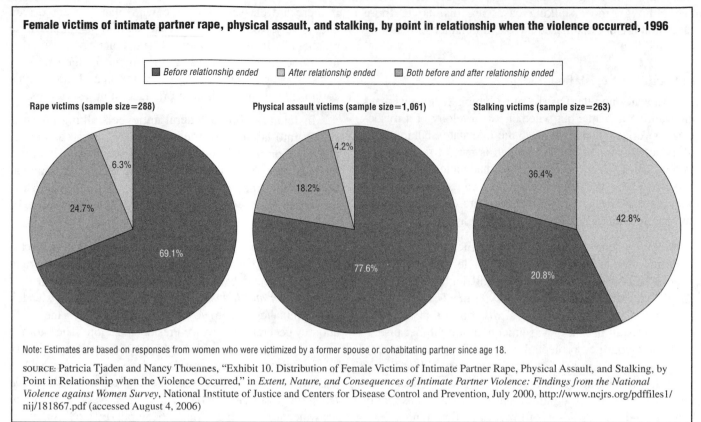

Female victims of intimate partner rape, physical assault, and stalking, by point in relationship when the violence occurred, 1996

■ *Before relationship ended*   ☐ *After relationship ended*   ▨ *Both before and after relationship ended*

Rape victims (sample size=288)   Physical assault victims (sample size=1,061)   Stalking victims (sample size=263)

Note: Estimates are based on responses from women who were victimized by a former spouse or cohabitating partner since age 18.

SOURCE: Patricia Tjaden and Nancy Thoennes, "Exhibit 10. Distribution of Female Victims of Intimate Partner Rape, Physical Assault, and Stalking, by Point in Relationship when the Violence Occurred," in *Extent, Nature, and Consequences of Intimate Partner Violence: Findings from the National Violence against Women Survey*, National Institute of Justice and Centers for Disease Control and Prevention, July 2000, http://www.ncjrs.org/pdffiles1/nij/181867.pdf (accessed August 4, 2006)

their wives than men who live with their spouses. These findings support the widely held belief that there is an increased risk of partner violence for both men and women once an abusive relationship ends.

While 43% of all stalking victims said the stalking began after they ended their relationship, only 6.3% of rape victims and 4.2% of physical assault victims reported victimization after they terminated their relationship. (See Figure 8.7.) These findings suggest that most rapes and violent assaults against women by their partners occur during the relationship, but stalking is more likely to occur after the relationship is terminated.

Legal Response to Stalking

Tjaden and Thoennes note in *Stalking in America* that about half of the stalking victims in the NVAWS (53.1%) reported stalking to the police. In most cases the victim made the report. Police were significantly more likely to arrest or detain a suspect stalking a female victim (25.1%) than one stalking a male victim (16.7%). Other police responses included referrals to the prosecutor or court (23.3%), referral to victim services (13.8%), and advice on self-protective measures (33.2%). In 18.9% of the cases police did nothing.

Of those victims who reported their stalking to the police, Tjaden and Thoennes report that about half were satisfied with the actions taken by the police, and about

the same proportion indicated they felt police interventions had improved their situations or that the police had done all they could. Victims who thought police actions were inadequate had hoped that their assailants would be jailed (42%) and that their complaints would be treated more seriously (20%). Another 16% had wanted police to do more to protect them from their assailants.

According to Tjaden and Thoennes, victims who chose not to report their stalking to the police said they felt their stalking was not a police matter (20%), they believed police would be unable to help them (17%), or they feared reprisal from their stalker (16%).

Not unexpectedly, because women were more likely to be stalked by intimate partners with a history of violence, female victims were significantly more likely than male victims to obtain protective or restraining orders. According to *Stalking and Domestic Violence: The Third Annual Report to Congress under the Violence against Women Act* (1998), of those who obtained protective orders, 68.7% of the women and 81.3% of the men said their stalker violated the order.

Carol E. Jordan et al. studied the disposition of stalking cases and published their results in "Stalking: An Examination of the Criminal Justice Response" (*Journal of Interpersonal Violence*, February 2003). They examine the cases of 346 males charged with stalking from fiscal year 1999 and find that most misdemeanor and felony charges of stalking were dismissed. Only 28.5% of the charged stalkers were convicted. Jordan et al. conclude that although most stalking cases are dismissed, those cases that are not dismissed have a fair chance of resulting in conviction.

Antistalking Legislation

All states and the District of Columbia have laws making stalking a crime, but whether it is a felony or a misdemeanor varies by state. In 1996 the Interstate Stalking Punishment and Prevention Act, which is part of the National Defense Authorization Act of 1997, made interstate stalking a felony. This federal statute addresses cases that cross state lines. In the past interstate offenses were difficult for state law enforcement agencies to take action against.

Several state legislatures have amended their antistalking laws after constitutional challenges or judicial interpretations of the law made it difficult to prosecute alleged stalkers. For example, in 1996 the Texas Court of Criminal Appeals, in *Long v. Texas*, ruled that the 1993 Texas antistalking law was unconstitutional because it addressed conduct protected by the First Amendment. Legislators amended the statute in January 1997 to stipulate that to violate the statute, an alleged offender must knowingly engage in conduct that he or she "reasonably believes the other person will regard as threatening."

According to the U.S. Department of Justice's Office for Victims of Crime, the variation in state stalking laws has to do with the type of repeated behavior that is prohibited, and whether by definition stalking must include a threat. Laws are also based on the victim's reaction to the stalking and the stalker's intent. The Department of Justice's legal series bulletin *Strengthening Antistalking Statutes* (January 2002) details state legislative changes to better define prohibited conduct so that supreme courts would not find the statutes "unconstitutionally vague." For example, the Oregon legislature removed the term *legitimate purpose* from its statute when its supreme court determined it did not adequately describe the prohibited behavior. Similarly, the Kansas Supreme Court sought increased precision when it requested that the state's stalking statute provide measures of behaviors such as "alarm, annoy, and harassment," arguing that actions that alarm or annoy one person may not alarm or annoy another.

Cyberstalking

Cyberstalking (online harassment and threats that can escalate to frightening and even life-threatening offline violence) is a relatively recent phenomenon. Brian H. Spitzberg and Greg Hoobler's study of college students, "Cyberstalking and the Technologies of Interpersonal Terrorism" (*New Media and Society*, March 2002), find that almost a third responded that they had experienced some degree of computer-based harassment and pursuit.

Spitzberg and Hoobler write that "it stands to reason that if there are classes of people who elect, or are driven obsessively, to pursue intimacy with others that these pursuers will seek whatever means are available that might increase their access to the objects of their pursuit, and that people's increasing exposure on and through the computer will make them more accessible as victims."

In January 2006 a federal anticyberstalking law was signed into law by President George W. Bush as part of the reauthorized Violence against Women Act. It prohibited anyone from using a telephone or telecommunications device (including a computer) "without disclosing his identity and with intent to annoy, abuse, threaten, or harass any person."

Although the extent of the problem is difficult to measure, by 1999 cyberstalking had generated enough concern to warrant the report *Cyberstalking: A New Challenge for Law Enforcement and Industry* (August 1999, http://www.usdoj.gov/criminal/cybercrime/cyberstalking.htm) by the U.S. attorney general to then Vice President Al Gore. The attorney general's report cautions that although cyberstalking does not involve physical contact, it should not be considered less dangerous than physical stalking. The report *Stalking and Domestic Violence: Report to Congress* (May 2001, http://www.ncjrs.gov/pdffiles1/ojp/186157.pdf) by the Department of Justice compares the similarities and differences between offline and online stalking. Most stalking cases, offline and online, involve stalking by former intimate partners, although there are cases of stranger stalking in each. Stalking victims, offline and online, are most often women, whereas stalkers are most often men. Most stalkers are motivated by a desire to control the victim.

The report also notes major differences. Cyberstalking is actually easier for the stalker than offline stalking; the online environment lowers barriers to harassment and threats. Offline stalking, for example, requires the perpetrator to be in the same area as the victim, whereas cyberstalkers can be anywhere. In addition, the online environment makes it easy for a cyberstalker to "encourage third parties to harass or threaten a victim." For example, a stalker can impersonate a victim online and post inflammatory messages, causing others to send threatening messages back to the victim.

CASES MAKE HEADLINE NEWS. The attorney general's report recounts three of many serious instances of cyberstalking that attracted attention in the media and among policy makers. The first successful prosecution under California's cyberstalking law was in Los Angeles, where a fifty-year-old man stalked a twenty-eight-year-old woman who had refused his advances. He posted her name and telephone number online along with messages saying she wanted to be raped. The Internet posts prompted men to knock on the woman's door, often during the night, in the hopes of fulfilling the fantasy her stalker had posted. In April 1999 the accused pleaded guilty to stalking and solicitation of sexual assault and was sentenced to a six-year prison term.

Another California case involved an honors graduate student at the University of San Diego who entered a guilty plea after sending, over the course of a year, hundreds of violent and menacing e-mail messages to five female university students he had never met. The third case cited in the report was prosecuted in Massachusetts, where a man repeatedly harassed coworkers via e-mail and attempted to extort sexual favors from one of them.

In July 2002 the CBS News program *48 Hours* investigated a lethal case of cyberstalking that shocked the nation. In 1999 a twenty-year-old New Hampshire resident named Amy Boyer was killed by a cyberstalker she had met, but never befriended or dated, years earlier in the eighth grade. Unknown to Boyer, her stalker had apparently obsessed over her for years and had constructed a Web site that described his stalking of Boyer and his plans to kill her. He used an investigation service to discover where she worked and ambushed her as she left, shooting her and then killing himself. Boyer's death inspired her parents to speak out and champion anticyberstalking laws.

Law Enforcement and Cyberstalking

> *Cyberspace has become a fertile field for illegal activity. By the use of new technology and equipment which cannot be policed by traditional methods, cyberstalking has replaced traditional methods of stalking and harassment. In addition, cyberstalking has led to offline incidents of violent crime. Police and prosecutors need to be aware of the escalating numbers of these events and devise strategies to resolve these problems through the criminal justice system.*

—Linda Fairstein, chief of the Sex Crimes Prosecution Unit, Manhattan District Attorney's Office

Cyberstalking presents some unique law enforcement challenges. Offenders are often able to use the anonymity of online communication to avoid detection and accountability for their actions. Appropriate interventions and recourse are unclear because often the stalker and his victim have never been in physical proximity to one another. Complicating the situation, the identity of the stalker may be difficult to determine. Furthermore, in many jurisdictions law enforcement agencies are unprepared to investigate cyberstalking cases because they lack the expertise and training. The attorney general's study finds that some victims had been advised by law enforcement agents to simply "turn off their computers" or to "come back should the offender confront or threaten them offline."

Finally, some state and local law enforcement agencies are frustrated in their efforts to track down cyberstalkers by the limits of their statutory authority. For example, the Cable Communications Policy Act of 1984 bars the release of cable subscriber information to law enforcement agencies without advance notice to the subscriber and a court order. Because a growing number of Internet users receive services via cable, the act inadvertently grants those wishing to remain anonymous for purposes of cyberstalking some legal protection from investigation. The attorney general's report calls for modifications to the act to include provisions to help law enforcement agents gain access to the identifying information they need while maintaining privacy safeguards for cable customers. "It may be ironic," write Spitzberg and Hoobler, "that to combat the risks of cyberstalking, law enforcement may need the very tools of electronic surveillance and intrusion that are currently the source of many citizens' fundamental fears of privacy invasion."

CHAPTER 9
DOMESTIC VIOLENCE, LAW ENFORCEMENT, AND COURT RESPONSES TO DOMESTIC VIOLENCE

POLICE RESPONSE TO DOMESTIC VIOLENCE

The police are often an abuse victim's initial contact with the judicial system, making the police response particularly important. The manner in which the police handle a domestic violence complaint will likely color the way the victim views the entire judicial system. Not surprisingly, when police project the blame for intimate partner violence on victims, the victims may be reluctant to report further abuse.

According to the 2004 National Crime Victimization Survey, the police came to the aid of victims for about three-quarters (75.3%) of all violent crimes. In about half the incidents of rape and sexual assault, police came to victims (52.8%); 25.6% of victims went to police. Table 9.1 shows that police came to the aid of more victims of aggravated assault (76.6%), simple assault (73.8%), and robbery (85.9%) than victims of rape and sexual assault.

Family disturbance calls constitute most calls received by police departments throughout the country. Historically such calls were not taken seriously, a reflection of society's attitude about domestic violence at the time. For instance, in the mid-1960s Detroit police dispatchers were instructed to screen out family disturbance calls unless they suspected "excessive" violence. A 1975 police guide, *The Function of the Police in Crisis Intervention and Conflict Management*, taught officers to avoid arrest at all costs and to discourage the victim from pressing charges by emphasizing the consequences of testifying in court, the potential loss of income, and other detrimental aspects of prosecution.

Changes in society's tolerance for domestic violence mean that these approaches to domestic violence no longer enjoy official support (although they may still influence the actions of individual officers). By 2006 every state had moved to authorize probable cause arrests (arrest before the completion of the investigation of the alleged violation or crime) without a warrant in domestic violence cases. (A warrant is a written legal document authorizing a police officer to make a search, seizure, or arrest.) Many police departments have adopted pro-arrest or mandatory arrest policies. Pro-arrest strategies include a range of sanctions from issuing a warning, to mandated treatment, to prison time.

REPORTING DOMESTIC VIOLENCE TO THE POLICE

It is well established that a significant amount of intimate partner violence is unreported or underreported. In the past most women did not report incidents of abuse to the police. Several studies estimate that only about 10% of battering incidents are ever reported to authorities. The 1985 National Family Violence Resurvey finds that only 6.7% of all husband-to-wife assaults were reported to police. When the assaults are categorized by severity as measured on a Conflict Tactics Scale, only 3.2% of minor violence cases and 14.4% of severe violence cases were reported.

There is some evidence that over time, slightly higher percentages of female victims have reported instances of intimate partner violence to the police. In "The 'Drunken Bum' Theory of Wife Beating" (*Social Problems*, 1987), Glenda Kaufman Kantor and Murray A. Straus estimate that between 7% and 14% of intimate partner assaults were reported to police. A 1995 study using National Crime Victimization Survey data made the most optimistic projections, estimating that 56% of battering incidents were reported to the police.

The women who chose not to report their abuse cited a variety of reasons, including fear of retaliation, loss of income, or loss of their children to child protection authorities. When abuse is reported to law enforcement agencies, it is often by health care professionals from whom the woman has sought treatment for her injuries. In many states health professionals are mandated by law to report all instances of domestic violence to law enforcement authorities.

TABLE 9.1

Police response to a reported incident, by type of crime, 2004

			Percent of incidents					
Type of crime	Number of incidents	Total	Police came to victim	Victim went to police	Contact with police—don't know how	Police did not come	Not known if police came	Police were at the scene
Crimes of violence	**2,194,380**	**100.0%**	**75.3%**	**5.3%**	**0.0%***	**10.3%**	**2.4%**	**6.7%**
Rape/sexual assault[a]	69,320	100.0	52.8	25.6*	0.0*	8.4*	13.2*	0.0*
Robbery	268,940	100.0	85.9	3.6*	0.0*	7.9*	0.7*	2.0*
Aggravated assault	532,420	100.0	76.6	4.4*	0.0*	6.8	2.9*	9.4
Simple assault	1,323,700	100.0	73.8	4.9	0.0*	12.4	2.0*	7.0
Purse snatching/pocket picking	88,050	100.0	38.3	23.8*	0.0*	30.5*	0.0*	7.5*
Property crimes	**7,110,270**	**100.0%**	**66.8%**	**5.8%**	**0.0%***	**23.8%**	**2.5%**	**1.1%**
Household burglary	1,764,690	100.0	85.3	1.9	0.1*	11.2	0.6*	0.8*
Motor vehicle theft	845,260	100.0	68.1	6.2	0.0*	22.6	2.2*	0.8*
Theft	4,500,320	100.0	59.3	7.2%	0.0*	28.9	3.2	1.3

Note. Detail may not add to total shown because of rounding.
*Estimate is based on about 10 or fewer sample cases.
[a]Includes verbal threats of rape and threats of sexual assault.

SOURCE: "Table 106. Personal and Property Crimes, 2004: Percent Distribution of Police Response to a Reported Incident, by Type of Crime," in *Criminal Victimization in the United States, 2004*, U.S. Department of Justice, Office of Justice Programs, Bureau of Justice Statistics, June 2006, http://www.ojp.usdoj .gov/bjs/pub/pdf/cvus04.pdf (accessed July 8, 2006)

The National Crime Victimization Surveys (NCVS) are ongoing, nationwide surveys that gather data on criminal victimizations from a national sample of eighty thousand household respondents over age twelve. The surveys provide a biannual estimate of crimes experienced by the public, whether or not a law enforcement agency was contacted about the crime. In *National Crime Victimization Survey: Criminal Victimization, 2004* (September 2005, http://www.ojp.usdoj.gov/bjs/pub/pdf/cv04.pdf), Shannan M. Catalano notes that 55.2% of female victims of violent crime in 2004 reported the crime to police. Only about one-third (35.8%) of women who were victims of rape or sexual assault reported the assaults to the police. African-American women (66.9%) and Hispanic women (65.1%) were more likely to report violent crimes to the police than were white women (52.1%).

Table 9.2 shows that women who were victims of violent crime at the hands of strangers were more likely to report the crime than were women who were victimized by nonstrangers (58.6% and 53%, respectively). However, recent data have not been broken down further to examine reporting behaviors of women assaulted by intimate partners. Using seven years of data from the NCVS, Callie Marie Rennison examines trends, including police notification, in *Intimate Partner Violence and Age of Victim, 1993–99* (October 2001, http://www.ojp.usdoj. gov/bjs/pub/pdf/ipva99.pdf). She finds that nearly three-quarters of intimate partner violence against females ages twelve to fifteen is not reported to police and that more than half of females ages sixteen to nineteen and over age fifty do not make police reports.

The reasons people give for their decision to report victimizations to the police are shown in Table 9.3. For all personal crimes, high proportions of victims said they reported the incident to stop this incident (18.5%) or to prevent further crimes by the offender against them (17.7%). One out of five (20.4%) reported the incident simply because it was a crime. Other reasons included to stop the offender from victimizing anyone else (10.9%), to punish the offender (7.2%), to catch the offender (4.9%), and a feeling of duty to notify the police (4.8%).

Other victims chose not to report personal crimes to the police. Nearly one out of five people who chose not to report a personal crime said they did not do so because it was a private or personal matter (19.2%). Others were afraid of reprisal (4.6%), an issue particularly salient for battered women. (See Table 9.4.) When the crime was perpetrated by someone the victim knew rather than by a stranger, victims were even more likely to say they did not report because it was a private or personal matter (21.8% versus 16.3%) or because they feared reprisal (6.2% versus 2.9%). (See Table 9.5.)

In *The Reporting of Domestic Violence and Sexual Assault by Nonstrangers to the Police* (March 2005, http:// www.ncjrs.gov/pdffiles1/nij/grants/209039.pdf), Richard B. Felson and Paul-Philippe Paré use data from the NCVS to examine the effects of the gender of the victim and the relationship between victim and offender on the victim's decision to report or not report a physical or sexual assault to the police. They find that victims are just as likely to report assaults by intimate partners as they are to report assaults by other people they know. Sexual assaults are less likely to be reported than are physical assaults.

Marsha E. Wolf et al., in "Barriers to Seeking Help for Intimate Partner Violence" (*Journal of Family Violence*,

TABLE 9.2

Victimizations reported to police by type of crime, by victim-offender relationship, and by gender of victims, 2004

| | Percent of all victimizations reported to the police | | | | | | | | |
| | All victimizations | | | Involving strangers | | | Involving nonstrangers | | |
Type of crime	Both genders	Male	Female	Both genders	Male	Female	Both genders	Male	Female
Crimes of violence	**49.9%**	**45.9%**	**55.2%**	**52.4%**	**49.0%**	**58.6%**	**47.6%**	**41.9%**	**53.0%**
Completed violence	62.1	63.0	61.2	69.7	71.6	66.6	56.5	53.5	58.7
Attempted/threatened violence	43.8	38.6	51.5	45.3	40.3	55.0	42.1	36.4	48.7
Rape/sexual assault[a]	35.8	0.0*	36.9	39.9	0.0*	43.0	32.8	0.0*	32.8
Robbery	61.1	51.9	79.6	60.6	54.7	76.2	61.7	46.0	83.4
Completed/property taken	73.0	66.7	80.8	75.5	77.0	73.2	69.8	50.1*	88.4
With injury	71.0	61.9*	77.3	84.9	100.0*	68.0*	61.2	17.6*	82.0
Without injury	74.2	68.6	84.1	72.0	69.9	75.7	78.3	66.1*	100.0*
Attempted to take property	43.4	37.3	74.9*	43.1	36.1	86.1*	44.0*	40.4*	57.3*
With injury	57.0	50.1*	100.0*	59.5*	54.1*	100.0*	53.5*	44.4*	100.0*
Without injury	36.1	30.1	64.3*	36.6	28.7*	81.7*	34.6*	35.9*	31.1*
Assault	49.4	45.2	55.1	51.7	48.3	58.3	47.2	41.6	53.1
Aggravated	64.2	61.2	70.1	71.0	68.0	79.0	56.5	51.3	63.6
With injury	70.6	71.3	69.4	88.8	91.9	79.1*	57.0	50.2	65.4
Threatened with weapon	60.4	55.6	70.5	63.5	57.6	79.0	56.0	52.1	62.0
Simple	44.9	39.5	51.7	45.0	40.3	53.1	44.8	38.5	50.8
With minor injury	59.6	57.3	62.0	62.1	58.5	69.2	57.9	56.2	59.3
Attempted threat without weapon	39.7	33.8	47.6	40.3	35.0	49.1	39.2	32.4	46.6

Note: Detail may not add to total shown because of rounding.

*Estimate is based on about 10 or fewer sample cases.

[a]Includes verbal threats of rape and threats of sexual assault.

SOURCE: "Table 93. Violent Crimes, 2004: Percent of Victimizations Reported to the Police, by Type of Crime, Victim-Offender Relationship and Gender of Victims," in *Criminal Victimization in the United States, 2004*, U.S. Department of Justice, Office of Justice Programs, Bureau of Justice Statistics, June 2006, http://www.ojp.usdoj.gov/bjs/pub/pdf/cvus04.pdf (accessed July 8, 2006)

April 2003), interviewed forty-one battered women to find out what kept them from calling police. The factors cited included the idea that they must have physical proof that battering had occurred, the desire to avoid a humiliating physical examination in the case of rape or sexual abuse, cultural attitudes about domestic violence, poor self-esteem, being physically prevented from calling the police by the batterer, poor police response when battering was previously reported, and fears of possible retaliation by the batterer or removal of children from the home by child protective services. These women also came up with a "wish list" for how they wanted police to treat them when they called about domestic violence. This list, in the words of Wolf et al., "reflects the women's desires to have responsive police who treat victims with dignity, listen to them, and send appropriate messages to victims and batterers." (See Table 9.6.)

OUTCOME OF POLICE INTERVENTION

In the early 1970s it was legal for the police to make probable cause arrests without a warrant for felonies, but only fourteen states permitted it for misdemeanors. Because the crime of simple assault and battery is a misdemeanor in most states, family violence victims were forced to initiate their own criminal charges against a batterer. By 2006, however, all states authorized warrantless probable cause misdemeanor arrests in domestic violence cases. However, more than half of the states have added qualifiers, such as visible signs of injury or report of the violence within eight hours of the incident. Most state codes authorizing warrantless arrests require police to inform victims of their rights, which include the acquisition of protection orders and referral to emergency and shelter facilities and transportation.

In "Determining Police Response to Domestic Violence Victims" (*American Behavioral Scientist*, May 1993), a landmark study of four precincts of the Detroit Police Department and their responses to domestic violence in 1993, Eve S. Buzawa and Thomas Austin document several factors that affected police decisions to arrest offenders:

- The presence of bystanders or children during the abuse

- The presence of guns and sharp objects as weapons

- An injury resulting from the assault

- The offender and victim sharing the same residence whether they were married or not

- The victim's desire to have the offender arrested (of victims who expressed such a desire, arrests were made in 44% of the cases; when the victim did not want the offender arrested, arrests were made in only 21% of the cases)

TABLE 9.3

Reasons for reporting victimizations to the police, by type of crime, 2004

Type of crime	Number of reasons for reporting	Total	Stop or prevent this incident	Needed help due to injury	To recover property	To collect insurance	To prevent further crimes by offender against victim	To prevent crime by offender against anyone	To punish offender	To catch or find offender	To improve police surveillance	Duty to notify police	Because it was a crime	Some other reason	Not available
All personal crimes	**2,251,370**	**100.0%**	**18.5%**	**1.0%***	**4.3%**	**0.3%***	**17.7%**	**10.9%**	**7.2%**	**4.9%**	**3.2%**	**4.8%**	**20.4%**	**5.6%**	**1.2%***
Crimes of violence	2,165,880	100.0%	19.0	1.1*	3.4	0.3*	18.1	11.2	7.4	4.9	3.3	4.6	20.1	5.4	1.2*
Completed violence	902,880	100.0%	17.0	2.0*	6.0	0.4*	14.9	11.0	10.9	3.8	3.9	5.3	18.6	5.6	0.6*
Attempted/threatened violence	1,263,010	100.0%	20.4	0.4*	1.5*	0.2*	20.4	11.4	4.8	5.7	2.9	4.1	21.1	5.3	1.7*
Rape/sexual assault[a]	92,000	100.0%	13.8*	2.0*	0.0*	0.0*	9.1*	15.1*	8.2*	5.0*	10.1*	4.7*	22.9*	9.2*	0.0*
Robbery	397,650	100.0%	15.3	0.0*	13.2	0.0*	8.2	15.8	12.0	3.5*	6.3*	8.4	14.8	1.3*	1.3*
Completed/property taken	309,950	100.0%	15.0	0.0*	16.9	0.0*	8.9*	14.8	10.7	3.7*	6.5*	8.5*	12.7	0.8*	1.6*
With injury	112,840	100.0%	16.7*	0.0*	11.4*	0.0*	15.5*	14.9*	7.9*	7.9*	6.0*	11.5*	5.8*	2.3*	0.0*
Without injury	197,110	100.0%	14.0*	0.0*	20.1	0.0*	5.2*	14.6*	12.2*	1.3*	6.7*	6.7*	16.6	0.0*	2.5*
Attempted to take property	87,700	100.0%	16.4*	0.0*	0.0*	0.0*	5.5*	19.4*	16.8*	3.0*	5.6*	8.0*	22.5*	2.8*	0.0*
With injury	20,230*	100.0%*	0.0*	0.0*	0.0*	0.0*	0.0*	14.4*	14.4*	0.0*	24.4*	0.0*	46.7*	0.0*	0.0*
Without injury	67,470	100.0%	21.3*	0.0*	0.0*	0.0*	7.2*	20.9*	17.4*	3.8*	0.0*	10.4*	15.3*	3.7*	1.3*
Assault	1,676,230	100.0%	20.2	1.3*	1.3*	0.4*	21.0	9.9	6.2	5.2	2.2	3.7	21.2	6.2	1.3*
Aggravated	479,500	100.0%	18.0	2.6*	3.0*	1.3*	15.5	9.4	6.5*	10.0	2.6*	2.7*	22.1	4.9*	1.3*
Simple	1,196,730	100.0%	21.0	0.7*	0.6*	0.0*	23.1	10.1	6.1	3.3	2.1*	4.2	20.8	6.7	1.3*
Purse snatching/pocket picking	85,490	100.0%	5.5*	0.0*	27.0*	0.0*	8.6*	4.0*	4.0*	4.0*	0.0*	7.9*	28.5*	10.4*	0.0*
All property crimes	**8,675,030**	**100.0%**	**7.5%**	**0.1%***	**23.2%**	**4.1%**	**8.8%**	**6.0%**	**4.5%**	**7.0%**	**6.3%**	**6.4%**	**22.6%**	**2.3%**	**1.2%**
Household burglary	2,574,250	100.0%	9.7	0.2*	19.4	3.3	11.0	7.2	5.0	7.4	8.7	6.4	20.1	1.1*	0.5*
Completed	2,324,600	100.0%	8.8	0.2*	21.4	3.6	10.2	7.0	5.2	7.3	8.1	6.1	20.6	1.0*	0.5*
Forcible entry	1,338,470	100.0%	8.4	0.0*	22.1	3.9	10.9	7.1	6.3	8.0	8.5	5.5	17.5	1.4*	0.6*
Unlawful entry without force	986,130	100.0%	9.4	0.5*	20.5	3.1*	9.2	6.8	3.8	6.4	7.6	7.1	24.7	0.5*	0.4*
Attempted forcible entry	249,650	100.0%	17.9	0.0*	0.9*	0.9*	18.2	9.7*	2.9*	8.1*	14.7	8.5*	15.9	2.2*	0.0*
Motor vehicle theft	1,073,240	100.0%	5.8	0.2*	36.0	7.5	6.0	3.7	4.3	8.0	5.3	5.3	15.8	0.9*	1.1*
Completed	945,090	100.0%	4.6	0.2*	40.6	7.6	5.6	3.7	4.9	8.0	4.5	5.0	13.3	1.1*	0.8*
Attempted	128,140	100.0%	14.9*	0.0*	2.3*	6.9*	9.1*	3.3*	0.0*	7.8*	10.7*	7.3*	34.2	0.0*	3.6*
Theft	5,027,540	100.0%	6.8	0.1*	22.5	3.8	8.3	5.9	4.2	6.6	5.3	6.6	25.3	3.1	1.6
Completed	4,849,970	100.0%	6.7	0.1*	23.3	3.9	8.5	5.6	4.3	6.5	5.4	6.6	24.5	3.0	1.7
Attempted	177,580	100.0%	9.8*	0.0*	0.0*	2.3	2.3*	12.2*	1.8*	8.4*	4.2*	5.8*	47.2	6.0*	0.0*

Percent of reasons for reporting

Notes: Detail may not add to total shown because of rounding. Some respondents may have cited more than one reason for reporting victimizations to the police.

*Estimate is based on about 10 or fewer sample cases.

[a]Includes verbal threats of rape and threats of sexual assault.

SOURCE: "Table 101. Personal and Property Crimes, 2004: Percent of Reasons for Reporting Victimizations to the Police, by Type of Crime," in *Criminal Victimization in the United States, 2004*, U.S. Department of Justice, Office of Justice Programs, Bureau of Justice Statistics, June 2006, http://www.ojp.usdoj.gov/bjs/pub/pdf/cvus04.pdf (accessed July 8, 2006)

TABLE 9.4

Reasons for not reporting victimizations to the police, by type of crime, 2004

Type of crime	Number of reasons for not reporting	Total	Reported to another official	Private or personal matter	Object recovered; offender unsuccessful	Not important enough	Insurance would not cover	Not aware crime occurred until later	Unable to recover property; no ID no.	Lack of proof	Police would not want to be bothered	Police inefficient, ineffective, or biased	Fear of reprisal	Too inconvenient or time consuming	Other reasons
								Percent of reasons for not reporting							
All personal crimes	**3,126,410**	**100.0%**	**13.9%**	**19.2%**	**20.3%**	**6.7%**	**0.1%***	**0.5%***	**0.5%***	**2.5%**	**4.8%**	**3.0%**	**4.6%**	**4.1%**	**19.9%**
Crimes of violence	2,949,790	100.0	13.9	19.3	19.9	6.6	0.1*	0.4*	0.3*	1.9	4.7	3.2	4.7	4.3	20.7
Completed violence	800,740	100.0	14.5	20.7	11.2	2.2*	0.4*	1.6*	1.2*	2.6*	5.4	3.6*	9.6	4.3	22.6
Attempted/threatened violence	2,149,040	100.0	13.6	18.8	23.1	8.3	0.0*	0.0*	0.0*	1.6	4.4	3.0	2.9	4.3	19.9
Rape/sexual assault[a]	163,980	100.0	8.7*	18.5*	8.6*	1.5*	1.9*	5.6*	0.0*	0.0*	5.3*	4.1*	12.1*	5.6*	27.9
Robbery	265,740	100.0	4.7*	8.7*	15.1	6.5*	0.0*	1.3*	3.6*	10.0*	7.0*	8.9*	10.0*	8.4*	15.7
Completed/property taken	110,850	100.0	6.6*	11.4*	7.5*	2.8*	0.0*	3.1*	8.6*	12.5*	10.2*	5.1*	16.8*	3.1*	12.3*
With injury	35,190	100.0	13.0*	7.9*	9.2*	8.7*	0.0*	0.0*	6.7*	0.0*	0.0*	0.0*	45.2*	0.0*	9.2*
Without injury	75,660	100.0	3.7*	13.0*	6.7*	0.0*	0.0*	4.5*	9.5*	18.3*	14.9*	7.4*	3.6*	4.5*	13.8*
Attempted to take property	154,890	100.0	3.3*	6.8*	20.5*	9.2*	0.0*	0.0*	0.0*	8.3*	4.7*	11.7*	5.2*	12.3*	18.1*
With injury	42,690	100.0	7.1*	0.0*	25.4*	0.0*	0.0*	0.0*	0.0*	9.9*	0.0*	0.0*	18.8*	19.9*	18.8*
Without injury	112,200	100.0	1.9*	9.3*	18.6*	12.7*	0.0*	0.0*	0.0*	7.7*	6.4*	16.2*	0.0*	9.4*	17.8*
Assault	2,520,070	100.0	15.2	20.5	21.1	7.0	0.0*	0.0*	0.0*	1.1*	4.4	2.5	3.7	3.8	20.7
Aggravated	423,170	100.0	14.6	19.3	19.7	4.0*	0.0*	0.0*	0.0*	2.5*	5.6*	2.5*	1.6*	4.6*	25.5
Simple	2,096,900	100.0	15.3	20.7	21.4	7.6	0.0*	0.0*	0.0*	0.9*	4.2	2.5	4.1	3.6	19.8
Purse snatching/pocket picking	176,620	100.0	13.8*	17.9*	26.8	7.7*	0.0*	1.4*	3.1*	12.0*	6.6*	0.0*	2.9*	0.0*	7.7*
All property crimes	**13,746,400**	**100.0%**	**8.6%**	**6.6%**	**28.2%**	**3.5%**	**2.7%**	**5.2%**	**5.8%**	**11.7%**	**8.4%**	**2.7%**	**0.5%**	**3.5%**	**12.6%**
Household burglary	2,092,470	100.0	4.3	6.6	22.8	3.6	3.2	6.5	6.5	14.1	9.4	4.4	0.9*	3.8	13.9
Completed	1,727,810	100.0	3.4	6.9	19.3	2.2	3.3	6.3	7.9	14.9	9.9	4.7	0.9*	4.4	15.8
Forcible entry	352,930	100.0	1.9*	11.8	16.8	3.2*	2.3*	7.2*	6.7*	10.9	4.7*	6.5*	0.7*	5.6*	21.6
Unlawful entry without force	1,374,880	100.0	3.7	5.6	20.0	2.0*	3.6	6.0	8.2	15.9	11.2	4.3	1.0*	4.2	14.4
Attempted forcible entry	364,660	100.0	8.9*	5.1*	39.4	9.3	2.7*	7.7*	0.0*	10.6	7.2*	2.7*	0.6*	0.7*	4.6*
Motor vehicle theft	207,330	100.0	2.8*	8.2*	32.7	3.5*	4.6*	2.2*	0.0*	14.3*	11.0*	4.5*	0.0*	5.2*	11.1*
Completed	42,500	100.0	0.0*	27.7*	13.3*	0.0*	5.6*	0.0*	0.0*	5.8*	5.8*	5.6*	0.0*	9.7*	26.3*
Attempted	164,830	100.0	3.6*	3.2*	37.7	4.4*	4.3*	2.8*	0.0*	16.4*	12.3*	4.2*	0.0*	4.1*	7.1*
Theft	11,446,600	100.0	9.5	6.6	29.1	3.5	2.5	5.0	5.8	11.2	8.2	2.3	0.4	3.4	12.4
Completed	11,013,380	100.0	9.7	6.6	28.5	3.4	2.6	5.1	6.0	11.1	8.5	2.4	0.4	3.4	12.3
Attempted	433,220	100.0	4.5*	6.8*	44.3	4.5*	1.2*	4.5*	0.5*	13.0	0.5*	1.8*	0.0*	2.3*	16.1

Notes: Detail may not add to total shown because of rounding. Some respondents may have cited more than one reason for not reporting victimizations to the police.

*Estimate is based on about 10 or fewer sample cases.

[a]Includes verbal threats of rape and threats of sexual assault.

SOURCE: "Table 102. Personal and Property Crimes, 2004: Percent of Reasons for Not Reporting Victimizations to the Police, by Type of Crime," in *Criminal Victimization in the United States, 2004*, U.S. Department of Justice, Office of Justice Programs, Bureau of Justice Statistics, June 2006, http://www.ojp.usdoj.gov/bjs/pub/pdf/cvus04.pdf (accessed July 8, 2006)

TABLE 9.5

Reasons for not reporting victimizations to the police, by victim-offender relationship and by type of crime, 2004

Relationship and type of crime	Number of reasons for not reporting	Percent of reasons for not reporting													
		Total	Reported to another official	Private or personal matter	Object recovered; offender unsuccessful	Not important enough	Insurance would not cover	Not aware crime occurred until later	Unable to recover property; no ID no.	Lack of proof	Police would not want to be bothered	Police inefficient, ineffective, or biased	Fear of reprisal	Too inconvenient or time consuming	Other reasons
Involving strangers															
Crimes of violence	1,338,570	100.0%	12.6%	16.3%	23.3%	8.3%	0.0%*	0.5%*	0.4%*	3.6%	6.1%	2.7%	2.9%	5.6%	17.7%
Rape/sexual assault[a]	59,990	100.0	12.4*	20.9*	8.7*	0.0*	0.0*	5.2*	0.0*	0.0*	0.0*	3.0*	14.8*	15.4*	19.6*
Robbery	161,600	100.0	5.9*	10.6*	19.3*	1.9*	0.0*	2.1*	3.0*	13.6*	5.8*	7.5*	6.7*	13.9*	9.7*
Assault	1,116,970	100.0	13.5	16.9	24.7	9.6	0.0*	0.0*	0.0*	2.4*	6.5	2.0*	1.7*	3.9	18.8
Involving nonstrangers															
Crimes of violence	1,611,220	100.0%	14.9	21.8	17.0	5.3	0.2*	0.4*	0.3*	0.4*	3.6	3.6	6.2	3.2	23.1
Rape/sexual assault[a]	103,980	100.0	6.6*	17.1*	8.6*	2.3*	3.0*	5.8*	0.0*	0.0*	8.4*	4.8*	10.6*	0.0*	32.7
Robbery	104,140	100.0	2.9*	5.8*	8.6*	13.7*	0.0*	0.0*	4.5*	4.5*	8.7*	11.2*	15.2*	0.0*	25.0*
Assault	1,403,100	100.0	16.5	23.3	18.3	4.9	0.0*	0.0*	0.0*	0.2*	2.8	2.9	5.2	3.7	22.3

Notes: Detail may not add to total shown because of rounding. Some respondents may have cited more than one reason for not reporting victimizations to the police.

*Estimate is based on about 10 or fewer sample cases.

[a]Includes verbal threats of rape and threats of sexual assault.

SOURCE: "Table 104, Personal Crimes of Violence, 2004: Percent of Reasons for Not Reporting Victimizations to the Police, by Victim-Offender Relationship and Type of Crime," in *Criminal Victimization in the United States, 2004,* U.S. Department of Justice, Office of Justice Programs, Bureau of Justice Statistics, June 2006, http://www.ojp.usdoj.gov/bjs/pub/pdf/cvus04.pdf (accessed July 8, 2006)

TABLE 9.6

Battered women's "wish list" for police response

- Have quick police response
- Provide consistency in response and take time to listen to women—take victim statement
- Have more female officers
- Avoid questioning parents in front of children
- Get translators for non–English-speaking victims (do not use the batterer or children as translators)
- Send strong message to batterer that battering is wrong, he will be watched, caught, and prosecuted
- Tell women that battering is wrong, it can escalate, and it will not stop without help; take time to inform them of rights and resources
- Arrest appropriate person
- Arrest on felony charges when possible
- Enforce protection orders
- If needed, have advocate at scene who can help victim after police leave
- Provide follow up with victim

SOURCE: Marsha E. Wolf, Uyen Ly, Margaret A. Hobart, and Mary A. Kernic, "Table II. Battered Women's 'Wish List' for Police Response," in "Barriers to Seeking Police Help for Intimate Partner Violence," *Journal of Family Violence*, vol. 18, no. 2, April 2003. Reprinted with kind permission of Springer Science and Business Media.

Mandatory Arrests

Arrest gained popularity as a tactic after the publication of the first in a series of six studies funded by the National Institute of Justice known as the Spouse Assault Replication Program. All the studies were designed to explain how arrest in domestic violence cases could serve as a deterrent to future violence. Lawrence W. Sherman and Richard A. Berk, the authors of the influential first study in the series, "The Specific Deterrent Effects of Arrest for Domestic Assault" (*American Sociological Review*, April 1984), find that "the arrest intervention certainly did not make things worse and may well have made things better."

Although Sherman and Berk caution about generalizing from the results of a small study dealing with a single police department in which few police officers properly followed the test procedure, they conclude that in instances of domestic violence, an arrest is advisable except in cases where it would be clearly counterproductive. At the same time, Sherman and Berk recommend allowing police a certain amount of flexibility when making decisions about individual situations, on the premise that police officers must be permitted to rely on professional judgment based on experience.

Sherman and Berk's study had a tremendous impact on police practices, although five other Spouse Assault Replication Program studies found arrest had little or no effect on domestic violence recurrence (J. David Hirschel, Ira W. Hutchison, and Charles W. Dean, "The Failure to Deter Spouse Abuse," *Journal of Research in Crime and Delinquency*, 1992). A survey conducted two years after the Sherman and Berk report found more than a fourfold increase in the number of police departments reporting arrest as their preferred policy in domestic violence disputes. Some police departments have adopted a presumptive arrest policy. This policy means that an arrest should be made unless clear and compelling reasons exist not to arrest. Presumptive arrest provisions forbid officers from basing the decision to arrest on the victim's preference or on a perception of the victim's willingness to testify or participate in the proceedings. Proponents point out that arresting an offender gives the victim a respite from fear and an opportunity to look for help. Furthermore, they claim it prevents bias in arrests.

By the 1990s as many as one out of three police precincts had adopted a mandatory arrest policy in domestic abuse cases. In "The Influence of Mandatory Arrest Policies, Police Organizational Characteristics, and Situational Variables on the Probability of Arrest in Domestic Violence Cases" (*Crime and Delinquency*, October 2005), David Eitle finds that mandatory police arrest policies do result in more arrests when called to the scene of a domestic assault. In addition, he notes that these policies reduce somewhat the overrepresentation of African-Americans among those arrested. However, do these arrests reduce violence against women?

Some studies find that mandatory arrest policies have positive effects. For example, Jacquelyn C. Campbell et al. find in "Risk Factors for Femicide in Abusive Relationships: Results from a Multisite Case Control Study" (*American Journal of Public Health*, July 2003) that previous arrest for battering actually decreased women's risk of being subsequently killed by the batterer. Christopher D. Maxwell, Joel H. Garner, and Jeffrey A. Fagan argue in "The Effects of Arrest on Intimate Partner Violence: New Evidence from the Spouse Assault Replication Program" (July 2001, http://www.ncjrs.gov/pdffiles1/nij/188199.pdf) that arrest of batterers is consistently related to subsequent reduced aggression against their intimate partners. Figure 9.1 shows that during the follow-up period after batterers had either been arrested for domestic violence or had an alternative intervention (including mediation counseling, a citation to appear in court, a restraining order, or a warning), those who were arrested consistently "survived" (or did not batter) at a higher rate than those who were not arrested.

However, some battered women's advocates do not support mandatory arrest. They fear that poor and minority families are treated more harshly than middle-class families and that if the police arrive and both spouses are bloodied by the fight, both will be arrested, forcing the children into foster care.

Some studies, such as Ellen Pence and Martha McMahon's *A Coordinated Community Response to Domestic Violence* (January 1997, http://data.ipharos.com/praxis/documents/ccrdv.pdf), show that mandatory arrests may actually increase violence, especially if the batterer is

FIGURE 9.1

Time between intervention and next aggressive offense recorded by police, by arrest or non-arrest of offender, selected years 1981–93

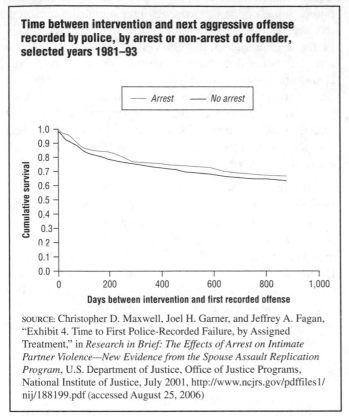

SOURCE: Christopher D. Maxwell, Joel H. Garner, and Jeffrey A. Fagan, "Exhibit 4. Time to First Police-Recorded Failure, by Assigned Treatment," in *Research in Brief: The Effects of Arrest on Intimate Partner Violence—New Evidence from the Spouse Assault Replication Program*, U.S. Department of Justice, Office of Justice Programs, National Institute of Justice, July 2001, http://www.ncjrs.gov/pdffiles1/nij/188199.pdf (accessed August 25, 2006)

unemployed or has a criminal record. Some observers suggest that mandatory arrest should be replaced with mandatory action, such as providing transportation to a shelter or granting the victim the option to have the offender arrested. Mandatory action would allow police officers to make decisions appropriate to each individual case.

Evan Stark, in "Mandatory Arrest of Batterers: A Reply to Its Critics" (Eve S. Buzawa and Carl G. Buzawa, eds., *Do Arrests and Restraining Orders Work?* 1996), offers reasons for a mandatory arrest policy other than deterrence. Stark asserts that mandatory arrest policies provide:

- A standard against which to judge variation in police responses

- Immediate protection from current violence and time for victims to consider their options

- Access to services and protection for victims that would not be available outside the criminal justice system

However, David Hirschel and Ira W. Hutchison, in "The Voices of Domestic Violence Victims: Predictors of Victim Preference for Arrest and the Relationship between Preference for Arrest and Revictimization" (*Crime and Delinquency*, April 2003), find support for a police policy of taking victim preferences into account in the decision to arrest. Victims based their preferences for arrest on the seriousness of the violence and the perpe-

trator's prior abusive behavior; in fact, victims proved to be good judges of the seriousness of the violence and the likelihood of it recurring. Hirschel and Hutchison find that victims who wanted their abusers arrested were more likely to suffer subsequent abuse than were victims who did not want their batterers arrested. "Based on these data," Hirschel and Hutchison state, "victim desire for arrest of the offender would appear to be a factor that police should take into account in determining subsequent action."

DO MANDATORY ARREST POLICIES DISEMPOWER THE VICTIM? In "Battered Women Add Their Voices to the Debate about the Merits of Mandatory Arrest" (*Women's Studies Quarterly*, 2004), Paula C. Barata and Frank Schneider look at the debate about mandatory arrest policies from a different angle: from the point of view of the victim. They find that a large proportion of battered women actually support a mandatory arrest policy, although they "were more likely to see the benefits of mandatory arrest for other victims/survivors than for themselves." Barata and Schneider hypothesize that the victims' support for mandatory arrest policies in their own situations were influenced by such factors as love for their battering partner, their fears about retaliatory abuse, or their worries about money.

Battered women whose partners had been arrested generally described a pattern of initial decreased violence when the batterer was removed from the home, but an increase in violence when the abuser, who was potentially angry about being arrested, returned home. Only about a third of the women interviewed (38.5%) believed the threat of another arrest would decrease the violence in the long run.

However, despite their disbelief in deterrence, a majority of women still thought that domestic violence was a crime, not a family problem, and several participants liked mandatory arrest policies because they proved to the abuser that assault is wrong and will be punished by the legal system. In fact, most of the battered women interviewed by Barata and Schneider did not view mandatory arrest policies as disempowering. Barata and Schneider argue that this is because of two reasons: first, victims do not want the responsibility for deciding if their battering partner will be arrested and were relieved when the decision was taken out of their hands, and second, victims of battering do not believe they have much influence over the decision to arrest, even without a mandatory arrest policy in place. Also, the vast majority of women believed that mandatory arrest policies made police take their abuse more seriously.

JoAnn Miller, in "An Arresting Experiment: Domestic Violence Victim Experiences and Perceptions" (*Journal of Interpersonal Violence*, July 2003), also studied victims' perceptions of empowerment or disempowerment as a result of arrest. She focused on the Spouse Assault Replication Program victims' perceptions of police interventions and arrest. She examined two concepts of power: personal power (control of economic and social resources) and legal power (perceived empowerment in response to police intervention).

Miller finds that women did not use their sense of personal power (derived from an independent income) to end domestic violence. However, she notes that victims' perception of legal power (derived from their satisfaction with the police action taken) could be used to feel safer and to control interactions with violent partners in the future. She concludes that "the most reasonable criminal justice and social service responses to domestic violence are those that consider the victim's needs by taking into account her subjective experiences, her cultural and social resources, and her personal and legal resources." In other words, in Miller's view, mandatory arrest policies tend to undermine victims' personal power because they do not take into account victims' needs.

Victims' Attitudes toward Police Response

Interviewing 110 victims as part of their study of the Detroit Police Department's response to domestic violence mentioned previously, Buzawa and Austin find that 85% of victims were satisfied with the police response. Not surprisingly, the victims were particularly satisfied when the police responded to their preferences for arresting or not arresting the offenders.

In "Perceptions of the Police by Female Victims of Domestic Partner Violence" (*Violence against Women*, November 2003), Robert Apsler, Michele R. Cummins, and Steven Carl investigate "what female victims of domestic violence wanted from the police, the extent to which they perceived they obtained what they wanted, and how helpful they found the actions of the police." They find that women in the study were satisfied with the police response to their call. The women believed the police had been helpful, and more than 80% of them said they would definitely call the police for help in the future. Apsler, Cummins, and Carl emphasize that the particular police department involved in the study had recently instituted policies specifically designed to help battered women.

NOT ALL VICTIMS WHO SEEK POLICE ATTENTION ARE THE SAME

Apsler, Cummins, and Carl speculate that the female victims who seek police aid are likely the most frightened women and that they are seeking assistance to prevent future instances of abuse. In "Fear and Expectations: Differences among Female Victims of Domestic Violence Who Come to the Attention of Police" (*Violence*

and Victims, August 2002), Apsler, Cummins, and Carl review police officers' interviews of ninety-five consecutive victims who came to the attention of a police department in a Boston suburb.

The study participants had either contacted the police department via telephone or by personal appearance at the police station to request intervention in a violent intimate partner dispute. Police officers administered a standardized questionnaire that included questions about the severity of the abuse victims had experienced, their level of fear, and their expectations about the future. About half the victims were living with their abusers at the time the incident occurred.

Apsler, Cummins, and Carl find that just one-quarter of respondents said they were afraid of their abusers. Another 6% were fairly afraid, 12% said they were slightly afraid, and 36% claimed they were not at all afraid of their abusers. Taken together, these latter two groups accounted for nearly half of participants reporting little or no fear of their abusers.

The results were similar in terms of participants' expectations of future abuse. Apsler, Cummins, and Carl find that just 21% of victims thought future abuse was likely, and well over half of women surveyed said future abuse was not at all likely or only slightly likely. These findings challenge long-standing beliefs that the victims who tend to come to the attention of the police are those who most fear future abuse.

Interestingly, there were no statistically significant relationships found between victims' expectations of future violence and whether they lived with their abusers, had children under eighteen years old, or were able to support themselves financially. A less surprising result was that victims' expectations of future abuse strongly influenced their desired future relationships with their offenders. A strong majority of the participants (90%) who thought future abuse was fairly likely or likely wanted to permanently separate from the offenders. In contrast, only about half of the women who thought further abuse was not at all likely wanted permanent separations.

Apsler, Cummins, and Carl conclude that the differences between victims of domestic violence and their varied expectations when seeking police attention point to a need for law enforcement agencies to offer a variety of police responses tailored to victims' needs. For example, they suggest that mandatory arrest of victims' aggressors might not help as a universally applicable strategy for all victims, especially women who do not fear further abuse. By contrast, fearful victims might be reassured and experience greater security if police maintained regular, ongoing contact with them following the incident. Apsler, Cummins, and Carl add that police follow-up might also send a powerful message to perpetrators—that they are under surveillance and that future violations will not be tolerated.

PROTECTION ORDERS
What Are They?

An abuse victim in any state may go to court to obtain a protection order. Also referred to as "restraining orders" or "injunctions," civil orders of protection are legally binding court orders that prohibit an individual who has committed an act of domestic violence from further abusing the victim. Although the terms are often used interchangeably, restraining orders usually refer to short-term or temporary sanctions, whereas protection orders have longer duration and may be permanent. These orders generally prohibit harassment, contact, communication, and physical proximity to the victim. Although protection orders are common and readily obtained, they are not always effective.

All states and the District of Columbia have laws that allow an abused adult to petition the court for an order of protection. States also have laws to permit people variously related to the abuser to file for protection orders. Relatives of the victim, children of either partner, couples in dating relationships, same-sex couples, and former spouses are among those who can file for a protection order in a majority of the states, the District of Columbia, and Puerto Rico. In Hawaii and Illinois, those who shelter an abused person can also obtain a protective order against the abuser.

Petitioners may file for protection orders in circumstances other than violent physical abuse, including sexual assault, marital rape, harassment, emotional abuse, and stalking. Protection orders are valid for varying lengths of time depending on the state. In thirty states the orders are in force for six months to a year. In Illinois and Wisconsin the orders last two years, and in California and Hawaii they are in effect for three years. Furthermore, some states have extended the time during which a general or incident-specific protective order is effective. For example, a no-contact order issued against a stalker convicted in California remains in effect for ten years. In Iowa five-year protection orders are issued and additional five-year extensions may be obtained. New Jersey offers permanent protective orders, and a conviction for stalking serves as an application for a permanent restraining order. Judges in Connecticut may issue standing criminal restraining orders that remain in effect until they are altered or revoked by the court.

Protection orders give victims an option other than filing a criminal complaint. Issued quickly, usually within twenty-four hours, they provide safety for the victim by barring or evicting the abuser from the household. Statutes in most states make violating a protection order a matter of criminal contempt, a misdemeanor, or even a felony. However, this judicial protection has little meaning if the police do not maintain records and follow through with arrest should the abuser violate the order.

The "full faith and credit" provision of the Violence against Women Act was passed to establish nationwide enforcement of protection orders in courts throughout the country. States, territories, and tribal lands were ordered to honor protection orders issued in other jurisdictions—although the act did not mandate how these orders were to be enforced. According to Christina DeJong and Amanda Burgess-Proctor in "A Summary of Personal Protection Order Statutes in the United States" (*Violence against Women*, January 2006), most states have amended their state domestic violence codes or statutes to reflect the new requirement, although the states vary widely on how easy it is for battered women to get their protection orders enforced. Courts and law enforcement agencies in most states have access to electronic registries of protection orders, both to verify the existence of an order and to assess whether violations have occurred.

Effects of Protection Orders

In "Protection Orders and Intimate Partner Violence: An 18-Month Study of 150 Black, Hispanic, and White Women" (*American Journal of Public Health*, April 2004), Judith McFarlane et al. report on their study of the effects on intimate partner violence of the application for and receipt of a two-year protection order against abusers. McFarlane et al. interviewed 150 women over an eighteen-month period to determine whether protection orders diminished violence. Although almost half (44%) of the women reported at least one violation of the order, McFarlane et al. find significant reductions in physical assaults, stalking, and threats of assault over time among all women who applied for a protection order, even if they had not been granted the order. McFarlane et al. hypothesize that it was not the protection order itself that led to the diminished violence but the contact with the criminal justice system that exposed the battering to public view.

Victoria L. Holt et al., in "Do Protection Orders Affect the Likelihood of Future Partner Violence and Injury?" (*American Journal of Preventive Medicine*, January 2003), came to a similar conclusion in their prospective study of 448 female victims of intimate partner violence. They measured the number of unwelcome calls or visits, threats, threats with weapons, psychological, sexual, or physical abuse, and abuse-related medical care among women who had obtained a civil protection order and those who had not. Holt et al. find that women who obtained a protection order following an abusive incident had a significantly decreased risk of contact by the abuser, threats by weapons, injury, and abuse-related medical care.

Holt et al. find in "Civil Protection Orders and Risk of Subsequent Police-Reported Violence" (*Journal of the American Medical Association*, August 7, 2002) that having a permanent protection order in effect was associated with an 80% reduction in police-reported physical violence in the twelve months following an incident of intimate partner violence. They also report that women who had obtained temporary protection orders, in effect for two weeks only, were more likely than victims with no protection orders to be psychologically abused in the six months after the reported incident of intimate partner violence. Holt et al. speculate that temporary protection orders may have restrained abusers from inflicting physical violence, producing a commensurate increase in psychological abuse. They observe that while temporary orders were linked to increased psychological abuse, the orders did not generate the increased physical violence that many victims and service providers fear will follow. Holt et al. conclude that concern about increased physical violence after obtaining temporary protection orders may be unfounded and that permanent protection orders may be more powerful deterrents to prevent violence recurrence than previously believed.

Enforcement of Orders of Protection

Robert J. Kane examines patterns of arrest of batterers who violate restraining orders in "Police Responses to Restraining Orders in Domestic Violence Incidents" (*Criminal Justice and Behavior*, October 2000). Although all violators in his study were required by Massachusetts state law to be immediately arrested, in reality only between 20% and 40% of violators of restraining orders were taken into custody. Kane finds that restraining orders had no significant effect on arrest rate; instead, police perception of imminent danger to the victim was the strongest predictor of arrest. He also finds that as the number of domestic violence calls from one victim to police increased, the rate of arrest decreased, regardless of whether a restraining order was in place. Kane suggests that further studies should be done into variations in arrest rates that include personal characteristics of police officers and the social contexts of the couples involved in domestic violence incidents.

George Rigakos, in "Constructing the Symbolic Complainant: Police Subculture and the Nonenforcement of Protective Orders from Battered Women" (*Violence and Victims*, Fall 1995), studies how police officers' attitudes influenced the nonenforcement of protective orders in a suburb of Vancouver, British Columbia. He finds that a traditional masculine culture contributed to negative stereotypes of women as liars, manipulators, and unreliable witnesses.

According to Rigakos, interviews with police officers and justice officials revealed four major themes. First, justice officials and police felt they were doing all they could for women but contended that other criminal justice institutions impeded their work. Second, the police in this study held conservative attitudes about marriage that resulted in their excusing men's abusive behavior. Third, because traditional beliefs influenced police attitudes toward the victims, many male officers seemed determined to make the women's behavior appear "unreliable." Some felt that the women were using restraining orders to manipulate their husbands to give themselves advantages in custody battles and divorces. Fourth, the officers made generalizations that were supported by their beliefs about the women but were not substantiated by official court records. The officers believed that after they had spent tremendous amounts of time and effort to prepare a case, the women frequently did not pursue the charges. These negative perceptions of the women produced "selective memory" that magnified every instance of a battered woman failing to appear to testify against a partner and diminished the number of times when the women followed through with legal action.

The U.S. Department of Justice, in the report *Enforcement of Protective Orders* (January 2002, http://www.ojp.usdoj.gov/ovc/publications/bulletins/legalseries/bulletin4/ncj189190.pdf), observes that while all states have passed some form of legislation to benefit victims of domestic violence, and thirty-two states have integrated these rights at the constitutional level, the scope and enforcement of these rights varies. The Department of Justice calls for law enforcement agencies, prosecutors, and judges to be completely informed about the existence and specific terms and requirements of orders and to act to enforce them. Furthermore, it asserts that "unequivocal standardized enforcement of court orders is imperative if protective orders are to be taken seriously by the offenders they attempt to restrain."

LANDMARK LEGAL DECISIONS

Before the 1962 landmark case *Self v. Self*, when the California Supreme Court ruled that "one spouse may maintain an action against the other for battering," women had no legal recourse against abusive partners. The judicial system had tended to view wife abuse as a matter to be resolved within the family. Maintaining that "a man's home is his castle," the federal government traditionally had been reluctant to violate the sanctity of the home. Furthermore, many legal authorities persisted in "blaming the victim," maintaining that the wife was, to some degree, responsible for her own beating by somehow inciting her husband to lose his temper. Yet even after the landmark California case, turning to the judicial system for help was still unlikely to bring assistance to or result in justice for victims of spousal abuse. Jurisdictions throughout the United States continued to ignore the complaints of battered women until the late 1970s.

Many victims of domestic violence have sought legal protection from their abusive partners. This section summarizes the outcomes of several landmark cases that not only helped to define judicial responsibility but also shaped the policies and practices aimed at protecting victimized women.

Baker v. The City of New York

Sandra Baker was estranged from her husband. In 1955 the local domestic relations court issued a protective order directing her husband, who had a history of serious mental illness, "not to strike, molest, threaten, or annoy" his wife. Baker called the police when her husband created a disturbance at the family home. When a police officer arrived, she showed him the court order. The officer told her it was "no good" and "only a piece of paper" and refused to take any action.

Baker went to the domestic relations court and told her story to a probation officer. While making a phone call, she saw her husband in the corridor. She went to the probation officer and told him her husband was in the corridor. She asked if she could wait in his office because she was "afraid to stand in the room with him." The probation officer told her to go to the waiting room. Minutes later, her husband shot and wounded her.

Baker sued the city of New York, claiming that the city owed her more protection than she was given. The New York State Supreme Court Appellate Division, in *Baker v. The City of New York* (1966), agreed that the city of New York failed to fulfill its obligation. The court found that she was "a person recognized by order of protection as one to whom a special duty was owed... and peace officers had a duty to supply protection to her." Neither the police officer nor the probation officer had fulfilled this duty, and both were found guilty of negligence. Because the officers were representatives of the city of New York, Baker had the right to sue the city.

Equal Protection

Another option desperate women have used in response to unchecked violence and abuse is to sue the police for failing to offer protection, alleging that the police violated their constitutional rights to liberty and equal protection under the law.

The Equal Protection Clause of the Fourteenth Amendment provides that no state shall "deny to any person within its jurisdiction the equal protection of the laws." This clause prohibits states from arbitrarily classifying individuals by group membership. If a woman can prove that a police department has a gender-based policy of refusing to arrest men who abuse their wives, she can claim that the policy is based on gender stereotypes and therefore violates the equal protection laws.

THURMAN V. CITY OF TORRINGTON. Between October 1982 and June 1983 Tracey Thurman repeatedly called the Torrington, Connecticut, police to report that her estranged husband was threatening her life and that of her child. The police ignored her requests for help no matter how often she called or how serious the situation became. At one point her husband attacked her in view of the police, and was arrested. Thurman obtained protection and restraining orders against him after this incident. But when her husband later came to her home and threatened her again, in violation of his probation and the court orders, police refused to intervene.

On June 10, 1983, Thurman's husband came to her home. She called the police. He then stabbed her repeatedly around the chest, neck, and throat. A police officer arrived twenty-five minutes later but did not arrest her husband, despite the attack. Three more police officers arrived. The husband went into the house and brought out their child and threw him down on his bleeding mother. The officers still did not arrest him. While his wife was on the stretcher waiting to be placed in the ambulance, he came at her again. Only at that point did police take him into custody. Thurman later sued the city of Torrington, claiming she was denied equal protection under the law.

In *Thurman v. City of Torrington* (1984), the U.S. District Court for Downstate Connecticut agreed, stating:

> City officials and police officers are under an affirmative duty to preserve law and order, and to protect the personal safety of people in the community. This duty applies equally to women whose personal safety is threatened by individuals with whom they have or have had a domestic relationship as well as to all other people whose personal safety is threatened, including women not involved in domestic relationships. If officials have notice of the possibility of attacks on women in domestic relationships or other people, they are under an affirmative duty to take reasonable measures to protect the personal safety of such people in the community.

> ... A police officer may not knowingly refrain from interference in such violence, and may not automatically decline to make an arrest simply because the assailant and his victim are married to each other. Such inaction on the part of the officer is a denial of the equal protection of the laws.

There could be no question, the court concluded, that the city of Torrington, through its police department, had "condoned a pattern or practice of affording inadequate protection or no protection at all, to women who complained of having been abused by their husbands or others with whom they have had close relations." Therefore, the police had failed in their duty to protect Tracey Thurman and deserved to be sued.

The federal court jury awarded Thurman $2.3 million in compensatory damages. Almost immediately the state of Connecticut changed the law, calling for the arrest of assaultive spouses. In the twelve months following the new law, arrests for domestic assault almost doubled, from 12,400 to 23,830.

Due Process

The Due Process Clause of the Fourteenth Amendment provides that no state can "deprive any person of life, liberty, or property, without due process of law; nor deny to any person within its jurisdiction the equal protection of the laws." It does not, however, obligate the state to protect the public from harm or provide services that would protect them. Rather, a state may create special conditions in which that state has constitutional obligations to particular citizens because of a "special relationship between the state and the individual." Abused women have used this argument to claim that being under a protection order puts them in a "special relationship."

MACIAS V. HIDE. During the eighteen months before her estranged husband Avelino Macias murdered her at her place of work, Maria Teresa Macias had filed twenty-two police complaints. In the months before her death, Avelino Macias sexually abused his wife, broke into her home, terrorized her, and stalked her. The victim's family filed a wrongful death lawsuit against the Sonoma County Sheriff's Department in California, accusing the department of failing to provide Macias equal protection under the law and of discriminating against her as a Hispanic and a woman.

The U.S. District Court for the Northern District of California dismissed the case because Judge D. Lowell Jensen said there was no connection between Macias's murder and how the sheriff's department had responded to her complaints. On July 20, 2000, the U.S. Court of Appeals for the Ninth Circuit reversed the earlier decision and ruled that the lawsuit could proceed with the discovery phase and pretrial motions. Judge Arthur L. Alarcon of the U.S. Court of Appeals for the Ninth Circuit conveyed the unanimous opinion of the court when he wrote, "It is well established that there is no constitutional right to be protected by the state against being murdered by criminals or madmen. There is a constitutional right, however, to have police services administered in a nondiscriminatory manner—a right that is violated when a state actor denies such protection to disfavored persons."

After this decision the case proceeded to trial. On June 18, 2002, Sonoma County agreed to pay $1 million to the Macias family to settle the case. The settlement agreement did not include an admission of any wrongdoing by the county. Nevertheless, domestic violence activists lauded the result. According to Katherine P. Califa in "Domestic Violence Civil Suit Settles for $1 Million" (July 5, 2002, http://www.now.org/issues/

violence/070502macias.html), Kim Gandy, the president of the National Organization for Women (NOW), stated, "This settlement shows that law enforcement cannot get away with denying equal protection under the law to victims of domestic violence."

TOWN OF CASTLE ROCK V. GONZALES. The U.S. Supreme Court reaffirmed in 2005 that governments are not required to offer citizens protection from violent abusers. In the case of *Town of Castle Rock v. Gonzales,* Jessica Gonzales's three children were taken from her home by her estranged husband in violation of an order of protection. When she alerted the police and repeatedly asked them for assistance, they made no effort to find the children or enforce the state's mandatory arrest law. The children were killed later that night. Gonzales sued the town, arguing that by failing to respond to her calls the police had violated her right to due process of law, and the case eventually reached the U.S. Supreme Court. In its review the Court found on June 27, 2005, that "Colorado law has not created a personal entitlement to enforcement of restraining orders" and that the state's law did not really require arrest in all cases, but actually left considerable discretion in the hands of the police. So while the Castle Rock police made a tragically incorrect decision in this case, they did not do so in violation of Gonzales's due process rights. The American Civil Liberties Union subsequently filed the case with the International Human Rights Organization, arguing that domestic violence victims have the right to be protected by the state from their abusers.

KEY DOMESTIC VIOLENCE LEGISLATION

While appealing to the judicial system for help will not solve all the problems an abused woman faces, the reception a battered woman can expect from the system—police, prosecutors, and courts—improved markedly in the late twentieth century. The Violence against Women Act, signed into law by President Bill Clinton in September 1994, did much to help. The act simultaneously strengthened prevention and prosecution of violent crimes against women and provided law enforcement officials with the tools they needed to prosecute batterers. Although the system is far from perfect, legal authorities are far more likely to view abuse complaints as legitimate and serious than they had in the past.

Violence against Women Act

A key provision in the Violence against Women Act, the civil rights provisions of Title III, declared that violent crimes against women motivated by gender violate victims' federal civil rights—giving victims access to federal courts for redress for the first time. In testifying in favor of the passage of the act, Sally Goldfarb (http://www.binghamton.edu/womhist/vawa/doc14b.htm), an attorney for NOW, told Senate members, "The enactment of civil rights legislation would convey a powerful message: that violence motivated by gender is not merely an individual crime or a personal injury, but is a form of discrimination, an assault on a publicly-shared ideal of equality. When half of our citizens are not safe at home or on the streets because of their sex, our entire society is diminished." When the Violence against Women Act was passed into law, the text of the civil rights provision was:

> Federal civil rights action as specified in this section is necessary to guarantee equal protection of the laws and to reduce the substantial adverse effects on interstate commerce caused by crimes of violence motivated by gender; and the victims of crimes of violence motivated by gender have a right to equal protection of the laws, including a system of justice that is unaffected by bias or discrimination and that, at every relevant stage, treats such crimes as seriously as other violent crimes.

In 1999 the civil rights section of the act was tested in the U.S. Supreme Court. Christy Brzonkala, an eighteen-year-old freshman at Virginia Polytechnic Institute, was violently attacked and raped by two men, Antonio Morrison and James Crawford, on September 21, 1994. Brzonkala did not immediately report the rape, and no physical evidence of the rape was preserved. Two months later, she filed a complaint with the school; after learning that the college took limited action against the two men, she withdrew from the school and sued her assailants for damages in federal court.

Brzonkala's case reached the Supreme Court in 1999. Briefs in favor of giving victims of gender-based violence access to federal courts were filed by dozens of groups—the American Medical Women's Association, the National Association of Human Rights Workers, the National Coalition against Domestic Violence, and the National Women's Health Network among them—as well as the briefs filed by law scholars and human rights experts. However, five of the Supreme Court justices decided in *Brzonkala v. Virginia Polytechnic Institute* (2000) that Congress could not enact a law giving victims of gender-motivated violence access to federal civil rights remedies. The majority opinion emphasized that "the Constitution requires a distinction between what is truly national and what is truly local"—and it ruled that the violent assault of Christy Brzonkala was local.

In October 2000 Congress responded to the Supreme Court decision by passing new legislation, the Victims of Trafficking and Violence Protection Act of 2000. The new statute included these titles: Strengthening Law Enforcement to Reduce Violence against Women, Strengthening Services to Victims of Violence, Limiting the Effects of Violence on Children, and Strengthening Education and Training to Combat Violence against Women. The act allocated $3.3 billion over five years to fund traditional support services along with prevention and education about dating violence, rape, and stalking via the Internet, as well as new programs for transitional housing and expanded protection for immigrant women. The new act did not mention women's civil rights. The

Violence against Women Act was reauthorized in 2005, providing funding to programs through 2009.

Other Federal Laws and Public Policies

The following are among other federal laws and public policies aimed at addressing violent crimes against women:

- The Hillory J. Farias and Samantha Reid Date Rape Drug Prohibition Act of 2000 made it illegal to manufacture, distribute, or dispense gamma hydroxybutyric acid (GHB, also known as "liquid ecstasy" and the "date rape drug") and created a special unit to evaluate abuse and trafficking of GHB and other drugs associated with instances of sexual assault.

- The Social Security Administration in 1998 changed its rules governing new social security numbers. Previously, a woman needed to provide evidence that an abuser was using her social security number to locate her or that the violence was life threatening. With the new law women need only to provide written corroboration of domestic violence from a third party, such as a doctor, lawyer, clergy member, or even a family member or friend, to obtain a new number.

- A Postal Service Release of Information Final Rule was published on January 25, 2000, and became effective February 24, 2000. If an individual postal customer presents the U.S. Postal Service with a court order of protection, then the postal service may not disclose identifying information such as address, location, or post office box, unless ordered by the court.

- A Final Rule on Documentation of Immigrants and Nonimmigrants—Visa Classification Symbols was published on June 18, 2001. This rule amended the Violence against Women Act to create new nonimmigrant categories for victims of trafficking for illicit sexual purposes and slavery and those who have suffered abuse, such as battering, and other forms of violence.

In addition, on January 26, 2001, the U.S. Sentencing Commission published the Sentencing Guidelines for United States Courts, which increased the base sentencing levels for offenses and required stricter sentences for stalking, domestic violence, and cases involving the use of GHB.

The International Marriage Broker Regulation Act of 2005 was geared to stop serial abusers of women who come to the United States as "mail-order brides." The new law requires all men seeking visas for a bride-to-be to disclose any convictions for domestic violence, sexual assault, or child abuse. In addition, men seeking a new visa for a second fiancée within two years will be denied, and no petitions for a third fiancée visa will be granted.

TABLE 9.7

Rejection rates of handgun applications under the Brady Act, by selected states, 1999–2004

	2004			1999–2004		
	Total transactions	Total rejections	Rejection rate	Total transactions	Total rejections	Rejection rate
Total	3,384,017	40,257	1.2%	18,062,231	268,219	1.5%
Alaska	40,504	816	2.0%	230,607	5,923	2.6%
Alabama	229,997	3,400	1.5	1,320,342	22,364	1.7
Arkansas	158,366	2,495	1.6	905,734	17,933	2.0
Delaware	16,424	255	1.6	100,708	1,591	1.6
Idaho	75,553	1,265	1.7	385,768	8,598	2.2
Kansas	99,007	920	0.9	577,177	6,367	1.1
Kentucky	234,974	2,567	1.1	1,351,916	19,031	1.4
Louisiana	172,421	3,046	1.8	1,029,466	19,817	1.9
Massachusetts	112,996	94	0.1	261,150	746	0.3
Maine	52,665	374	0.7	293,892	2,001	0.7
Minnesota	227,846	2,438	1.1	1,000,363	11,722	1.2
Missouri	209,316	1,921	0.9	1,183,929	14,272	1.2
Mississippi	152,294	1,520	1.0	908,048	11,396	1.3
Montana	83,545	1,234	1.5	421,958	7,781	1.8
North Dakota	34,690	386	1.1	182,027	2,026	1.1
New Mexico	81,546	1,156	1.4	474,077	7,595	1.6
Ohio	327,040	4,122	1.3	1,771,068	27,708	1.6
Oklahoma	173,188	1,875	1.1	930,241	13,270	1.4
Rhode Island	10,054	79	0.8	60,590	502	0.8
South Dakota	50,323	607	1.2	245,250	3,537	1.4
Texas	672,995	8,103	1.2	3,493,357	53,641	1.5
West Virginia	132,846	1,077	0.8	747,225	7,388	1.0
Wyoming	35,427	507	1.4	187,338	3,010	1.6

Note: States are those for which the FBI conducted all checks under permanent Brady (The Brady Handgun Violence Prevention Act). The total for the 6-year period includes December 1998.

SOURCE: Michael Bowling, Gene Lauver, Matthew J. Hickman, and Devon B. Adams, "Table 3. Rejection Rates for Selected FBI States, 1999–2004," in *Background Checks for Firearm Transfers, 2004,* U.S. Department of Justice, Office of Justice Programs, Bureau of Justice Statistics, October 2005, http://www.ojp.usdoj.gov/bjs/pub/pdf/bcft04.pdf (accessed July 26, 2006)

DOMESTIC VIOLENCE GUN BAN. Federal law includes batterers convicted of domestic violence crimes or those with domestic violence protection orders filed against them among the people who are prohibited from owning or carrying guns. Since 1994, most people attempting to purchase guns in the United States have had to pass a background check first. According to the report *Background Checks for Firearm Transfers, 2004* (October 2005, http://www.ojp.usdoj.gov/bjs/pub/pdf/bcft04.pdf), Michael Bowling et al. note that from March 1, 1994, through December 31, 2003, 61.6 million applications for firearm permits or transfers were subjected to background investigations by the Federal Bureau of Investigation (FBI) and state and local agencies. Of these applications, about 1.2 million were rejected. While the rejection rate is low (Table 9.7 shows that the FBI rejection rate for selected states was only 1.2% in 2004), a substantial proportion of those rejections are because of prior domestic violence convictions. In 2004, about 16% of those rejected were rejected because the FBI or state or local police agencies found that applicants had either been convicted of a domestic violence misdemeanor or had a restraining order issued against them. (See Table 9.8.) After prior felony convictions, domestic violence was the second-leading reason for rejecting applicants' gun permit requests.

Loopholes in state and federal laws allow batterers to purchase guns despite the federal ban. In many states private gun owners can sell their firearms without background checks. In addition, many states keep incomplete records of domestic violence offenders and orders of protection. Still other evidence suggests that some gun dealers knowingly allow people who are not legally eligible to purchase firearms to buy them through a third party.

DIFFICULTIES IN THE COURT SYSTEM

An appeal to the U.S. judicial system should be an effective method of obtaining justice. For battered women, however, this has not always been the case. In the past ignorance, social prejudices, and uneven attention from the criminal justice system all tended to underestimate the severity and importance of battering crimes against women. Although society has become significantly less tolerant of domestic violence, and laws in many states criminalize behavior previously considered acceptable, old attitudes and biases continue to plague intimate partner violence and spouse abuse cases in the courts.

Intimate partner abuse cases are often complicated by evidence problems, because domestic violence usually

TABLE 9.8

Reasons for rejection of firearm transfer applications, 1999–2004

Reason for rejection	FBI		State and local agencies						
	2004	1999–2004	2004	2003	2002	2001	2000	1999	1999–2004
Total	**100%**	**100%**	**100%**	**100%**	**100%**	**100%**	**100%**	**100%**	**100%**
Felony indictment/conviction	37.6	51.9	49.6	44.8	51.8	57.7	57.6	72.5	57.2
Other criminal history[a]	25.0	16.6	—	—	—	—	—	—	—
Domestic violence									
Misdemeanor conviction	11.5	13.0	12.6	11.7	10.4	10.6	8.9	9.0	10.3
Restraining order	5.1	4.5	3.4	3.8	3.5	3.7	3.3	2.1	3.2
State law prohibition	—	—	9.0	10.4	9.9	7.0	4.7	3.5	6.9
Fugitive	4.6	3.5	8.3	7.8	8.0	5.8	4.3	5.0	6.2
Illegal alien	2.0	1.2	0.6	1.1	0.8	0.4	0.2	0.2	0.5
Mental illness or disability	0.5	0.4	2.7	2.4	1.4	1.2	1.0	0.5	1.4
Drug use	9.1	6.3	1.5	1.8	1.3	1.0	0.7	1.0	1.1
Local law prohibition	—	—	0.1	1.2	0.9	0.5	0.2	0.2	0.5
Other[b]	4.7	2.5	12.3	14.9	12.0	12.1	19.2	6.0	12.7

—Not available or not applicable.

[a]Includes state prohibitors, multiple DUI's (driving under the influence), non-NCIC (National Crime Information Center) warrants, and other unspecified criminal history disqualifiers.
[b]Includes juveniles, persons dishonorably discharged from the armed services, persons who have renounced their U.S. citizenship, and other unspecified persons.

SOURCE: Michael Bowling, Gene Lauver, Matthew J. Hickman, and Devon B. Adams, "Table 5. Reasons for Rejection of Firearm Transfer Applications, 1999–2004," in *Background Checks for Firearm Transfers, 2004*, U.S. Department of Justice, Office of Justice Programs, Bureau of Justice Statistics, October 2005, http://www.ojp.usdoj.gov/bjs/pub/pdf/bcft04.pdf (accessed July 26, 2006)

takes place behind closed doors. The volatile and unpredictable emotions and motivations influencing the behavior of both the abuser and victim may not always fit neatly into the organized and systematic framework of legal case presentation. Finally, the varying training mandates to ensure that prosecutors and judges are better informed about the social and personal costs of domestic violence, along with society's changing attitudes toward abuse, influence the responses of the judicial system.

The victim-offender relationship is an important factor in determining how the offender is treated by the criminal justice system. On the one hand, strangers are treated more harshly because stranger offenses are considered more heinous and the true targets of the justice system. As a result, criminal law is strictly enforced against them. On the other hand, the justice system has traditionally perceived nonstranger offenses as a victim's misuse of the legal system to deal with strained interpersonal relationships.

Several studies confirm that while intimate partners are frequently charged with and convicted of more serious offenses, stranger offenders generally receive longer sentences. In addition, most intimate partner crimes never go to sentencing, because victims drop charges or settle out of court. Those cases that do proceed through the judicial system are likely to be the more serious crimes.

Willingness of Victims to Prosecute

One of the most formidable problems in prosecuting abusers is the victim's reluctance to cooperate. Although many abused women have the courage to initiate legal proceedings against their batterers, some are later reluctant to cooperate with the prosecution because of their emotional attachment to their abusers. Other reasons for their reluctance are fear of retaliation, mistrust or lack of information about the criminal justice system, or fear of the demands of court appearances. These reasons are among the findings by Lisa Goodman, Lauren Bennett, and Mary Ann Dutton in "Obstacles to Victims' Cooperation with the Criminal Prosecution of Their Abusers: The Role of Social Support" (*Violence and Victims*, Winter 1999) and by JoAnn Miller in "An Arresting Experiment: Domestic Violence Victim Experiences and Perceptions" (*Journal of Interpersonal Violence*, July 2003). A victim's fear and ambivalence about testifying, and the importance of her behavior as a witness, can undoubtedly discourage some prosecutors from taking action.

However, a victim might choose not to move forward with the prosecution because the violence ceases temporarily following the arrest while the batterer is in custody. In most cases, a woman does not want her husband to go to jail with the attendant loss of income and community standing. She simply wants her husband to stop beating her.

Religious convictions, economic dependency, and family influence to drop the charges place great pressure on victimized women. Consequently, many prosecutors, some of whom believe abuse is a purely personal problem and others who believe winning the case is unlikely, test the victim's resolve to make sure she will not back out. This additional pressure drives many women to drop the charges because after being controlled by their husbands, they feel that the judicial system is repeating the pattern by abusing its power. Hence, the prosecutors' fears contribute to the problem, creating a self-perpetuating cycle.

Goodman, Bennett, and Dutton explore the reasons many domestic violence victims refuse to cooperate in the prosecution of their abusers. Surprisingly, they find that the relationship between emotional support and cooperation with prosecutors was not significant. Similarly, institutional support, whether from police or victim advocates, was also unrelated to cooperation. Neither level of depression nor degree of emotional attachment to the abuser had an effect. These findings refute the common perception that the battered woman is too depressed, helpless, or attached to the abuser to cooperate in his prosecution. Instead, Goodman, Bennett, and Dutton's findings show that many domestic violence victims persevere in the face of depression and the sometimes complex emotional attachment to their partner.

Consistent with findings from earlier studies, Goodman, Bennett, and Dutton find that the more severe the violence, the more likely the abused women were to cooperate with prosecutors. Participants rearing children with the abuser were also more likely to cooperate, perhaps because these women hoped that the criminal justice system would force the abuser into treatment. In contrast, women with substance abuse problems were less than half as likely as other women to cooperate with the prosecution. Goodman, Bennett, and Dutton conclude that the women who used alcohol or drugs believed that the abuse was partly their fault or that a judge would not take them seriously. Some also feared that their substance abuse might negatively affect the court proceedings and possibly even lead to criminal charges or the loss of their children.

Factors Associated with Prosecutors' Charging Decisions in Domestic Violence Cases

In "Modeling Prosecutors' Charging Decisions in Domestic Violence Cases" (*Crime and Delinquency*, July 2006), John L. Worrall, Jay W. Ross, and Eric S. McCord investigate what factors influenced the decisions of prosecutors to charge a batterer and what factors influenced the decisions of prosecutors to pursue a misdemeanor or a felony charge. They collected data on 245 domestic violence cases filed by police officers, examined the impact of characteristics of the victim, offender, and the offense, and determined how these characteristics influenced the prosecutors' charging decisions.

Worrall, Ross, and McCord find that prosecutors were more likely to charge offenders if they had been arrested, or if they had inflicted serious injuries on the victim. They find that criminal charges were more likely to be filed against a male batterer than against a female batterer. They also find that if the victim supported prosecution, felony charges were more likely to be filed against the batterer.

TREATMENT FOR MALE BATTERERS

Rather than serving a prison term, many convicted batterers enter treatment programs. As a requirement of probation, most courts will order a batterer into an intervention program. Regardless of an intervention program's philosophy or methods, program directors and criminal justice professionals generally monitor the offenders' behavior closely. Most batterers enter intervention programs after having been charged by the police with a specific incident of abuse.

The criminal justice system categorizes offenders based on their potential danger, history of substance abuse, psychological problems, and risk of dropout and rearrest. Ideally, interventions focus on the specific type of batterer and the approach that will most effectively produce results, such as linking a substance abuse treatment program with a batterer intervention program. Other program approaches focus on specific sociocultural characteristics, such as poverty, race, ethnicity, and age. In "Analyzing the Studies" (*Batterer Intervention Programs: Where Do We Go from Here?* June 2003, http://www.ncjrs.gov/pdffiles1/nij/195079.pdf), Shelly Jackson argues that the effectiveness of batterer intervention programs might improve if the programs were seen "as part of a broader criminal justice and community response to domestic violence that includes arrest, restraining orders, intensive monitoring of batterers, and changes to social norms that may inadvertently tolerate partner violence."

Several states require that the victim be notified at various points of the intervention and that programs with a strong advocacy policy contact victims every two or three months. Victims may be asked for additional information about the relationship, given information about the program's goals and methods, and helped with safety planning. In addition, the batterer's counselor will inform the victim if further abuse appears imminent.

Batterers leave the program either because of successful completion or because they are asked to leave. Reasons for termination include failure to cooperate, nonpayment of fees, revocation of parole or probation, failure to attend group sessions regularly, or violation of program rules. Successful completion of a program means that the offender has attended the required sessions and accomplished the program's objectives. With court-mandated clients a final report is also made to probation officials. To be successful, batterer intervention programs must have the support of the criminal justice system, which includes coordinated efforts between police, prosecutors, judges, victim advocates, and probation officers.

Program Dropout Rates

Dropout rates in battering programs are high, even though courts have ordered most clients to attend. Several studies, such as that by Jennifer Rooney and R. Karl Hanson in "Predicting Attrition from Treatment Programs for Abusive Men" (*Journal of Family Violence*, June 2001), record varying dropout rates, some finding that as many as 90% of the men who begin short-term treatment programs do not complete them.

High dropout rates in batterer intervention programs make it difficult to evaluate their success. Evaluations based on men who complete these programs focus on a select group of highly motivated men who likely do not reflect the composition of the group when it began. Because a follow-up is not conducted with program dropouts—the men most likely to continue their violence—research generally fails to accurately indicate the success or failure of a given treatment program.

Certain characteristics are generally related to dropout rates. Bruce Dalton, in "Batterer Characteristics and Treatment Completion" (*Journal of Interpersonal Violence*, December 2001), finds that the level of threat that the batterer perceived from the referral source (for example, the court) was, surprisingly, not related to program completion. Unemployment was the one characteristic most consistently related to dropping out of treatment. Dalton theorizes that these men have both trouble paying for the treatment and a lower investment in the "official social order."

Other researchers find that factors influencing completion rates of batterer intervention programs include youth, not being legally married, low income and little education, unstable work histories, criminal backgrounds, and excessive drinking or drug abuse. Voluntary clients, especially those with college educations, remain in treatment longer. Some researchers find better attendance among college-educated men, regardless of whether their enrollment in a program is court ordered or voluntary (see Rooney and Hanson, above; and Edward W. Gondolf, "A Comparison of Four Batterer Intervention Systems: Do Court Referral, Program Length, and Services Matter?" *Journal of Interpersonal Violence*, January 1999).

Nearly all professionals involved in domestic violence prevention and treatment programs concur that batterer intervention programs must address the issue of dropouts. Reducing or eliminating intake sessions and immediately engaging batterers in useful interventions may help to promote attendance and participation. Counselors should provide more information about the purpose of the program in the preprogram orientation sessions. Other suggested retention measures include courtroom assistance, mentors, and harsher and quicker punishment for dropouts. One study finds that home visits after a batterer misses a meeting also help decrease dropout rates. Researchers on this subject include Bruce Dalton in "Batterer Characteristics and Treatment Completion" (*Journal of Interpersonal Violence*, December 2001) and A. DeMaris in "Attrition in

Batterers' Counseling: The Role of Social and Demographic Factors" (*Social Service Review*, 1989).

Recidivism Rates

Recidivism (the tendency to relapse to old ingrained patterns of behavior) is a well-documented problem among people in intimate partner violence treatment programs. In "Predictors of Criminal Recidivism among Male Batterers" (*Psychology Crime and Law*, December 2004), R. Karl Hanson and Suzanne Wallace-Capretta examine risk factors associated with recidivism of 320 male batterers within a five-year follow-up period. Of those men, 25.6% recidivated with a battering offense. Risk factors included being young, having an unstable lifestyle, being a substance abuser, and having a criminal history. Batterers were not deterred by expectations of social or legal negative consequences. However, maintaining positive relationships with community treatment providers was associated with deterrence of future battering.

Julia C. Babcock and Ramalina Steiner report some cautiously optimistic findings in "The Relationship between Treatment, Incarceration, and Recidivism of Battering: A Program Evaluation of Seattle's Coordinated Community Response to Domestic Violence" (*Journal of Family Psychology*, March 1999). Their research measured recidivism of domestic violence after arrest and completion or noncompletion of a mandatory, coordinated program of treatment involving the courts, probation officers, and treatment providers.

Babcock and Steiner followed 387 people arrested for misdemeanor domestic violence offenses, thirty-one of whom were women. More than three-quarters of participants had no prior domestic violence convictions and 69% had no prior criminal history. Participants were referred to one of eleven certified domestic violence treatment programs. The majority attended programs that use the Duluth model (based on the feminist idea that patriarchal ideology, or men's desire to oppress women, causes domestic violence), whereas the remainder participated in feminist, psychoeducational, and cognitive-behavioral men's groups. About 31% completed at least twenty-four sessions of treatment, and those batterers considered to have completed treatment attended an average of thirty-two sessions. In contrast, batterers who did not complete treatment attended an average of just 5.8 sessions. Treatment completers were generally first-time offenders, better educated, employed, and had less prior criminal involvement. Of the noncompleters, 58% did not attend any sessions, and the majority were not legally punished, despite their failure to attend court-ordered treatment.

Program completion was related to lower rates of recidivism—treatment completers had significantly fewer domestic violence arrests at follow-up than noncompleters, and this difference remained even when Babcock and

Steiner controlled for differences in prior criminal record and history. Batterers who had been court ordered to attend treatment and failed to complete it were more likely to commit further offenses than treatment completers. Babcock and Steiner conclude that their findings support the premise that completing treatment is directly related to reduced rates of domestic violence. They caution, however, that participants who completed treatment were probably not representative of the entire population of batterers—they likely had more to lose as a result of failure to complete treatment than the treatment dropouts.

In "The Effects of Domestic Violence Batterer Treatment on Domestic Violence Recidivism" (*Criminal Justice and Behavior*, February 2003), Jill A. Gordon and Laura J. Moriarty study the effect of batterer treatment on recidivism. They find that attending treatment had no impact on recidivism when comparing the treatment group as a whole with the experimental group. Christopher I. Eckhardt et al., in "Intervention Programs for Perpetrators of Intimate Partner Violence: Conclusions from a Clinical Research Perspective" (*Public Health Reports*, July–August 2006), concur in their review of the literature concerning batterer intervention programs and recidivism rates. However, Gordon and Moriarty also find that among the treatment group, the more sessions a batterer completed, the less likely he was to batter again. Batterers who completed all sessions were less likely to be rearrested for domestic violence than were batterers who had not completed all sessions.

IMPORTANT NAMES AND ADDRESSES

ABA Center on Children and the Law
740 Fifteenth St. NW
Washington, DC 20005-1019
(202) 662-1000
URL: http://www.abanet.org/child

Administration for Children and Families
370 L'Enfant Promenade SW
Washington, DC 20201
URL: http://www.acf.dhhs.gov/programs/cb

Center for Effective Discipline
155 W. Main St., Ste. 1603
Columbus, OH 43215
(614) 221-8829
FAX: (614) 221-2110
URL: http://www.stophitting.com

Center for Women Policy Studies
1776 Massachusetts Ave. NW, Ste. 450
Washington, DC 20036
(202) 872-1770
FAX: (202) 296-8962
E-mail: cwps@centerwomenpolicy.org
URL: http://www.centerwomenpolicy.org/

Child Welfare Information Gateway
1250 Maryland Ave. SW, Eighth Floor
Washington, DC 20024
(703) 385-7565
1-800-394-3366
FAX: (703) 385-3206
E-mail: info@childwelfare.gov
URL: http://www.childwelfare.gov/

Child Welfare League of America
440 First St. NW, Third Floor
Washington, DC 20001-2085
(202) 638-2952
FAX: (202) 638-4004
URL: http://www.cwla.org/

Children's Defense Fund
25 E St. NW
Washington, DC 20001
(202) 628-8787
1-800-CDF-1200

E-mail: cdfinfo@childrensdefense.org
URL: http://www.childrensdefense.org/

Crimes against Children Research Center
University of New Hampshire
126 Horton Social Science Center
Durham, NH 03824
(603) 862-1888
FAX: (603) 862-1122
URL: http://www.unh.edu/ccrc

False Memory Syndrome Foundation
1955 Locust St.
Philadelphia, PA 19103-5766
(215) 940-1040
FAX: (215) 940-1042
E-mail: mail@fmsfonline.org
URL: http://www.fmsfonline.org/

Family Research Laboratory
University of New Hampshire
126 Horton Social Science Center
Durham, NH 03824
(603) 862-1888
FAX: (603) 862-1122
URL: http://www.unh.edu/frl/index.html

Institute on Violence, Abuse, and Trauma
6160 Cornerstone Ct. E.
San Diego, CA 92121
(858) 623-2777
FAX: (858) 646-0761
URL: http://ivatcenters.org/

International Society for Prevention of Child Abuse and Neglect
245 W. Roosevelt Rd., Bldg. 6, Ste. 39
West Chicago, IL 60185
(630) 876-6913
URL: http://www.ispcan.org/

National Center for Missing and Exploited Children
Charles B. Wang International Children's Building
699 Prince St.
Alexandria, VA 22314-3175

(703) 274-3900
1-800-843-5678
FAX: (703) 274-2200
URL: http://www.missingkids.com/

National Center for the Prosecution of Child Abuse
American Prosecutors Research Institute
99 Canal Center Plaza, Ste. 510
Alexandria, VA 22314
(703) 549-4253
FAX: (703) 836-3195
E-mail: ncpca@ndaa.org
URL: http://www.ndaa-apri.org/apri/
programs/ncpca/ncpca_home.html

National Center for Victims of Crime
2000 M St. NW, Ste. 480
Washington, DC 20036
(202) 467-8700
FAX: (202) 467-8701
URL: http://www.ncvc.org/

National Clearinghouse for the Defense of Battered Women
125 S. Ninth St., Ste. 302
Philadelphia, PA 19107
(215) 351-0010
FAX: (215) 351-0779

National Coalition against Domestic Violence
1120 Lincoln St., Ste. 1603
Denver, CO 80203
(303) 839-1852
1-800-799-7233
FAX: (303) 831-9251
URL: http://www.ncadv.org/

National Council on Child Abuse and Family Violence
1025 Connecticut Ave. NW, Ste. 1000
Washington, DC 20036
(202) 429-6695
URL: http://www.nccafv.org/

National Criminal Justice Reference Service
PO Box 6000
Rockville, MD 20849-6000
(301) 519-5500
1-800-851-3420
FAX: (301) 519-5212
URL: http://www.ncjrs.org/

National Domestic Violence Hotline
PO Box 161810
Austin, TX 78716
(512) 794-1133
1-800-799-7233
URL: http://www.ndvh.org/

National Resource Center on Domestic Violence
Pennsylvania Coalition against Domestic Violence

6400 Flank Dr., Ste. 1300
Harrisburg, PA 17112-2778
1-800-537-2238
FAX: (717) 671-8149
URL: http://www.nrcdv.org/

National Runaway Switchboard
3080 N. Lincoln Ave.
Chicago, IL 60657
(773) 880-9860
1-800-344-2785
FAX: (773) 929-5150
URL: http://www.nrscrisisline.org/

Prevent Child Abuse America
500 N. Michigan Ave., Ste. 200
Chicago, IL 60611
(312) 663-3520

FAX: (312) 939-8962
E-mail: mailbox@preventchildabuse.org
URL: http://www.preventchildabuse.org/

Rape, Abuse, and Incest National Network
2000 L St. NW, Ste. 406
Washington, DC 20036
(202) 544-1034
1-800-656-4673
FAX: (202) 544-3556
URL: http://www.rainn.org/

Survivors Network of Those Abused by Priests
PO Box 6416
Chicago, IL 60680-6416
1-877-762-7432
URL: http://www.snapnetwork.org/

RESOURCES

The National Child Abuse and Neglect Data System (NCANDS) of the U.S. Department of Health and Human Services (HHS) is the primary source of national information on child maltreatment known to state child protective services (CPS) agencies. The latest findings from NCANDS are published in *Child Maltreatment 2004* (2006). The most recent national incidence study, the Third National Incidence Study of Child Abuse and Neglect (NIS-3; 1996), is the single most comprehensive source of information about the incidence of child maltreatment in the United States. NIS-3 findings are based on data collected not only from CPS but also from community institutions (for example, day care centers, schools, and hospitals) and investigating agencies (for example, public health departments, police, and courts). Other HHS publications used include *The AFGARS Report* (2005), *Children Living with Substance-Abusing or Substance-Dependent Parents* (2003), *National Survey on Drug Use and Health, 2004* (2005), and *Major Federal Legislation Concerned with Child Protection, Child Welfare, and Adoption* (2003).

The Child Welfare Information Gateway, which is maintained by the Children's Bureau of the HHS, provides two helpful publications used in the preparation of this book: *The Child Welfare System* (2004) and *2003 Child Abuse and Neglect State Statute Series Statutes-at-a-Glance: Mandatory Reporters of Child Abuse and Neglect* (2003).

Different offices of the U.S. Department of Justice produce publications relating to child maltreatment and domestic violence. The Bureau of Justice Statistics published *Intimate Partner Violence* (July 2000), *Intimate Partner Violence, 1993–2001* (February 2003), *Sexual Assault of Young Children as Reported to Law Enforcement: Victim, Incident, and Offender Characteristics* (July 2000), *Criminal Victimization, 2004* (2005), *Homicide Trends in the United States* (2006), and *Criminal*

Victimization in the United States, 2004 (2006). The Office for Victims of Crime published the *Children at Clandestine Methamphetamine Labs: Helping Meth's Youngest Victims* (2003) and *Background Checks for Firearm Transfers, 2004* (2005).

The Office of Juvenile Justice and Delinquency Prevention published *The Decline in Child Sexual Abuse Cases* (January 2001) and *Crimes against Children by Babysitters* (September 2001). The Office of Justice Programs published *The Sexual Victimization of College Women* (2000). The Federal Bureau of Investigation published *Crime in the United States, 2004: Uniform Crime Reports* (2005). The Violence against Women Grants Office published *Stalking and Domestic Violence: The Third Annual Report to Congress under the Violence against Women Act* (1998).

"Risky Mix: Drinking, Drug Use, and Homicide" (2003), "Prosecutors, Kids, and Domestic Violence Cases" (2002), "Childhood Victimization: Early Adversity, Later Psychopathology" (2000), "Assessing Risk Factors for Intimate Partner Homicide" (2003), and "Explanations for the Decline in Child Sexual Abuse Cases" (2004) were all published in the *National Institute of Justice Journal*. The National Institute of Justice also published *An Update on the "Cycle of Violence"* (February 2001), "The Effects of Arrest on Intimate Partner Violence: New Evidence from the Spouse Assault Replication Program" (July 2001), *Extent, Nature, and Consequences of Rape Victimization: Findings from the National Violence against Women Survey* (January 2006), and *Extent, Nature, and Consequences of Intimate Partner Violence: Findings from the National Violence against Women Survey* (July 2000).

Other federal government publications used for this book include *National Survey on Drug Use and Health, 2004* (Office of Applied Studies, Substance Abuse and Mental Health Services Administration, 2005), "Physical

Dating Violence among High School Students—United States, 2003," *MMWR Weekly* (May 19, 2006), *Educator Sexual Misconduct: A Synthesis of Existing Literature* (U.S. Department of Education, 2004), "Statutory Rape Laws by State," *OLR Research Report* (April 14, 2003), *Child Welfare: HHS Could Play a Greater Role in Helping Child Welfare Agencies Recruit and Retain Staff* (U.S. Government Accountability Office, March 2003), *The Foreign-Born Population in the United States: 2003* (U.S. Census Bureau, August 2004), *U.S. Legal Permanent Residents: 2005* (Office of Immigration Statistics, April 2006), and *A Nation Online: Entering the Broadband Age* (U.S. Department of Commerce, September 2004).

Online Victimization: A Report on the Nation's Youth (Crimes against Children Research Center, June 2000) discusses the findings of the first Youth Internet Safety Survey. *Teenage Life Online: The Rise of the Instant-Message Generation and the Internet's Impact on Friendships and Family Relationships* (Pew Internet and American Life Project, June 2001) finds that adolescents who have Internet access do communicate with strangers they meet online.

A number of studies were conducted on domestic violence when spouse abuse first became a public issue during the 1970s and 1980s. Since that time, however, there has been little government-funded statistical research on domestic abuse. The pioneering work done at the University of New Hampshire's Family Research Laboratory (FRL) in Durham, New Hampshire, has become an authoritative source of information and insight about family violence. Murray A. Straus, David Finkelhor, Linda Meyer Williams, Kathleen A. Kendall-Tackett, Lisa Jones, Richard K. Ormrod, and many others associated with the laboratory have done some of the most scientifically rigorous research in the field of abuse. Studies released by the FRL investigate all forms of domestic violence, many based on its two major surveys: the National Family Violence Survey (1975) and the National Family Violence Resurvey (1985). Much of the research from these two surveys has been gathered into *Physical Violence in American Families: Risk Factors and Adaptations to Violence in 8,145 Families* (Murray A. Straus and Richard J. Gelles, 1990). Straus is also widely known for his studies on corporal punishment. Several of Straus's journal articles, his book *Beating the Devil out of Them: Corporal Punishment in American Families and Its Effects on Children* (2001), and papers presented at meetings on domestic violence in various countries were helpful in the preparation of this book.

Chief among the University of New Hampshire researchers who perform the landmark studies and in-depth work on intimate partner violence are Murray A. Straus, David Finkelhor, Richard J. Gelles, and Suzanne Steinmetz. Studies released by the FRL investigate all forms of domestic violence, many based on the National Family Violence Survey and the National Family Violence Resurvey. Murray A. Straus and Glenda Kaufman Kantor published data in "Changes in Spouse Assault Rates from 1975 to 1992: A Comparison of Three National Surveys in the United States" (paper presented at the Thirteenth World Congress of Sociology, Bielefeld, Germany, July 1994). Martha Smithey and Murray A. Straus published the report "Primary Prevention of Intimate Partner Violence" (July 2002). Murray A. Straus published "Prevalence of Violence against Dating Partners by Male and Female University Students Worldwide" in *Violence against Women* (July 2004).

Many journals published useful articles on child maltreatment and domestic violence that were used in the preparation of this book. They include the *American Journal of Drug and Alcohol Abuse, American Journal of Psychiatry, American Psychologist, Archives of Pediatrics and Adolescent Medicine, Child Abuse and Neglect, Child Maltreatment, Journal of Child Sexual Abuse, Journal of Family Violence, Journal of Interpersonal Violence, Journal of Marriage and the Family, Journal of the American Academy of Child and Adolescent Psychiatry, Journal of the American Medical Association, Journal of Trauma and Dissociation, Journal of Traumatic Stress, Maternal and Child Health Journal, New England Law Review, Pediatrics, Psychology of Women Quarterly, Psychoneuroendocrinology, Violence against Women,* and *Violence and Victims.*

Helpful books used for this publication include *Against Our Will: Men, Women, and Rape,* by Susan Brownmiller (1975); *Terrifying Love: Why Battered Women Kill and How Society Responds,* by Lenore E. Walker (1989); *What Parents Need to Know about Sibling Abuse: Breaking the Cycle of Violence,* by Vernon R. Wiehe (2002); *Confronting Chronic Neglect: The Education and Training of Health Professionals on Family Violence,* edited by Felicia Cohn, Marla E. Salmon, and John D. Stobo (2002); *When Battered Women Kill,* by Angela Browne (1987); *Wife Rape: Understanding the Response of Survivors and Service Providers,* by Raquel Kennedy Bergen (1996); *The Epidemic of Rape and Child Sexual Abuse in the United States,* by Diana E. H. Russell and Rebecca M. Bolen (2000); *Understanding Family Violence: Treating and Preventing Partner, Child, Sibling, and Elder Abuse,* by Vernon R. Wiehe (1998); *Do Arrests and Restraining Orders Work?,* edited by Eve S. Buzawa and Carl G. Buzawa (1996); *Issues in Intimate Violence,* edited by Raquel Kennedy Bergen (1998); *The Book of David: How Preserving Families Can Cost Children's Lives,* by Richard J. Gelles (1996); and *The Secret Trauma: Incest in the Lives of Girls and Women,* by Diana E. H. Russell (1986).

INDEX